teaching reading
in secondary school
content subjects:
a bookthinking process

teaching reading in secondary school content subjects:

a bookthinking process

Carl B. Smith
Indiana University

Sharon L. Smith
Communications Consultant,
Indianapolis Public Schools

Larry Mikulecky
Indiana University

Holt, Rinehart and Winston
New York   Chicago   San Francisco   Dallas
Montreal   Toronto   London   Sydney

For Madonna, Tony, and
all the young people who challenged
us to think about their learning.

Library of Congress Cataloging in Publication Data
Smith, Carl Bernard.

Teaching reading in secondary school content subjects:
a bookthinking process

1. Reading (Secondary education)   I.   Smith,
Sharon L., joint author.   II.   Mikulecky, Larry,
joint author.   III.   Title.
LB1632.S557   428'.4'0712   77-18957
ISBN 0-03-019381-8

Special thanks to the Cleveland, Ohio, Public School
System and the Martha Holden Jennings Foundation for
the use on pages 161–163 and 383–391 of sample study
guides from *Science Reading Units*.

preface

Show me a widely read person and I'll show you someone able to cope with the vicissitudes of life!

From the time of Newman's classic *The Idea of a University*, the well-read person has stood as a symbol of intellectual growth and capability. Schools and teachers encourage the growth of a person who reads and learns, and yet they are under increasing criticism for not producing readers. Some state legislatures have demanded a minimum literacy test as a prerequisite for a high school diploma.

This text helps upper-grade teachers to promote a student's ability to process written information. It shows classroom teachers how to incorporate bookthinking into their classes on science, mathematics, English, social studies, vocational education, and so on. Examples from these subject areas are interspersed liberally throughout. Bookthinking, the ability to extract information and interact reasonably with a written message, may be the most significant skill a teacher can develop in his students.[1] It is truly the process from which mature learning springs, a teachable idea that fits into the goals of every concerned teacher.

EVERY TEACHER'S GOAL

Every teacher looks for ways to provide success for his students, not only to answer a quiz but also to continue to read and learn. That's why content teachers and this text have mutual interests.

Basic to bookthinking is an appreciation that the organization of prose writing from one subject to another may be different. On that premise, a teacher can seek out and teach the bookthinking skills appropriate to writing in his content area. Writers with specific content orientations construct pas-

---

[1] The authors recognize the concern for identifying male and female persons in general references. But in lieu of a smooth solution we will use the convention of a masculine pronoun when both male and female persons are included in a reference.

sages according to those orientations. A science writer schooled in scientific inquiry may organize his writing to report data, categorize them, and draw conclusions from them. If writers follow patterns, or if textbooks follow patterns in presenting information, the teacher should demonstrate for students what those patterns are and how to use them for independent learning. Aside from a teacher's personal interest in the subject, teaching a youngster how to conceptualize content thinking and writing may be the most valuable contribution he can make to a student. It is in that sense that every teacher teaches reading-thinking. The authors of this text are convinced that a concern for writing structure, for different prose forms, constitutes an important aspect of reading content texts. That idea is illustrated in various ways throughout the text. And it represents one of the significant differences in approach between this text and others that discuss how to read content texts in middle and secondary schools.

WHOSE JOB?

Excuses multiply whenever the question of responsibility for teaching reading arises. Naturally, no one wants to accept responsibility for failure, and no one wants to take in a child who has failed. For that reason when a reading problem is spotted in the upper grades, the responsibility is laid on the elementary teacher, or the parents, or the textbook writer. Or the content teacher looks for a remedial consultant or a reading lab to deal with the problem, when he personally should try to promote continuing growth in reading, in the manner of our concept of bookthinking.

That growth in bookthinking can and should occur throughout a student's years in school, making him continually more and more able to interact reasonably and efficiently with authors in all fields of endeavor. Showing the student how to do that is the responsibility of each teacher he meets. This book is organized to help the content teacher make decisions about reading-thinking; that is, defining the bookthinking process, finding strategies to teach it with subject matter, and evaluating teaching and learning.

USING THE BOOK

As with any text, a teacher has the option of listing topics he wants to discuss and then assigning chapters from this text to match his list. Though the Contents indicates the logic of organizing the chapters the way we did, the chapters could be used selectively to suit the perspective of the course. Perverse as it seems to us, an instructor may also decide that one or the other chapter does not fit his particular course. We would hope, then, that the instructor would announce to the class that the chapter has evil, subversive ideas in it.

That probably will seduce the students to read it on their own—without assignment. Where independent learning modules are used, sections of the text can form an information base which the student reads to complete a module. Chapters 2 and 3, "The Bookthinking Process" and "Mature Reading Behavior," give basic concepts that a teacher needs for understanding the processing of printed information and the development of language and cognition in adolescent and mature readers. The text could also be used in its given sequence, following the logic used in its development. Chapters in this book were written in response to major instructional questions that content teachers ask about reading. To demonstrate our intent to keep the reader in touch with reality, the first chapter analyzes the common problem of a textbook that is too difficult for many students in the class to read. The teacher must decide whether he will permit the mismatched readers to stumble and fall or make some adjustment to keep them on their feet.

From that practical beginning the text provides four major categories of discussion:

I Bookthinking—a teacher's perspective:
In which the student's problem with subject-matter texts, his language and cognitive growth, and the characteristics of a mature reader are discussed in terms of a teaching model for content teachers.
II Student experience and competence:
In which the students' attitudes, interests, and competencies are analyzed, and techniques are given for observing them.
III Strategies for coping with books:
In which the major strategies for solving word, comprehension, and study reading situations are related to the adolescent's reading competence.
IV Organization and evaluation:
In which are discussed ways of achieving bookthinking objectives through book materials and classroom organization.

Through that sequence the text provides answers to the major instructional decisions a content teacher has to make.

How do I define reading in a way that I can use it to promote growth?
How do I adjust to the various reading levels in my class?
How can I adjust to the ways kids think?
What will motivate kids to read my subject?
What skills or competencies should be emphasized? How do I teach them?
How should the class be organized to emphasize books as important tools for learning?
What should be done with very poor readers?
How do I know if students are making progress?

Other decisions are examined, but the list above indicates the intent of this text to examine reading as it affects the content teacher and the learner. Many chapters have appendixes that will serve as continuing references for the classroom teacher.

This text is designed to show middle and secondary school content teachers how to be more effective teachers of their subject texts. It can be used as a reading-methods text for preservice teachers or for a beginning in-service (graduate) course. It emphasizes the content teacher's role in bringing the student and the book together effectively. It involves techniques that content teachers can use to help students read better, but with a difference. Because the content teacher often feels that he has no responsibility for teaching reading, the book will emphasize *better teaching* by showing the student how to interact with the book, how to interact with the message on the printed page.

TO THE READER

Your sense of competent teaching certainly involves communication and interaction with students. You and your students must engage in a discourse over topics in chemistry, history, literature, auto mechanics—else there is no learning. But your sense of competent teaching also dictates that you help each student become an independent learner. Once your students are out of the range of your voice, you want them to know how to find information and engage different kinds of teachers—the authors of the books and articles in your subject area. Unless your students learn to interact with those authors, they cannot become independent learners, and you will fail to achieve an important objective of teaching.

How to teach students to read and to learn from subject-specific texts is the point of this book. It is a book about bookthinking—how to engage in discourse with a book, with an author. Bookthinking does not occur automatically. A student expects you, the teacher, to demonstrate how to think in his subject area and how to transfer those skills to thinking within a book. Having discourse with an author means the student-reader can follow the author's language patterns, can analyze the organization of his ideas, understands his vocabulary, and is interested enough to interact with the author. Part of your role as teacher is to guide students in those aspects of bookthinking.

This book will present ways to guide you and your students in the fundamental process of reading and thinking in subject-matter texts. Reading is defined here as an interaction between the reader and the writer, an interaction based on a mutual vocabulary, sense or organization, and interest. This interaction raises a dozen different instructional questions which are reflected in the chapter headings of this book:

How do you match a student with a book he can learn from?
What role does motivation play?
How does a teacher analyze students' bookthinking behavior?
Can the classroom teacher help the poor reader?
What strategies can be used to promote vocabulary and comprehension growth?

What books and classroom organization help students cope with books?
What can be done to help the student who cannot be assisted by the classroom teacher?

You are a subject-matter teacher. This text is designed to make you a
better teacher of your subject; it does not aim to make you a reading teacher.
But we intend to make you conscious of students' strengths and weaknesses
in reading and of how your regular teaching activities can promote student
effectiveness. Our objective is to help you bring your students and their books
together in a systematic fashion. A systematic approach, as in most aspects of
learning, is extremely important and will help immensely in promoting effective content reading.

As a prelude to using the strategies suggested in this book, you may
want to apply them to your own reading and study. Each chapter in this text
gives you an opportunity to create for yourself a vigorous triangular interaction among you, the textbook, and your instructor. We believe that the
major question you should ask as you apply the strategies is: What are my
responsibilities in helping students think as they read print materials in my
subject area? Your answer must go beyond a set of techniques and strategies,
because the students in your class will approach any one book with a wide
range of abilities and experience. Finding an appropriate response to their
uniqueness is the marvelous challenge we all face as teachers. This text will
help you formulate a system and give you many practical suggestions for
meeting the challenge, no matter what subject is your major.

For suggesting ways to improve the manuscript of *Teaching Reading in
Secondary School Content Subjects: A Bookthinking Process*, we thank Peggy
Elliott, Indiana University Northwest, and John Mangieri, Ohio University.
At Holt, Rinehart and Winston we thank Richard Owen, Senior Acquisitions
Editor, and Francoise Bartlett, Senior Project Editor, for their editorial direc-
tives and their help in marshaling the manuscript from concept to finished
book.

Bloomington, Indiana   C.B.S.
January 1978   S.S.
                                                                 L.M.

contents

part 1

Bookthinking-A Teacher's Perspective

1

Matching Students and Books

Why are many students unable to use the textbooks provided for them in middle and secondary schools?

How does one determine the difficulty of a book?

How can a teacher prepare a student to think through a book?

TV AND BOOKS

In my family room I found four teenagers watching a rerun of *Star Trek* on television. So engrossed were they that they didn't pay me a nod or a "hi," not even a glance. Some of these same kids had told me often that "school is boring, there's nothing to do, we don't learn nothing." So when the program finished, I asked: "What do you do different when you watch TV from what you do when you read a book?"

I got those looks that said, "Always a teacher! Always worried about school questions." But Tony answered anyway. "I don't know," he said. "I don't think I do anything different. I watch TV and read a book to have a good time. No questions, no themes; just enjoying myself."

"How about textbooks?" I continued to play the teacher.

"Are you kidding? I don't like those. They're dull," he said.

"Why do you say they're dull?"

"All they do is give you a lot of facts that you have to memorize for tests. They don't take you anywhere. They just give you background."

Tony thought he had escaped, but I pushed him again. "You obviously read them a little. How do you know which parts to read?"

"Well, if the teacher gives us a study guide, like in American history this year, I skim over everything to get the answers that the study guide asks for. Sometimes we use that stuff in class discussions, but that too is mostly to prepare for the exams."

What happens after the exam? "That's just the point," he jabbed. "I don't remember from one test to the next what happened on the last one. Once the exam is over, I forget it—so what good was the reading?" That question stirred up one of the others who had remained silent. Beth responded: "Tony must have a secret. I found that history book so tough that I couldn't even find the answers most of the time. My dad said it looked more like a college book than one for high school. And I sure agree."

Boring and Difficult

There sits the content teacher on the horns of the dilemma: How can a subject be made interesting and easy for students who insist that the text is boring and difficult? Yet the teachers of those kids would say that they already have excellent textbooks—new, attractive, scholarly. Maybe the problem could be resolved if the teacher abandoned the textbook and used television instead. After all the kids didn't even turn to acknowledge my presence when I walked in on their TV watching.

Perhaps if we set up twelve different TV sets each tuned to a different channel and had kids gather around the set that appealed to them most we could determine what it is that makes TV programming more attractive to teenagers than reading their textbooks. But probably there would be some kids stationed at each of the sets, each watching what made him or her feel best. Then we would know only that a lot of different students had a lot of different programs that made them feel good. How does that information aid us in instruction? No one ever said that school was organized on the premise that all activities were to make the students feel good. Besides, consider the advantage television has. TV programs have to hold audience attention only ten or eleven minutes, and then there are commercials to give everyone a break from the heavy stuff he has been watching. On news broadcasts, where the really heavy stuff comes at you, the commercials are even more frequent. And no more than one minute is ever spent on a single item in the news. Broadcasters know that if they have to hold the interest of the mass audience, they have to change the information load and the scene every thirty seconds or so. Of course, no one has suggested here that adolescents even watch the news.

Television programmers have done everything possible to make viewing as interesting and easy as possible. Though teachers can learn many things from television's success, it should be a truism that televiewing and school learning are aimed at two different targets. Television must take the viewer along for a ride. "Sit on my magic carpet, and I will give you a thrill a minute." Whereas learning, as educators such as Piaget, Dewey, and Montessori have described it, is a constructive activity. "Here are some building blocks and some tools. Let's see what kind of structure you can put together." Books and thinking are basic ingredients in that construction process.

Books and Thinking

Books contain the ideas and information from which our educated society works. They may be hard cover, soft cover, or no cover, for books here mean connected discourse—a continuous flow of ideas or facts—in print. In books, magazines, newspapers, bulletins, and letters, a literate people can find the stuff to build lives, design technology, weave a philosophy, make sense out of existence. Being able to interact with books, being able to think while reading, therefore, constitutes the literate person's basic skill in advancing his or her own development and that of society as well. "Book-thinking" is a term coined by the authors to represent the way a mature reader interacts with a printed message. It is a person's basic academic skill and the key to independent growth.

If being able to think through and to interact with written discourse contributes substantially to one's growth, and hence to one's progress in school, then teachers need to know how they can promote bookthinking in the subject they teach. Theoretically, at least, most teachers would not work simply "to get answers for an exam," as Tony said he did. Most teachers hope their students will get involved with their subject. In doing so, a teacher needs to demonstrate how to use the books in building something of value in science or social studies or math or vocational education. In that sense, reading the subject matter book is not a matter of pronouncing words (a decoding process); reading requires knowing how to approach the ideas in a book and how to make use of the book in a mature fashion. Demonstrating or explaining how to do that is the responsibility of each teacher in his own subject area.

What about the complaint that the books are boring and difficult? If you are not a physicist or an electrical engineer, a chapter from a college text on solid-state electronics would probably be boring and difficult for you. In defense of your inability to read it easily and discuss its content, you just might say, "It's boring. All I do is read to get answers for the test." Might it not be wise for every teacher to start the school year with the premise that the main text for his course may be "boring and difficult" for many students in his class? Acceptance of this notion would certainly force the teacher to realize that student interest and ease are never given and must be included, therefore, in all instructional plans.

Nonreaders

The authors of this text have conducted an in-service workshop with fourteen science and social studies teachers in which it was revealed that, in conducting their classes, eight of them had abandoned the use of books. "The kids can't read," they said. "I have to communicate by word of mouth or they don't get it."

"All of the kids can't read?" we asked.

"Well," they replied, "either that, or some of them just won't tackle a difficult book."

Maybe they think it is boring? Or maybe that's their defense. Who wants to admit that a text at his grade level is too difficult for him. We asked the teachers to examine their textbooks to see if they could determine the nature of the difficulty. We had the social studies teachers read the science textbooks and the science teachers read the social studies textbooks. Each was to open the text at random and read the chapter where the book opened. Privately, each person wrote what his reactions to the chapter were—words, concepts, writing style, background. The results indicated that many of these teachers would have had difficulty with the text. It wasn't simply a lack of familiarity with technical words that slowed them down. It was also a lack of background or a frame of reference from which to work and an impatience with the style because it was different from what they were used to. "I found it very boring," admitted one teacher. "It did not hold my attention."

Perhaps restating a question would clarify a point. Is it true that many middle school and secondary school students literally cannot read, or is it that they simply have little or no preparation for or strategy for reading (bookthinking) a subject matter text? Certainly there are adolescents and adults who have not mastered the skills of translating a written message into its spoken counterpart. In fact they cannot pronounce the words on the page. But those few do not account for the large numbers that teachers say cannot read the subject-matter text. When eight teachers out of fourteen in a typical school system abandon books because the students cannot read them, there is something more at work than a handful of kids who cannot pronounce words.

Education via Headband

In the movie *The Magic Kingdom,* information was transmitted via headband. All knowledge was communicated from a programmer to those who needed information. Thus the society produced exact duplicates of the programmer.

Zardoz was another movie that depicted a similar kind of direct transfer of knowledge. Though the inhabitants had tremendous quantities of knowledge from the super programmer in the sky, their lives had lost meaning and they needed a "barbarian" to break into their society to show them that another style of life, though imperfect, was preferable because an individual was permitted, nay expected, to think and plan for himself. We naturally identify with the barbarian in *Zardoz* or the Savage in Huxley's *Brave New World* because we rebel against the notion of thought control. Instinctively we know that it leads to our disintegration as human personalities. How repugnant, then, the consequences of masses of teachers hiding books on the shelves under the guise that the students cannot read, that they must get all knowledge from the teacher's voice or from a film. When the teacher abandons the textbook as a source of independent knowledge and the discussion that results from it, he is indeed preventing individuality instead of promoting it.

HOW DIFFICULT ARE BOOKS?

It would be a valuable exercise for each teacher to analyze the basic text he uses or to analyze those that are on a state-adopted list, where state adoptions are used. State-adopted or locally adopted texts are not proposed here as the only books that should be used in the classroom. On the contrary, we recommend the use of a variety of books. Where adopted texts exist, however, they are the ones purchased first by the school corporation and thus form a major resource. Since the practice of adopting a text is quite common, teachers can gain valuable insights into the kinds of bookthinking expected of their students by examining those texts. Various analyses should be conducted to get the kinds of information that tell us something about the difficulties of the text.

Readability Formulas

Certain aspects of textual difficulty can be determined in a reasonably consistent way from one passage to the next. For example, one could assume that the one thousand most frequently used words in English writing are easy words simply because they occur so often that the reader develops an automatic response to them. All other words arbitrarily could be assumed to be difficult. In any randomly selected one-hundred-word passage, then, one could count the number of difficult words—those outside the one thousand most frequently used. Passages with more difficult words could thus be assumed to be more difficult to read.

One way to measure the difficulty of prose passages, then, is through a vocabulary frequency measure. Some formulas use a combination of difficult words and sentence length. Others are based on estimates of semantic and syntactic complexity. No matter which formula is used, it is important for teachers to realize that they are only attempts to quantify prose difficulty and must be couched in the experience and personal judgment of the teacher. There is no formula that provides an in-depth measure of experiential background, maturity, interest, and purposes for reading.

With those cautions in mind, let's examine two simple formulas that measure a combination of difficult words and sentence length. These formulas attempt to account for some aspects of vocabulary, sentence complexity, and concept load and thus produce a rough estimate of passage difficulty. Though only two aspects of reading difficulty, vocabulary and sentence length contribute to the ease of the difficulty of the prose. Though vocabulary difficulty and sentence length account for only part of what is called "level of readability," a teacher can apply a readability formula across passages or books to compare that kind of difficulty. More than a dozen formulas of this type have been used by researchers. One of the simplest is the Fog Index, which involves four simple steps:

Fog Index

To estimate readability follow these steps:

1. Take three 100-word passages; one from the beginning, one from the middle, and one from the end of the chapter or book.
2. Count the number of words in each passage that has three or more syllables. Do not count proper names, compound words or verb forms that become three syllables by adding *ed* or *es*.
3. Determine the average sentence length of each passage, for example, 18 words per sentence. For a partial sentence, estimate the percentage that is included in the 100-word passage, for instance .6 of a sentence.
4. Total factors 2 and 3 (the number of three or more syllable words and the average sentence length), and multiply the sum by 0.4. The result is the Fog Index for that passage. The score (Fog Index) represents the approximate level of education needed to read the passage.

Robert Gunning (1968), the developer of the Fog Index, claims that the resulting figure is a grade equivalent of difficulty for the passage. He said that he found a good correlation between his index and the difficulty of writing. For example, his sampling indicated that the *Atlantic Monthly* has an index of 12; *Harpers,* 11; *Time,* 10; *Reader's Digest,* 9; *Ladies Home Journal,* 8; and *True Confessions,* 7. In actual practice, grade-equivalent numbers have little value because there are so many other powerful forces that contribute to the cumulative difficulty of a passage. (Dawkins, 1975) Measuring vocabulary and sentence length is akin to measuring the legs and arms of a weightlifter and thereby predicting what he can lift. The score from a formula provides one bit of evidence to be coupled with others in deciding on the readability of a passage. The readability formula is simply a convenient way of making objective comparisons among various passages.

As a concrete example, try the Fog Index. Apply it to the paragraph above that begins: "It would be a valuable exercise for each teacher. . . ."

Count off 100 words for the vocabulary total and then average the sentence length by including the sentence where the one hundredth word occurs. If the same three-syllable word appears several times, count it on each occurrence. So far as the reader is concerned, it is difficult every time he sees it if he does not already know it.

Number of difficult words: _____
Average sentence length: _____
Multiply by 0.4
Level of difficulty according to index: _____

What is your judgment? Is this text too difficult?

Another formula, closely related to the Fog Index in its elements, is the Fry Graph for estimating readability. Any discussion of readability should use at least two methods to show that there is going to be variation in the estimates of difficulty from one formula to another. The Fry Graph was developed to be a quick, easy reference for estimating the reading difficulty of extended prose from grades one through college. The graph uses the average sentence length and the total number of syllables in a one-hundred-word sample as the means for determining difficulty. Look at Figure 1–1 and notice that the top heading is "Average number of syllables per 100 words." The graph will work on those passages that have at least 108 syllables but not more than 172 syllables. It is invalid for passages outside those limits. On the left side of the graph are indicated the average number of sentences per one hundred words. A one-hundred-word passage may contain from 3.6 to 25.0 sentences. Outside those limits the Fry Graph does not work.

Background

Research on readability levels using this type of formula shows tremendous variation from one formula to another (Klare, 1974). This is one good reason to use such information only as a general indicator of difficulty. The experience of teachers and case studies remind us that numerous other, probably more significant factors determine the true level of difficulty for any given reader. Experience and background with the topic, interest and enthusiasm for the topic (whether preformed or stimulated by the teacher), the density of concepts in the text, the amount of inference the writer requires the reader to apply—all are involved in measuring difficulty. To date there are no formulas that approach these other factors, but an example may help to clarify some of the features beyond the word count and sentence average.

Concept Load

Kellogg Hunt (1964) demonstrated the density of concepts in various prose passages. He explained the difference between the way a very young child might write about *Moby Dick* to make it comprehensible to his peers and the

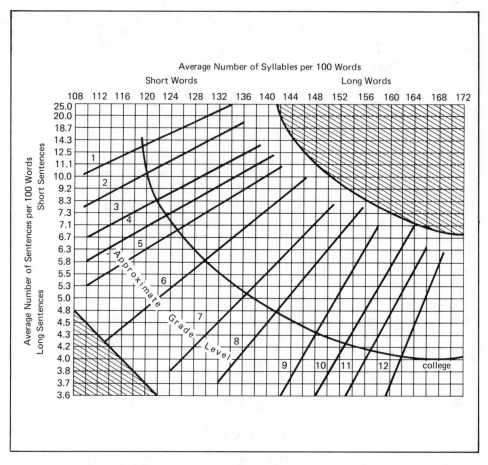

Figure 1-1. Graph for estimating readability. From Edward Fry, *Reading Instruction for Classroom and Clinic*. New York: McGraw-Hill, 1972.

way a mature person might write about *Moby Dick* for his peers. Thus, a young child might need this series of statements:

> Moby Dick is a whale.
> He is all white. He is big.
> Captain Ahab is a sea captain.
> He hates Moby Dick.
> Moby Dick hates Ahab.
> Captain Ahab tried to kill Moby Dick.
> Moby Dick got mad and he killed Captain Ahab instead.

For a mature audience a similar message might be expressed as follows:

Moby Dick, a great white whale, pursued by Ahab, leaped across a watery abyss and in retaliation slew him with vengeance.

The differences between the two passages, one for the immature and one for the mature, one for the neophyte and one for the schooled, help us understand the kinds of difficulties students encounter in their march across school years and school books. The passage for the young child presents one concept at a time, in concrete language, with only a minimum of inference required. The unfolding of the message proceeds one step at a time, allowing the child time and mental space to grab hold and put the ideas into recognizable order. Naturally, the vocabulary is simple and the sentences short. That kind of writing makes some fundamental assumptions about the background, language, and thinking of the young reader.

The second statement also makes assumptions about the mature reader in the passage that begins, "Moby Dick, a great white whale. . . ." The fact that he puts in apposition, "a great white whale, pursued by Ahab . . . ," makes some assumptions about the reader's language facility and his thinking facility. The writer assumes that the reader can compress ideas and can zip through transformations without verbalizing them. He also assumes that the reader's background will enable him to fill in the logical gaps not provided directly in that one-sentence summary of the battle between Ahab and Moby Dick. Notice also, only one polysyllable word appears, but the sentence is longer than the ones written for the young child. The words "vengeance" and "slew" are not commonly used and so could cause some trouble even though they do not fit into the Fog Index readability formula.

Fistful of Words

Some teachers use a quick and dirty method for estimating the apparent difficulty of a text for a class; they have the students in the class read several passages silently and independently. As he reads, a student closes a finger into his fist when he encounters a word he cannot pronounce or does not understand. On a piece of paper he writes the number of difficult words (number of fingers) for each of the one-hundred-word passages read. The rule of thumb is: Two fists or ten difficult words indicate slow frustrating reading for that student. That passage may be too difficult for that student to read on his own. True, the method is not highly scientific, but it alerts the teacher to the vocabulary and concept needs of the group in a highly efficient way. The teacher can make adjustments in text selections and in assignments on the basis of the "fistful" that each student records.

All these observations have been made about potential readability problems, and we haven't yet gone beyond the sentence. But we begin to see why it is presumptuous of a teacher to hand out books written for mature readers and expect every teenager to read and comprehend sufficiently well to carry on intelligent discussions or to write synthesis papers. Learning and bookthinking, with all the factors mentioned, are involved in the process. It is because students frequently need help in those and other aspects of book-thinking that school systems hire teachers. Otherwise, students could travel alone accompanied only by a few faithful books.

Boring Books

Are school books difficult and boring? Perhaps.

James Herndon, in his book *How to Survive in Your Native Land,* said he gave his students complete freedom to do what they wanted. They could roam the halls, hang out in the restrooms, go to the library, read, draw, create. Neither books nor tasks were imposed by the teacher. Even so, the kids kept complaining that it was boring: "There's nothing to do in here (when they stayed in the classroom) and there's nothing to do out there" (when they roamed the halls and did whatever). The text is boring when assigned, and school is boring when there are no assignments. What do the words actually mean? What do students mean: "It is boring"? Perhaps that is a student's way of defending himself—or of attacking school. Perhaps the students simply need ways of growing in vocabulary and language facility, need experience to bring their backgrounds into concert with the content, and need to be shown how to interact with the book—which is an example of the way people in that discipline think. After all, until a student begins to see how he can place his mind side by side with the author of the book, he cannot view the book with any interest. With those considerations, the teacher has a better chance of matching students and books—either in a prescribed text or in the myriad of other material available. *Bookthinking may be difficult work, but it should not be boring!*

MATCHING UP

In the powerful musical *Fiddler on the Roof,* the Jewish community has a matchmaker, a person who helps to get the right boy and the right girl together. No small task in view of pleasing two sets of parents and two young people. It is hinted that after many compromises were made the result was usually workable and perhaps quite satisfactory. The teacher plays a similar role with a corresponding need to adjust in deciding which book to place with which student.

When the teacher puts together the data he collects on the textbook and the background of the students, he can make the judgments that will lead to effective learning through reading. He knows, too, that a student's experience and a teacher's enthusiasm determine what a student reads. After the movie *Jaws* roared across the screens in the mid-70s, sharks made a big splash in biology classes. As one teacher put it, "Even the kids who previously

couldn't read the word *shark* now are interested in their *omnivorous* habits."
Motivation and interest are not everything in reading instruction, but they
certainly display marvelous compensatory powers when they are present.
As a teacher reviews books and magazines, he must remember that, if student
enthusiasm, vocabulary, and experience operate at a low level, the teacher
and the text must shoulder a tremendous load to move the student forward.
Choosing the books to be read, then, demands more than a quick perusal
to see if major concepts and topics are covered. Given the experience of
your students, can they relate to the manner and the style in which the
concepts are presented?

Technical Is Not Difficult

A misconception associated with reading subject-matter texts is that, once
technical vocabulary is identified, pronounced, and defined, the student has
his reading problems solved. Not true. Some of Malinson's studies (1972) of
science texts indicate that the major problem lies in nontechnical vocabulary.
Sandbagged around many of the unique, technical words are other difficult
words loaded with associated meaning. Take this passage for example and
see if you can separate the technical from the support language:

> Through the *experience-story approach* the teacher leads the child to proceed
> from the known—his oral language—to the unknown—the graphic represen-
> tation of that language. The teacher helps the child conceptualize that what
> he can say can be written, and what can be written he can read. (Harris and
> Smith, 1976, p. 162)

This passage appears in a chapter that describes elementary teaching methods.
"Experience story," the new technical term which a teacher might define,
does not reduce the weight of other words (graphic representation, conceptualize) that slow the reader or stop him in his efforts to encapsulate the
message.

Valuable dividends can be gained from anticipating the nontechnical
vocabulary that may cause problems and include them in a prereading
discussion. One diagnostic technique for identifying difficult words is to have
students search for the problem words. For example, for each new chapter
or selection, ask a representative from each group in the class to make a
list of the words he thinks might trouble him or his classmates. Or the entire
class might skim and list words. From the resulting list of words, the teacher
develops techniques to aid the student. One example is to have each member
of the group be responsible for a word. Each person presents his word as
follows:

1. He writes it on the board or locates it on a duplicated list.
2. He pronounces it.

3. He defines it and uses it in a sentence.
4. He reads the sentence where it appears in the lesson.

Variations on that technique include developing a growing glossary. Each person places his word on a file card headed by the word and its phonetic spelling. The definition and sample usage fill out the card. When filed alphabetically in a file box, the words are available for daily use as students need them.

---

1. diaphanous   2. (di af a nus)
3. Delicate quality so as to be transparent or translucent.
4. The dragonfly darts quickly over the pond on diaphanous wings as it captures mosquitoes and flies.

Sample student-made glossary card

Going Beyond the Sentence Level

In connected prose, some ideas are quite explicit and some require considerable inference. By estimating the amount of inference needed, the teacher has an idea, too, of the amount of difficulty that students will have with a particular writing style. The more inference required, the more difficult it will be for the average student. On the other hand, there are readers who prefer working with a high degree of inference. They can leap to the heart of the matter before it is whipped to death by a verbose author.

For example, in the paragraph quoted above concerning the experience-story method, the authors make several assumptions about the reader's background and therefore require the reader to infer rather than give him an extended explanation. Reread that quotation and note the places where it is assumed the reader has background in educational psychology and in teaching methodology.

If the authors believed that the readers needed more help in understanding that selection, they could have added explanatory phrases that required less of the reader. Thus, the paragraph could have been written as follows:

Through another teaching method called the experience-story approach, the teacher leads the child from the known—his oral language—to the unknown —the written representation of that language. He asks the child to dictate a story or an experience and writes it as the child dictates. The technique guides the child in making associations between talking and writing. Thereby, the teacher helps the child conceptualize that what he can say can be written, and what can be written he can read.

Being cognizant of more or less inference in writing style gives a teacher another significant factor that accounts for difficulty in reading topical prose. Matching student capabilities with the style in a textbook is achieved through trial and error. But in a broad sense the more inference, the more abstract the reading. Abstract reading requires a person trained in or accustomed to abstract thinking. Thus, training in a type of reading-thinking activity becomes an issue. Teacher and student need to work together to construct approaches that enable them to manipulate the ideas in their text. Either that, or find a text that the student can already use with minimal teacher guidance.

HOW DOES A TEACHER ADJUST TO THE RANGE OF READABILITY IN A CLASS?

An analysis of different kinds of writing and an application of a readability formula to texts in a given field should demonstrate that there are inherent difficulties in prose. A student isn't necessarily stupid when he struggles and perhaps even fails in reading a particular selection or text. Apart from the potential problems in subject-matter prose, the students come to a class with a range of abilities—some the result of genetics and some the result of their experience in school. Every teacher's professional conscience dictates a concern for each student's growth. That's why teaching is more than distributing morsels in an academic bread line. That's why the teacher analyzes the student as well as the textbook in bringing the two together.

Take the class listed in Table 1–1, for example. How would you respond to the wide range of reading scores in that group? For a secondary class it is not unusual to see a spread of eight to twelve years in the reading scores achieved on a standardized reading test. No matter what subject you teach, the effect of this range has significant implications for your teaching. Review these scores and consider some alternative means for helping these students make progress.

Class of 22

After reviewing the class scores found in Table 1–1, a teacher might typically react: "Great! Small class of only 22; IQ scores are normal or above. It looks like easy sailing."

But look at the reading scores. They represent a wide range from third grade through twelfth grade on the grade-equivalent table. Therefore, any intention that a teacher had of treating that group as a homogeneous class evaporates. Even assuming that those above the fiftieth percentile can

TABLE 1-1
Summary of Ability and Reading Achievement

MISS MILLER

	CALIFORNIA TEST OF MENTAL MATURITY			NELSON-DENNY READING TEST	
	VERBAL	NONVERBAL	TOTAL IQ	PERCEN-TILE	GRADE EQUIVA-LENT
Name					
1. Tom A.	98	102	99	47	9.0
2. Bobby B.	94	115	106	65	9.5
3. Nancy C.	88	110	98	13	3.7
4. Neil D.	109	93	101	52	9.1
5. Sharon E.	133	119	125	93	12.7
6. Phillip F.	104	91	98	42	8.4
7. Greta G.	109	98	104	65	9.5
8. Helen H.	98	93	90	47	9.0
9. Larry I.	136	139	136	89	11.8
10. Mary J.	111	99	106	59	9.3
11. Jerry K.	115	89	101	47	9.0
12. James L.	90	94	93	47	9.0
13. Marilyn M.	121	95	110	82	10.7
14. Joseph N.	109	96	103	65	9.5
15. Kathy O.	99	101	100	70	10.0
16. Peggy P.	121	108	114	59	9.3
17. Sandra Q.	95	101	99	42	8.4
18. Robert R.	88	98	93	29	5.4
19. Nila S.	91	95	94	25	5.0
20. Audrey T.	118	101	111	74	10.2
21. Virginia U.	90	105	99	22	4.6
22. Ralph V.	86	92	90	29	5.4

read the ninth-grade textbook (and that is not usually a wise assumption), that means that eleven students or half the class cannot read the text without frustration. Moreover, the teacher does not know what caused the students to get low or high scores on the test. Are they caused by differences in vocabulary, background concepts, language-usage differences, memory, inferential reasoning? The bald grade-equivalent score doesn't whisper a hint about the nature of the difference and therefore what the teacher should do about those differences. (See Chapter 5 for a discussion on the vagaries of using grade-equivalent scores for classroom decisions.) So the question about teaching this class can't be solved with a simple sweep of a hand, but rather leads us into the points to be made in this text.

Standardized tests are rightfully criticized for many weaknesses and misuses, but they do show adequately, as does Table 1–1, that a class has a wide range of performance in reading—a range to which each teacher must adjust in order to offer valuable experience to the individuals in that class.

Standardized tests, like the readability formulas discussed earlier, report information to you on a very limited sample of reading tasks. Like the formulas, the tests are concerned with vocabulary, usually a general-use vocabulary, and with the comprehension of short paragraphs, again usually on topics related to general life activity. The grade-equivalent scores on these tests, therefore, will not tell you with any precision what kind of responses a student will make to written discourse in a specific subject area. It is quite conceivable that a youngster scores 9.5 on a standardized reading test but cannot read past the first page of his ninth-grade science book. His background and vocabulary may not match that kind of reading, or he may have so little enthusiasm for the teacher or for the subject that he cannot crank up enough energy to work on the concepts presented. Or perhaps the writing style of the book baffles him or disgusts him and he cannot respond as he did for the general content on the reading test.

For the time being those cautions suffice to continue with your analysis of how to teach that group of kids. Concerned with the student's welfare, you want to help him as an individual, but you are naturally worried about the mechanics of meeting a range of abilities in each of the classes that reports to you. As you examined the reading scores given above, you probably made certain assumptions. For example, (1) the textbooks are suitable for those who scored at grade level, (2) those who scored above grade level certainly can read the text without difficulty. Those are not always valid assumptions. But in the guise of efficiency, let them stand for now. Your assumptions direct you to those students whose scores registered below the reading level for their grade. That's more than half the class—and not unusual.

If students cannot read one text, the most sensible thing to do is give them a text they can read. With today's plethora of books, magazines, and pamphlets, almost every reading level can be accommodated on almost every standard topic. For legitimate reasons, though, a teacher may want all students to use the same book as part of an activity. It may be integral to a group experiment, or the school library may not have adequate material on a specific topic. At those times the teacher could differentiate the reading assignments in such a way that each student uses the book according to his capability.

If you analyzed those ninth-grade scores in that fashion, you did acknowledge the need to adjust to the different levels of reading ability in the class. Your analysis identified two major options: finding books that match the reading level of the youngsters and, when desirable, using the same book for all, but giving different assignments to different individuals. Some can read it for a full integrated discussion; some can read the heads and the summary to get the main thrust and the major concepts; while others can search for a few specific details—perhaps found in the heads or in a specific graph or chart. A series of studies done by Herber and his students demonstrated the viability of using differentiated assignments through the development of study guides for each group (Herber et al., 1970). Developing those guides requires effort, of course, and they do imply a classroom organization that flows from identified class groups. The mechanics of preparing study guides appears in a later chapter. What is important here is to realize that a wide range of reading abilities must be met by constructive action.

The second option mentioned (there are many) was to find other books for those students who did not have the vocabulary and organizational skills needed to perform in the adopted text. Though it once might have been valid to say that subject-matter texts were quite limited, that is no longer true. Almost every topic in every subject is written about in various formats at various levels of difficulty. Some publishers even specialize in producing mature books for students with a limited vocabulary (Spache, 1970). Having a multitude of books in the libraries and publishers' warehouses, however, does not solve the problems in the classroom. A teacher who thinks he has only one text because the school adopts a single text for each grade should expand his peripheral vision. There are usually budgets for supplementary books if a teacher presses for them; there are always library funds that can be used to supplement a teacher's resources; there are library loans, magazines, newspapers, and home libraries that can serve learners.

Student-Made Texts

One of the cleverest ways we have seen for solving a multitext problem and for getting youngsters involved in their own learning at the same time was what the teacher called "Build your own text plan." Steve Baker, an English teacher in a small town in southern Illinois, told his students that they had the first nine weeks of the year to build their own textbook for the remainder of the year. They were allowed to use selections from textbooks, library books, magazines, newspapers, journals—any sources. Whatever they used had to be provided in sufficient quantities so each member of a project group could use it over a two-week period. And the selection had to fit defined literary periods and genres. That gave Baker an opportunity to show samples of writing and to convey the basic ideas he wanted to emphasize. After that, he played the role of adviser and idea stimulator.

There were five groups in the class, each composed of about six students. Each group was to develop its own text without reference to what the other groups were doing. After looking at available short stories, poetry, plays, essays, human-interest items, and so on, the students were to make a selection of what they wanted to read and discuss as a small class. In the process they read a much larger volume of material than they ever would have tolerated if their teacher had assigned it. Also, they read with a critical eye to decide whether to bring a selection to the entire group to include as part of their text.

What's more, each student had to be conscious of the various needs and interests of the group. Each group was given the responsibility of finding at least one selection of each literary type that could be read by every member of the group. That's when Baker applied the fistful of difficult words technique to them for estimating what might be too difficult. If any member of the group determined that a selection was too difficult for him, the group had to find a supplemental selection that he could read, or they had to agree to tutor that individual. That gave Baker an opportunity to show the students how to read selections in different ways, depending on what they had to get out of it or what they wanted to get out of it.

Selecting Groups

The five groups in the class (Table 1–2) were partially teacher selected and partially self-selected. First the teacher divided the whole class into three groups based on his observations of their ability to read in the field of English, because one of his objectives was to mix ability levels within groups. To accomplish this, he formed five planning trios, each containing one person from the three ability levels. He made sure the sexes were mixed as well. In a sense he had a fast group, a middle group, and a slow group.

TABLE 1-2
Groups for Student-Made Text

PERFORMANCE LEVEL	GROUP 1	GROUP 2	GROUP 3	GROUP 4	GROUP 5
High 10	Boy	Girl	Boy	Girl	Boy
Average 10	Girl	Boy	Girl	Boy	Girl
Low 10	Boy	Girl	Boy	Girl	Boy

GUIDELINES
15 students are assigned to 5 groups as above.
15 other students then choose a group to be in based on the
   emphasis the group will take.
No group may have more than 7 members.
Each group works independently on building a text that
   suits its emphasis.
Numbers in groups are adjusted to match total class size.

Then he drew a name from each of the groups to form the nucleus for one of the five working groups. The sexes had to be mixed in each group as well. He did that four more times so that each of five teams had a member from the fast, middle, and slow categories. Then he posted the names, gave each trio a day in which to discuss their interests, after which they posted areas of emphasis they would pursue. Then the remainder of the class signed up by alphabetical order with the trio they wanted to join. Each group could have a maximum of seven members. First signed, first served.

The results? Baker said they were fantastic. Doesn't know why he hadn't thought of it before. Not only were the intellectual results superior to any he had achieved when he personally tried to "run" the class, but the attitude of the students toward American literature, was the most positive of any group that he had worked with. Problems? Sure. But they were minimal compared to the results. Not only did the students read more, they read with greater purpose. Malcontents who seemed to retreat into a corner or voice their objections through obnoxious behavior were practically nonexistent. Remember, each group had to make sure that each member of the group participated and was gaining something of value. Peer tutoring was a natural and accepted part of the routine.

Baker found that he had plenty of time for talking with the students and guiding them on their individual projects. If they needed direction, practice, suggestions, or his reactions to a possible selection, he was available. They even taught him about American literature. They brought in selections that he hadn't read before and wanted to know what he thought of them. The students and teacher were learning together. That happened because they were each building something, each actively pursuing topics and trying to put them into some sensible form.

Baker also had time to work with two kids who came into his class labeled "nonreaders." He had time to discuss the cases with the school's reading specialist and to work out some techniques that kept the two kids participating in the class.

Though other examples of effective secondary school teaching appear throughout this text, the student-made-text approach emphasizes a truth that often slips out of mind: secondary schools are "print schools." Student success and teacher success, therefore, are tied to their effectiveness in teaching and in learning print strategies, that is, bookthinking strategies.

Matching the Student and the Book

One of the attractive values in the "build-your-own text" plan is the combination of mature direction and student choice and initiative. A sense of self-determination has strong, nay, mandatory dimensions in the life of the teenager. Yet he has little experience that shows him how to take hold and put things together. When the teacher said, "Build your own text," the satisfying juices of self-determination flowed. When the teacher said, "Here are types and periods to build on," and "Come to me if you need book titles or direction," the security of the ages bolstered the students.

There may be pitfalls in a build-your-own text technique, as there are in all teaching methods, but the technique contains the germ of all the positive elements in bookthinking.

1. Purposes are clear.
2. Personal interests are appealed to through self-selection.
3. Reading is active, critical, constructive.
4. Reading-learning activity is interactive, involving books and people.
5. A community sense arises from recognition of varied abilities in the group and the responsibility for each group to help its own members succeed at varying levels.

TEACHER JUDGMENT

Exactly how a teacher responds to the need to adjust to the variety of reading abilities in his class depends on his philosophy, his subject, and his experience. There is no question about the existence of a wide range of reading levels in every class.[1] As a teacher gains experience with youngsters and with books in his subject area, he develops more options and is strategically in a better position to aid students. The beginning teacher can use his awareness of the variance in books and in students to establish a few techniques to adjust to those variances. The results should greatly benefit the class because it demonstrates the variety of materials and the variety of ways to approach a topic.

As mentioned earlier, a beginning teacher would do well to build a file on available materials, with student help, it may be hoped. A card file and a reference shelf should grow conveniently out of the search for information and opinions in the books and magazines that surround the subject. Beginners may want to try writing experimental study guides to help two or three different categories of students read and use a common text.

Experience helps develop a teacher's antennae, makes her more alert to the cues of youngsters. For example, there is the kid who complains loudly about the class and the school but listens intently while slouching. He wants to impress everyone as antiestablishment and yet doesn't want to miss any ideas in an area that interests him. Then there is the kid who answers all the questions in class and on the test but never reads on her own. What is it that's only skin deep? Or there's the one who pretends to read whenever the teacher is looking; otherwise his gaze wanders around the room. And he

---

[1] The very nature of standardized test norms mandates that half the population in any one age group will score below the mean, will have a grade-equivalent below the grade in question. For a more precise indication of what a student can read, the teacher must evaluate his performance in class-assigned texts.

can't answer any questions about the book. Perhaps the most common indicator of trouble is the kid who avoids reading in class by "forgetting" his book. "It's in the locker or in Mrs. Schwartz's room." And, finally, there's the kid who closes his book, slumps in his chair, and announces, "This is a pile of crap."

Those behaviors are not always what they appear to be at first. Their meaning for reading needs the interpretation of experience and the perspective of where they are acted out. What the teacher can be sure of is that every one of those behaviors is a message, and that learning the language of behavior is an important part of his or her professional development.

As a teacher learns to shift and use information from people and from books, the chance of bringing them together in a workable combination improves. The teacher knows that books, like people, have distinguishing characteristics. As to readability, the teacher might use the following as a checklist for reviewing materials or for mentally cataloging them for use with his students. (A more detailed text analysis format is given in chapters 10 and 12.)

Book Characteristics

1. Interest area or type. What kinds of interests [topics] are emphasized?
2. Inference requirements. Does the writing style require a large amount or small amount of inference?
3. Vocabulary. Is the vocabulary difficult or technical or both?
4. Organizational aids. Does the format use numerous heads or other means to help the reader organize his thoughts and guide the movement of ideas?
5. Readability level. If a readability formula was applied, where would it rank this material? Is it sensibly close—within a couple of years of the grade in question?

To use an analysis of a book, the teacher must know the students well enough to bring books and students together. In a sense, the thrust of the present book lies in that direction. It is a continuing analysis of how to align books and students. The students' minds and emotions—how they work and their classroom manifestations—are integral to success in bookthinking. So, too, the features of books and their possible effects on teenage learners must be analyzed and used.

SUMMARY

One of the most challenging and yet most necessary tasks for the middle-school or secondary-school teacher is to match students with books they can use effectively. For students to become independent learners, they must learn how to use books. Because books vary in difficulty and students vary in ability, the teacher needs mechanisms for estimating a reasonable match between books and students. Two simple formulas were presented as tools for calculating the difficulty of a book. In addition, the teacher is encouraged to use her own insight and experience with prose syntax and conceptual complexity in making judgments about which books are appropriate for different students.

The concept of bookthinking, a process for extracting information from subject-matter texts, is proposed as a framework in which secondary and middle-school students and teachers can work. Capsulized techniques for bringing students and books together were presented. They are previews of expanded discussions in other chapters in the text.

DISCUSSION QUESTIONS

1. Using a reading difficulty formula, estimate the readability of state or locally adopted textbooks. Discuss the implications for teaching.
2. Using a list of book characteristics, such as the list in this chapter, describe the state or locally adopted books and the students who could benefit most from them.
3. If you wanted students to read independently in your subject area, how would you guide them in self-selecting books that were easy enough for them to read?
4. What difficulties do you see in matching students and books? What proposals would you make for solving those difficulties?

Suggested Readings

For an extensive bibliography on readability see "Assessing Readability" by George Klare, Reading Research Quarterly, X/1, pps. 98–102, 1974–1975.

Botel, M., and A. Granowsky. "A Formula for Measuring Syntactic Complexity: A Directional Effort," *Elementary English*, April 1972, 49, 513–516.

Dawkins, John. *Syntax and Readability*. Newark, Del.: International Reading Association, 1975.
   This informative short book expands the concept of readability beyond counting words and sentences. Though not offering simple formula solutions, it provides insights and procedures for making a person sensitive to passage difficulty. Not a beginner's book.

Flesch, Rudolf. *How To Test Readability*. New York: Harper, 1951. This book explains simply one of the early popularized means for estimating readability.

Gunning, Robert. "The Fog Index After Twenty Years," *Journal of Business Communication*, Winter 1968, 6, 3–13.
   Discusses findings of the very simply applied Fog Index in many popular magazines.

Jacobson, Milton D. "Reading Difficulty of Physics and Chemistry Textbooks," *Educational and Psychological Measurement*, Summer 1965, 25, 449–457.

The Bookthinking
Process–
A Cognitive Map

Bookthinking: What does it mean in the classroom?

What will a workable definition enable the teacher to do?

How do reading and bookthinking grow across the school years?

EXTRACTING INFORMATION
—STUDENTS

Most teachers anticipate that their students will gain knowledge and a sense of how to solve problems in their subject area. On that premise, we asked several high school students how they garnered information from certain courses—for instance, from lectures or reading or other media. One of those interviews was with two boys together, completing their tenth year in school and both "probably going to college."

Student Interviews

Question: In school where do you get information about a subject matter?
Tony: Combination of information from lectures and books.

Steve: I remember things I hear and so I use lectures as my main source of information. I read books as reinforcement of what I heard in class or in a discussion.

Question: What new things are you learning from your high school courses?

Tony: Most of the courses are just refining skills that you already have, especially in English where you are always "writing a theme" that is never defined any more specifically than that. We've been doing the same thing over and over again since the seventh grade without doing anything except getting practice.

Steve: In literature I guess we have started to analyze minor themes in a story instead of only analyzing the major ones.

Tony: In science, the teacher only baby-sits. He says, "Go through the chapters and do the experiments. Take the tests when ready. If you pass, go on to the next experiment and do the work on your own." Then he waits. Everybody cheats like crazy.

Steve: Math is all teacher because the book is all problems. The teacher explains how to solve problems and then you practice in the book.

Question: Does practice help you?

Steve: Yeah, it gets you ready for the tests, I guess.

Question: What do you think you get out of high school?

Steve: High school is a preparation for college, I guess, and teaches you to work on your own.

Question: Do your teachers guide you in working on your own, or how do you learn to do that?

Steve: The teachers say, "We'll give you this time to get it done." After that it's up to you.

Question: Do you find any social values in high school?

Tony: Socially, you have lots of time to rap with your friends and see people from all parts of the city. That's a big help in learning about life and in becoming mature.

Steve: All that talking and seeing different cliques lets you see people and shows you that you have to take care in selecting your friends.

Question: Where do you find all this time to talk to the kids at school?

Steve: In every class there is free study time, and so you talk.

Tony: While the teacher is talking, you talk to a neighbor if you want to.

Steve: In some classes, like biology, you can talk all the time because the whole class is free except for the last three weeks when you are working for a grade. Then it's business.

Question: Are you saying that the teacher only expects you to work the last three weeks of the semester?

Steve: Oh, no. But teachers just say read, and then they leave you alone. They don't know whether you do, except for an occasional test.

These two boys have adequate time but little sense of direction in using books. They see the school's main value, perhaps even main emphasis, as social contacts and not books. This interview, when coupled with the one in the previous chapter where teenagers were comparing televiewing to reading a textbook, gives us some notion of the esteem that teenagers have for subject-matter reading and their corresponding lack of sense of how to proceed intelligently in subject-matter reading.

From the students' perspective, television and social contacts at school had clear purposes and evident values—relax and enjoy programs; meet new people and learn how to get along in life. When it came to books, the only purpose seemed to be pass certain exams, and those didn't seem to retain a very high value. The response of some teachers to this problem seems to be to make the books more like TV programming. Make them so stimulating and exciting and colorful that they will have the same allure as "Charlie's Angels." If our purposes and those of TV program executives were the same, that might not be a wasteful idea. But books in school play a variety of roles—sometimes including entertainment—yet those roles do not appear clear to students. Perhaps they are not clear in the minds of teachers.

We must remember that a textbook was not meant to compete with TV. Purposes and intellectual styles are different. Textbook reading is generally serious reading. On the other hand, many of us probably read the newspaper and watch TV at the same time. Each permits a casual search for something that interests us. The mature reader is thus in control and turns one off and the other on as the stimulus of the moment engages his mind.

That doesn't mean that a teacher should be satisfied with ugly, raggy books as textbooks. Textbooks ought to be as attractive in format and as engaging in style as one can find for the students that one teaches. But subject-matter reading is not casual, and students have to be taught to approach the text as a distinct kind of discourse, one that does not follow the habits of televiewing. When books have clear purposes in the mind of the teacher, then they will probably take on significance in the minds of the students. They quickly learn where the values are and how to succeed. The teacher tells them how to do well in class through numerous personal remarks or attitudes.

TEACHER EXPECTATIONS

Let's look at this problem through the eyes of teachers. What do they expect students to do as a result of a reading assignment?

In one workshop for sixteen secondary teachers who expressed interest in reading methods, we asked them to describe what they expected students to do when they gave the students a reading assignment.

Teachers' answers were open and not limited to categories, but here they are categorized in terms of *literal, critical,* and *elaborative* expectations. (See Table 2–1.) The *literal* category included descriptions of memory tasks —recall of details, getting basic facts, identifying the thrust of theme. The *critical* category included analysis and evaluation tasks—comparing, arriving at conclusions, judging worth. The *elaboration* category included predictions

TABLE 2-1
Secondary Teachers' Expectations
for Textbook Reading

EXPECTATIONS	NUMBER TESTED
Answer literal questions	10
Answer critical questions	13
Elaborate on text	4
Total subjects = 16	

and applications—new endings, following directions, hypothesizing. The sixteen answered almost exclusively in terms of having students respond to questions (Smith and Smith, 1976). They hoped, they said, that their students would recall basic information, but especially that they would be able to answer critical reading questions. Only four teachers listed expectations that required an elaboration.

Then we asked: "What do you actually get from the students?" Their responses are summarized in Table 2–2.

TABLE 2-2
Teachers' Evaluation of Student Responses

TYPE OF RESPONSE	NUMBER
Literal	12
Critical	5
Elaboration	1
Number of teachers surveyed = 16	

As they expressed it, these sixteen teachers tended to get literal comprehension although they hoped for critical thinking. These teachers agreed that the results from students are disappointing when compared to teacher expectations. For the most part these teachers settled for literal responses. Only a handful got critical and elaborative responses.

Further discussion among the teachers and the high school students interviewed revealed an attitude of passivity toward reading, almost as if the reader were a sponge soaking up the print and being able to wring part of it back upon request. Yet teacher expectations required analysis, evaluation, and elaboration—hardly passive functions. Teachers do in fact expect directed and controlled thinking to take place during reading. The reader is expected to tackle a passage with purpose and energy. For directed, controlled thinking to take place, the reader must be as active as the writer when he wrote the passage. There is an I/you relationship between the author and the reader that must be identified and acted out if reading is to occur as most teachers expect it to.

The active role that a reader plays presupposes that, if a student doesn't know how to answer a type of question, the teacher will explain or demonstrate how to think through that question to a solution. Have we teachers, in defining our tasks, ever asked ourselves what literal, critical, and elaborative questions require of a student to answer them? Do we know how to formulate questions (or tests) to help the student grow? Or do we ask the vague kinds of questions we answered when we were in high school?

If teachers' expectations are rather vague or hidden, it is no wonder that students have nondescript means for using texts and other resources.

READING AS AN INTERACTION

When reading a subject-matter text, one tries to extract information, that's true. But more. Reading is not a random absorption by which one lets ideas flit through his consciousness hoping that some of them will tickle his fancy and lodge in his memory. While reading, it is certainly possible to engage in a fuzzy kind of mental activity characterized by a general flow of thought, a sort of stream of consciousness. Television viewing, for example, is often akin to a sort of mental drifting. But that is not what a teacher expects when he asks his students to read. He anticipates that their thoughts will be direced and controlled so that they can put the ideas of the subject into an orderly pattern for future work—whether a test or some other application. Reading can then be defined as an interaction, a communication in which the author and the reader each brings his background, language, and a common desire to reach the other person. No matter how else one defines reading, it must involve ideas, backgrounds, common language, common interest, and a mutual point of departure.

The teacher's job is to promote that interaction, especially to show students how to engage the authors in a given subject. See Figure 2–1 for an illustration of the author-reader relationship.

Thus, *reading is an interactive communication involving background experience, language, and an organization of ideas.*

The reader goes through a number of processes to accomplish an interactive communication (reading). He pronounces words and uses the conventions of writing to relate print and speech, follows words in an orderly sequence, associates them with ideas, and puts them together into a complete message. Over years in school, a student is trained in these processes and practices them until he becomes proficient. Along the way he develops automatic responses to a large number of word symbols and learns to predict what an author will say next by using clues from context, syntax, and the tone

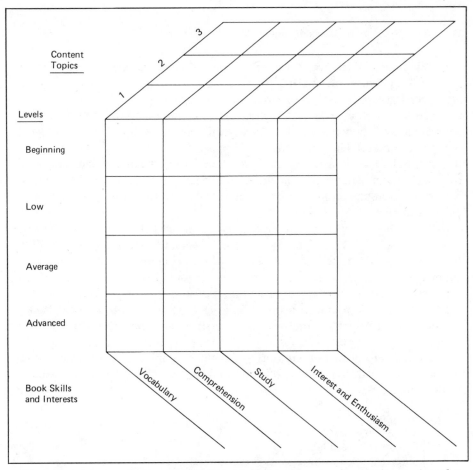

Figure 2-1. Author-reader relationship. Mature reading requires author and reader to bring related concepts, language, and purposes to the communication process. Their interaction should produce new ideas for the reader.

and style of the author. It is hoped that a student will achieve that minimum level of proficiency during his elementary school years. But some will not.

Beyond Grade Five

Suppose for a moment that all children did arrive in the upper grades with a sense that reading was an interaction, a communication with the writer. Wouldn't that accomplish all that's necessary for him to succeed in reading the books and magazines used in subject-matter classes? Suppose elementary teachers did show each child that reading is "like talk written down" by having him dictate his experiences and then printing or typing his words on a piece of paper. The student thereby sees that he can read back the message or someone else can read it. With his words printed in front of him, he can talk back to himself, so to speak, or someone else can talk back to him, just as people do when they converse. Suppose through similar techniques the young child developed an awareness of the interactive process of reading.

What then is left for the upper grades? Could not the same query be posed for thinking, for English, for science? Once the rudiments have been introduced, what is left to be done beyond grade five? For one thing an awareness of author-reader interaction must be elaborated into more specific competencies, competencies that have variations from one kind of subject matter to another. The vocabulary of English, for example, is different from the vocabulary of science. Each is different from the daily neighborhood language the student uses. The teacher, therefore, must show the student what the vocabulary of a subject means and how to learn it in the most efficient manner.

Consider the teacher as a learner. What would happen if a large group of teachers were asked to read a chapter on solid state electronics? With few exceptions, the teachers would find the chapter extremely difficult, if not impossible, to read and comprehend; not only because there are words for which they do not carry meanings, but because they would bring a nontechnical background to a task requiring a whole set of technical background. How can one interact with a writer if he and the writer do not start with a common base.

Vocabulary growth, therefore, is just the beginning of work to be done in the upper grades. The stuff of bookthinking includes growth in all these growth areas:

1. Background and concepts
2. Vocabulary and language
3. Organization of ideas
4. Sufficient practice for easy use of terms and ideas
5. Special skills, such as using maps and charts

All teachers are concerned with these areas because they represent better learning and better teaching. Thus, beyond a simple awareness of writer-reader interaction, there remains a considerable range of reading/thinking operations for student growth. Teachers need to define what that growth means for the students and for the subjects that they teach. For example, most upper-level students who are labeled "poor readers" do not suffer from lack of training in word-pronunciation techniques (phonics, structural analysis, context), but rather they cannot manipulate the vocabulary and ideas in their subject-matter texts (Strang, 1969; Davis, 1972). Here is an area for all subject-matter teachers to concentrate on and to develop instructional techniques to help their students succeed.

BOOKTHINKING CONCEPT

The subject-matter teacher chose to specialize in a discipline that involves a system of knowledge with procedures for arriving at that particular knowledge. Though not a reading teacher, the subject-matter teacher is certainly a "bookthinking" teacher—for reasons already stated. What he needs, then, is a bookthinking pedagogy, a teaching definition, and a plan that will guide him in making decisions about student needs and course activities. Figure 2–2 shows the dimensions of what the content teacher needs to include. There are topics or subject-oriented procedures to be learned by students who have various levels of abilities to study them independently and who also have a need to learn or to exercise skills and interests which, in turn, make them more capable of learning in that subject area. In a simplistic sense, then, Topic 1 must be organized so that the four levels of student abilities can be accommodated. Those accommodations extend across vocabulary, thinking operations, study approaches, and an appeal to student interest. With that view in mind, the teacher can make the teaching process as simple or as complex as he wishes—at least the dimensions of his choices are pictured in his mind.

Assuming that every teacher encourages student independence, considers books essential to the process of learning his subject content, and wants to find ways to helping students at all levels to think through books in his field, what, then, is needed for teaching his subject? The basic question is: How does a teacher get students to read and think about his subject so that they achieve reasonable objectives? ("They're mine," you say; "so naturally they're reasonable.") For example, a teacher wants a given student to answer typical questions about what he reads. (What happened? What is the theme? How can it be used?) A teacher also wants students to read maturely, that is, to adjust for various purposes. (Mature reading is described in Chapter 3.) And somehow, with the text material, the student is expected to grow in his ability to think.

Asking Questions

Consider for a moment what it means to answer typical questions. What does question-asking mean in the typical classroom? Does it take place after reading a mechanical workbook type of exercise or is it a time for searching and learning?

Typical questions are those that flow easily. They reflect the teacher's desire to remind students to pay attention and to think while reading. As reflected in the survey of teachers' expectations mentioned above, the highest percentage of questions expected and received is literal, a recall of details. Yet all teachers would say they want students to do more than recall information. They want them to think. If students do not answer critical questions, however, or have to answer them only infrequently, one can understand why teachers would tend to increase literal questions. They get responses. Following the way of the flesh, the teacher is led by the student instead of the reverse. The result

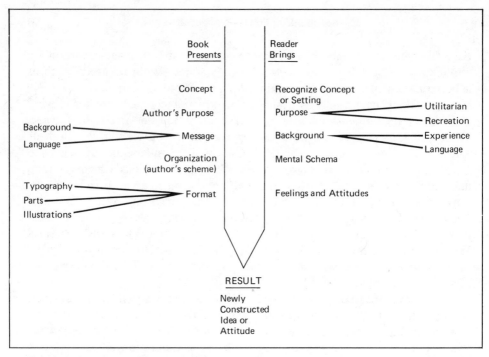

Figure 2-2. Bookthinking decisions. For any study topic the teacher decides on the level of reading to assign students and selects the skills or interests to emphasize during that lesson.

is that students cannot answer critical thinking questions unless someone shows them how.

Suppose that over a year or two of learning, a student came to expect that, while he read, the only things he had to look for were items of recall. (What color were the dog's eyes?) What happens to him when he reads thereafter?

According to learning theorists, such as B. F. Skinner, the constant repetition of a behavior leads to a pattern or a habit. By regularly answering the same type of question, the student learns to respond to reading in a very limited way. It isn't that he can't do more. It's just that the teacher has convinced him that he will be successful if he reads to recall those fascinating details. The longer that kind of reaction continues, the more ingrained is his expectation that he should read that way. The student's pattern is established by the teacher who consistently and regularly asks the same kinds of recall questions.

Or suppose a teacher does ask a range of discussion questions following each reading assignment. The student learns to expect that different types of questions will be asked and learns inductively that he can manipulate the selection in many ways to answer critical questions. He then comes to each passage prepared by dint of consistent questioning to make analyses and interpretations. If he personally cannot answer all the questions, he sees others responding to them. A group discussion among students of varying talents serves that purpose.

We must conclude, therefore, that the consistent expectation of the teacher and his systematic question behavior is an extremely important attitude. If he expects grains of sand, typical Henry will dribble out grains of sand endlessly. If he expects cacti and orchids, old Henry will plow and disc to try to produce those beauties.

If that were all that had to be done, this discussion could end very quickly. Each teacher could develop a series of question prototypes that would cover the range of literal, critical, and elaborative thinking and ask them regularly, and the long-range benefits would be considerable. Our colleagues in the grades above us would no longer chastise us for not teaching the students. Fortunately for the teaching profession, there is more to learning than that. Haven't each of us had the experience of hearing the same question asked again and again and yet some youngsters cannot figure out how to give a satisfactory answer? It is apparent, then, that a teaching plan for bookthinking involves more than simply asking a range of questions that extend from simple to complex.

A Map for the Teacher

To develop a teaching plan that will encompass the major comprehension tasks, we need to find handles on the barrelful of comprehension (bookthinking) tasks listed in behavorial objectives catalogs. No subject-matter teacher can hold six or seven hundred thinking-comprehension objectives in his head and incorporate them into a teaching plan for his content. Sheer numbers get in the way. The teacher needs a concept of comprehension short and simple enough to remember and to apply on a daily basis. To that end a brief examination of the major comprehension-thinking operations is in order.

In his description of children's thinking, Jean Piaget (1952) speaks of mental operations, a term he uses to distinguish major mental functions that require clearly different manipulations. Bookthinking expectations could be analyzed in a similar way. What major, different mental manipulations are expected from the competent reader?

Though comprehension-thinking operations may be described in many different ways, teachers will usually want readers to do the following with any given passage:

1. *Recognize* that he has some experience or purpose that enables him to associate with the content of the passage.
2. *Recall* important details.
3. *Analyze* the information in order to achieve a specific purpose.
4. *Judge* the worth of the passage.

5. *Use* the passage in some logical or emotional (affective) way and thus extend its value for him. (Harris and Smith, 1976.)

Those five statements represent thinking operations, different mental manipulations that range from simple to complex, and each can be represented by questions, that is, by a comprehension test. With only five categories, every teacher has an outline he can recall as he works with students. Under each of those first statements one could categorize any number of activities that are found in the comprehension exercises in teacher's guides. Consult Table 2–3 for typical questions and activities for each of the five

TABLE 2-3
Comprehension Operations

OPERATION	ACTIVITIES AND QUESTIONS
Recognize	Identify the reality or purpose of the topic. Place oneself in the setting, in the conceptual framework of the passage. *Sample question:* In what sense does space travel have meaning for you?
Recall	Search for and select information. Remember details or find them in a second reading, including sequence of events and location of major topics. *Sample question:* What are the primary characteristics of deciduous plants?
Analyze	Make inferences and manipulate information to determine main ideas, comparisons, cause and effect, organizational patterns, and similar tasks that require the reader to create a mental scheme for sorting information and relating it to purpose of the schema. *Sample question:* What is the theme of this chapter?
Judge	Select criteria and apply them to the passage to decide on worth, feasibility, esthetic appeal, and other purposes that require standards for making evaluative decisions. *Sample question:* Would you recommend that book to your best friend?
Use	Extend the information or the feeling of the passage (book) by applying it, creating an art form, or adjusting the intellectual base to which it relates. *Sample question:* How has your view of life (the world) changed as a result of this book?

operations mentioned here. Under the third, *analyze*, for example, we can place activities that call for comparison and contrast, finding the main idea, identifying a writer's organization, and making an inference.

By asking a range of questions covering the five thinking operations, a teacher guarantees that there is at least one question requiring analysis for each passage discussed.

As a teacher, you may want to modify either the number or the description of reading-thinking operations. Other models for categorizing comprehension processes are available. Bloom (1956), Barrett (1972), Smith (1963), and Davis (1972) have all published an outline or a model of comprehension. One of these may better suit an inclination or a background that you bring to teaching bookthinking. What is eminently important is that the teacher have a clear, operational definition of what those thinking operations are, because the clarity with which he perceives them dictates his effectiveness in getting his students to use them. Rosenshine and Furst (1971), for example, found that cognitive clarity in a teaching situation was the teacher characteristic that correlated most highly with student success.

Teaching-Learning Functions

By delineating comprehension into manageable segments, a series of important teaching-learning functions can be dealt with. Once the teacher has delineated what needs to be accomplished, students and teacher can work together toward their mutual objective.

1. *A positive attitude can be constructed.* Once the handles are there, the package can be picked up more easily and securely. "We know what we have to work on and we'll get to work."

2. *Diagnosis of the students can be accomplished.* For any given reading selection the teacher can ask a question for each of the five operations and get an estimate of the student's ability to answer and presumably to carry out that operation.

3. *Teaching explanations and demonstrations can be designed.* With only five categories or thinking operations, a teacher can devise clear explanations or concrete demonstrations of what the mind must do to answer questions of recall, analysis, evaluation, or extension.

4. *Student progress can be evaluated.* By using a rating scale or a plus-and-minus recording system, a teacher can identify instances of achievement or lack of achievement when the system has been reduced to only five categories. Interestingly enough, we do have significant evidence that reading comprehension skills are quite limited in number (Davis, 1972). It would seem, therefore, that the hundreds of "comprehension skills" listed in various teacher's guides are activities or instances of the few different operations employed in understanding and applying what we read.

With the cognitive map described above, a teacher has a relatively simple yet powerful tool to guide him in making important decisions about teaching and learning with a book—decisions that start with a first principle for teaching bookthinking: *Define operationally a range of mental operations (thinking skills) that can be included easily in daily teaching.* Aspects of that map are outlined in Table 2–3.

A Sense of the Learner

Thinking operations ordinarily are classified as cognitive functions. They are skills or operations that can be performed while reading. From experience, everyone knows there are also personal factors that influence a reader's response to any one passage. A reader may react enthusiastically to one subject and not to another. Thus he analyzes or judges with clarity and with energy because he has developed an interest in a subject, or he fails to respond adequately because he has not developed an interest in a topic or lacks background. His potential for response is not diminished, only his practical energy to do the job.

The same holds true for previous experience. Because of personal and intimate contact with politics, the son of a congressman may extend the usefulness of an editorial (see operation number five) by writing letters or by forming a political-action group, whereas another child without that kind of experience with political forces, barely grasps the concept in the editorial, much less knows how to extend those concepts into real-world action. To gain a full sense of the learner, therefore, one cannot tally his thinking skills on an academic bridge score sheet and make decisions on that score alone. Feelings, interests, and attitude constitute a powerful drive that may overshadow the cognitive learning. No matter what thinking operation is applied to a selection, the personal background of experience and training of the individual as well as his attitude about the subject or his interest in the subject will color his response.

What is the teacher's job? Adjust to all those circumstances. Provide variety; talk to kids about their interests; discuss books with them; encourage their individual interests and values. A second principle about teaching bookthinking is now revealed. *The use of thinking operations must be adjusted to the personal background of each individual learner*, a base that includes conceptual background, interests, and attitudes toward the subject being read about.

The teacher's plan for teaching bookthinking, then, revolves around applying those five operations to different kinds of content. The child who can apply them at his particular level of development would then be described as a successful reader, that is, he can construct meaning in various selections by applying those five reading-thinking operations.

What is a workable teaching plan for that definition of bookthinking? What teaching strategies are appropriate? The plan must lead to the objective and include the major principles that have been identified. All discussions about teaching begin with a question about how to help the learner be more successful. A reading-thinking pattern that covered a range of thinking operations is described, as is the fact that each learner brings a unique background to the task. Moreover, each content or each situation generates its own purpose for reading. Though a teacher has all five thinking operations in his repertoire, he doesn't have to use them for each selection read. What is reading, then, for subject-matter teaching? Reading becomes an interaction with a printed message across a range of thinking operations as guided by a purpose for that reading. This leads to our third major teaching principle: *Get a teachable definition of comprehension.* Each part of the definition gives directions on a map for learning.

GROWTH IN BOOKTHINKING

If reading is an interaction, the child must construct meaning on the basis of the words provided by the author and that which the reader personally provides. He constructs meaning and concepts at a given instant and gradually builds his long-range power to think. As the concepts become more abstract, as the learner becomes older, as the subjects become broader, the learner deserves the opportunity to grow in his own right. Teachers, therefore, provide opportunities for him to struggle, to fail, to succeed, and to share. Which suggests a fourth principle for teaching bookthinking: *Comprehension-thinking operations grow through time and multiple practice opportunities.* All the answers cannot be wrapped up in the pages of a workbook, nor in one class discussion, nor in the elementary grades.

How does reading develop across the years? An analogy may shortcut a detailed explanation of the complex development of reading competency.

Walking and talking are clearly essential to the normal life. Except for those with organic defects, everybody walks and talks. Persons even accomplish these feats close to the same age. At about twelve or thirteen months most children begin to walk. The range is narrow between those who walk early versus those who walk late. From eight months to sixteen months of age, almost all children learn to balance themselves and develop biped locomotion.

The same is true of talking. By the age of two years, English-speaking children have learned the rudiments of speech communication: labeling, sentence utterances, and word order. As the years pass, children improve their walking and talking through practice and by learning refinements from parents and other teachers.

Virtually everyone walks and talks, but not everyone swims and not everyone reads.

Consider swimming. Fun! Excellent exercise! But not necessary. Some persons learn at six months; some at 600 months. One lady recently told us that she just learned to swim at age sixty-two. Some normal, healthy people never learn to swim. Depending on the activities of family and friends, or perhaps on the availability of a pool, we either learn to swim or we don't.

Reading and swimming are analogous in two ways: Cultural imperatives determine their desirability and similar learning procedures help in their acquisition. Once a person wants to swim—whether influenced by parents, a doctor, friends, or the nearness of a swimming pool—how does he learn? How is he taught? As with other skills, there are many successful methods, but generally the process begins with a concept (swimming is moving through water) and becomes operational through practice, including the practice of specific skills. For purposes of comparison let's divide the teaching of swimming into stages.

Step 1: Get a concept of what swimming is: "Watch those people move through the water. See them churn their arms and legs. That's what swimming looks like."

Step 2: Feel the thrill of moving through the water: "I'll hold you up and push you through the water. Crank your arms and kick your legs so you get some sense of what swimming is like."

Step 3: Develop skills for independent locomotion: "If you are going to propel yourself, you must learn to move your arms, legs, and head in a helpful way. Let's learn how to move the legs first. Hold onto the side of the pool and practice kicking your legs in this fashion so you can get your legs to help move you through the water."

Step 4: Practice the whole act of swimming: "Now try to swim all by yourself. And practice and practice." Repeat steps 3 and 4 for for each basic skill.

Step 5: Learn refinements and practice: "I'm going to teach you the S stroke (or the flip turn). Do it in the air with me. Now practice it in the water. And practice and practice."

Step 6: Enter races (and practice and refine and practice): "Each Wednesday we'll have a race. Swim hard. Let's see who has the smoothest stroke for five lengths of the pool."

Step 7: Win an Olympic gold medal and become a TV personality.

After any one of those steps a person may bow out. For any number of reasons: "My toes get wrinkled. The teacher is mean. The water is too cold. All the kids at the pool are ugly. It gives me a headache. I will not display my body in public." And then swimming is dead until something or someone entices the dropout (or is it dripout) back into the water.

Elementary Reading

Reading possesses many characteristics similar to swimming. Not only are there basic and gold medal performances, but there are numerous places and reasons for kids to bow out. Even though American society places high academic emphasis on reading, unlike walking and talking, a child does not see reading in constant use (does not see swimming in constant use) and so has neither a cultural nor a biological imperative to read. He figures he can get by without it or, when pressed, he can stand in the water briefly while the others splash and swim.

Applied to reading, the steps from the swimming analogy proceed as follows:

As a start, a child needs to see that reading is desirable. His parents read, his friends read, and there are books and newspapers in his house, in the stores, and in the houses of his friends. It is clear that some of these reading materials are useful in daily activities. TV programs are listed in a guide. Movies and their times are printed in the daily newspaper. Some foods are prepared by following recipes, toys are assembled from written directions, and so forth. Those kinds of circumstances making reading desirable. But the desire does not occur at the same age for every child. Once it occurs, the child is ready, and the teacher can proceed with a development similar to what can be seen in the reading curriculum of the elementary school, usually begun in kindergarten or first grade.

Step 1: *Develop a concept*. Reading is similar to putting your own speech into written symbols and then reading it back. "Someone put his story in this book. Listen as I read his words to you."

Step 2: *Feel the thrill of reading*. "Tell me a story about something that happened to you. I'll write it down and then you can read it back." Using the child's dictation and having him pretend to read back his own words is the beginning stage of what is called an experience-story technique. The child has a sense of reading because he is looking at written symbols and is saying once more what he's just dictated to the teacher or to an aide. (See Appendix A at the end of this chapter.)

Step 3: *Develop basic skills for initial movement*. At this point the child learns the major symbol distinctions that identify sentences, words, and the sound-spelling patterns of the English language. Over years of instruction and practice the child increases the discriminations he can make within the symbol system and thereby gains sharper control. As in swimming, the child is always reading stories and books in conjunction with the exercises that make him more proficient. He is kicking his feet in the water. And it feels good.

Step 4: *Practice, practice*! Reading is a search for meaning, a search that requires skill and practice. To develop the automatic responses that enable the reader to have fluency in print the child practices and practices. Language facility of any kind demands numerous repetitions to gain fluency and efficiency. Sometimes alone and sometimes in group-reading activities, the child practices the basic skills and reinforces the concept of reading.

Step 5: *Learn refinements*. As books become more important in the elementary student's life he needs to know how to become more fluent, how to follow a theme, how to analyze to get the main idea, and so on. While he practices reading daily, the teacher and the basal reader give him explanations and demonstrations of how to accomplish or improve those important thinking operations. Significantly, the operations need to be refocused each year in each subject that the student takes. For example, take this question: "What are some of the major details (important things) that you can remember from that selection?" In the child's early years a teacher may be satisfied to permit the child to flit randomly through his memory to see what he can recall from what he has just read. As he grows in his ability to construct meaning, however, the student should have a way to make his recall of important details more systematic and better organized.

To teach her students how to search and select details from a passage, one teacher used the following demonstration: She dumped the contents of her purse on her desk and covered the pile of "three hundred" items with a towel. Then she selected three pairs of students and told them they were to view the pile for five seconds before working together to make a list of the items they saw. The three pairs averaged thirteen items, though she did not announce to the class what the items were.

Then she selected three other pairs and told them that she was going to show them how to recall more than thirteen items, even though they were to see the pile for the same five-second count. With her hand she simply divided the pile into three parts and told the new group that they were to remember what was in part one, what in part two, and what in part three. When they wrote their lists, they averaged twenty-two items. Why? Because she had given them a simple way of organizing their viewing and their recalling.

The teacher then pointed out that they should use a similar mental operation when they read. When asked to recall major details, they should mentally divide the article into three parts and pick out from each part what seemed important to them. That example can be extended in a dozen different directions. Some of those will be discussed in other parts of this text.

Step 6: *Enter races and refine as needed.* For the reader the competition comes from books. The reader competes with himself—to finish more books; to read a wide variety; to deal with each type in a proficient way. The challenge comes from the vocabulary and from an increased control over the thinking operations needed to enjoy or to use the book or magazine or newspaper. The teacher who says, "I found a special book for you," creates part of the challenge—at all levels. In the elementary school and the middle school, the basal reader, with its multiple levels of books, also adds to the challenge and to the sense of successfully competing in a personal race. Each new book (level) represents to the child a symbol of advancement in reading proficiency and of success in school. One of the major advantages of having numerous "skinny" books in the elementary program is that they represent achievement and success in the child's competition with himself to move forward and to do better.

Step 7: *A gold medal:* We don't want to overemphasize the notion of competition, but each of us appreciates a personal star, a personal awareness that "I'm in charge." In reading, that awareness comes from the recognition that we have complete flexibility to adjust to personal and imposed purposes for reading over a wide range of content. It is the sense of one who knows how to approach and proceed through whatever kind of content or organization or style he encounters. The flexible, proficient, purposeful reader is the mature reader. That's what each teacher works toward, but it is a goal that almost certainly *cannot* be achieved in the first seven or eight years of schooling.

Just as swimmers have coaches (teachers) throughout steps 1 through 7, so readers (bookthinkers) need teachers to demonstrate, guide, and prompt the practice that leads them toward mature reading. Not all are going to become gold medal readers, but the teaching-learning relationship in bookthinking continues all the way through college and graduate studies.

Content of the Elementary Program

The preceding seven-step description depicts the teaching-learning cycle in the elementary reading program and should indicate that there is more to the teaching of reading than a set of mechanical drills in phonics or in pronouncing words on cards. Reading, in a broad sense, goes on throughout the years, no matter what developmental aspect is being emphasized.

An elaborate and complex curriculum for teaching reading is followed by most school systems. Usually the developmental reading curriculum is represented in a series of coordinated books called "the basal reader series." It is estimated that more than 90 percent of the schools in the United States use a basal reading series to guide teachers and children in developing reading competency. From kindergarten through the sixth or eighth grade, these basal programs provide vocabulary growth, listening and language activities, practice in word recognition skills, questions for discussion and comprehension testing, and story content that reflects the age of the child as well as the values of society.

Basal Reader Content

Starting in the mid-seventies, basal readers have undergone a noticeable shift in content. The Dick and Jane type of stories that portrayed a nice suburban family from infancy through all the joys and trials of school attendance for eight years have practically disappeared. Now the stories in readers reflect many of the concerns of our society in showing people in a variety of economic and cultural settings. The stories do in fact reflect the multicultural nature of our society without abandoning the fun and enthusiasm associated with writing for young children. Recent writers are also conscious of eliminating sex bias and try to show males and females in a number of roles that do not stereotype women as housewives or men as automated wage earners. Women are shown as lawyers and bus drivers, and men, in a single-parent household, are shown cooking meals.

Much of the artificial and stereotyped language of the Dick and Jane readers has likewise given way to a more natural language, the kind of language people speak. (Wardhaugh, 1975). In the beginning books the characters now say: "Come on in. This is my house. Come on in and see it." Whereas readers of a previous generation said: "Oh, oh, oh. Run, run, run. Run, Jane, run."

From kindergarten on, the new breed of basal readers brings in real-world content. The child is shown that reading enables him to do things and learn things as well as enjoy himself in an adventure. Recipes, construction projects, space flight information, problem-solving situations, and many selections characteristic of those he will meet in math, science, and social studies now appear in his basal reader. These selections enable the teacher to encourage the child to transfer his reading skill to many kinds of reading and to develop some of the special skills he will need in those subjects where he must read to learn.

By following the plan of the basal reader, the child emphasizes different aspects of reading and content as he proceeds through his years in school. What is emphasized varies from series to series, but a typical sequence might include:

Kindergarten:	Listen and retell. Develop language-experience stories.
First grade:	Language-experience stories. Develop a sense of what a story is. Discriminate words and sounds, for example, the difference between *mad* and *made*. Build a reading vocabulary of frequently used words. Learn the rudiments of English sound-symbol correspondences.
Second grade:	Continue sound-spelling pattern generalizations. For example, the consonant-vowel-consonant pattern usually stands for a short vowel sound as in *cat, bed, hit, cot, but*. (See other generalizations below.) Develop language fluency and expand automatic recognition (reading vocabulary) of high-frequency words. Learn to respond to simple questions about story details and its main idea.
Third grade:	Expand language through an interest in words and word parts, such as prefixes and suffixes. Use figurative language. Evoke the child's interest in content reading. Teach him how to respond to more analytic and judgmental questions.
Middle grades (4,5,6):	At this point the child meets a mass of content in science, social studies, health, and so on. Demonstrate

the transfer value of reading skills to those subject-matter selections. He must learn to deal with technical vocabulary and special reference tools, such as the glossary. He learns to respond to application and elaboration questions about his reading, and to identify styles and types of writing.

Middle grades (7,8,9): Language flexibility is emphasized—vocabulary and writing style. Student learns to be flexible in reading connected discourse according to his purpose and the organization of the author.

Phonics and Decoding

Though there are hundreds of possible sound-symbol correspondences existing in English, only a few have a high frequency of utility. Knowing them enables a teacher to explain the notion that the English spelling system is highly regular. It therefore can be analyzed for reading and for spelling purposes and can be the source of a systematic analysis of new words read in context. Here is a list of generalizations useful for classroom teaching. The rest of the generalizations do not have to be memorized in the form of rules; they will become internalized through practice in reading.

Useful Phonics Generalizations

1. Short vowel rule: When there is only one vowel in a word or syllable, that vowel usually has a short sound, if the vowel stands at the beginning or in the middle of the word; for example, *at, but.*
2. Long vowel, rule 1: When a two-vowel word or syllable has a silent "e" at the end, the first vowel in the word usually has a long sound; for example, *made, side.*
3. Long vowel, rule 2: When there is a double vowel in a word or syllable, the first vowel usually has a long sound and the second vowel is silent; for example, *maid, beat.*
4. Murmur rule: When a vowel is followed by an "r," it has a modified sound that is neither characteristically long nor short; for example, *car, hurt.*
5. Diphthong rule: Certain double vowels have linked sounds that make use of both vowels; for example, the "ou" in *house,* "ow" in *now,* "oi" in *oil,* and "oy" in *boy.*

A System for Word Recognition

In helping students work out word problems, the teacher should adopt a pattern of questioning that will direct the student to develop a systematic procedure for unlocking unknown words. For example, the teacher should ask in sequence:

1. What makes sense in that spot?
2. What is the beginning sound of the word?
3. What is the ending sound in the word?
4. Do any sound-spelling patterns show up in the word?
5. Ask someone or look it up in the dictionary.

This routine suggests that the student use as few cues as possible to achieve the accurate word and then continue his reading. At any point where he figures out what the word is, he proceeds without using the remaining steps in the system.

Through the activities associated with the basal reader or through the curriculum guides developed by a school system, the emphases listed above are translated day by day into activities that bring children, books, and teachers together. Some of those activities are aimed at developing a good feeling and positive attitudes toward reading, and some of them are aimed at learning or practicing specific language-reading skills. In Appendix B, a list is given of the cognitive skills that are emphasized in the intermediate grades of the basal reader published by the Macmillan Company. This list shows the range and the specificity of activity typical for that age level. For a more comprehensive list of the skills exercised in the primary grades, see the list of objectives displayed in the teacher's guide of any basal reader.

SUMMARY

Success in every subject matter demands the intelligent use of books and other print material. Bookthinking, therefore, stands right in the midst of every teacher's instructional responsibility. Any definition that includes the reading of a variety of subject matter texts must necessarily be broad. Reading or bookthinking is not a single act but encompasses several functions or operations. For a given purpose, the reader interacts with the language and ideas of an author, extracts stated and implied meanings, responds critically and emotionally, and uses perceived ideas in a variety of ways. From the teacher's point of view the functions of bookthinking must turn into an instructional or operational definition that enables the teacher to observe the student and interpret his behavior. Thus a teacher's working definition describes the interaction between reader and writer in terms of the reader's ability to pronounce words in sequence (in context), understand their accepted meaning, answer a range of questions across the text and discuss them in a real life context, for purposes of study, information, and joy.

This chapter emphasizes the need for teachers' expectations to be realistic and pedagogically sound, that is, to recognize the developmental nature of bookthinking and to provide a wide range of questions and activities commensurate with the skills of the students and the style of the author. To accomplish that end the teacher needs a cognitive map that will guide him in making instructional decisions—a map that incorporates bookthinking into the procedures for his class. A map was presented in this chapter as was a description of the development of reading and bookthinking across the elementary grades into the middle and secondary schools.

DISCUSSION QUESTIONS

1. What is a workable definition for bookthinking in the subject that you teach?
2. What marks the essential difference between bookthinking in middle and secondary schools and reading instruction in the elementary schools?
3. Most teachers use questions as a way of stimulating discussion about a subject. What patterns of questions would help students interact with the textbooks in the subject that you teach?
4. How could language experience techniques be used in your subject?

Suggested Readings

Emans, Robert. "The Usefulness of Phonics Generalizations above the Primary Grades," *The Reading Teacher* (Feb. 1967), 419–425.

Gibson, Eleanor J., and Harry Levin. *The Psychology of Reading*. Cambridge, Mass.: MIT Press, 1976.

Chapter 3, "The Development of Cognitive Strategies," provides an excellent review of the research related to the organization of intellectual tasks and the concept of transfer of learning in cognitive tasks. It provides substantial support for the value of working toward a mental set. The application to reading is assumed in the discussion. Provides valuable distillation.

Harris, Larry and Carl B. Smith. *Reading Instruction, 2d ed*. New York: Holt, Rinehart and Winston, 1976.

For additional information on decoding and phonics generalizations, Chapter 9 reviews the background of the English spelling system and methods for teaching decoding in the elementary school and lists the generalizations that have a utility high enough to develop in an elementary school program. Chapter 9 also contains a phonics test for teachers that would be interesting for secondary teachers to try. Easy reading.

Appendix A

Language Experience Techniques for All Ages

A technique known as the "language-experience" approach has gained popularity in recent years, and it clarifies the relationship between speech and print in a way that makes it quite usable in teaching book-thinking. The basic logic of the technique is this: *What I can think, I can say. What I can say can be written and others can read it back. What others can read, I can read.*

In its simplest form the language-experience technique has a student dictate a story which is immediately transcribed by a tutor or a teacher. The tutor then asks the student to "read it back." Since these stories are deliberately quite brief, the student, even if he cannot decipher all the symbols, can usually "read" back what he has dictated. He experiences an immediate sense of success and has learned a valuable lesson about the relationship between ideas, speech and print. Using the base of the dictated story, the teacher then helps the student discover the cues in the printed symbols that enable him to conquer the writing of others. Details for using this approach as a beginning reading technique can be found in *Learning to Read Through Experience* by Lee and Allen (1963).

For older students the technique also has considerable value, both for individual students and for group instruction. First, take the example of an eighth-grade boy with whom one of the authors worked in the inner city of Cleveland. Randy, after seven years in school receiving social promotions, had not learned to read. Upon entering the eighth grade, he could not easily read a first-grade book. He didn't seem to have any strategy at all for analyzing the printed page. To establish the relationship between speech (ideas) and print, the teacher asked Randy to dictate stories, which the teacher typed as the boy dictated: "Randy, tell me what you did over the weekend." And this is what he said:

Randy
What I did on the Weekend
I would get in the car and turn the wheel and push on the gas. I keep acting like I'm driving.

My buddy came to see what I was doing. We got some tires from a junkyard and tried to sell them for $.50. We made $5.00.

On the way back from the junkyard, we stopped at the store and spent $1.00.

Then we busted out a window in an old car in the junkyard. We found a tool case with some tools in it. We tried to turn the old car over but couldn't.

I took the tools home and started working on my bike.

Randy's dictation was comparatively long, and he did not read back correctly every word. But he got the sense of reading by taking that typewritten sheet and saying again what he had just told—with a little help from the teacher. And from that base, Randy became interested enough to attend to things like sentence markers (periods and capitals), important words, and sound-symbol correspondences. His attitude altered, too. He became more alert; his eyes watched more carefully; the lines in his face relaxed—almost in a smile. What had happened was that his language became real—because it was there in print—and it became valuable: other kids were interested in reading what he had "written." Other stories were dictated, and Randy's facility and reading ability grew with his stories. "Randy, tell me about some of the interesting people in your neighborhood." And guess who he talked about?

Randy

The Policeman

The policeman is one of your best friends. He will keep you out of trouble. He will keep you from getting killed. He helps everybody.

He knows how to shoot. He takes target practice and he wrestles. When he goes around, he carries a stick, a badge, a gun and handcuffs.

He wears a blue suit all the time. He walks up and down the street to see what is going on. He watches the groceries.

He shoots at people who shoot at him. Then he sneaks up on them and catches them. When he catches them, he puts handcuffs on them and takes them to jail. When he needs help, he calls more policemen.

When it's all over, the policemen can go home.

The end.

Randy's case provides an instance of how a dictation technique enables a teacher to work out some problems for an individual. But a language base can be used with a group as well.

Language in a Group

It is helpful to recall that children four, five, and six years old have a working knowledge of the basic structures and rules of language, that is, they can use all the basic sentence patterns and the basic transformations. The average child of six has also learned to hear and respond to a large number of words, perhaps as many as twenty thousand. Thus personal language is an excellent base for successful growth in school. Teachers across the grades then have the responsibility ever to increase the student's vocabulary and to make him more facile with language so he can deal with school books and the language of the world which comes to him through books, television, and business contacts. The marvelous advantage to the educator of using the student's own language is that it gives him a success base from which to build. It is akin to saying, "Your language is good. Start with your language and learn how to improve it."

In a group setitng, the language-experience idea has values related to those for the individual. When a number of students are studying a common factor or have engaged in a common experience—a field trip, a play, an experiment—they can summarize it, list its highlights, give brief critical reactions, or outline its conceptual framework. The teacher solicits student language to make up the summary or the reaction and writes their responses on the board. After a trip to the museum to view the art and artifacts from King Tut's tomb, for example, the teacher might ask the students to summarize what they saw by categorizing the objects.

As the students begin to offer suggestions and come up with the categories the teacher lists them on the board.

Treasures of Tutankhamun
1. Coffins
2. Jewelry
3. Religious journey through death
4. Royal comfort

Under each of the categories, the students then recall and describe those items which fit. But that's only a list, you say. No, not really. The students must think and organize their ideas and then express them in language that communicates (and perhaps convinces). New words are used and their pronunciation and use make them part of the language of the student. Then they are written on the board for all to see and read. The items that go under the categories above could be expressed in sentences or phrases: For example, "A golden statuette of the goddess Selkert had a scorpion on her head," or "An alabaster chalice shaped like a lotus bloom was a wishing cup." Once the group agrees that the statement is appropriate for a given category, the teacher (or a student scribe) writes the phrase on the board, on chart paper, or an overhead projector. Those words remain there, then, for reading and discussion.

The teacher uses opportunities during the exercise to teach words, such as *a/la/bas/ter*; elicit definitions, such as wishing cup; and encourage the reserved student to contribute his analysis of the field trip.

Small groups within the class could accomplish similar results. Each group could post and discuss its outline and explain aspects that interest the rest of the class. The small-group approach encourages wider participation and diversity of response. The teacher is then free to roam through the groups eliciting responses, especially from students having difficulty with language and reading.

As an alternative, each could work on his own and make his own book on King Tut, using a combination of language and illustrations. These books could be shared or displayed and each student then discusses at least two things that he learned from reading the books from other members in the class.

Charts, outlines, summaries, and dictations can all be used as a means for using student language as a base for growth in vocabulary, precision, fluency, and organization of ideas. Whether in a group or with individuals, this logic guides the activity: *Think it. Say it. Write it. Read and share it. Teach as the need and opportunity present themselves.*

Appendix B

Intermediate Skills[a]

Word and Language

1 Recognizing basic words in content areas
2 Identifying accented syllable
3 Identifying and analyzing compound words
4 -le as a syllabication clue
5 Recognizing alliteration
6 Recognizing common suffixes
7 Using common suffixes
8 Identifying picturesque language
9 Recognizing common prefixes
10 Using common prefixes
11 Recognizing basic words in content area
12 Identifying figures of speech
13 Distinguishing homophores
14 Distinguishing homographs
15 Identifying antonyms
16 Recognizing basic words in content area
17 Distinguishing between definite and indefinite terms
18 Recognizing possessives: singular and plural
19 Identifying word function: verbs, adjectives, nouns
20 Changing adjectives to adverbs
21 Recognizing basic sight words in the content areas: pioneer, explorer, territory, century, trapper, trail, travel, immigrant, distance, region, mountain, southern, eastern, westward, northwest, plains, wilderness, migration, crater, expedition, caravan, etc.
22 Changing root words to nouns
23 Identifying synonyms
24 Analyzing words through prefix meanings
25 Changing root words to adjectives
26 Recognizing multiple meanings of words
27 Analyzing words through suffix meanings

Comprehension

28 Identifying cause and effect
29 Recognizing author's purpose

---

[a] C. B. Smith and R. Wardhaugh, *Series R.* New York: The Macmillan Company, 1975.

30   Noting author's word choice
31   Recognizing story plot, character, and setting
32   Recalling story sequence
33   Distinguishing fact, fiction, opinion
34   Recognizing one's personal biases and preconceptions
35   Extending ideas and topics
36   Judging authors' qualifications
37   Visualizing a description
38   Using context for word meaning
39   Drawing conclusions
40   Following sequence
41   Interpreting information in newspaper
42   Locating answers to specific questions
43   Comparing sources of information and detecting discrepancies
44   Recognizing the organizational pattern of writing in science
45   Noting sensory images
46   Noting details
47   Predicting outcomes
48   Using context to determine word meaning
49   Making comparisons
50   Following the organizational pattern of writing in social studies
51   Identifying main ideas
52   Classifying
53   Applying personal standards (probably not testable)
54   Recognizing propaganda, making generalizations
55   Identifying motives (of characters)

Literary

56   Recognizing different types of fiction
57   Identifying different types of fiction
58   Identifying climax
59   Recognizing mood through word choice
60   Identifying historical fiction
61   Identifying myth
62   Recognizing story element: characterization
63   Identifying style
64   Recognizing story elements: plot
65   Identifying different types of nonfiction
66   Recognizing story elements: setting

Study Skills

67   Outlining ideas
68   Using dictionary: entry words, guide words, illustrations
69   Reading maps
70   Reading graphs
71   Reading tables
72   Determining exact dictionary definition to use
73   Using pronunciation key

74 Keeping simple records
75 Encyclopedia: selecting dsecriptor terms—locating entires—using headings
76 Summarizing
77 Reading charts
78 Recognizing parts of newspaper
79 Locating information in newspaper
80 Reading diagrams
81 Using Dewey Decimal System
82 Using different types of dictionaries: authors, sports, slang, places
83 Using an almanac
84 Following cross-references in encyclopedia
85 Outlining
86 Using an atlas
87 Taking notes

3

Mature Reading
Behavior

What are some characteristics of mature reading behavior?

Is textbook reading a "special case"?

How can students learn to relate to textbooks in mature fashion?

Follow These Directions

[*From instructions sent by the Veterans Administration to vocational schools explaining how to conduct a job survey*]
DVB Circular 20-74-113
Appendix B
Exhibit C (Con.)

(1) Establish the total number of graduates from which the selection is to be made. In this example, assume that the number on line 5 of VA Form 22-8723 is 1276.

(2) Establish the number of digits involved in this number. In this example the number is 1276, so the number of digits involved is four.

(3) Pick any arbitrary place on any page of the "book" of random numbers as a starting point. For example, the tenth row in the eleventh column of the sample page of random numbers might be picked as the random starting point (85).

(4) From this starting point, select consecutive groups of numbers equal to the number of digits in the total number of graduates (see subparagraph (2)). For example, the random starting point shows the number 8513. A sequential pick of other four-digit numbers results in the following picks: 9924, 4449, 1809, 7949, 7416, 3223, 0257, 3527, 3372, 2453, 6394, 0941, 1076, 4791, 4404, 9549, 6639, 6004, 5981, 4850, 8654, 4822, 0634, etc. The numbers underlined are to be used for selecting the sample; all the other num-

bers cited do not fit within the total number (1276) from which the sample is to be drawn, so they will be discarded.

(5) From the random numbers which will be picked to select a sample of 300, exclude "0000," any duplicate numbers, and any numbers higher than the total number of graduates reported on line 5 of VA Form 22-8723. Thus, from the random numbers cited in subparagraph (4) above, only four would be used (257,

941, 1076 and 634).

(6) The process illustrated in subparagraph (4) above would be continued until 300 usable numbers are selected, all of which must be different.

5. The example cited in paragraph 4 above is illustrative only and the schools *will not* use the attached page of random numbers as a basis for their sample selection. However, the method illustrated is to be used.

Question: What would you do with this set of instructions?

One student's answer: If I had to read it, I would go sentence by sentence, back and forth between the sample sheet and the instructions. I think it would be possible to follow them, but I'm not sure. If I didn't have to read it, I wouldn't.

Question: Do you mean that none of your normal reading behaviors would apply to the reading of this passage?

Answer: They would not.

WHAT IS MATURE READING BEHAVIOR?

By the time students reach middle or junior high school, they are expected to be able to read. In the earlier grades they were taught *how* to do this important thing, and now it is time for them to get down to the business of using reading to learn from textbooks. In other words, they are expected to demonstrate "mature reading behavior." But what assumptions lie behind this expectation?

Rudolf Flesch provided us with a simple answer to this question when he said that Johnny is reading when he accurately translates printed into spoken words. That is, according to Flesch, reading is purely a matter of decoding. In the fifties, the educational profession (and its political guardians) gladly embraced this simple judgment, along with another judgment that students were being deprived of a valuable skill. Reforms were instituted at the primary-grade levels, and content teachers in later grades awaited a new strain of readers who would be able to do what was expected.

Twenty years later, however, we must acknowledge that the expected miracle did not occur. Many students still are not making the great leap from basals to content textbooks on their own. In teachers' lounges the complaint goes on that these kids just can't read. An assembly of skills learned in initial reading instruction, apparently, is not all that is involved in interacting with books.

It is true that a proficient reader has internalized the decoding process so that it is generally automatic, so he can attend primarily to the task of making sense out of connected discourse. Beyond this very minimal requirement, however, there is no succinct way of saying what a capable reader does. This is because, for mature reading, variation is the rule.

Sometimes a teacher expects, rather vaguely, that students will do what the teacher does when he reads. But does he know himself how he deals with various kinds of prose? Perhaps a little introspection would be useful here. As a mature reader yourself, consider how you would respond to the following passages, all from the same magazine feature on the human brain.[1] Following each passage give the reading a grade (A, B, C, D, or F) on interest, readability, and usefulness to you:

I

Biochemically, the disease [Tourette's syndrome] appears to be a deficiency of an enzyme which functions in reusing uric acid and which is normally found in the basal ganglia of the brain. The enzyme is hypoxanthineguanine-phosphoribosyltransferase. The drug of choice is haloperidol, which helps restore the enzyme balance by clocking the action of one of the brain's half-dozen known neurotransmitter substances—dopamine. The drug does not cure the disease but certainly does alleviate the symptoms. Precise dosages are warranted, because the side effects of haloperidol may be harmful. In a fifty-two-year-old female patient, for example, it was found that 0.8 milligrams of the drug induced Parkinson-like shakes and twitches, while 0.6 milligrams did nothing at all. When the woman was treated with 0.7 milligrams, the symptoms disappeared—not, however, before the debilitating psychological effects of being a long-time sufferer of Tourette's syndrome had taken their toll in other ways. (Samuel E. Bleecker, p. 117)

Your Response
    Interest: _____
    Readability: _____
    Usefulness: _____

II

A solitary ant, afield, cannot be considered to have much of anything on his mind; indeed, with only a few neurons strung together by fibers, he can't be imagined to have a mind at all, much less a thought. He is more like a ganglion on legs. Four ants together, or ten, encircling a dead moth on a path, begin to look more like an idea. They fumble and shove, gradually moving the food toward the hill, but as though by blind chance. It is only when you watch the dense mass of thousands of ants, crowded together around the hill, blackening the ground, that you begin to see the whole beast, and now you observe it thinking, planning, calculating. It is an intelligence, a kind of live computer, with crawling bits for its wits. (Lewis Thomas, *The Lives of a Cell*, 1974, p. 119)

---

[1] *Harper's*, December 1975, 251 (1507).

Your Response
    Interest: _____
    Readability: _____
    Usefulness: _____

III

Chronic alcoholics were administered the Wisconsin Card Sorting Test. It was found that these subjects who admitted to an alcoholism history of greater than ten years were impaired at set persistence, set shifting, and error utilization relative to normal controls, while those subjects who described themselves as alcoholics for a period of less than ten years were deficient only in set persistence. Neither group of alcoholics were impaired in their ability to identify simple concepts or in learning to learn capacity. The manifest behavioral deficits are consistent with the anatomical and neurological evidence for a frontal limbic focus on the pathology of chronic alcoholism. (Ralph E. Tarter, *Journal of Nervous and Mental Diseases* (August 1973), 119)

Your Response
    Interest: _____
    Readability: _____
    Usefulness: _____

IV

Give your right brain a break. While your left cerebral hemisphere goes out every day and discusses, analyzes, or manipulates reality for the sake of earning a living, the right hemisphere nags and complains about being dragged along on mundane errands. Stop that right brain ennui! Give the right side of your brain its favorite treat—music. As any rock buff knows, stereo headphones permit a luxurious self-indulgence in music. They connect you to the music; wire you for sound; your mind becomes infused with the textures and rhythms. A few minutes under the set can be as relaxing as a shot of bourbon, or as invigorating as a hot shower. (Advertisement, p. 122)

Your Response
    Interest: _____
    Readability: _____
    Usefulness: _____

How can you describe your responses to these four passages? Did you react differently? What factors within the passages seemed to affect your reaction to it? These factors might include topic (was it a subject you had some prior interest in?), terminology (did you understand key terms well enough to be able to follow the sense of the passage?), level of conceptualization (was the writing focusing on a particular fact or a more general concept?), and the writer's view of his audience (did he assume an audience of specialists or of general readers?).

    These are only a few of the factors that might enter into your response to a given short passage. Also, you were probably comparing the passages with each other and could choose one that you liked and understood best. A reader will find himself attracted more to one level of conceptualization than to another, just as surely as he will find some topics much more interesting than others. In both instances, his preferences will reflect what he already knows. It is a highly personal reaction that is developed through individual experience. *The fact that an individual reader does have differentiated reactions to different kinds of prose is one characteristic of mature reading.*

One Adult Response

One adult reader, a graduate student, describes below his reactions to the four passages. One way to analyze this reader's response is to look at certain decisions he made while reading the passage.

I

The first passage was clear and obscure at the same time. That is, I could follow the general logic of the explanation, but I didn't know any of the key words, so in the end I could only say that it takes so much of a certain medicine to cure a certain disease. I don't know what Tourette's syndrome is; method hrdl bgk bgk bgk bgktab gktabgk gktabg tabgk abg abg bmf m and I'm pretty vague on the "basal ganglia" of the brain; and that long word—that enzyme with more letters than the alphabet—it doesn't seem like a word at all. There is no way I could pronounce it, and if I can't pronounce a word, I feel as if I haven't really read it. In this case, I don't feel particularly motivated to find out the meanings of all the terms I don't know because it doesn't seem important to me. If I were a doctor interested in neurological disease, it would make sense to know about these enzymes and chemicals. But I know I'm not going to retain it anyway, so why go to the trouble of looking up those technical terms—even if I knew where to look?

In reading this passage, the reader decided not to find out the meanings of the technical terms used. He gives two reasons for this decision: (1) he was not interested enough in the subject to dig for details, and (2) he knew he would not retain the details even if he did dig them out. The two reasons are obviously interrelated. The reader would forget the meanings because he had never had the interest to develop the background necessary to retain them.

II

The second passage was quite different. I enjoyed reading it after reading the one before. It seemed to involve a kind of metaphor, and I felt that I wasn't just reading about ants but about a lot of things in nature. It was about a process that seems universal: different organisms coming together to form a kind of superorganism. I noticed that the style was kind of literary—the writer builds up an image of all these ants coming together, blackening the ground, and becoming increasingly organized. It conveys a suspenseful, almost

ominous feeling. But ants aren't really the point. The implications of the passage are more important than what is actually said. Thoreau's piece about
ants comes to mind. And I once saw a science fiction movie which was a
pseudo-documentary about insects to show how they are taking over the
world. But that's just one line of thought that comes to mind after reading
this passage. There's also the metaphor to intelligence. I think I could go on
making associations from this passage. It seems to call up a lot of ideas of my
own and more or less extend my thinking.

In response to the second passage, the reader made the decision not to
confine himself to the material on the page but to let his mind go in various
directions suggested by the statements given. He decided that the author's
purpose was not simply to provide information about ants, but to make some
very comprehensive points about the function of intelligent behavior. The
reader also decided to relate the ideas in this passage to the other knowledge
that he had. It seemed relevant to his "mainstream" of cognition. That is, it
was personally valuable to him.

III

The third passage seems much more cut and dried, more like straightforward
information. The main difference between this and the first passage is that
here I understand everything pretty well; there aren't any really strange words.
I think I can say that I know something about the performance of alcoholics
on certain tests. Still, I don't know exactly what some of the terms mean. I
think I'd have to read over the article again and make sure I understand the
distinctions that are being made. I think I'd have to check on some terms, too.

The reader's main decision regarding the third passage was to consider it a
discrete item of information for later use. The reader also decided that he
needed to go over the points being made before he could say that he "knew"
the information, and probably check his understanding of some terms. His
response suggests a study-skills approach to this passage.

IV

The last passage is funny. It's a commercialization of a popular concept, the
split-brain concept that is getting a lot of publicity these days. This is funny
because of the relationship between the two hemispheres it suggests—one out
earning a living while the other complains about being bored and not having
any fun. It's like an old stereotyped view of marriage. I never take advertisements seriously anyway, and I really hate to see an idea used like this. It
seems silly. When I read this, I feel as if someone were trying to wire *my*
brain, and I don't like it.

In response to the fourth paragraph, the reader has made a quite definite
decision to respond to the writer's motive rather than to the content of the
passage as such. He believes that whatever information is contained in the
passage has been degraded by the attempt to use it for commercial purposes.
He seems willing to reject the idea itself on that account. Despite his resistance

to the writer's motive, then, he is still allowing himself to be swayed emotionally by the passage. Responding in a primarily emotional manner is also a decision made by the reader.

A second important characteristic of the mature reader, then, is that *he is continually making decisions.* He begins, usually, by deciding what to read, and then he decides whether to continue reading it. Even if the material is required reading, he is aware of some definite benefit that will accrue from the effort to read. Perhaps it will help him in his occupation. Once he is launched into the reading, the decision-making process is continuous. It is an important part of the active process of deriving meaning from print.

In this regard, you might ask yourself what you did when you encountered the 44-letter word in the first passage, the enzyme hypoxanthineguaninephosphoribosyltransferase. What decision did you make? If you decided to try to pronounce the word, chances are that your decoding skills were not adequate to the task. As this word rather preposterously illustrates, any reader can reach the limit of his automatic decoding skills and be obliged to return to the level of sound/letter correspondences. When this happens (to take issue with Mr. Flesch), the question of meaning tends to fade away. Even in terms of its minimal definition, mature reading is a relative concept that depends upon both the reader's background and the content of the text. When a reader encounters an unfamiliar symbol system, or an unusual way of combining familiar word elements, he may feel very immature indeed.

Flexibility

The mature reader, then, learns to be flexible. When he finds himself challenged by a particularly difficult or unusual text, either he decides to disregard it, or he figures out some way of dealing with it. In the case of the first passage, a reader with more curiosity about the subject than the student interviewed might decide to look up some of the terms in the text. For example, he might want to find out about Tourette's disease itself. Or he might want to clarify the concept of neurotransmission. To do this he could consult his undergraduate textbook in general psychology, which he kept to use as a reference. He might also decide to look up the word *enzyme* without worrying about the particular one named. For this purpose he might consult a dictionary.

Inventing Strategies

The point is that *the mature reader will invent appropriate strategies— strategies that are appropriate to his purpose for reading.* If a person is truly self-directed in his reading, there is little need to tell him what to do. If his purpose has been set for him by an assignment, however, he may need direction.

A mature reader is also engaged in a process of selection, what might be called a great husking operation as he makes his way through all the printed material to which he is exposed. The more clearly a person has set his own purposes, the more precise he will be in selecting relevant material. As a simple example, suppose that a seventh-grade teacher wants to learn about the maturational problems of twelve-year-olds. If he consults a book on adolescent psychology, he will not read it from the beginning until he comes to the desired information. By some other means, probably using the index, he will find the relevant material in the book. And even then he is not likely to read an entire section until he finds what he initially wanted to know. Chances are that he will skim until he spots precisely the information he started out to find, and then go back and pick up other interesting information

---

Applications

1. Find passages from textbooks in four different content areas, at any level you choose, and read these as if you were trying to learn the content. As you read, consider the following questions:
   a. How well does this content connect with what you already know?
   b. What decisions are you making as you read?
   c. Would you read this material if you didn't "have to"?
   d. Do you think you will remember what you have read a week from now? A month? A year?
2. Suppose you are a substitute teacher who has been assigned to a class that is *not* in your content area. (If you ever substitute, you will probably have this experience.) Select a two- to three-page reading assignment from a book in this subject and decide how you would relate to this material in order to lead a good class discussion. This exercise will put you in the position of being both student and teacher at the same time. How do your mature reading behaviors apply to this task?
3. Now suppose that you have your own classes in your own content area for which a textbook has been assigned by the administration. Find any appropriate textbook for playing this role. Sit down with the text and see what happens when you read it. Do you like the style? Does it have interesting content? Are you inclined to skim over it because you already "know" the content? Can you look at the text from the student's point of view?

on the same general subject. Of that information, he may be concerned with retaining very little for the simple reason that the book is available to him. So long as he is able to understand the information that might become useful and knows where he can find it again, there is no compelling reason to store it in memory. This brings out two further points regarding the mature reader. *He selects what he needs for his purposes, and he reads to comprehend, not necessarily to remember, and certainly not to memorize.* If a person wants a certain body of information to be conveniently accessible, it is mature behavior to purchase the book that contains it.

To return to the analysis of the four passages by the graduate student quoted earlier, it seems easy to predict how he would rate them in order of preference. He has clearly conveyed his attitudes toward each. It follows from all that has been said about the behavior of the mature reader that he is always responding in an evaluative, emotional way as well as intellectually. Reading sets into motion his deepest thinking processes, calling up attitudes as well as many other associations stored in his cognitive memory. If this does not happen, he is not reading. When the reader has little or nothing in his own experience to which he can relate the content of the material, he becomes bored and concerned with other thoughts. His response to the material is negative. In general, it can be said that the mature reader looks for what he wants, is happy when he finds it, and is impatient with irrelevant material.

HOW DOES AN ANALYSIS OF MATURE READING APPLY TO TEXTBOOK READING?

In the previous discussion, certain characteristics of mature reading were identified:

1. As a minimal definition, mature reading is characterized by the automatization of the decoding processes and concentration of the meaning of connected discourse. However, this is always a relative situation.
2. The mature reader responds differently to different kinds of prose.
3. He sets purposes and selects material accordingly.
4. He invents strategies appropriate to his purposes as he goes along.
5. He is likely to disregard material irrelevant to his purposes.
6. In these and other ways, he is engaged in a continuous process of decision making.
7. He reads to comprehend rather than to remember.
8. He is always responding emotionally as well as intellectually to what he reads.

But what about reading for school? Can this also be a self-directed, purposeful activity? At first glance, at least, it seems that reading for school is qualitatively different—different in a way that might thwart the mature behaviors discussed so far. For one thing, the reading is assigned, not self-selected. Purposes are set by the book and/or the instructor. When motivation to read is external, strategies must be selected differently.

Think of your own experience. Think of a class in college in which you found it difficult to apply yourself to the reading. If you still have the textbook from that class, take it out and look it over again. What was it that made that textbook difficult to read? Maybe the book was densely written. Maybe your own background in the subject was insufficient. Or maybe you just didn't particularly care about the subject. These are all good reasons for having trouble reading a book, but when test time came around, they didn't seem to matter. The material was there, and you were expected to "know" it.

If you have had this experience and can recall it vividly enough, you can put yourself in the place of the student who has difficulty reading in *your* class.

Much of the apparent difference of textbook from other kinds of reading comes from certain attitudes toward textbooks which students and teachers commonly hold. Almost by definition, a textbook is something a student reads because he is supposed to, and this attitude can pose a formidable obstacle. To many students, a textbook represents a thick package of knowledge that must somehow be transferred from between the two covers of the book to the reader's mind via the visual process. This view encourages a particular attitude toward learning. It is regarded as something that happens *because* a person reads, not *while* he reads.

From this point of view, the content of a textbook seems uniformly important. Everything in it at least ought to be learned, an implied mission that must fail and leave the reader with a sense of inadequacy. When everything in a book is presumed to be important, the usual mature strategies won't work. And the fact that students and teachers tend to confound "learning" with "remembering" makes the situation worse. A person reading a story, a magazine article, a set of instructions or a letter typically does not try to memorize it, either verbatim or in substance. Rather, he or she responds to it.

Mature reading might be compared to a mining operation, suggesting the pursuit of thin veins of significance through densities of material. Consider, for example, your approach to reading the evening newspaper or consulting a reference work. For many students, however, the textbook is all density with no precious veins evident. For others, it is all material to be chunked out and carried away in whatever form one can manage. These are the students for whom the reading of textbooks often seems a futile enterprise.

What Does a Teacher Expect
Students To Do When They Read?

An easy and natural thing for a teacher to do is to tell students, simply, to read such-and-such assignment, assuming that the students will know *how* to read in order to learn. Perhaps the teacher expects them to do what he himself does when he studies—or did, if he no longer has occasion to do this kind of reading any more. Chances are, however, that the teacher himself doesn't really know what students are supposed to do to learn from reading. If asked, he might be able to construct a list: extract information, identify main ideas, summarize in one's own words, connect new material to past learning, and so on. And it is true that these are the activities that enable students to learn from written materials—but they do not necessarily come naturally with the act of reading.

It is important for the teacher to keep in mind that these are sophisticated activities that only some readers are able to arrive at independently. While it is true that a wholly self-directed, mature reader does not need to be told what to do to achieve his purposes, a reader whose purposes are being externally determined very often does.

Again, think about your own experience as a student. Perhaps you were never given formal instructions on how to study, and perhaps there were times when you thought for sure you didn't know how. For almost everyone, some potential lines of intellectual development are dropped early because the person finds a subject too boring, too heavy, or too overshadowed by more interesting subjects. In the long run, this does not seem regrettable because some lines of development were pursued. You have found a field and a profession. But what made the difference? What influenced your choice?

Undoubtedly, a large element in your development was guidance, however subtle or diffused. Parents, siblings and friends, teachers and other trusted persons provided models, dropped hints, gave reinforcement, and in other ways helped you to build up your own set of motivations and strategies for formal study. Even without a course in study skills or how to read a book, it all came together in your mind, to the point where you became a mature consumer of school materials as well as of the other kinds of reading a literate person enjoys.

But can this inductive development of study strategies be taken for granted? Only in some instances—with some students in some subjects. There are a few who operate most productively on their own, with as little interference as possible, and these students should be respected for what they can do. But they should not be viewed as representative of all young learners. They are not evidence of what all students could do if they would only try. Most students need to know what is expected of them and how they can go about accomplishing it. Indeed, it is crucial for them to have this information if they are to do what is necessary for learning to occur. An important part of the teacher's role is simply to show students what to do.

HOW CAN A TEACHER HELP STUDENTS DEAL MATURELY WITH TEXTBOOKS?

While a student's mature behavior generally is not the same as that of his teacher or of other adults, the concept of maturity does apply. The individual learner is now at a point of his development where he uses information. What he already knows provides the point of departure for what he will learn. He has also formed a concept of school learning, and, unless he has been badly discouraged, he also wants to be able to do it. He wants to succeed, but by absolute necessity this must be on his own terms.

In *How to Survive in Your Native Land,* James Herndon describes an out-of-school encounter with a student who was a member of the "dumb class" in school. In fact, he was regarded as "the dumbest kid in the dumb class," because in school he couldn't do anything right. In casual conversation, however, Herndon found out that the boy was going to his job, which was keeping score in a bowling alley. Here was food for thought. How could a "dumb kid" keep up with the scoring procedure for several games going on simultaneously? Could it be that he was only dumb in school, where he had been defined as such?

Herndon also describes what happened when he himself tried to take a standardized reading test. He scored at a seventh-grade level. This was not because he couldn't read the passages, but because he gave answers that were different from those prescribed by the test writers. Further investigation on his part revealed that many students who were testing out as hard-core nonreaders were in fact reading all kinds of things on their own, from *Mad* magazine to paperback novels. From these and other observations, Herndon concluded that students were not being encouraged to read and think in their classes, but rather to search through printed material for specific answers. If they could do it, they adapted to the situation given. Others adapted by tuning the situation out.

To encourage reading that is also thinking, the teacher should place emphasis on encouraging mature student response. That is, the student should be encouraged to interact with the material in a personal and deliberate way. Therefore, it is important to get the student actively involved in the task of learning, and this means placing one's emphasis on the student rather than on the book.

Old conceptions of the sacredness of the textbook as an authority on some segment of knowledge are, it is hoped, passing. Students should be encouraged to look at any form of printed material as having its ultimate origins in some human mind. It represents the thought processes of some other person. This consciousness of print as a form of interpersonal communication can be important in the establishment of a mature attitude toward reading. It can also increase the reader's awareness of his own participation in the communication act.

Too often a text is given by the administration to the teacher who in turn hands it out to the student with the assumption that he is now ready to start learning from it. The books are carted in, each student is assigned one with a particular number, and the transaction has taken place. But this approach encourages the view of textbooks as prefabricated parcels of knowledge. Instead of merely handing out the book, the teacher should orient the students to it as an article of human thought by discussing with them both its virtues and its limitations as a basis for learning. There are many aspects of a text that can be brought to the student's attention once the teacher himself has given the book a thorough critical evaluation. Some of these are suggested in the following questions:

1. *How is the textbook organized, and why did the writer decide on this particular organization?* Some indication of this choice can usually be found in the author's introduction, but often a teacher's own inferences will be even more useful for discussion with students.
2. *What is the writer's point of view toward the subject?* Since every textbook writer has to select from a vast range of possibilities the material and concepts he presents, something can be said about his point of view simply by observing what he has selected.
3. *What is the writer's attitude toward his readers?* Too often, textbook writing comes across as flat or patronizing, an attitude of which students are likely to be keenly aware. Since textbook writers are rarely the cream of the literary crop, teachers can sympathize with students' reactions to textbook prose. Then the next step can be taken: concentration on the underlying meaning—appreciation of what the author does have to say. When the textbook is written in a good style, this too can be appreciated.
4. *What do you know about the writer himself?* And what do you think motivated him to write this book? Any information along this line should be helpful, especially items that help to establish the author's credibility as an authority in the field. Speculation on why he wrote the book can lead back to a second consideration of his attitude toward his readers.
5. *What parts of the book are good and what parts are weak?* Although the teacher may be the only one in the classroom capable of making a judgment like this at the beginning, realizing that a critical, selective response is possible will encourage students to do the same as they read.
6. *How does the writer expect students to learn from this book?* The class can discuss whether the graphics (pictures, charts, tables, etc.) are an important part of the whole presentation, and why the author included the particular ones that he did. Check to see if a book has the aids necessary to make it a useful reference work: descriptive chapter titles, a strong subheading system, chapter summaries, and a topical index to mention some. Look at the study questions, practice problems, suggested projects and other means of organizing learning provided by the author.

An orientation discussion that considers questions like these can help a student come to his own terms with a textbook before he tries to learn from it. Also it should help to relieve the attitude toward the text as a special case that can't be approached in a normal way. These questions can also be applied to textbook selection. Textbooks do, of course, tend to have certain properties that set them apart. But the negative effect of these can be reduced by showing the student that his personal response is appropriate.

Applications

1. Select a content area textbook at any level and read through randomly selected parts of it, keeping in mind the six questions given above. Can you formulate good answers to these questions?
2. Look at the questions provided in the text as aids to student learning. What kind of response do these questions seem to elicit?
3. Elsewhere in his book, Herndon suggests that students are badgered by the sheer *amount* of questioning they get on what they read. Do you agree with this? What are some alternatives to questioning for getting students to respond to or use textbook material?

THE ROLE OF PURPOSE
IN LEARNING

As noted earlier, purposefulness is a characteristic of mature behavior, and purpose should be a primary feature of instruction. Both the learner and the teacher must have definite purposes that they wish to and believe they can achieve. Because a textbook is a repository of information, the student's purposes should call for the use of this information in some productive way.

To help the student set such purposes, the teacher must first ask himself the question, What can information be used for? A quick, common-sense inventory of possible answers to this question might be as follows:

1. Solve problems.
2. Support ideas and requests.
3. Argue against ideas and requests.
4. Clarify a complex or vague issue.
5. Answer specific questions.
6. Participate in conversations.

These are not the only possible answers, and the reader is encouraged to continue the list on his own. He should especially examine uses of information that are specific to his subject field. One might also add that information is used to construct a knowledge base, to interpret reality, and to increase the student's chances of becoming a philosopher or at least of getting a good job. But these more general uses of information cannot really be addressed in the classroom. They represent what is happening within the individual's mental world if things are going right, and he is being given good opportunities to deal with information in a practical way. The teacher should be concerned with uses of information that suggest assignments and activities possible in the classroom. In effect, the textbook should be used as a reference book to the greatest possible extent. This is what it most nearly resembles in the world of mature reading.

Once it has been established that a textbook can be approached with normal reading strategies and attitudes, students can be helped to develop workable techniques for dealing with this kind of prose. Among these characteristics are the following:

1. A textbook generally presents information and concepts in a straightforward manner with some explanation and supporting evidence.
2. Its format emphasizes its organization, which is often one of its strongest features. Most textbook writers try conscientiously to present material in a logical structure.
3. It makes use of a variety of typographical devices to cue the reader into an understanding of its content (sometimes to the point of distraction).
4. It attempts to engage the reader directly by asking questions, posing problems, and suggesting projects.
5. Frequently it presents vocabulary instruction as a separate but concomitant feature paralleling the prose content.
6. In general, it tries to accommodate the reader in many ways, perhaps to the point of interfering with his own need to *impose* order, draw inferences, and reach conclusions.

A textbook has both advantages to exploit and shortcomings to be aware of. The teacher should be aware of both.

Application

Look again at a textbook in your content area and try to answer this general question: How does this book encourage mature reading, and how does it discourage it?

GOING BEYOND TEXTBOOKS

Another way to encourage mature reading behavior among students is to avoid dependency on a single text and expand the kinds of materials available in the classroom. This society has a highly productive press, and the amount and variety of reading material issued in soft cover—magazines, newspapers, and trade books—are overwhelming. Indeed, a teacher may well be overwhelmed just at the prospect of getting a grasp on what is available and making a reasonable selection within the budget constraints of his school. Nevertheless, this possibility should be pursued to its practical limits. And beyond these materials there are rich resources available in accessible libraries, both school and public. Students will benefit if the teacher is knowledgeable on the kinds of literature currently being published in his field, both for classroom use and for the public at large.

In this respect, magazines are a particularly good medium for connecting the student to the adult world of reading. Magazines speak in the present tense. The articles have been recently written and selected for their relevance to current concerns. Even a recently published textbook has something of the past built into it. Trade books, especially paperbacks, share some of the magazine's aura of currency, even when, in fact, they are reissues of earlier hard-cover editions. Paperback publication implies a popular demand for a book and gives it an informal, unimposing format. Even a classic seems less formidable in paperback. The whole phenomenon of the paperback press, which greatly facilitates book ownership and book trading, provides an excellent means for developing an interest in self-directed, independent reading.

Applications

1. Go to a local or campus bookstore and make a survey of paper-back books or trade books in your field.
2. Write to paperback publishers and ask for a list of titles that might be appropriate for students at whatever grade level you plan to teach. The addresses of some paperback publishers are given at the end of this chapter.

PERSONAL RESPONSE

Throughout this chapter the point has been emphasized that mature reading involves a personal, judgmental response to written materials. Students who are able to deal with school materials on their own terms will develop definite preferences which may inhibit learning in some subjects while they establish the potential for unlimited development in others. This development of clear preferences is also a part of maturing in bookthinking. In the following two paragraphs, a college freshman describes how she studies in two school subjects, conveying attitudes that were developed during her secondary school years.

Asked how she would go about reading a history assignment, she wrote:

> If this assignment is something that I am interested in, which history usually is, I read the entire assignment straight through and try to get as much out of the reading as I can. Long assignments, no matter how interesting, always call for a break or two between chapters. I never put off something that really interests me or builds up my curiosity. If the assignment deals with American history I am even more interested and will read more slowly and carefully to grasp everything possible.

About science, however, she was considerably less enthusiastic:

> Whenever I study for a science test, I always do something else at the same time, such as put up my hair, file my nails, eat, or iron my clothes. Science, my most dreaded subject, interests me in no way whatsoever, and therefore does not deserve all of my time. I would flunk a science test if I did not do something else while studying for it, because I would become so frustrated after a while that I would give up and put the books away.

Although one might prefer to have this student engage in activities that are more directly involved with the reading assignment, at least she has grasped the principle that it is necessary to be active while reading. And while she will probably never become an avid fan of science, she has discovered the value of interacting with books on her own terms and is ready to pursue this value for as far as she cares to go.

Application

If you are in a practicum or student-teacher situation, ask your class to write a brief (one-page) essay on the following topic: Why I read (or do not read) textbooks. Look over the responses to this topic to see how many answers seem to reflect the student's own thinking and how many seem to reflect what the student believes he should say. What else can you learn from reading these student responses?

SUMMARY

There is no single definition for mature or competent reading. However, it can be said that the mature reader attends primarily to meaning, responds differently to different kinds of prose, reads selectively according to specific purposes, generally ignores material not related to his purposes, reads to comprehend rather than to remember, has attitudinal as well as intellectual responses to reading, and is continuously making decisions. Textbooks may tend to thwart mature reading behavior, primarily by setting the reader's purpose for him rather than letting him set his own, and also by seeming to contain nothing but important material.

A teacher can help a student deal with textbooks in a mature way by treating the textbook first as a book—an article of human thought—and then as a repository of information to be used as a reference source. The teacher should look at a text with these questions in mind: How is the textbook organized? What is the writer's point of view toward the subject? What is the writer's attitude toward his readers? What do you know about the writer himself? What parts of the book are good and what parts are weak? How does the writer expect students to learn from the book? Textbooks have certain characteristics, and students can learn strategies for dealing with these kinds of books. Above all, students should be encouraged to make a personal response to textbook reading—to evaluate the text and the experience of reading it as well as try to gain information from it.

DISCUSSION QUESTIONS

Spread throughout this chapter are application exercises that should be used as the basis for discussion of concepts presented here.

Suggested Readings

Gibson, Eleanor, and Harry Levin. *The Psychology of Reading.* Cambridge, Mass.: MIT Press, 1975.
This book represents the point of view of experimental psychologists looking at reading. The authors cover a comprehensive range of topics under three broad categories: concepts underlying the study of reading, the study of reading, and questions people ask about reading. They provide an extensive review of the literature in each discussion, making this book an excellent introduction to reading research and theory. Chapter 12 deals with "Models of the Reading Process in the Mature Reader."

Schulwitz, Bonnie Smith, ed. *Teachers, Tangibles, Techniques: Comprehension of Content in Reading.* Newark, Del.: International Reading Association, 1975.
This book contains a collection of papers selected to provide insight into the comprehension process and how it can be developed in content classes. The first section deals with issues and models of comprehension, the second with the teacher's role, the third with media and materials (tangibles), and the

fourth with techniques. Among issues discussed in the various articles are readability, information retrieval, reading and writing, and critical reading.

Smith, Frank, *Understanding Reading.* New York: Holt, Rinehart and Winston, 1971.

The author's purpose in this book is to establish a theoretical foundation for understanding the reading process with an emphasis on what the reader himself does in his mastery of print as a medium of communication. In describing the characteristics of fluent reading the author develops, his basic thesis is that "the information that passes from the brain to the eye is more important in reading than the information that passes from the eye to the brain."

Weiss, M. Jerry, *et al.,* eds., *New Perspectives on Paperbacks,* Monograph No. 1, published by The College Reading Association, 1972. 98 pp. (Available from Strine Printing Co., Inc., 391 Greendale Road, York, PA 17403. $2.00 or $1.75 in lots of 10 or more).

This monograph on the potential value of paperbacks for classroom use presents a number of writers' views, each focusing on a particular issue. Topics covered include censorship and ways to cope with it; books dealing with the experience of the physically or mentally different; the black experience for young children; teachers' attitudes toward contemporary literature and how these attitudes turn students off reading; the problem of television as a competitor to books and ways that both TV and movies can be used to encourage reading; the issue of the "obsolescence" of print and suggestions for countering this trend; the flexibility that paperbacks make possible in particular subject fields; and advice on choosing literature that will help adolescents mature into perceptive adults. This is a stimulating collection of ideas presented in short discussions, with ample reference to current paperback literature. Each chapter is followed by a substantial bibliography of materials available, and the monograph features title and author indexes and a publishers' directory.

Appendix A

Selected Paperback Publishers

Anchor Press/Doubleday: 245 Park Avenue, New York, NY 10017.
    Adult level trade books on problems of living and contemporary ideas.
Archway Paperbacks (Published by Pocket Books): 630 Fifth Avenue, New York, NY 10020.
    Fiction and nonfiction of interest to young readers.
Avon Books: 959 Eighth Avenue, New York, NY 10019.
    Both fiction and educational nonfiction.
Bantam Books, Inc.: 666 Fifth Avenue, New York, NY 10019.
    Wide variety of subjects at various levels.
Camelot Books (A Division of Avon Books): 959 Eighth Avenue, New York, NY 10019.
    Fiction and nonfiction for young readers.

Collier Books: 866 Third Avenue, New York, NY 10022.
    Wide range of nonfiction subjects.
Dell Books: 1 Dag Hammarskjold Plaza, 245 East 47th St., New
    York, NY 10017
    Wide range of both fiction and nonfiction.
Delta Books (A division of Dell Books): 1 Dag Hammarskjold Plaza,
    245 East 47th St., New York, NY 10017.
    Nonfiction of general and academic interest. Also features Laurel
    Editions, covering the same area.
Fawcett World Library: 1515 Broadway, New York, NY 10036.
    Books for secondary schools and colleges (Fawcett Premier
    Books).
New American Library: 1301 Avenue of the Americas, New York,
    NY 10019
    Signet Books feature popular fiction and topical nonfiction.
    Plume Books: nonfiction on current topics.
    Mentor: nonfiction for high school and college levels.
Penguin Books: 7110 Ambassador Rd., Baltimore, MD 21207.
    Adult nonfiction.
Pinnacle Books, Inc.: 275 Madison Avenue, New York, N.Y. 10016.
    Topical nonfiction and high-interest fiction.
Reward Books (A Subsidiary of Prentice-Hall, Inc.): Englewood Cliffs,
    NJ 07632.
    Nonfiction on popular subjects.
Vintage Books (A division of Random House): 201 East 50th Street,
    New York, NY 10022.
    Variety of subject matter, fiction and nonfiction.
Warner Paperback Library: 75 Rockefeller Plaza, New York, NY
    10022.
    Fiction based on contemporary life; controversial nonfiction.
Washington Square Press (A division of Simon & Shuster, Inc.): 630
    Fifth Avenue, New York, NY 10020.
    Books of educational interest for high school market and general
    public.

part 2

Student Experience and Competence

4

Motivating Positive Reading Habits

What is the sense of teaching people how to read if the way we do it destroys their inclination to read independently?

What can be done at the middle school and high school levels to combat the trend toward "aliteracy," a characteristic of students who can read but choose not to read?

Quiz

Complete and self-correct the following quiz. The results are to be filed in your permanent record for future use.

1. Why is it that the most exciting, relevant, well-planned lessons can be completely upstaged by:
   The first snowfall,
   A bee or butterfly entering the window,
   An ordinary dog or cat that has found its way into school,
   The custodian raking leaves outside the window,
   A motor-head, car-jockey squealing tires in front of the school, or
   Almost any detail from the world at large?

2. What happens to students between sixth grade and twelfth grade to consistently lower reading-attitude scores with each year spent in school?

3. What's the result of continually forcing a person to read material too difficult for successful comprehension?

4. What difference does it make if students don't read anything on their own so long as they can satisfactorily do their assignments?

5. Read any good books lately?

Answers

1. The upstagers are real and, in comparison, most school activities have little reality outside the classroom. To paraphrase James Herndon—How often would most teachers voluntarily do what they ask most students to do?

2. So far research hasn't been able to isolate exactly what is causing the decline in reading-attitude scores. There are, however, several aspects of the secondary school experience which seem to discourage reading, and there are several things teachers could do to reverse the trend.

3. Avoidance of reading is the result of forcing someone to read to frustration level. Most secondary texts are too difficult for independent reading by most students and, as a result, many students are forced to read at their frustration levels.

4. The difference it makes is that the current products of schools are often adults who can read but choose not to. According to a 1969 Gallup poll, 58 percent of the population "never read, never finished" a book.

5. If your answer is no, you might be a part of the problem. Research indicates that many teachers are poor reading models. Such teachers read only rarely, and then not very well. Improving this situation could go a long way toward improving students' reading attitudes.

EDUCATION'S DOUBLE BIND

What we as educators want and what we are getting don't seem to be the same things. Most of us want to contribute to the creation of a literate society in which individuals have the ability and inclination to be interesting, informed, responsible citizens. We'd like our efforts to contribute to the shaping of well-rounded individuals who can be independent, continue learning, and make responsible decisions. This means, in practical terms, developing people who are able to *and* choose to read regularly.

For the last decade or so, standardized tests of reading ability have been the measure of a school district's success in teaching reading. From the first grade through twelfth grade we've been monitoring reading ability. Results of the recent national reading assessment indicate that reading ability for younger readers improved over the period from 1971 to 1975.[1] This data contradicts the viewpoint held by many that reading scores are in a constant state of decline. Some improvement seems evident at lower grade levels, and problems seem equally evident at higher grade levels. More of our national resources in terms of funding and teacher training are beginning to be directed toward producing similar gains for secondary school students whose scores did not improve during the assessment period.

These gains in reading ability are gratifying and ought to be encouraged. But they bring to light a double bind which our educational efforts are currently ignoring. We are creating a nation of "aliterates," people able to read but choosing not to do so. Readership surveys of adults are startling. Meade (1973) cites a Harris poll that indicates that only 26 percent of all adults read *in* a book during a 30-day period, and a Gallup poll (1969) reports that 58 percent of the population indicate having "never read, never finished" a book.

In effect, this information implies that the product of American education is a population trained in the ability but not the habit of reading. It seems curious that so much effort should be so narrowly expended to accomplish what amounts to only half the task of creating a literate society.

The emphasis on reading ability at the expense of reading attitude[2] and the reading habit becomes even more wasteful when one considers the vicious cycles being created. Children with no reading models (parents, older siblings) at home tend to read less well than other children. If a child does not read well, he often receives skills training that ignores reading habits and attitudes. That child leaves school with negative reading attitudes and habits that influence younger siblings and the next generation (see Figure 4–1). More emphasis on reading scores cannot break this cycle, but emphasis on ability and on reading attitudes and habits might be able to do it.

A Student's Perspective of What Occurs in School

Not much research has been done on the reading attitudes of students. What has been done, however, seems to indicate that the average score of students on reading-attitude measures drops with each grade in school. Why? At present nobody really knows why reading-attitude scores drop or why adults so rarely choose to read beyond what is necessary for survival. As teachers,

---

[1] *National Assessment of Education Progress: Reading and Literature General Information Yearbook*, Washington, D.C.: Government Printing Office, 1976.

[2] The term "attitude" has been subject to a variety of definitions, none of which has proven totally satisfactory. In this chapter, reading attitude refers to the sum of behaviors, feelings, and cognitive values an individual has in relation to reading.

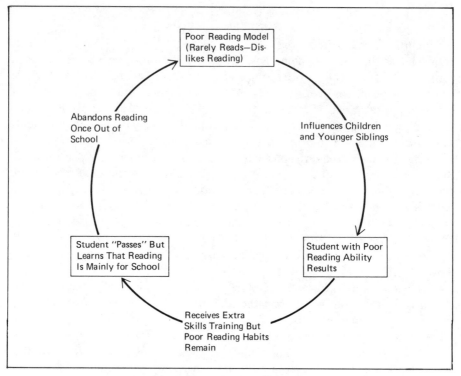

Figure 4-1. Modeling effects

however, we might be well advised to look at what happens to students in schools. That is one area, at least, in which we have some degree of control.

Occasional anecdotes and transcripts of conversations with students in previous chapters should remind you in a fragmentary sense what school is like for the average or below-average reader. This perspective is important for us as teachers since most of us found school a success-filled experience and rarely found ourselves classified as below average. For a few moments, then, allow yourself to imagine what a school day is like for an average secondary school student.

Groups of friends and acquaintances talk and laugh as they walk toward school. A waft of strange-smelling smoke drifts from somewhere ahead. Laughing comments are heard about who is high again and do you remember what happened last year in Miss Baumann's class when Ricky came really stoned.

Bells . . . always bells . . . warning bells, passing bells, lunch bells, shower bells, cleanup bells. Hey look at her. Look at him. I wonder if he/she is looking at me. The sound of tires squealing is heard and a cigarette butt is flipped from an open car window.

Inside. Up to the third floor to the locker and down to the first for math class. 36 right—22 left—32 right. Missed it. 36 right—22 left—32 right —click. Got to hurry. A winter coat's too heavy to fit in the narrow locker with everything else there. The coat is pushed in and several books fall out. A quick but foggy inventory of the day's needs is performed.

Math class—Got the book, homework stuffed inside.
Drama—What do we need?—Can't remember.
Sociology—Don't need anything. The dumb book is already in the room.
Gym class—Damn!—My shoes are at home.
English—Got to get a library book sometime before English class.
Biology—I forgot to read it, but she'll tell us all about it anyway.
Driver's ed.—Boy, that book is dull. Why don't they just let you drive.

Hallways . . . faces . . . faces . . . a din of conversation.
Room 107—Three rows over and four desks back.
In the front of the room a white-haired teacher begins to write algebraic equations on the chalkboard. He calls over his shoulder, "Pass your assignments to the front, please." Students sleepily begin to rustle through books and looseleaf binders searching for assignments.

In a monotone, the teacher begins explaining the term "binomial" and addressing questions to the class. Three or four students toward the front give the answers and ask most of the questions.

Students jerk to attention as the teacher's tone of voice changes, "All right, then, turn to page 106, problem 7."

. . . The day continues with more classes, more instructions, more explanations, more assignments, and more sitting. Occasionally a bright spot flashes through . . . lunch, a chat with a close friend, a classroom group activity that allows a chance to laugh, or a discussion topic that lures students into sharper awareness. End-of-chapter questions have been answered, two worksheets have been completed, one informal basketball game has been lost, two chapters have been paraphrased by teachers, and one movie on the Danai tribe has been viewed. A bell and time to walk home. A special announcement over the P.A. system on parking-lot use and a prolonged re-explanation on the use of topic sentences at paragraph beginnings preempted use of the library book which was obtained from your cousin's friend Jerome at lunch.

Goals

These discussions of reading education's double bind and the tone and flavor of a secondary student's day have been admittedly sketchy and impressionistic. They do capture a germ of truth, however, in reflecting that, for an average student, school can be a somewhat dull social event. On a daily basis, little occurs to encourage reading or even allow time for it. Only 2 percent (Lowe, 1974) of students can remember having seen a teacher read. In general, with some magnificent exceptions, that's where we are.

Given this state of affairs, teachers need a clear conception of where they are headed if good teaching is to thread its way through the mire of random school experiences. Higher mean scores on standardized tests shouldn't be our main goal. Watching to be sure that book reports are properly done shouldn't consume our energy. What we, as teachers, should hope to foster are independent, mature readers. Our aim should be to develop students independent of us, students who seek out new interests and enjoy reading and learning about those new interests. The goal isn't for every content area teacher to teach reading. The goal is for each content teacher to foster student independence by encouraging students to *read* and *enjoy reading* more about the content area.

This goal isn't particularly lofty or abstract. Education should produce literate adults who are able to read and regularly do choose to read. Getting lost in a forest of curriculum objectives, course outlines, test criteria, and departmental directives will no longer do. When viewed as part of a twelve-year schooling experience, the teacher must decide which practices, activities, materials, or methods foster literacy and which do not. This doesn't necessarily mean deemphasizing content, but it does mean making books living entities for students and for teachers. The teacher must judge which school experiences foster positive attitudes toward real-life reading and which experiences actually discourage such positive attitudes.

SCHOOL IMPEDIMENTS TO DEVELOPING READING ATTITUDES

Several factors in the adolescent experience contribute to the steady decline of students' reading attitudes. Some of these factors, such as home influence, peer influence, job demands, and the increased time demands of an active adolescent social life, are probably beyond the influence of schools and teachers. There are, however, several concrete aspects of "schooling" at the secondary level which can be charged with discouraging positive reading attitudes and habits.

Change in Type of Reading Material

Starting about the middle school grades, there occurs a marked change in the reading diet of students. Early grades provide students primarily with narrative or story material. Even social studies or science material is often couched in the discoveries of one or two familiar characters who are exploring the woods and streams. By middle school, however, expository writing and textbooks have become the norm. These texts seem to be much less interesting in format, the concept load is usually much more dense per page, and the general readability of many texts is so high that only a small percentage of a class can independently read and comprehend them. In a very real sense, students encounter a sort of literacy shock when they encounter upper-grade textbooks. The shock is all the more destructive for the fact that usually little is done to prepare students for the transition from narrative to expository writing. Most assigned reading at the secondary level is a special kind of exposition—textbook writing.

Frustrational Reading Levels and Failure Experiences

Nobody likes to fail, and most of us without masochistic bents try to avoid failure-producing situations. Adolescents are no exception.

It doesn't take much time for average and below-average students to discover that most textbooks are too difficult for them to understand without a lot of help. They probably don't understand that the books are too difficult because of vocabulary usage that exceeds five to ten unknown words per hundred. The students may not know that overly involved complex sentences are too long for slow readers to retain in memory long enough to comprehend. In all likelihood, most students haven't the faintest idea that many of their textbook authors are writing to impress colleagues first, to educate adolescents secondarily. They do know, however, that in social studies class, English class, science class, math class, and perhaps even in shop class, they are being asked to read pages that make no sense and provide recurrent experience of failure. Typically they have no well-defined concept of why they are reading particular assignments. It is little wonder that teachers hear excuses like I left my book at home, or it's in the locker, or the dog chewed it, or my cousin has it in the back of his car.

Departmentalization and Anonymity

Another shock that students experience between elementary and secondary school is that of moving from a secure family of some thirty classroom personalities to a much more anonymous academic setting populated by hundreds and perhaps thousands of people. Instead of a single teacher with her known expectations and idiosyncracies, students face six or seven teachers daily. This deluge of personalities is compounded by the fact that many classes change at semester's end, and, especially in large schools, each new class may be filled with a new set of peers whose expectations need to be learned and taken into account.

Since the classes are departmentalized, the flavor of the student-teacher relationship is also likely to change. Each teacher is a minor "expert" in his or her field. The tendency for each teacher to be more content or material oriented and less individual-student oriented is very high. Because the teacher sees a student only an hour per day, heavy emphasis is likely to be placed upon "covering material." Each teacher, as a result of several years of specialized training, has come to see his or her subject area as the most important thing to be learned by students. Western civilization must be transferred through appreciation of literature. Technology can only be mastered by a scientifically trained citizenry. And critical evaluation of historical and current events is the only hope for an improved world. Depending upon the teacher, the crying need is for healthier bodies, tighter paragraphs, or a greater sensitivity to the arts. A new focus occurs seven different times with each new period in a secondary student's day. It's not surprising that few students are flexible enough to make daily that many transformations of purpose.

The tendency to concentrate more on material than on individual students is fueled by the massive numbers of students faced by secondary teachers. A teacher of semester courses may encounter 150 students per day and up to 300 students per year. That much personal contact tends to make individual work seem overwhelming. A secondary teacher who only becomes close to five or six favorites per semester class can justifiably be accused of having teacher's pets and favorites. It should be noted, however, that such a secondary teacher would still be getting to know twice as many students per year as his or her elementary teacher counterpart.

In short, departmentalization and the student anonymity that usually accompanies it encourage an emphasis on tasks and content at the expense of a slowly developing understanding between student and teacher. If rapport between student and teacher encourages positive reading attitudes and an appreciation of the living ideas behind the textbooks, the odds are against that rapport having enough time and contact to develop for many secondary students.

Teachers as Reading Models

For many students, teachers are likely to be their only reading models. If a student is lucky enough to encounter a teacher with good reading habits, research (El Hagrasy, 1962) suggests that the reading habits of these students will improve. Not all students are fortunate enough to encounter teachers with strong positive reading habits, attitudes, or even abilities, however.

Survey information on teachers' reading abilities, attitudes, and habits has usually shown teachers in a poor light. Many studies (Simpson, 1942; Dinnam and Hafner, 1970; Geeslin and York, 1970) show a large percentage of teachers to be reading less well than many of the high school students they are hired to teach. Surveys of some teacher groups (Cline, 1969; and

Mikulecky and Ribovich, 1977) show above-average reading abilities. But though some teachers read well, many, many teachers read less well than an average high school graduate.

Research on teacher reading habits and attitudes reveals the same sort of picture. Some studies indicate that most teachers read less than a book a month (Odland and Ilstrup, 1963) and up to 20 percent read no books even over the summer (Hawkins, 1967). Most other studies of teacher reading habits and attitudes suggest that an uncomfortably large number of teachers reads rarely and then only when required.

Logic and some research indicate that teachers' reading abilities, attitudes, and habits have an influence on those same characteristics of students. A large number of teachers do not read well or often and do not particularly like to read. This fact may well be a significant factor in the decline of student reading attitude.

Lack of Time Equals Low Priority

All of us speak with our actions as well as our words. A student doesn't have to be particularly bright to conclude that reading can't be very important if so little time is made for it during the school day. Time is the one resource we share as humans. It is only natural for students to assume that reading has a low priority if it is only allocated the few minutes of time at the end of a class period when all other work has been completed. When a teacher exhorts a student to read more because reading practice is important and perhaps even essential for success in school, most students will give verbal agreement. For that matter, so will most parents. Everybody knows reading is important. They've been told so thousands of times and verbally agreed that it's important several hundred times. Too many people also feel, however, that reading is something you don't really do except when there is absolutely nothing else to do. You might read, for example, when trapped in a doctor's waiting room, but certainly not when there is anything else to be done.

The problem of having little available reading time during school hours is compounded by the fact that almost no out-of-school reading time is present in the lives of many adolescents. One of the phenomena of adolescence in our society is the heavy increase in time demands as the youth begins to abandon a family-oriented culture and enter a peer-oriented culture. Clubs, organizations, athletic events, social events, religious training, dating, jobs, and just hanging around with friends all absorb the out-of-school hours of adolescents. In addition, research (Waters, 1977) shows that the average television viewing time is in the range of thirty to forty hours per week. The shape of our society is such that the average adolescent is going to find or make little out-of-school time for reading. For many, many students, reading takes place in school or not at all.

WHAT CAN BE DONE

A number of approaches, techniques, and methods can be used to encourage reading and halt the deterioration of positive reading attitudes. Most of these approaches are based on the recognition that a key goal of education is to develop lifelong learning habits which, in most cases, means lifelong reading habits. Reading in schools should not be seen as teaching students to sound out words or to answer end-of-chapter questions. School is rather the place to begin using books in the ways we expect literate adults to use them the rest of their lives.

At the Individual Level

Effective teachers try to gather as much information about their individual students as they can before making decisions or setting educational goals and objectives. Teaching students to develop positive reading habits and attitudes ought to be built on a solid information base. This information base is especially important when teachers are dealing with reading attitudes, because research indicates that there is a strong tendency for teachers to misjudge students' reading abilities to be equivalent with their reading attitudes (Mikulecky, 1976). Teachers often mistakenly assume that good grades mean good reading attitudes. Secondary teachers who, of necessity, spend less time with more students are especially prone to make this type of mistake.

The most natural way to gather information about students' reading habits and interests is to talk with them, observe what they are reading, and get to know their interests so appropriate reading suggestions can be made. Given the overwhelming numbers of pupils facing a secondary teacher each day, however, such methods are not satisfactory if they are the only methods used. There is not enough time in a semester for a teacher to become familiar with the reading attitudes and interests of each student through conversation and direct observation.

Reading-Attitude Measures

A teacher can, however, gather information using a number of formal and informal reading-attitude measures and reading-interest inventories. Such paper-and-pencil measures can provide a teacher with information about how a student's reading attitude compares with that of his peers within the classroom or across the nation. Several secondary-level reading-attitude measures have appeared in the last few years. The Estes Scale (1971)[3] is

[3] An updated version of this scale is available from T. H. Estes, J. P. Johnstone, and H. C. Richards, *Estes Attitude Scales.* Charlottesville, Va.: Virginia Research Associates, 1975.

available and Kennedy and Halinski (1975) have created a seventy-item reading-attitude measure which can be divided into two forms. The *Mikulecky Behavorial Reading Attitude Measure* (reprinted as an appendix in this chapter), is a twenty-item measure which provides guidelines for interpreting numerical scores. The attitude measure is based on Krathwohl's *Taxonomy of Educational Objectives* (1964) which describes various stages a person passes through in developing an attitude. The guidelines help teachers to interpret a student's stage as well as his score. A teacher who administers this measure at the beginning of a semester has access to information about the comparative reading attitudes of each student in class. In addition, the information provided by the stages of the measure can help a teacher to decide what approach to take in encouraging a student's reading. A student low on the continuum, for example, might be introduced to easy, high-interest materials. A student at the middle stages has already gained some pleasure from reading and needs to discover new ways in which reading can be a more valuable, pleasurable experience. Finally, students at the higher stages can be assumed to be hooked on reading. The teacher's task, described later, is to broaden the reading diet and experiences of such students.

Interest Inventories

Another paper-and-pencil tool that can prove quite helpful is an interest inventory. These can easily be constructed by teachers (see samples in chapter 5 on Analyzing Students) to determine what each student's interests are. With this information as a basis, a teacher can match a student with material in which he or she is already interested. Such a practice is desirable for two reasons. Initially, there is much intrinsic motivation in reading about something already relevant and familiar. Vocabulary and concepts may already be known, the rate may increase with excitement, and the likelihood of a successful, pleasurable experience is high. When reading material is matched to their interests, students tend to comprehend at from one to two grade levels above their tested reading levels (Estes and Vaughn, 1973). Second, matching students with reading material dealing with their life interests helps to initiate life-long reading habits. One of our main goals as teachers is to produce persons able to continue their learning without us. A student who has discovered interesting and helpful information in print is likely to seek out more printed information as his interests change, broaden, and develop. Interest inventories given early in the semester can provide a teacher with the information necessary to make important connections between students and materials. This is especially important to content-area teachers. If an overly difficult text is the only print source of information available to students in a class, that text may permanently discourage students from pursuing interesting aspects in that subject. Biology and social studies teachers usually read a lot more than textbooks covering their subject areas.

Students, however, often encounter only overly difficult texts. What conclusions can they reach?

Once information has been gathered about student interests, attitudes, and abilities, that information can also serve as a starting point for contact between teacher and student. Appropriate books and magazines can be recommended, and questions can be directed to students' areas of interest. A coach can suggest a particular magazine article, and a shop teacher can have do-it-yourself articles available. Nearly everyone likes to talk about and learn about things that matter to them.

Individual Conferences

In chapter 1, the teacher who had students work out their own text found time for chats, that is, conferences with students about books and ideas. Talking about and sharing what one reads *can* be enjoyable and can help anchor the book experience into a social reality. Experiencing this sharing and social anchoring is especially important for students who see reading primarily as a task or as a sort of unreal interval during which one passively stares at words. Reading is a communication between author and reader. Personal communication between teacher and student about books can enliven and add a shared importance to the communication between author and student reader.

Brief exchanges between student and teacher can add life to a student's interaction with a book. Since the purpose isn't to quiz a student's comprehension, the teacher doesn't necessarily have to have read what the student has read. Being familiar with the reading material can help a teacher sort through the verbiage of a student who hasn't really read the material or can enable a teacher to spot where a student missed the main thrust, but such familiarity isn't necessary. As a matter of fact, students who have something "new" and unfamiliar to show the teacher often come alive and feel less threatened about "saying the wrong thing." Teacher questions should be open-ended like: "What's been happening in your book?" or "How do you think the main character would make it at this school?" or "What do you think is going to happen next?" or even "If you were making a movie of this book, whom would you choose to play the main characters?" Exchanges of this kind can be accomplished in two or three minutes while the rest of the class is working on a weekly project. In that way a teacher can usually manage to meet with each student during any given month. Content teachers in business classes, home economics classes, or almost any other content area can ask students to contribute articles and pamphlets to a growing classroom library. A conference assignment could be to bring in and be able to talk about several articles. These articles may even be plastic coated by audio-visual departments in some schools.

There can be several variations to the individual conference. Lyman

Hunt (1970), for example, suggests using questions that ask students to assess their growth. Content is virtually ignored and teachers ask questions like: Did you read better today than yesterday? Did the ideas in the book hold your attention? Did you get mixed up in any place? Did you have to go back and straighten yourself out? The emphasis is on process and encouraging the reader to be aware of when he is reading well and when not.

Perhaps the simplest variation is to make time for regular individual conferences between students. About ten minutes before the end of a reading period, the teacher might say, "Find someone you feel fairly comfortable talking with. Take turns and talk about what you've been reading for at least five minutes." Talking about what has been read immediately after reading tends to improve comprehension—it makes the reading experience more real and vivid. Students are usually comfortable talking with each other, and an added spin-off is that students learn about the existence of additional reading materials from sources they can trust—their peers. By walking among students as they talk to each other, the teacher can gather a great amount of information in a short period of time. As students turn up current bits of reading on a given content area, the teacher may even decide to read interesting selections to the class.

Training Students for Self-Selection

If students are to become readers independent of their teachers, self-selection becomes extremely important. Many students, perhaps most, are either in awe or at least confused about how to choose something to read. By modeling methods for selecting reading material, a teacher can help to overcome the especially frustrating hurdle of "getting a book."

Initially, the teacher can demonstrate a technique for finding books of appropriate difficulty. Some teachers have long used the "ten-finger technique." This technique simply asks students to cover each unknown word on a page with a finger. If the child runs out of fingers, the book is too hard. As homespun as the technique appears, it approximates Emmet Betts' definition of five unknown words per hundred as being indicative of a frustrational reading level.

The technique is easily applied. Books can be randomly opened, and students can check off unknown words. If more than seven to ten unknown words per page are encountered during a couple of trials, the book is most likely too difficult. This doesn't mean the student shouldn't read it; it just means that perhaps an easier book ought also to be selected. A student who insists on reading difficult books should be allowed to try. Daniel Fader recounts the story of one student with low reading ability who persisted and somehow managed to read all the way through *The Scarlet Letter* by Hawthorne because he'd heard it was a story about a prostitute.

Other helpful self-selection techniques are often ignored by teachers—

perhaps because they seem too obvious. For example, many students rarely consider reading "come-on" blurbs on the back cover or introductory pages of paperback books. The idea of lightly skimming through a book several pages at a time and dipping in on occasion to get a "feel" for the book is unknown to most secondary students. It's almost as if they feel, "Once you touch it you have to take it." By modeling some of these ordinary-sounding techniques for self-selection, a teacher can introduce helpful tools to students and go a long way toward letting students become more familiar and comfortable with books.

Address Recommendations to Realistic Reasons for Reading

As much as possible, books should be read for realistic reasons—reasons that have validity outside the school setting and within the students' personal framework. So long as grading exists, tests seem to be necessary in education. If, however, the only reason a student is encouraged to read is to pass a test, that student is not likely to read after the test is completed. The same result is likely if the only reason for reading is completion of worksheets or end-of-chapter questions.

If students are to continue reading past the school experience, reading must be motivated by reasons that continue past the school experience. There are many such reasons on which a teacher can build reading motivation. Among these reasons and realistic motivations are:

1. Curiosity
2. Pleasure and excitement of the new
3. Utility (that is, explanations of how to handle difficulties or accomplish specific goals)
4. Prestige and social status with peers
5. Escape and vicarious experiences
6. Expanding and reinforcing present attitudes and interest areas
7. Reflection of personal situations and dilemmas.

Curiosity Curiosity is one of the easiest emotions to stimulate. A teacher might orally read a portion of a story or a passage from a text and stop at a crucial point. Curiosity and a need for closure will often do the rest. Sometimes placing students in situations similar to those about which they are to read may produce curiosity about how others handle similar situations. For example, simply describing a crucial conflict in the plot of a novel and asking, "What would you do in a situation like that?" can be foundation enough. Once students have involved themselves to the point of saying what they would do, curiosity about how the author dealt with the situation is likely to arise. The same process can work for readings in history or science. When students have read about data collected in an experiment, ask them for their own conclusions before reading the researchers' conclusions.

Pleasure and Excitement of the New Novelty is attractive to most of us. Our attention is drawn to traveling in exotic places, encountering unusual ideas, finding unique solutions to problems. Much of the popularity of science fiction or detective stories with ingenious solutions to puzzling crimes can be explained by the pleasure of the new. Such motivation can easily be used to encourage reading. This is especially true in problem-solving subjects like the sciences. The teacher might say, "Here is the problem—How do you suppose this life form solves it?"

Utility Even the least-enthusiastic reader will read when he must. The remedial reader thumbing through an auto repair manual is perhaps the cliche example of this. How-to-do-it books outsell most novels because people *will* read to find out how to do something. Next to the Bible, Benjamin Spock's book on child care is America's best seller. Nonreaders will spend hours trying to memorize a dull and difficult driver's-education manual to obtain a driver's license. A lesson in all of this for teachers is: Capitalize on utility as a motivation by showing students where they can find printed material on subjects they need to master. Driving and auto repair have already been mentioned as examples. Teachers can also help students to connect with materials on carpentry, sports, music, hobbies, consumer information, self-help, crafts, or any other field in which the students display an interest. If it is possible to do it, someone has written a book on *how*. Your aim is to help students realize this and get to those books.

Prestige and Social Status Reading to gain prestige and attention from others is common. Sometimes adults will participate in blatant name and title dropping, and at other times adults will read what friends are reading so they can participate in conversations. This sort of activity is less common among adolescents, but the motivation is present. If a star athlete reads a book and talks about it, others will also read that book. A teacher can facilitate this kind of activity by becoming aware of friendship groups within a class and focusing attention on the "opinion leaders" of each group. Reading to impress peer groups goes on, to some extent, with or without the teacher's encouragement. An example comes to mind from this author's inner-city teaching experiences. One day, Terry, a young dude with expensive clothing and rumored dealings outside of school, brought to school a copy of *Pimp: The Story of My Life,* by Iceberg Slim (Robert Beck). Within the week a half-dozen copies had somehow made their way into the hands of most of the poor reading males in class. This title is not being recommended here, but the power of peer-group prestige for motivating reading certainly is.

Escape and Vicarious Experience As early as the sixteenth century, Sir Philip Sidney advised that reading should be for either "entertainment or enlightenment." Reading to escape or to experience adventures otherwise impossible is a driving motivation for many readers. Years ago the *Hardy Boys* and *Nancy Drew* mystery series supplied an almost addictive reading habit for thousands of adolescents. Now those books are the basis of a television series. Titles change with the times, but the same need is present today. Tolkien's *Lord of the Rings* and Carlos Castaneda's *Don Juan* are read in many high schools. Various authors of science fiction or spy thrillers or romance novels each have their followings. Though too much escape can be undesirable, and the content of some reading is extremely superficial, most students should be encouraged to immerse themselves in escape reading at some time during their adolescence. Have you ever met a highly proficient adult reader who didn't at some time during his youth get hours of reading practice while escaping to a fictional world between the covers of a book?

Expanding and Reinforcing Present Interests This motivation has already been mentioned in the discussion of reading-interest inventories. Stated simply: People like to read about what they like. It feels good to have what we know or what we believe reinforced. Commercial publishers are quick to capitalize on this phenomenon by marketing books on sports, snow-mobiling, racing, and so forth. In addition, research shows that if material is of high interest to readers it is significantly easier to comprehend.

Reflection of Personal Situations and Dilemmas A prime human motivation is self-discovery and self-enjoyment. We like to find out about ourselves and enjoy seeing others handle situations and overcome difficulties similar to our own. Children, according to psychologist and educator Bruno Bettel-heim (1976) in *The Uses of Enchantment,* enjoy fairy tales, in part, because they portray heroes overcoming threatening, powerful adversaries who are much like the threatening, powerful objects of fear present in a child's world. Robert Carlsen (1972) notes that adolescents are particularly interested in books that deal with the transition to adult life, searches for personal value, and adventures of social significance. It is helpful and encouraging to read about others solving problems similar to our own.

This same need to see reflections of personal situations is present in self-help books. Teenagers read books that give advice on dating, positive thinking, dealing with adolescence, and achieving peace through religion, yoga, meditation, hypnosis, or whatever. The teacher who knows a student well enough to understand that student's personal goals and conflicts can often suggest appropriate books.

At the Classroom Level

Most of the above suggestions have been aimed at what a teacher can do at the individual student level to set the stage for improved reading habits and attitudes. Diagnosis, individual contact, training students to be independent, and creating realistic student motivation to read are all important aspects of the teacher/student relationship. School, however, is much more than an individual teacher/student experience—it is also a total group or classroom experience.

This latter experience of schooling is seldom given the emphasis it deserves, and teachers rarely recognize the power they have to create a classroom world, a learning oasis. A teacher's expectations, choice of activities, behavior guidelines, and incentives create an atmosphere that can inspire and foster learning, often in spite of outside societal influences. Samuel Taylor Coleridge coined the phrase, "that willing suspension of disbelief," to describe an attitude or state of mind evoked in us as perceivers by the poet or playwright when we respond esthetically to the artist's work. A similar phenomenon can occur in classrooms. To an extent, students willingly allow teachers to shape their worlds and their reactions during the classroom experience. The way students think, feel, and behave can change significantly as they pass from one classroom to another.

There are several things a teacher can do to create an atmosphere and space that encourage reading. These range from simply being an active reader oneself—who is a model for students—to creating, organizing, and managing a number of activities that play up books.

Being a Model Who Makes Time

For many students, teachers are likely to be the only available models of literate, regular readers. Lowe (1974) reports that only 10 percent of the students surveyed could remember anyone at home choosing free or hobby reading. Unfortunately for the great majority of students who could benefit from contact with regular readers, teachers rarely serve as models. Lowe also reports that only 2 percent of these same students recall seeing a teacher read. It doesn't take students very long to suspect that some sort of hypocrisy is going on when they encounter only words of advice and no evidence of regular adult reading even among their teachers.

Teachers who really expect students to become independent literate, regular readers can go a long way toward helping students reach that goal by showing students how it's done. A teacher who regularly reads and talks to students about what he has been reading bridges the credibility gap. A teacher who makes time during the school day for student reading and then reads himself clearly demonstrates the high importance and priority of reading. Simply being seen carrying personal books or magazines can stimulate conversations.

More reasonable ways to provide time for reading in school are available. Allowing regular free reading during which everyone, including the teacher, reads is one such way. Book reports and lengthy comprehension checks ought to be avoided. If some sort of record keeping seems necessary, use a book log in which the amount read and a few summary remarks (no more than one or two sentences) are jotted after a reading period. By having the log turned in after each reading period and passing it out at each beginning, the teacher can notice who is reading and who is not. Special-interest reading within a content area could be handled the same way. Follow-up activities in the form of individual conferences and conversations with class-mates have been mentioned earlier in the chapter. It is important that students have such reading experiences (without being quizzed) with several different teachers and in several different classes. A teacher who uses newspapers or has available magazines related to his subject area is a model for students. They will pick up and even imitate his enthusiasm and habit of reading interesting articles.

Grouping for Interaction

Grouping lends itself to being a reasonable follow-up to free reading. A biology teacher, for example, could group students according to interest in reading about a particular species, or environmental problem, or promising new area in the field. The process of talking about a book or article with friends tends to make a person a more active reader; comprehension seems to increase, and reading tends to increase as students sell each other on new titles and old favorites. Discussion of interest-area reading with peers is a positive experience that is less contrived than many school experiences. It could easily be the start of a habit that continues past school.

In *The New Hooked on Books,* Daniel Fader presents a discussion of another kind of grouping that can be useful at the secondary level. Students are assigned heterogeneously to groups of three whose main charge is to take care of each other and make sure everyone learns as much as possible. This group becomes a sort of "home" for the student. Being responsible to and for two other people does much to dispel the anonymity of the secondary-school experience and gives learning a much more human setting. Talking about and sharing what one has learned with a group one comfortably knows and trusts increase the potential capacity for learning of all types. Improved reading habits can result from discussing reading in groups like this since reading becomes entwined with positive interpersonal relationships.

Motivational Activities

The topic of motivation and motivational activities is one that has been overdiscussed and often advised. Too often gimmicks, games, rewards, hard-ware, and teacher tricks have been used to lure students into one academic area or another. These gimmicks usually tend to be a moment of "flash" that passes quickly because the moment isn't grounded in any realistic reason for continuing the activity. Little follow-up activity occurs, and the teacher soon must resort to a new motivational technique to hype up the students. Still, there is a place for motivational gimmicks and techniques in getting student attention and creating an atmosphere where reading is encouraged.

Oral Reading One such motivational activity is brief oral readings to students. Most of us enjoy listening to someone read, especially someone who reads well and is interested in what is being read. A teacher can share passages of favorite books, current articles, or relevant newspaper stories and thereby encourage students to further sample books and other reading. A more diabolical version of this technique is to read a particularly exciting passage and stop, as does an old-time movie serial, at a crucial or a crisis point. Frustrated students may grow angry at their teachers, but they are highly likely to continue reading. A less flashy but equally effective technique is for science teachers to read a brief description of a key experiment and ask students to predict the result before reading the full report. Discussion can follow reading. The important point here is that after the students have been lured into reading, there should be outlets for the realistic sharing and enjoyment of what is read.

Games and Gimmicks Almost every issue of professional journals in virtually every content area includes at least one teacher activity, game, or innovative use of materials designed to motivate students. In addition, most faculties have a few creative individuals in each department ready to share their newest ideas. Rather than list several of these activities, this section will present some principles for evaluating good motivational activities, and will then present a few specific working examples.

Initially, a motivational technique ought to be grounded in a realistic ongoing reason for reading. This can range from curiosity through escape to reflection of a personal dilemma. Several such reasons are listed on page 88.

Second, the motivational technique should require some form of commitment action on the part of the student. Several research studies in attitude change indicate that even artificially contrived commitment and behavior change can serve to change attitude and long-term behavior patterns.

Finally, the motivational technique should have built into it an ongoing follow-up of some kind that continues to address a realistic reason for reading. Motivational techniques that are used in isolation can be colossal wastes of energy and may serve only to create jaded students.

Virtually any motivational technique that meets these three requirements can be of use. An excellent example of a technique that fits these requirements is the tried-and-true "book auction." Students are each given an arbitrary amount of credit or classroom currency, which they may use to "bid" on books that fellow classmates are attempting to sell or auction off. Each student is expected to do a good job of "talking up" or "selling" his book before the bidding begins. The book is given to the highest bidder, who has the first chance to read it before the next week or month's book auction. If books seem too cumbersome, content classes using the auction can draw on pamphlets, magazine articles, biographies, do-it-yourself manuals, and other appropriate forms of print of interest.

Students may read for a variety of reasons. The auction adds peer prestige to the list of reasons. To have read material that everybody wants or something that does well during bidding can be motivating. In addition, the auction framework demands a commitment from everyone involved. Sellers must appear convincing to succeed. Buyers have had to compete for the "opportunity" to read the book or article first, so they also have made a commitment. Several follow-up activities can be added to the auction. Students may participate in several groups in which they hear new titles discussed and have opportunities to discuss their own reading. Reading time can be set aside during the week so students can be prepared for the next auction.

Social studies classes have used planning a trip, attaining a goal, or having an adventure as a motivating technique. Reading done in the process of planning is done both for utility (how to do it) and for escape (getting a feel for a place or a fantasy). The process of having to hunt for information and organize realistic budgets entails a certain level of commitment. Commitment is also involved in such follow-up activities as placing your plan before a group for scrutiny, or perhaps working with a partner to gather and read necessary information. As the ultimate follow-up, a few students from previous semesters can return to the classroom to describe successful trips or projects they have completed based on the planning done in class. Cross-country bike hikes, trips to see European relatives, and renovated city lots have grown to realities from such plans.

TV, Movies, Tapes, and Records The use of nonprint media as motivation for reading is a topic that deserves special mention. In brief—use these media for all they are worth. Teachers often complain that TV and movies keep students from reading, gobble up too much time, and, in general, are destructive to literacy. Booksellers, on the other hand, are more attuned to the buying habits of the public. They publish one *Star Trek* novel after another, market print versions of other weekly TV series, and prepare simultaneous campaigns for books and movies of the same title. *Rich Man, Poor Man, The Money Changers, Roots, Gone With the Wind, Jaws,* and *The Omen* are just a few titles whose sales have spurted to the top of the paperback market partially as a result of media motivation. The promotional campaign for the Streisand/Kristofferson movie, *A Star is Born,* included the simultaneous release of the movie, the book, and the LP recording. Authors know that the mere mention of a title on the Johnny Carson show guarantees next-day sales of several thousand books. Scholastic/Scope magazines have even been publishing condensed versions of current television scripts from the more popular shows. Schools in Philadelphia (Waters, 1977) report gains in reading ability after having students read scripts of such TV shows as *The Missiles of October* and *Eleanor and Franklin* while viewing those shows.

To a lesser extent, classroom use of tapes and recordings of stories and poetry can serve to spark student interest and student reading. Many school and public libraries have recordings of titles already included in most school curricula. Because some productions are of very low quality, teacher previewing is highly recommended.

There are several strong reasons for capitalizing on media motivation for reading. Initially, media motivation has proved to be workable for the public at large and could be the start of an ongoing reading habit for students. Second, using media motivation counters the problem of frustrational reading level for students. Even though many students read at a frustrational reading level all through secondary school, Hamilton (1973) reports no complaints of comprehension problems from students who have viewed a movie before reading the book of the same title. Apparently a cognitive framework is established which makes understanding the book possible. In any case, media-stimulated reading could help to reverse the deadly vicious cycle of failure to understand print, which traps many students.

Materials

Having books readily available is essential in creating a classroom atmosphere conducive to reading. Supermarket paperbacks reach an audience almost never reached by libraries simply because of accessibility. Printed material should have the same sort of accessibility in the classroom.

A teacher can draw upon a wide variety of sources for classroom material. The librarian of a school can often be helpful in setting up rotating classroom libraries. Several educational corporations have book services that sell paperbacks at inexpensive prices when entered as a classroom order of twenty or more books. Sometimes local newspapers can be persuaded to deliver classroom sets of yesterday's paper.

In addition, students can help build their own classroom libraries. A classroom project that gives credit for bringing in old magazines and paperback books will turn up hundreds and sometimes thousands of publications from the attics and garages of a community. The teacher and perhaps a few students, should sort through the material to see what is useful for the classroom, but the work is happy work and a little like examining presents.

There are several "book lists for adolescents" to help teachers, departments, and school systems in ordering books for students. A list of these publications can be found in Appendix B at the end of this chapter. One could be cautioned, however, that such lists are quickly outdated. Checking with the libraries, examining current issues of *English Journal* for book lists, or simply surveying students about favorite books can be more appropriate ways to compile book orders.

The focus of these materials is surrounding students with reading materials. Earlier in this chapter, Krathwohl's *Taxonomy of Educational Objectives* was discussed. Krathwohl's model of how attitudes develop clearly recognizes an *acceptance* or *recognition* stage as the first step toward attitude change. Before change in reading attitude is at all possible, students need to *get used to* or *accept* reading material as a regular part of their world. This even precedes actual reading for some students. Being in a library surrounded by books, for many students, is an uncomfortable and alien experience. Helping students to build a classroom world of their own in which books and magazines are everywhere can help to ease this discomfort. Simply seeing that there are magazines on art, music, science, sports, and so forth can make a difference. Building a reading habit is a slow process. Having reading material readily available is the necessary first step in that process.

At the School Level

A teacher who is interested in reading improvement at the secondary-school level will usually be identified as a strength to the faculty, especially if he or she has had some training in secondary reading. Being asked to sit on a committee to deal with reading problems is not at all atypical. In such positions, a teacher has opportunity for contributing input to school-wide changes.

A principal or a school-wide reading committee can do much to improve reading attitudes and habits at a school-wide level. It is a simple matter for an administrator to ask for evidence that curriculum objectives referring to reading appreciation, habits, and attitudes are being met. Administering a pre-post test of reading attitudes and habits (such as was mentioned earlier in the chapter) emphasizes, through testing, that improving reading habits and attitudes is important. Activities designed to improve these traits should be given as much attention as activities directed at isolated reading-skill development. Budget decisions about whether funds are used for paperbacks or skill-development programs may also be influenced by principals or reading committees. Libraries can be encouraged to bring more students into contact with material they are likely to read.

Perhaps the most important effect a principal or reading committee can have at a school-wide level is in influencing teachers. If the reading abilities and habits of teachers can be improved, the spin-offs for students should soon follow. Here are ten suggestions for principals and reading committees whose goal is improvement of teacher reading abilities and habits:

Suggestions for Improving Teacher Reading Habits and Abilities

1. The principal can pay special attention to the reading abilities and habits of teachers to be selected for the school. Building a core of teachers who read well and often has the multiple benefits of providing good models for children, providing alternate models for nonreading teachers, and creating an atmosphere more conducive for change on the part of nonreading teachers. Hearing other teachers talk about what they've read exerts a subtle peer pressure.

2. Many teachers, especially those who have read little over a long period of time, are slow readers. If your district employs a reading specialist, perhaps that person can be persuaded to offer speed-reading tips at faculty meetings or in-service sessions. Mass-media advertising about speed reading has made it easier for sensitive, proud adults to accept reading help, and teachers who learn to read faster are likely to read more often and become better readers.

3. On a personal basis, the principal or committee can begin recommending books and articles to individual teachers. A tactful method might be to say, "I'm looking for something new to read. Have you read anything interesting lately? I just finished ——(title)——."

4. A more subtle, behind the scenes, method to encourage teacher reading is to lend books to teachers in person or through mailboxes with a note saying, "I thought you might be interested in this." Later one can ask what the teacher thought of the book. At worst, nothing is lost, and at best some interesting conversation, more reading, and perhaps even some new books in return will be gained.

5. Three or four minutes may be spent at the beginning or end of faculty meetings having individual teachers recommend to the staff an interesting book or article. Being tactfully asked beforehand by the principal to do this could grow into an honor and could encourage nonreading teachers to read lest they be asked and found wanting.

6. Lyman Hunt (1967) has recommended a program called *Uninterrupted Sustained Silent Reading*. Once a week for one hour, the entire school reads. Students read and are given the important and unusual opportunity of seeing teachers and other adults reading. The teacher's excuse of "I haven't time" disappears, and the principal has shown to teachers and students through policy that reading is important enough for *all* to spend time upon it.

7. If there is an already-existing core of teachers who regularly read or if such a core can be developed, small discussion groups can be organized around group-selected books. If using whole books seems too formidable, the discussions could center on the practical implications for your school of certain articles or chapters from new education texts. Again, this is easier to implement if the excuse of "I have no time" is undercut by the principal's

policy of providing a small amount of reading time for both students and teachers.

8. Recommendations and comments by teachers about books could be additions to daily or weekly printed bulletins. A few minutes of writing by the faculty at an early-in-the year faculty meeting could provide the principal with ammunition for several weeks' worth of bulletins. In addition to the recognition provided by the bulletins, most teachers will be interested in what other teachers are reading.

9. Some schools on small budgets have started the creation of professional libraries made up of books and texts contributed or loaned by teachers. Many districts also have professional libraries centrally located from which traveling collections could be gathered. If the principal can begin the library with a little seed money, so much the better. The point is that accessibility must precede use.

10. Finally, the teachers' lounge is an excellent place for a put-and-take paperback library made up entirely of contributed books. If teachers page through books in shopping centers and grocery stores, why shouldn't they page through and select a few in the teachers' lounge?

Beyond the School

The clear message of common sense and research is that what occurs at home greatly affects what the school can hope to accomplish. Examples of how the school and community can work together more closely may be found in other cultures. In Japan, for example, several community groups sponsor home reading programs. Michio Namekawa (1976) has described two such programs that began as early as the 1940s in Japan. In "the twenty-minute mother-child reading movement," parents and children sit together for twenty minutes a day, the child reading a book to the mother. In another movement, reading hours are scheduled at home once a week, when everyone in the family reads. Such programs as these could easily be adopted by such groups as the Parent-Teachers Association or the American Association of University Women. Though originally designed for elementary students, middle school versions could easily be designed.

To a certain extent, the PTA and AAUW in some cities are already working with the schools to improve reading abilities and reading habits. In Racine, Wisconsin, and other cities, for example, the American Association of University Women sponsors one-on-one reading programs. In these programs, students receive often-needed individual attention as they either read or are read to by AAUW members who work a few hours each week in the schools. Some members have worked effectively at the high school level.

There are many potentially useful ways for the school and community to interact. Members of the community from a variety of professions might be asked to appear in classrooms to discuss, among other things, the role that reading plays in both their personal and professional lives. Some schools use journalism classes to produce a newsletter that is sent to parents. Included in the newsletter and in features in the student newspaper could be mentions of what parents and students are currently reading. In addition, teachers might be encouraged individually or by departments to contribute titles and brief book reactions to both publications.

SUMMARY

Education seems to be in the double bind of training students to read in ways that discourage them from actually reading. At the secondary-school level, there exists a host of impediments to positive reading habits and attitudes. These impediments often include materials, the departmental structure, and even the poor reading model presented by many teachers.

In spite of such obstacles, much can be done to motivate reading and improve reading habits. At the individual level, the teacher can use reading-attitude measures and interest inventories to gather diagnostic information about each student. This information can help teachers prepare students to be independent readers who read for realistic reasons and develop their own individual interests.

At the classroom level, the teacher can be a model who makes time for reading. Also, the teacher has access to a wide variety of grouping and motivational techniques that have proven effective.

On a school-wide level, administrative decisions on testing, budget, and teacher selection can be used to create an atmosphere where reading attitudes are likely to improve. In addition, school and community groups can work together emulating the example of such cultures as Japan where a nonreader isn't a low test score but rather a person who didn't read a book during the month of May.

In conclusion, it should be noted that most successful reading motivation techniques are based on reasons for reading that extend beyond the classroom and are entwined with personal and social realities that will continue when schooling has finished. Luring students to read or bribing them or tricking them may work for a time. Such practices, however, run counter to the goal of developing literate, independent adults who use books and other printed materials in pursuing pleasures, interests and tasks.

DISCUSSION QUESTIONS

1. To what would you attribute the steady decline in reading attitude scores for each successively higher grade in school?

2. By pre- and post-testing with a reading attitude measure, it should be possible to determine what is effective in developing positive reading attitudes and what is not. What factors or variables in the school experience ought to be checked for their effect on reading attitude?

3. What changes would you expect to see if schools and teachers were held "accountable" for their effect on reading attitude as they are now held accountable for their effect on reading ability?

4. Choose at least two content areas not usually associated with heavy reading. What could be done by teachers in those areas to improve the attitudes of their students toward reading in general and the content area in particular?

Suggested Readings

Alexander, J. Estill, and Ronald C. Fuller. *Attitudes and Reading*, Newark, Del.: International Reading Association, 1976.
   This book helps teachers identify attitudes related to reading, provides suggestions for assessing attitudes, and suggests behaviors and instructional strategies which may help students form more positive attitudes toward reading. A nice joining of research and practical application.
Fader, Daniel N. *The New Hooked on Books*, New York: Berkley Medallion Books, 1976.
   This book contains a description of a workable program for encouraging reading among adolescents. This volume is "one decade after" the original *Hooked on Books* appeared (1966) and summarizes some of Fader's newer ideas, including a special grouping technique mentioned in this chapter.
Strickler, Darryl J., ed. *The Affective Dimension of Reading: Resource Guide*, Bloomington, Ind.: Indiana University Reading Programs, 1977.
   An anthology of readings authored by, among others, Bill Martin, Jr., Charlotte Huck, and Daniel N. Fader. The readings suggest ways to implement teaching ideas at various levels with improved attitudes toward reading being the common goal. The resource guide stands by itself, but was designed to accompany a series of videotapes available through Indiana University.

Appendix A

Mikulecky Behavioral
Reading Attitude Measure

Name _____   Instructor's Name _____

Age _____ Sex _____   School _____

On the following pages are 20 descriptions. You are to respond by indicating how much these descriptions are either unlike you or like you. For "very unlike" you, circle the number 1. For "very like" you, circle the number 5. If you fall somewhere between, circle the appropriate number.

Example

   You receive a book for a Christmas present. You start the book, but decide to stop halfway through.
   VERY UNLIKE ME   1   2   3   ④   5   VERY LIKE ME

1. You walk into the office of a doctor or dentist and notice that there are magazines set out.
   VERY UNLIKE ME   1   2   3   4   5   VERY LIKE ME

2. People have made jokes about your reading in unusual circumstances or situations.
   VERY UNLIKE ME   1   2   3   4   5   VERY LIKE ME

3. You are in a shopping center you've been to several times when someone asks where books and magazines are sold. You are able to tell the person.
   VERY UNLIKE ME   1   2   3   4   5   VERY LIKE ME

4. You feel very uncomfortable because emergencies have kept you away from reading for a couple of days.
   VERY UNLIKE ME   1   2   3   4   5   VERY LIKE ME

5. You are waiting for a friend in an airport or supermarket and find yourself leafing through the magazines and paperback books.
   VERY UNLIKE ME   1   2   3   4   5   VERY LIKE ME

6. If a group of acquaintances would laugh at you for always being buried in a book, you'd know it's true and wouldn't mind much at all.
   VERY UNLIKE ME   1   2   3   4   5   VERY LIKE ME

7. You are tired of waiting for the dentist, so you start to page through a magazine.
   VERY UNLIKE ME   1   2   3   4   5   VERY LIKE ME

8. People who are regular readers often ask your opinion about new books.
   VERY UNLIKE ME   1   2   3   4   5   VERY LIKE ME

9. One of your first impulses is to "look it up" whenever there is something you don't know or whenever you are going to start something new.
   VERY UNLIKE ME   1   2   3   4   5   VERY LIKE ME

10. Even though you are a very busy person, there is somehow always time for reading.
VERY UNLIKE ME 1 2 3 4 5 VERY LIKE ME

11. You've finally got some time alone in your favorite chair on a Sunday afternoon. You see something to read and decide to spend a few minutes reading just because you feel like it.
VERY UNLIKE ME 1 2 3 4 5 VERY LIKE ME

12. You tend to disbelieve and be a little disgusted by people who repeatedly say they don't have time to read.
VERY UNLIKE ME 1 2 3 4 5 VERY LIKE ME

13. You find yourself giving special books to friends or relatives as gifts.
VERY UNLIKE ME 1 2 3 4 5 VERY LIKE ME

14. At Christmas time, you look in the display window of a bookstore and find yourself interested in some books and uninterested in others.
VERY UNLIKE ME 1 2 3 4 5 VERY LIKE ME

15. Sometimes you find yourself so excited by a book you try to get friends to read it.
VERY UNLIKE ME 1 2 3 4 5 VERY LIKE ME

16. You've just finished reading a story and settle back for a moment to enjoy and remember what you've just read.
VERY UNLIKE ME 1 2 3 4 5 VERY LIKE ME

17. You *choose* to read nonrequired books and articles fairly regularly (a few times a week).
VERY UNLIKE ME 1 2 3 4 5 VERY LIKE ME

18. Your friends would not be at all surprised to see you buying or borrowing a book.
VERY UNLIKE ME 1 2 3 4 5 VERY LIKE ME

19. You have just gotten comfortably settled in a new city. Among the things you plan to do is check out the library and book stores.
VERY UNLIKE ME 1 2 3 4 5 VERY LIKE ME

20. You've just heard about a good book but haven't been able to find it. Even though you're tired, you look for it in one more book store.
VERY UNLIKE ME 1 2 3 4 5 VERY LIKE ME

SUMMARY STATISTICS

Junior High School (7–9 Grades) and Senior High School (10–12 Grades) Urban, Suburban, and Rural Subjects MBRAM Scores

Level	URBAN				SUBURBAN				RURAL			
	N	Mean	Range	S.D.	N	Mean	Range	S.D.	N	Mean	Range	S.D.
Jr	127	55.93	27–90(63)	12.11	276	59.60	25–98(73)	14.33	182	60.81	22–92(70)	13.91
Sr	332	55.24	20–90(70)	12.51	144	58.29	24–95(71)	15.55	190	59.28	29–97(68)	15.17

Attitude Bands for Junior and Senior High School by Location

Attitude Level	URBAN		SUBURBAN		RURAL	
	Jr. High	Sr. High	Jr. High	Sr. High	Jr. High	Sr. High
Above Average	66–100	62–100	68–100	67–100	69–100	68–100
Average	53–65	49–61	52–67	50–66	54–68	52–67
Below Average	20–52	20–48	20–51	20–49	20–53	20–51

Stages of Krathwohl's Taxonomy
as Reflected by
Mikulecky Behavioral Reading Attitude Measure
Items

Stage I (Attending) of the taxonomy is reflected by items 1,3,5,7. Each item provides from 1 to 5 points. A perfect score at this stage would be 4 items × 5 points—20 points. A student can be said to have attained a stage if he/she has 75 percent of the possible points at that stage. By interpreting items and stages, a deeper understanding of a student's reading attitude is possible.

KRATHWOHL STAGES	ITEMS (1–5 POINTS POSSIBLE EACH ITEM)	CRITERION SCORE (75 PERCENT OF POSSIBLE POINTS)
I. Attending: The individual is generally aware of reading and tolerant of it.	1,3,5,7	15 pts.
II. Responding: The individual is willing to read under certain circumstances. He or she begins to choose and occasionally enjoy reading.	11,14,16	11 pts.
III. Valuing: The individual begins to accept the worth of reading as a value to be preferred and even to extend to others.	13,15,17, 18,19,20	23 pts.
IV. Organization: For the individual, reading is part of an organized value system and is so habitual that it is almost "instinctive."	9,10,12	11 pts.
V. Characterization: For the individual, reading is so much a part of life that both the reader and others see reading as crucial to this person.	2,4,6,8	15 pts.

Appendix B

Book Lists for Teachers and Students

Basic Book Collection for High School—Published by the American Library Association and compiled by Eileen F. Noonan, in 1963, this includes 1,400 books and 70 periodicals arranged by subject area and then alphabetically by author. A wide range of topics is covered and the types of works are noted. Also, a brief résumé indicates the basic sketch of the plot. This list is rather extensive and will be helpful to the *average* student, because there are no references for books for slow or reluctant readers. In addition to the fiction section, much technical information is indicated. The reading levels are not specified and, in general, these are not high-interest books.

Basic Book Collection for the Junior High Student—For the American Library Association, Margaret V. Spengler wrote this list of books which ranges from the classical to the popular, arranged alphabetically by author and according to themes within content areas. Short résumés follow each title. Also, there is included a short story collection and the prices are listed. There are really no books for mature readers but mostly for the average readers, grades seven to nine. Few recent books are listed and most of the books are hardbound. Finally, these are not high-interest books.

Book Bait—Elinor Walker has compiled for the American Library Association a list of adult books that are popular with teenagers. The annotations are very long and excellently written. The books are intended to be those which are popular with young adults. The list is arranged in alphabetical order by author with no thematic divisions. The selection is rather limited. The popularity of each is specified for males and females. Each book has appropriate grade level indicated. There is no method to distinguish between paperbacks and hardbound books.

Doors to More Mature Reading—Elinor Walker, along with Donald W. Allyn, Alice Johnson, and Helen Lutton worked for the American Library Association to compile this list of 600 books which is alphabetically arranged by authors with no thematic divisions. The sections these books are organized into are: plays, poetry, science, etc. This source is great for its extensive annotations of mostly very well known books.

English Journal (Jan. 1975, pp. 29–40) "Literature/Reading/Paperbacks"—This section of the magazine gives some content books for teachers such as "Understanding the Old Testament"; some anthologies (for example, *Modern Black Stories*); and several descriptions of reading series. One of these is the Target Book series for students with perceptual learning disabilities and reading problems. This list is compiled according to publishers and includes the price of the book as well as a three- or four-line description of each book.

English Journal (Jan. 1975, pp. 112–115) "1974 Honor Listing: Books for Young Adults"—Compiled by Carlsen, Manna, and Tucker, this collection classifies books under six thematic listings and alphabetically according to author under each heading. A six- to ten-line description is offered with each book, including the book's importance within this theme. These books are those which are most popular with young readers. Students' comments are given with the book talks with sample readers.

English Journal (Jan. 1976, pp. 20–29) "Literature/Reading Paperbacks"—Compiled according to most of the major and some of the minor publishers. This list includes a brief description of many of the books given. The books mentioned are for the junior and senior high school student, and the overwhelming majority are high-interest books.

Fiction Catalog—Published in 1971 by the H. W. Wilson Co., and edited by Esterle A. Fidell, this is very useful for finding books on specific subjects. It is arranged according to author but includes a title and subject index. One-paragraph descriptions and one-paragraph commentaries are also given. Sometimes the reading level is listed for these 4,315 books. The list contains young adult and adult books and is more descriptive than many others. The annotations are quite helpful. "A guide to the best fiction in the English language."

High Interest—Easy Reading—This book was edited by Raymond Emery and Margaret B. Houshower for Citation Press for slow or reluctant readers. All the books are listed according to reading and interest levels. The books are not too recent (1965) but are very high-interest selections for young adults. This collection is arranged by their interests, and short résumés follow each title. This is a good selection for the slow and unmotivated reader. There is even a sample inventory for the student to fill out, indicating his/her interests.

Kliatt Paperback Book Guide—Editors Doris Hiatt and Celeste Klein compiled this list for Kliatt Paper Book Guide Co. (Published quarterly in Massachusetts.) This collection of books has been organized according to five sections: The Arts, Literature, Reference, Social Studies, and Misc. (according to author in each area). Following each title, there is a four- or five-sentence description and a one- or two-line commentary, indicating the striking elements. The looseleaf, section-colored format gives this book nice flexibility. The prices are given, along with the reading and interest levels. The annotations are superior. This list is for all young adults and, in general, is a list of high-interest books. Useful for students as well as teachers and librarians.

The Paper Back Goes to School—The Bureau of Independent Publishers and Distributors employed Alan P. Ford to devise a list of 5,000 inexpensive paperbacks, listed alphabetically by book title according to subject headings and title listings. Book prices are included. Elementary titles are given in a small section. No age levels are specified except in the elementary section. Many of these nonleisure books would be suitable for classroom teaching.

Patterns in Reading—Jean Carolyn Rose compiled this book list for the American Library Association. It consists of 1,600 titles selected from best literature to simple junior novels. The books are arranged according to themes. Both fiction and nonfiction are included. The book list starts with the most readable books and continues to the more difficult. Each includes a one-sentence résumé. There is an author and title index in the back. This is not a particularly recent list (1961). There are many books on foreign countries and historical periods.

Reading Ladders for Human Relations—Published in 1972 by the American Council of Education and edited by Virginia M. Reid, this list is divided into four sections: Creating a Positive Self Image, Living with Others, Appreciating Different Cultures, Coping with Change. The focus of these books is to help a reader understand his/her lifestyle and the styles of others. Within each section, the books are arranged by maturity levels and then listed alphabetically by author. Very full listing of books supplemented with a brief résumé of each one. Paperbacks are distinguished from hardbounds and price information is given. There is also a good section on planning book discussions which indicates how to suggest books to students.

Teacher's Guide to World Literature for High School—Published by the National Council of Teachers of English in 1966 and compiled by Robert O'Neal and Berry College, this book gives 150 book reviews, indicating the importance, author, résumé, comparative analysis, and translation of each. The prices are included for each of these classics. Thematic suggestions are offered in the back. This book is mostly intended for teachers but would give exceptionally advanced junior high or motivated high school students an opportunity to scan résumés of classics in order to narrow their choice selections.

Your Reading—Charles Willare, working for the New York American Library, Inc., devised this book list arranged by themes (animals, sports, adventure, etc.) and then alphabetically according to author in these sections. Short résumés are given. There are few books per theme, however. The level of difficulty of each book is given and fiction is distinguished from nonfiction. Again, these books, although 1,300 of them are listed, are not too recent.

5

Analyzing
Bookthinking Behavior

How does a teacher analyze the bookthinking behavior of students when he meets several classes each day?

What are major indications of specific difficulties in comprehending the textbook?

What major decisions does a teacher make related to bookthinking?

From time to time a youngster will slam his book shut and announce dramatically: "This is a lot of crap and I'm not going to read anymore!" The whole class then looks to the teacher to see how he will defend himself. For that's what such an outburst seems to indicate—an attack on the subject, the teacher's love, and the teacher must come to its defense, perhaps to his own defense.

"What do you mean?" the teacher may shout back. "That's the best high school text on that subject we can buy!" or "Who do you think you are to make that kind of judgment? You know so little about the subject you can't even carry on an intelligent conversation about the simplest topics." Maybe the teacher will show enormous patience and restraint: "Now, Henry, you are just tired and irritated. Let's talk about it and you'll feel better about it tomorrow."

To which Henry will probably say again: "I will not. It's boring and just a lot of stupid crap!" He likes that word (or one a little more vulgar) because all the students' eyes perk up, and it puts the teacher on the defensive, not Henry. Besides, it provides him with a continuing excuse for not reading that text. It's clearly against Henry's esthetic principles to fill his mind with that kind of load.

How would you react if this incident occurred in your classroom?

Assuming Henry is not simply trying to give the teacher a vengeful trauma, and assuming he is not reacting to a personal emotional problem, he is probably telling his teacher that the text he is reading frustrates him, that he can't handle it. Similarly, the girl who puts her head on her desk and sleeps whenever reading is assigned, and the boy who comes forward during a reading assignment and admits he can't quite understand what the message is—these youngsters are crying for help. At least they are crying in distress over the reading load. Those cries cannot be ignored; they are disruptive. They may not be belligerent, but they are certainly disruptive. Most teachers will respond to those students even though they don't recognize the reading problem. Teachers need to calm the class as well as work for the benefit of the individual student.

When a student sends up an obvious distress signal, the teacher's easiest and most efficient means for determining the nature of the problem is to ask the student to describe it. "What seems to be the trouble? Do you understand the technical vocabulary? Can you follow the diagrams? Are you able to see the author's line of reasoning? What do you do when you come to a word you don't know or can't pronounce? What is happening in your mind as you follow the author's thought?" With questions like this, the teacher encourages the student to concentrate on the book and to be introspective. What is it that causes me the most trouble? Those questions often will gain the information needed to start the student on a more successful experience. Introspection often provides valuable information in analyzing a student's behavior.

Responding to overt cries for help, however, does not constitute competent teaching. When someone yells in pain, everyone becomes a Good Samaritan. The competent teacher does more. He finds ways to analyze the behavior of all his students so he can aid them, even if they have not created an ugly scene. How does the competent teacher analyze the bookthinking behavior of his students? How does he examine that behavior when he meets several classes of youngsters each day? Those are the questions this chapter seeks to answer.

INSTRUCTIONAL DECISIONS

The classroom teacher was not meant to operate as a clinical diagnostician. Specialized tests and detailed case reports fall into someone else's domain, not the teacher's. But the teacher makes decisions daily about how to teach students. Decision making about teaching implies the use of diagnostic skills. In fact, the professional training of teachers provides a considerable background for diagnosing the problems of learners. Pertinent teacher decisions should guide the teacher in assessing the student. The teacher determines what important instructional decisions can and should be made about his students and then bases his analysis of student behavior on information collected in those decision areas. Teachers can carry that process forward out of professional judgment. For example, because the vocabulary load and the level of readability affect the students' ability to use a textbook, the teacher should decide whether a chosen text can be used successfully by some, all, or none of the students. Obviously, the reading level of the student must be equal to that of the book or the student cannot be successful. He will be frustrated and turn his interest elsewhere. This notion frightens many teachers because it obliterates the traditional notion of assembly-line teaching. The single text, read or presented at the same pace to all students, constitutes an activity on the assembly line. To suggest a variety of books or that a book be used in different ways for different students brings the conveyor belt to a halt and demands that the teacher rethink how he constructs learning for students. Yet it is quite clear, even to the untrained observer, that any typical upper grade has a wide range of reading levels, and some students will be frustrated and certainly not learning if asked to read the typical text along with every other student. (Techniques for assessing instructional levels are discussed in chapter 1.)

Identifying students' levels of reading performance constitutes significant data for making one major teaching decision. Each teacher has to identify his own instructional decisions and assign them priorities. Selected decisions and their priorities depend to some extent on a person's teaching philosophy and on the nature of the subject-matter experience in the school curriculum— whether the courses are required or elective, for example. Or what are the major instructional decisions for bookthinking in science or in home economics? What expectations does a teacher hold for reading the content text?

Decision Questions

A teacher's bookthinking decisions flow from these questions:

Level: At what difficulty level can the student succeed?
Interest: Is he curious enough about the subject to expend effort?
Recall: Can he locate and/or remember significant details?
Interact: Can he analyze and evaluate an author's ideas?
Apply: Can he use the special features, such as charts and formulas, pertinent to texts in this field?

These questions are coincident with the wishes and expectations of every teacher. The objectives for reading a content text complement the objectives a teacher has for knowing and using subject-matter information. The difference proposed here is that the subject-matter teacher must make decisions and plan lessons based on the students' abilities and skills in processing book information. The Decision Work Chart (Table 5–1) outlines the steps a teacher can use to work out each area in which he must make a decision. Where there is a decision to be made, information must be collected to help the teacher determine which available alternative is best for his students. Part of the work chart is completed. As an application exercise, the reader may wish to fill in the rest. Ideas from the first four chapters of this text provide possible answers for the open categories.

The assembly-line teacher operates under the assumption that the teacher's job is to issue a single application of information as students pass through the teacher's daily classes. As each one moves through, the teacher sprays him with information. And, like the paint sprayer at the conveyor belt, he finds that some items take a smooth, high-gloss finish; others turn out with bubbles and cracks; and some let all the paint run off in a disgusting puddle. Since the paint sprayer pulls the trigger for the same length of time for each item, the outcome or final product is dependent on the quality of the item when it is sprayed. Maybe a foul breeze interferes occasionally or the sprayer sneezes, but usually someone else screwed up, right? Probably

TABLE 5-1
Decision Work Chart

AREA	QUESTION	DATA	CHOICE AMONG ALTERNATIVES
Level	What level for success?	Observe student with different levels.	Use range of books; differentiate assignments.
Interest	Curious about subject?	Interest inventory; informal talks.	Group enthusiastic or uninterested. Offer projects to induce curiosity.
Recall	Remember details?		
Interact	Analyze and evaluate		
Apply	Can it be used?		

Note: A teacher might collect responses from all the students by constructing an assignment that calls for responses in the areas of recall, interaction, and application. The assignment assumes that all those responding can read at the level of the textbook assigned.

the one who forged the base metal did it all wrong.

On the other hand, the teacher who makes decisions about how a student processes information and adjusts his instruction accordingly is akin to the custom builder. How big a home do you need? How fancy? Where should the rooms be placed to suit the way you think and live? After getting answers to those questions, the custom builder uses standard construction techniques to construct a custom product. A major difference lies in his attitude, not necessarily in his tools or lumber. Each teacher acts in class on the basis of his concept of teaching, his concept of how to build learning in students. Trying to make decisions about bookthinking, for example, would mark the teacher as a custom builder and lift him off the assembly-line approach. Customizing classroom instruction for 150 students each day requires an attitude and sense of organization that revolves around student success. Success is here defined as the student's belief that he is making progress in something important. The teacher's job is to convince the student that book-thinking in social studies, English, or business law is important. Each of the 150 students can evaluate himself according to his sense of progress in bookthinking. That reduces the time and effort a teacher has to spend. Through study units, projects, and other self-directing learning activities (discussed in chapters 12 and 13), teacher and student work together to ensure a continuing sense of progress.

Defining Learning Outcomes

Though one's expectations are based on his teaching philosophy or theory, the classroom teacher's interest in bookthinking should focus on learning outcomes, not a theoretical stance. By picturing a student doing the experiments or displaying the desired knowledge, the teacher is able to direct his observation and plan the instruction with greater precision. What is it that a teacher expects the learner to do with a book in his subject area? He probably wants him (a) to have sufficient interest to read the text, (b) to extract information from the text, (c) to interact with the author's idea, and (d) to answer questions about the text and to discuss those ideas in class across a range of thinking operations. Statements like those lead the teacher toward an operational definition. This definition of bookthinking, then, includes:

Interest in reading about a topic
Reading for the purposes of finding information, interacting with the author's ideas, or recreation
Answering questions about the text and discussing ideas in class
Using various resources related to a topic.

Those aspects of bookthinking can be observed in student behavior, and an outline similar to that in Figure 5–1 begins to formulate in the teacher's mind as a scheme for observing student behavior. He has thus

Operations	Observations	Student - *Dan B.* *Biology Class* Level
Interests *Sports*

Use science of body building as a handle. Also effect of exhaust on plants | 9/30 *Lifts weights - has exercise books*

Fixes up old cars - lots of tools | Primary (beginner) |
| Locate and recall | 10/3 *Could not use index and table of contents.*

10/5 *Good recall on muscles chapter* | |
| Interact | 10/9 *Takes passive posture when reading.*

10/10 *Inadequate answers to analysis questions* | Intermediate *Only missed 5/100 words* |
| Subject-special tasks | 10/5 *Took great care in examining chart of torso muscles*

10/6 *Passive posture & no sense of eye muscles chart* | Upper *Missed 14/100 words* |
| Using other resources | 10/6 *Did not know there was a science encyclopedia*

Uses an encyclopedia like a dictionary | Advanced (competent adult) |

Figure 5-1. Observing bookthinking operations

identified the mental operations he expects students to perform while reading
and therefore must decide what he can do to help them. Lacking those competencies, a student will need instruction in how to develop them. After all,
a student who does not know how to react to the writer of a social studies
text will not gain that skill by having the same question asked of him a
second time. Someone needs to show that student how to interact with a
writer. And that's the teacher's job. So the teacher should select carefully
the major competencies he expects students to exhibit, for not only is the
teacher observing them, he should also be ready to explain and demonstrate
them.

Each decision area is observed through specific reading tasks or competencies. The area of interaction may be observed, for instance, as a student
tries to analyze the characters in one of John Updike's short stories. In no
case does the teacher try to observe all related behaviors, only those that he
thinks are significant manifestations of the competency in focus. That
shouldn't surprise anyone. To test means to take a sample of behavior, and
it must always be interpreted as a sample. It is hoped that the test maker
and the teacher/observer are sampling significant learner behaviors, but
they are only samples, nonetheless. If the teacher doesn't see any evidence
in a given student of an ability to analyze, he teaches the student how to
analyze through explanations, categorization activities, and problem-solving
activities. In other words, the teacher decides to teach him instead of simply
giving him additional practice.

Interest

Each area of behavior a teacher wants to observe should be described by
manifestations that he or she can find in classroom activity. Often a type of
behavior can be seen in graded stages, low to high. A positive interest in
reading provides an excellent example. Every teacher wants his or her students to express a positive interest in reading about the subject of the course.
It is reasonable to list positive interest in the following gradations. The
student:

1. Is aware of the scope and implications of the subject
2. Accepts the fact that others may have a high positive interest in the subject even if he does not
3. Shows a respect for others' interest in the subject
4. Pursues his interest in the subject independently
5. Has a well-organized sense of values related to the subject.

Each of these manifestations of interest in or attitude toward the subject
can be sampled (tested) in various ways. The first item given above states
that the student is aware of the scope and implications of the subject. One
way of collecting relevant information is to construct a knowledge-and-

interest inventory from the table of contents of the book the student will be using. Table 5–2 shows how that subject-matter inventory might be constructed to collect data simultaneously from an entire class. Those students who exhibit weak or nonexistent knowledge about the subject and its implications need to have some exposure that will give them a sense of direction and purpose, thus opening the door for their enthusiasm to build.

Most teachers and learning specialists would agree that developing and maintaining interest in a subject is an important objective. Therefore it should be worked on. High interest in a topic will give a student the extra mental energy he needs to extract information from a difficult text. And everyone faces that situation from time to time. (For further discussion on motivation, see chapter 4.)

Frequently it is helpful to know the student's attitude toward reading

TABLE 5-2
Subject-Matter Inventory

Directions to student:
Check the category that best describes what you know or how you feel about each topic. All of these terms are about physics.

TOPICS	DON'T KNOW IT	HAVE HEARD IT BUT DON'T KNOW WHAT IT MEANS	I CAN TALK ABOUT IT OR USE IT	IT IS A STRONG INTEREST OF MINE
Concepts of motion				
1. The idea of motion	_____	_____	_____	_____
2. Galileo describes motion	_____	_____	_____	_____
3. Dynamics and Newton	_____	_____	_____	_____
Motion in the heavens				
4. Where is the earth?	_____	_____	_____	_____
5. Does the earth move? Copernicus	_____	_____	_____	_____
6. Unity of Earth and sky. Newton	_____	_____	_____	_____
Models of the atom				
7. Chemical base of atomic theory	_____	_____	_____	_____
8. Electrons and quanta	_____	_____	_____	_____
9. Modern physical theory	_____	_____	_____	_____

Note to teacher: These chapter titles or rephrased chapter titles could give you an indication of students' perceptions and also give you an opportunity to introduce the scope of a course by reviewing the topics that appeared in this inventory.

and specific interests in reading. Lack of interest in a particular subject may, in fact, represent the student's general feeling about school and books. On the other hand, disinterest in a subject may reflect a specific bias or a failure of the teacher to bring the subject and the student's interest together. To collect information over a broad picture of interests and reading, a teacher can have students complete an interest inventory similar to the one shown in Figure 5–2.

Extracting Meaning

As important as personal interest is in pulling the student into reading about a given topic, the teacher must attend to the continuing purpose of using written material—that is, to extract some information to further the student's progress in the field. For centuries teachers have been administering tests to students to see what they have learned from their reading. Typically, that test data is recorded as a percentage or as an "ABC" grade and interpreted as an indication of the quality of the student's performance. But for purposes of making decisions about what a student can do, most of those tests yield little or no useful data.

Asking questions about information in a book is one obvious way of determining what a student knows. But questions about written discourse can range from the inane (What was the first word in the second line?) to the universal (In the cosmos of knowledge about this subject where would you place the information contained in chapter 10?). To be of diagnostic value, the questions must be targeted. The teacher should want to know what kinds of questions the student can answer, not how many. When the type of question is known, the teacher can direct instruction and future reading assignments toward helping that student grow.

If a student can fathom the main idea of what he reads but can't remember important details, the teacher then can teach him how to select, organize, and hold for future reference the salient facts from the reading. A student will have to be shown that it is not enough simply to breeze through a passage to get an indication of its intent and theme. He must learn to highlight items and store them for use in solving particular problems. The same principle applies to other types of questions. How, for example, does a student make judgments about the value of a passage? If he doesn't know how to establish criteria and apply them, the teacher has a further instructional obligation.

Answering Questions

Questions, then, should be asked systematically in order to develop a profile on the student's ability to think as he reads a book or passage. A question outline to match the thinking operations described in chapters 2 and 3 gives the teacher a diagnostic tool to probe the student's ability to think as he

1. Apart from lessons, about how much time each day do you spend reading? _____

2. Do your parents encourage you to read at home? _____

3. Have you read a book in the past two or three months? _____

    3.1. What are the titles of some books you have been reading? _____

    3.2. How many books have you borrowed from friends during the last month? _____ Give titles of some. _____

    3.3. How many books have you loaned to friends during the last month? _____ Give titles of some. _____

4. Do you have a card for the public or school library? _____

5. How many books do you have of your own? _____

6. About how many books do you have in your home? _____ Give the titles of some. _____

7. From what sources—other than your home, libraries, and friends—do you obtain books?

    1. Buy them _____   3. Rent them _____

    2. Gifts   _____   4. Exchanges _____

8. Underline the kinds of reading you enjoy most: history, travel, plays, essays, adventure stories, science, poetry, novels, detective stories, fairy tales, mystery stories, biography, music, art.

9. What kind of work do you want to do when you finish school? _____

    Are you going to college? _____ Where? _____

10. What newspapers do you read? _____

11. What sections of the newspaper do you like best? Check below.

    1. Sports _____   4. News   _____

    2. Funnies _____   5. Editorials _____

    3. Stories _____   6. Other   _____

12. What magazines are received regularly at your home? _____

    (Underline those which you read.)

13. Name your favorite magazines. _____

14. Name the comic books you read and underline your favorites. _____

15. Where do you get your magazines and comic books? _____

16. Name the three movies you last saw. _____

17. Name the three radio or TV programs you like best. _____

18. Name the state or country farthest away that you have visited. _____

19. Which of the following have encouraged you to read? Check below.

    1. Parents   _____   6. Pals   _____

    2. Teacher   _____   7. Club leader _____

    3. Librarian _____   8. Relatives   _____

    4. Hobby   _____   9. Club work _____

    5. Friends   _____   10. Other   _____

Figure 5-2. Interest inventory

reads. The categories and broad sample questions given below need to be translated by a particular teacher to fit the topic and the sophistication level of his students, but the resulting information will almost certainly be valuable and challenging.

CATEGORY	GENERAL QUESTION
Identification	What experience do you have that enables you to relate to this subject?
Recall	What were the important details in this passage?
Analysis	What is the theme? What conclusions can you draw?
Judgment	Was it worth reading?
Extension	In what ways can you use those ideas?

A question checklist, illustrated in Figure 5–3, might be used to record acceptable and nonacceptable responses, giving the teacher a rundown on who needs help in answering certain types of questions.

No teacher should make a snap judgment about a student's ability to extract meaning from a text on the basis of a single response or on evidence

Directions to the Teacher

When a student gives an acceptable response to a type of question, mark +; if unacceptable, mark−. Those who accumulate several minuses should be gathered for instruction in working with that type of question.

Students	Identification	Recall	Analysis	Judgment	Extension
1. Harry A.					
2. Bic B.					
3. Red C.					
4. Sandra D.					
5. Tec E.					
6. Emmon M.					
7. Tally O					
8. Hugh S.					
9. Mark X.					
10. Telly Y.					

Question Categories

Figure 5-3. A question checklist

from one article. But, over a period of time, over several readings and their discussions, the teacher puts together a profile on each student. Whether through a log or a brief checklist, the teacher gathers information systematically and is enabled to make decisions on the basis of information rather than random hunches.

Subject-special Tasks

Each subject has vocabulary, charts, graphs, tables, and other special features which contribute to the reading difficulty of that subject. A teacher must decide on the critical tasks for his subject and his level of instruction in order to know which ones to observe. Vocabulary plays a crucial role in all subject-matter reading. Do the students know how to tackle new words? What skills should be observed by the teacher? During one grading period, a teacher may decide to focus attention on the development of vocabulary skills. A brief checklist like the one below can then serve as a self-evaluation tool for the student, or as an observation checklist which the teacher fills out on each student or each group of students.

Vocabulary Skills

_____Uses context to define
_____Uses word parts to define
_____Uses the glossary
_____Uses technical dictionary (other resources)
_____Identifies process words (erosion, photosynthesis, parsing, compounding, reclamation)
_____Identifies content words (carbon, onomatopoeia, polygon, philanthropist)

These and other aspects of vocabulary may be examined. As a rule, the teacher should concentrate on one or two, observing them carefully and teaching those students who need assistance. As for the other vocabulary skills, a brief exercise in each would alert students to their existence. For example, students might preview a chapter of the textbook to see if the writer uses a consistent way to define important words. He may regularly use content definitions or the glossary or an analysis of word parts. Having students check for those routine ingredients not only alerts them to helpful cues about the author's style but also reminds them of ways to solve daily vocabulary problems. Many students will continue to use them even when they are no longer emphasized by the teacher. In vocabulary, as in other aspects of bookthinking, students should be prodded regularly into self-evaluation. The sample subject-matter inventory, shown earlier, might serve as a model form. The important words from a chapter could be listed in the left-hand column. Then, by using the same column headings as in that inventory, each student checks his sense of the word. Resulting information would guide the teacher in supplying appropriate background to class members. The fact that the teacher pursues vocabulary growth in a systematic fashion will in itself encourage students to seek other avenues of vocabulary development. (Chapter 7 provides numerous ideas on teaching vocabulary in all subjects.)

Subheads Textbooks and technical writing normally employ subheads. Do students know how to use them efficiently? Can students separate main heads from subheads? Do they try to preread the subheads to get a sense of the content and the movement of ideas in the chapter or in the article? The teacher can find out which students know how to use headings properly by asking them to take the heads in a chapter and arrange them in outline form. Further, a student might be asked from the arrangement of the heads to predict what will occur or what he will find in a passage. With a simple written exercise and a follow-up discussion, the teacher thus learns without an official text whether his students know how to analyze the text through the quick, efficient means of analyzing the subheads. Subsequently, of course, he will need to remind the students to make use of that skill as they read.

A quick way to discover which students are able to use subheads is to give them an exercise like the following:

Use of Heads

The terms and phrases below are headings taken from a selection in your textbook. Look at them and see if you can answer the questions.

DYING TREES

Poisons in the air
Exhaust from cars and trucks
Cement and superhighways

MAN'S LUNGS

Smog
Cigarettes
Sprays

What do you think is the general topic being discussed in the selection that uses these heads? _____

What are the major areas that are emphasized in this selection? _____

How does "cement and superhighways" fit with the rest of the heads?

_____

If you were asked to find out something about *insecticides* in this selection, where would you look? _____

Why did you choose that section? _____

In just a few minutes of class time, then, the teacher can determine how many youngsters need help in thinking through the headings of the text. It not only helps them get a sense of how the chapters are organized but gives them a way of previewing the chapter for a sense of direction. (Other overview and preview activities are presented in chapter 13.)

Tables and graphs The teacher who knows the purpose of a table or a chart or a graph and knows how to use it doesn't think twice about those devices as used in the student's textbook. They are there as a simplified form of giving information, or are there to help the reader visualize a concept or more easily understand an idea. But the student/reader often doesn't recognize those purposes and may not know how to read those illustrative devices. When asked how he used tables and charts in his textbooks, one student said he treated them like pictures—he didn't even look at them unless the teacher directed him to do so.

Knowing that a table is often intended to be a handy reference that classifies similar elements and shows their relationships might help science students, for example, get a handle on using to advantage the material shown in Table 5–3.

The horizontal lines in the table aid the reader in using it. Finding a

TABLE 5-3
Facts About the Solar System

PLANETARY BODIES	AVERAGE DISTANCE FROM SUN IN MILLIONS OF MILES	DIAMETER IN MILES	REVOLUTION AROUND SUN	ROTATION ON AXIS	MOONS AND SATELLITES
Sun		864,400		25 days	
Mercury	36	3,100	88 days	88 days	0
Venus	67	7,700	225 days	Not sure	0
Earth	93	7,920	365¼ days	23 hrs., 56 min.	1
Earth's moon	93	2,160	365¼ days	29 days, 12 hrs.	
Mars	142	4,220	687 days	24 hrs., 37 min.	2
Jupiter	483	88,600	11⅞ yrs.	9 hrs., 50 min.	12
Saturn	887	75,000	29½ yrs.	10 hrs., 14 min.	9 (3 rings)
Uranus	1,784	29,600	84 yrs.	10 hrs., 49 min.	5
Neptune	2,793	27,700	165 yrs.	15 hrs., 40 min.	2
Pluto	3,670	3,600	248 yrs.	16 hrs.	0

wanted fact is a matter of locating the intersection of a horizontal axis and a vertical axis. Inexperienced readers may need to have that procedure demonstrated for them. Perhaps more important for the table is its system of relationships. Relative sizes, distances from the sun, rotation periods, and so on are given. These tend to create a concept of the solar system that may help the student understand the text he is reading or give him specific answers to discussion questions and laboratory exercises. Whether a student sees those opportunities or not can be determined by a question that invites him to explain in his own words what can be done with the table. "Henry, how does that table enable you to visualize the solar system?" When no cogent explanation comes forth, the teacher can explain and demonstrate or have some other student do so.

Charts, Maps, and Diagrams The function of most charts is to help a reader visualize a place, an event, or a procedure. A map, for example can be viewed as a kind of chart that is designed to help the reader see places, directions, and related geographic or demographic information. The legend on a map or similar chart gives the reader the keys he needs to interpret accurately the information contained on a map. It is up to the teacher to ask whether the student knows some of the basic purposes for using charts and therefore has a sense of how to read them. Many charts, for example, use the technique of comparison. The writer is trying to help the reader compare something he knows to something he may not comprehend clearly. A picture of the Great Pyramid of Egypt alone, for instance, in no way conveys its size. But the diagram in Figure 5–2 compares the pyramid to some modern structures and thus gives the student a mental image to use for discussion. If the teacher wants to see how many students can use that kind of chart, he might ask his class to look at Figure 5–4 and in their own words (or in their own diagram) tell about the size of the Great Pyramid. They should not be allowed, however, to use the comparisons in Figure 5–4.

OBSERVATION TECHNIQUES

Informal Observation

After choosing the points he wants to emphasize, a teacher needs to collect information about how students perform. This is accomplished through informal techniques or direct situations.

The content teacher usually has no difficulty in formally testing students on what they have acquired. Formal tests, whether prepared commercially or prepared by the teacher, tap the students' knowledge of the facts and inferences of the subject. But formal tests are not so readily available for the processes a student uses in bookthinking. Calculating percentages is a process

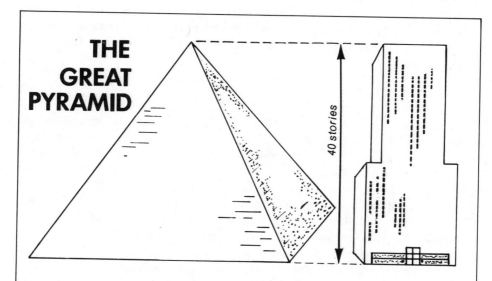

One is awed on contemplating the size of the Great Pyramid, constructed in about 2600 B.C. The pyramid's top reaches to the fortieth floor of a modern skyscraper in New York City. It covers an area equivalent to more than eight soccer fields—approximately 13 acres of land.

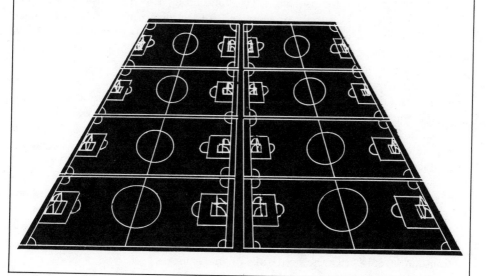

Figure 5-4.

in mathematics. Just as the math teacher determines the student's ability to figure percentages by watching the steps he takes in the problem solution, so the teacher needs to find similar ways to observe the student's processes or work habits in using a book—in bookthinking, for example—through introspection, problem solving, assignments, oral reading, and daily class observation.

Introspection

Most of us teachers grew up with the idea that teaching meant actively presenting ideas, working problems in front of the class, or reading aloud along with the students. When that was finished, teacher and students each did private work without bothering the other. Assume for a change that teaching can also mean having students work independently or in groups while the teacher circulates to see how he or she can help students improve their work habits, thus enabling them to learn the subject more efficiently. As students work on projects or assignments or solve problems, all sorts of opportunities arise for observing bookthinking processes. One technique is introspection, a student's self-examination of how he works out a particular bookthinking problem, his personal analysis of what his mind does when that kind of problem comes up. A direct question during a brief conference may pinpoint immediately why, for example, the student misinterprets a graph in his social studies text. He failed to use the legend. Or the entire class may be asked to examine themselves and respond on a "self-inspection" form, such as the one shown. A supply of these self-inspection forms can be distributed periodically when some new process is examined. They tend to call a student's attention to the process and may act as an instructional prod as well as give the teacher information for a decision on who needs help in the process.

Because he often meets 125 or more students a day, the content teacher may not think there are opportunities for conferences with students and ways to use those conferences to learn about the strengths and weaknesses of students. Rather than think of a conference, which has overtones of formality, appointments, and the like, let's call such meetings "individual instructional contacts." Most teachers have numerous "individual instructional contacts" every day, while circulating to observe work, for example, or in those brief chats before and after class. The teacher can turn those contacts into observation periods by refocusing his attention when the original purpose of the contact is achieved. Depending on the question the student asked or the reason for the teacher-student contact, the teacher can redirect the conversation and how he uses the textbooks or magazines.

"Henry, when you see a word for which you have no workable definition, how do you figure out what it means?—or, When I give you a reading assignment, how do you tackle it? How do you get the theme or know what is the author's point of view?—or, If I ask you to describe the climate in northern Brazil, how would you use the map to help you give me an accurate picture?"—and so on.

These questions, asked at a time when a brief contact is made during the school day, cause the student to search his own techniques for extracting information from print and to explain what he knows about his reading ability (see Figure 5–5).

Problem Solving

The old axiom still holds: "As a man solves a problem, so goes the man." To see how a student uses a book, give him a problem that requires book usage and watch how he proceeds. He doesn't know that his bookthinking techniques are being observed. Without making him self-conscious about the procedure, the teacher can observe him informally and know whether or not he needs help, for example, in relating a chart to the text. Consider this example:

> "Henry, I want you to determine what a small Italian farm community can produce when they must use a small valley and the mountains rising on either side. Their existence depends on maximum use of the valley and the mountains. Is there some way that they could farm it all? Read chapter 10 on farming in Italy and work out your answer."

BOOKTHINKING	I DO THIS WELL	I NEED TO LEARN MORE ABOUT THIS	I CANNOT DO THIS
Can you: 1. Use context clues to define words?			
2. Define a word from its word parts?			
3. Obtain information from a graph?			
4. Follow directions in the text?			
5. Select the best reading speed for reading different parts of the book?			
6. Select the best reading speed for each kind of reading?			

Figure 5-5. Self-examination on bookthinking

The student must then read the chapter that discusses "farming by zones." The text is clarified by a diagram similar to that in Figure 5–6.

A teacher has two ways of observing the student solve the problem. One is to watch his eyes and his fingers as he shifts, one would hope, between the text and the diagram that illustrates what zone farming looks like. The other comes during his explanation. Does he refer to the diagram as a means of explaining the concept and in solving the problem? If his explanation is written, he may even reproduce the diagram. If the explanation is oral, he may gesticulate to indicate the levels or zones that the diagram portrayed.

Open-Book Tests

The problem-solving technique just described bears strong resemblance to an open-book test. A teacher, needing a classroom exercise to serve double duty, could use an open-book test in the first unit in the school term to get both content and bookthinking feedback on the students. While the students are taking the test, the teacher roams around the room with a checklist or note pad, trying to see which book skills the students use to solve the problems posed in the test. Such observations have considerable value because they reflect a real-world situation for students, that of taking a test. Several checklists in this chapter could serve as models for observing students and logging results. Other books on informal assessment can provide the teacher with forms and checklists for observing the kinds of behavior discussed in this book. *Reading, What Can Be Measured* (Farr, 1969) and *A Source Book of Evaluation Techniques for Reading* (Laffey, 1972) offer many useful observation techniques.

Figure 5-6. Zones for farming

Assignments

Worksheets, compositions, lab reports and other student work products may also reflect a student's procedures in using a text. That depends, of course, on the nature of the assignment. By reviewing his work with a specific procedure or thinking operation in mind, the teacher can get a sense of the student's ability in that area. An outline-summary of an article or a chapter, for example, should indicate the student's ability to determine its organization. His arrangement of major and minor topics demonstrates his ability to analyze the author's organization. An outline, however, does not guarantee that the student analyzes while he is reading. It simply means that he is able to analyze. Occasionally, he may need a reminder to transfer that skill to reading: "Do you ever think about the organization of ideas when you read?"

"Are you kidding! I only do this when you tell me!"

"Well, think how much more control you would have over the material if you tried to outline it in your mind as you read."

Oral Reading Miscues

Reading aloud by students may not occur often in the content class, but reading aloud does offer the teacher an insight into the student's fluency or ease with vocabulary and ideas. For those who seem to have considerable difficulty with reading, an oral reading activity could help the teacher identify more specifically the problems or patterns a student displays. Some of his miscue patterns or apparent error patterns can direct the teacher to aid the student—through both advice and practice.

Research in analyzing oral reading miscues (Goodman *et al.,* 1967) cautions us to determine which miscues interfere with meaning or indicate a consistent lack of skill in identifying and pronouncing words and in extracting ideas accurately. All competent readers become intent on getting ideas and therefore sometimes say things different from the actual printed words—yet the meaning stands clearly in their minds. A person's natural language may at times superimpose itself on the language of the text. Thus the student sees these words: "He climbed up into the truck bed," but says these words: "He hopped up into the truck bed." Or he might even say: "He hopped up into the flatbed." It is clear that he knows what is going on in the passage. The automaticity of his own language and background simply overpowered the words the author had used. A competent reader is always reaching ahead for ideas, is actually predicting the ideas and language to express those ideas. He sometimes predicts with his own language, which may cause him to substitute for the author's words.

In similar fashion, a reader's dialect may cause certain oral reading miscues that are not significant errors; they do not constitute errors that interfere with meaning. Some dialects, for example, do not pronounce the final /s/ on the third-person-singular verb. "Mercury runs on winged feet" is then read: "Mercury run on winged feet." That is not a reading problem. No meaning was lost; no pronunciation skill is missing. The dialect simply imposed itself on the oral delivery of the text.

With that caution about the difference between an error and a language misuse, the teacher can create occasions for observing unobtrusively the oral reading of students to analyze for the heart of a problem. He can ask a student to find the answer to a question and to read aloud the paragraph where the answer occurs. Or he can ask all students to select the most interesting, most exciting, most descriptive, or most bizarre passage and read it to the class. What to the student appears to be an idea-sharing exercise can serve the teacher's purpose of observing samples of oral reading.

As the student reads aloud, the teacher can note any miscues by using a simple notation system such as that illustrated in Figure 5–7. In this way a teacher can keep track of miscues and later decide if they represent an error pattern that requires work. A notation system thus helps the teacher make notes about the students' oral reading performance and make inferences about patterns of oral reading. The system in Figure 5–7 is adapted from Harris and Smith, 1976.

Here are some typical miscues and a comment about each:

Mispronunciations may range from a misplaced accent (hardly of great concern unless the student has no feeling at all for accenting new words that he meets) to gross sounds that do not even resemble the word in print. One student, for instance, saw the word "probably" and said "stibbled." Upon examination, we learned that he had no way to solve an unknown word. "Stibbled" didn't make any more sense to him than it did to those of us listening. But there was a word there, and he made a sound for that space. We had to teach him a systematic approach to solving new words.

Substitutions should be examined in the same way that additions are. When numerous substitutions can be identified as cover-ups for not knowing the word in print, the teacher should act on the situation; but not when the substitution is a slip of the tongue.

Awkward phrasing and long *hesitations* may indicate that the selection is too difficult for the student. Either the vocabulary or the concepts are so far beyond him that the student stumbles, reads a word at a time, fails to put ideas together in natural or related phrases, and generally exhibits the symptoms of frustration. For beginning readers, awkward phrasing may only be an indication of their inexperience in reading aloud, but, for older students, other explanations have to be pursued. Students who are just learning English, of course, might resemble the beginning reader. With practice and increased command over English, their fluency will improve.

Substitution or mispronunciation	*lonely* / ~~lovely~~	She was a ~~lovely~~ *lonely* girl.
Awkward phrasing	/	It was / a cat in / the window.
Word supplied by the teacher	_____	Give me a field of <u>daffodils</u> for my bed.
Repetition	∿∿∿	Three molecules <u>swirled</u> in orbit.
Reversal	ꙅ(a w) (ʍɒꙅ)	He ꙅaw the horse leap over the fence.
Hesitation (3 seconds)	√	The pinto √ galloped. . . .
Omission	⬭	I had written (but) he ignored me.
Addition	∧	He *had* wrote to Jane. ∧

Total number of miscues: _____

The total number of miscues becomes important only in a comparative sense. The more miscues per one hundred words, the more likely the student will falter in comprehension tasks. No one miscue in itself, however, predicts failure to comprehend. The observer looks for patterns of miscues that will guide recommendations for helping the student become more proficient.

Use of this notation system is demonstrated below. No serious reading difficulties are evident in this sample. In two instances (*quickly* and *jockey*), the reader did not attempt to pronounce a word. Other words with the same beginning consonants might be presented to this student to see if he is able to associate sounds with "qu" and "j."

Oral Reading Sample

The bay horse moved <u>quickly</u> to the inside of the track. His ~~hooves~~ *hoofs* splattered mud as he hit the soft, wet ground. ~~Several~~ *some* other horses raced alongside the big bay ∧ *horse* forcing him to stay on the soft ground. Slowly the <u>jockey</u> moved the bay away from the wet ground back / to the firm / *part* ~~place~~ on the track.

(As) the / crowd / cheered, the bay / caught and passed the leaders. / Ahead, the finish line waited. √ Victory seemed certain.

Total miscues = 15

Though there are no serious problems seen in the miscues made by this student, the total number of miscues for such a short passage indicates that the student is not a fluent, proficient reader. Direction, encouragement, and practice are certainly in order.

Figure 5-7. Oral reading notation system

Word supplied means that the student asked for help or paused so long that the teacher gave him the word in order to keep the ideas flowing. Those instances are opportunities for checking on the student's ability to use context and to apply phonics principles. The teacher might ask: "What makes sense there?" or "Try to pronounce the word." If there are no satisfactory responses to those questions, the teacher should, of course, supply the word. Afterwards, the teacher wants to see if the words supplied were common, frequently used words or were words that belong in an esoteric category. Vocabulary and word-practice activities flow from that analysis.

Repetition of words or phrases during oral reading occurs for a number of reasons. The reader stumbles momentarily and repeats himself in order to provide smooth phrasing and a sense of coherence. Almost everyone repeats words and phrases for that purpose. A reader may come to a difficult or unfamiliar word and back up a few words as if to get a running start on the challenge of the difficult word. It is a way of providing a semantic and syntactic context for solving the problem of the unknown word. A whole phrase may sound awkward or obtuse and the reader will back up and repeat to see if a second attempt will clear up the confusion. Thus an occasional repetition is understandable. If the repetitions occur frequently, however, they indicate many interferences with the student's flow of thought and ought to result in directions to the student on ways to improve flow of thought and fluency in presentation.

Reversals. The best of readers now and then reverse letters within words or words within phrases. A momentary loss of attention or some other lapse in one's language processing may cause the reader to say "board" for "broad," or to read "Color yellow the duck," instead of "Color the duck yellow." When a student makes those reversals frequently or in a regular pattern, the teacher needs to call attention to the matter and perhaps refer the student to a special reading teacher for systematic help in that problem.

Hesitations of three seconds or more indicate that the reader has met a considerable obstacle to reading a particular phrase or passage fluently. A word has stopped him or the ideas he is working on don't make sense. Stumped, the reader stops to analyze the word or idea, or he is simply waiting for help. After noting the hesitation, the teacher may give him the word or may want to find out what caused the hesitation. Can the reader pronounce the word? Does he know what it means? Is he experiencing incongruence and can't make sense out of the passage?

Omissions may be accidental or they may be indications of a student's inability to deal with the omitted part. Clinical experience shows that poor readers sometimes try to cover up their inability to deal with the omitted part. Clinical experience shows that poor readers sometimes try to cover up their inability to pronounce a word or to define a word by skipping right over it, saying the next word in sequence, or saying the next word that makes sense. If the student claims he is not aware of the words he skips, he may be suffering from visual or psychomotor problems that should be referred to a specialist for investigation.

Additions during oral reading usually represent the reader's attempt to make the passage sound sensible to his own ears. But when the student adds words that make little or no sense, or adds words in an apparent effort to cover up his inability to understand the text, the teacher is given an opportunity to build the background or the vocabulary or to change the book for something more suitable for the reading level of that student.

Oral Reading Inventory

On noticing a student who has difficulty with reading, a teacher can pursue the problem by giving him an individual inventory composed of a series of graded passages as described in chapter 1, Matching the Student with a Book. The teacher can select a series of passages (150 to 200 words each) that range in reading difficulty from easy (lower elementary) to difficult (adult) and ask the student to read aloud while the teacher makes notations as described earlier in Figure 5–7. In that way, the teacher discovers an instructional reading level (where the student can be taught without undue frustration) and also learns about his specific strengths and weaknesses. Commercial informal reading inventories have been published by Cooper *et al.* (1972), Silvaroli (1976), and McCarthy (1977), among others. Each contains a student profile sheet to help the teacher organize the information he has collected about a reader. Johnson and Kress (1965) discuss the uses and interpretations of informal reading inventories, and Goodman and Burke (1972) discuss oral reading miscues and their numerous categories in their *Reading Miscue Inventory*.

Teachers who prepare their own informal reading inventories by selecting passages from the materials used in the school and arranging them in order of difficulty should write four to six comprehension questions about each passage. The comprehension questions should cover a range of thinking operations (as discussed in chapter 2) thus giving the teacher a sense of the kinds of responses a student can make at a given level of difficulty. Combining the comprehension questions and the notations made while the student was reading aloud gives the teacher a composite picture of how the student performs with that kind of reading passage. Through research (Betts, 1957; Johnson and Kress, 1965) and through the experience of reading specialists, some rules of thumb have been developed that may guide the classroom teacher in using an oral reading inventory. First, unless the student does outrageously badly in either comprehension or in reading aloud, the two factors should be considered together to determine an instructional level. Second, for instructional purposes, a student should be able to answer 80 percent of the comprehension questions and have no more than ten miscues per one hundred words. As with any rule of thumb, the teacher modifies it according to his daily observations. Table 5–4 gives additional guidelines for evaluating informal reading performance.

Daily Observation

Each day the teacher has opportunities to observe a student's bookthinking performance. Written papers, answers to questions, brief informal conferences, class discussions—all these provide information for the teacher who has trained his eye and tuned his ear to pick up the cues. Opportunity for observation is not the problem; a system for collecting the data usually is.

A system for observing bookthinking performance starts with a definition or with a list of behaviors to focus on. No one can observe everything, and so the successful diagnostic teacher fixes in his mind those aspects of bookthinking that he thinks are important to his subject and that he is willing to work on. After all, a teacher doesn't want to collect information that he doesn't intend to use. Why, for example, would a teacher make systematic

TABLE 5-4
Standards for Individual Reading Levels

	INDEPENDENT LEVEL	INSTRUCTIONAL LEVEL	FRUSTRATION LEVEL
Comprehension	90% score	80% score	Less than 80%
Vocabulary (based on 100 running words)	Pupil able to pronounce 99 words	Pupil able to pronounce at least 95 words	Pupil unable to pronounce 10 or more words
Oral reading	Natural, rhythmical, well phrased	Natural, rhythmical, well phrased	Jerky, many substitutions, unnatural, omissions and repetitions
Tensions	None	None	Finger pointing, frowning, breath control poor, etc.

Note: Independent level is the book level at which a student can read independently with ease and excellent understanding. This is the level at which he should do extensive supplementary reading and unsupervised library reading for pure enjoyment or for information along lines of his own interest. *Instructional level* is the highest book level at which the pupil is able to read with success under the teacher's guidance. *Frustration level* is the book level at which the child stalls because he is unable to comprehend what he is trying to read.

judgments about the adequacy of a student's vocabulary unless he intended to upgrade the vocabulary of one he found wanting? A list of critical competencies could serve the teacher as a class observation list. Figure 5–8 shows how one teacher listed competencies for her history students. What she was trying to do was give herself a simple method for making notes. From the notes she was able to make judgments about student needs. The method gave her a way, she said, of zeroing in on those kids who seemed to need extra help in processing the information that came to them through the textbook and other readings.

Reciprocal Questions

Teachers are so accustomed to asking questions they may overlook a reverse strategy: having students formulate questions and asking them of the teacher. The advantage of having the students think more carefully about the message is matched by the opportunity the strategy gives the teacher to

Students	Harry O.	Olivia N.	John B.	Jeannette M.	Archie B.	Laverne R.	Shirley S.	Henry F.	
Technical vocabulary									1
General vocabulary									2
Categorize events									3
Determine themes									2
Relate cause-effect									
Use time line									
Interpret maps									
Use index to locate details									
Apply past to present conditions									

Rating notations. Each time a sample of student behavior is seen make a notation according to the following scale. As the student's abilities change, erase previous notations and insert a more current estimate.

1. Almost no evidence that he can perform
2. Performance is less than adequate for this class and book
3. Adequate for average work in this class
4. Above average competence.

Figure 5-8. Competencies for history students

see what kinds of questions individual students can find to ask. Some experimenters, for example, Manzo (1969), have examined the technique of having students ask questions of the teacher. The situation can be set up by the teacher announcing that he will ask questions on the first section to be read. Then a group of students (perhaps those the teacher wants to observe) can ask questions of the teacher about the next section.

At first, students may be dizzy with a sense of power and ask the teacher to sit on his hands so he can't cheat in trying to find the answers. But after some initial silliness, they will begin to ask serious questions. Besides the high positive interaction established by that kind of reciprocal questioning, the teacher can see who can ask questions that reveal the substance of a passage, its value to the learner, and possible applications. Such an arrangement provides the teacher with a natural opening. He can show the students how to analyze a passage in order to develop questions which reveal details, analyze ideas, require judgments, and extend the information into the reader's life space. (See chapter 2 for details on questioning and a range of questions.)

Questions constructed by students don't have to be aimed only at the teacher. They can be directed to other students as well. An interesting technique is to have groups of students prepare questions about various passages that they will ask another group. Each group develops questions, asks them of other students, and makes decisions about the adequacy of the answers. Recording answers can be done by group captains or row captains in a manner described later (in chapter 12 on organization). Reciprocal questioning builds on the principle that the student must take an increasing responsibility for his own learning, and that groups of students must take responsibility for learning within the group. It is another procedure that gives a teacher time to observe and then to react with valid instructional techniques to help the student.

Other forms of informal observation present themselves daily. An alert teacher collects the anecdotes, the glimpses, the unstated but visible signs of frustration and stores them on paper or in his head and designs instruction out of that information. No one teacher is expected to use all of these informal techniques, but everyone should know that there are alternatives for evaluating student competency.

FORMAL ASSESSMENT

"I freeze when I take a test." "I turn to jelly; my mind is like a wet noodle." Most of us have felt like that in the presence of an exam or have heard classmates and students describe the results of test anxiety. And that's only the beginning of the litany of why formal testing leaves so much to be desired. Nonetheless, formal tests are efficient: They sample a group of students under similar conditions, and they give the teacher data to work from.

To understand the relationship among various types of testing, examine Figure 5–9. This chart shows the kinds of information that schools and teachers can realize from group versus individual tests, from formal versus informal tests.

Normed Tests

Normed tests, which give grade equivalent scores and other ranking data, are the most frequently used. They are administered to every child again and again and again. What does a normed reading test measure? What does it show besides a ranking arrangement which marks some children low, some high, some in the middle?

Group-administered reading tests are built essentially by joining a vocabulary subtest with a paragraph comprehension subtest and using the total score from those tests to reflect *reading*. Even those tests that have one or two additional subtests are still sampling a very limited performance and calling it a *reading score*. The resulting grade-equivalent score reflects what the average eighth, ninth, or tenth grader would do with the limited

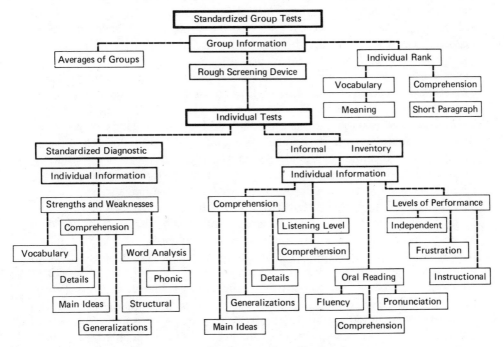

Figure 5-9. Types of reading tests

samples of reading activity presented by that test. But the norms (the grade-equivalent rankings) do show the teacher the range of performance in a class over those selections in the test. Dozens of the commercial secondary school reading tests are reviewed in the Buros' Mental Measurement Year-books and in a booklet on secondary tests published by the International Reading Association (Blanton *et al.*, 1972). That information is especially useful in grouping the students for work in a basic text and for funding related books and periodicals which subgroups in the class can read without undue frustration.

Criterion Tests

Criterion tests differ little in appearance from the norm-referenced tests, but they differ considerably in their intent. Where a norm-referenced test samples general reading behavior in order to rank test takers from low to high scorers, criterion-referenced tests focus test items on specific kinds of reading behavior. For example, a student may be asked to respond to ten items about the use of prefixes as a word-analysis strategy. If he gets eight of the ten correct, he will have met the criterion for success on that specific reading behavior. Similarly, if he gets the main idea for four of the five paragraphs in a section of the test, he will have met the criterion, and it is therefore assumed that he knows how to get the main idea in similar passages. The criterion for success in a specific behavior has been met. That doesn't necessarily mean that he can whiz through everything he reads. But it tells the teacher that the student appears competent in determining main ideas. For instructional purposes, the teacher can move on to other areas.

Teachers can make up their own criterion tests, and, of course, there are commercial tests available. Some criterion tests are available in the cassette tape format. A different reading skill or set of skills is described and directions given on each tape. The directions come through a head-phone instead of aloud in the classroom (Blanton *et al.*, 1974). Under the teacher's direction, a student goes to the cassette which tests the skill he has been working on. In this way testing becomes quite individualized.

The content teacher interested in specialized activities—such as use of the table of contents and index to find information in a book, use of a glossary, ability to find information in reference books, the use of maps, charts, graphs, and so on—can develop his own tests for specialized competencies, if he has the time and the inclination. He should keep in mind, of course, the guidelines for constructing valid and reliable tests (Farr, 1969). For the purpose of evaluating the student's reading competency, the test items should focus on the student's ability to process information. It should not merely be a test of knowledge of the subject. It is difficult to keep those two notions separate. So the teacher must regularly remind himself that he is teaching a bookthinking process, and he is teaching a body of information at the same time.

Cloze Tests

The *cloze procedure* provides the teacher with a simple technique for testing comprehension of a passage and for determining whether the text is written at an instructional level for the student. As described in chapter 1, by eliminating every fifth _____ in a text and _____ the student try to _____ in the exact word _____ that the author used, _____ teacher can get a _____ accurate idea of how _____ the student comprehended the _____.

The term 'cloze' is taken from the concept of closure in psychology. Closure refers to the human tendency to fill in or complete an entity which appears to be incomplete. For example, when you see a broken circle, your tendency is to draw a line in the blank space. With language, the same thing happens. In class, for instance, when a speaker is searching for a word to finish a statement, a student will often come up with a word to fill the language gap. "You're putting words in his mouth" is a complaint one hears now and then. "Let him talk for himself." Husbands and wives and others who know each other's thoughts or speech patterns often help one another finish a sentence. Occasionally one reads about a divorce case that resulted from this tendency. One spouse would never let the other finish a sentence. The one was always putting words in _____ spouse's mouth.

To construct a cloze test, take a selection of at least 275 words which is not dependent upon immediately preceding information. Begin with the second sentence and delete every fifth word, using standard-length blanks for those deleted words. The students then fill in the blanks. You count as correct only those words that match exactly the words of the original. That strict counting procedure enables you to use the scoring criteria developed by researchers in this field (Bormuth, 1962). Students able to place correctly 41 percent or more of the words deleted are considered able to comprehend the text. Below 41 percent, adequate comprehension is doubtful. Bormuth found the following equivalencies between successful cloze responses and answers on a typical multiple choice comprehension test:

PERCENT OF CLOZE BLANKS CORRECT	PERCENT OF COMPREHENSION ITEMS PASSED
50	95
40	80
35	65

Because the student must think along with the language of the author and make heavy use of context to get the correct responses in a cloze test, the teacher can make educated inferences about the student's familiarity with the vocabulary and about his ability with context on the basis of this simple test strategy. Rather than develop hard-and-fast rules from a cloze test, however, it makes more sense to use resulting insights as a way of identifying individuals who need close and more detailed observations.

Of what value is a cloze test for deciding about an instructional reading level? The table above would indicate that an achievement of 40 percent of correct cloze responses qualifies for an instructional level. Below 40 percent there is doubt, and some adjustments in the material seem to be in order.

TEACHER JUDGMENT

Because bookthinking is a complex process and because it varies somewhat from subject to subject, no single test or testing procedure will capture the total picture. The only one who can develop a comprehensive picture of a student's performance is the professional teacher. With a background in human psychology, methodology, and learning psychology, and given the demands of a subject discipline, the teacher has all the tools for making reasonable judgments about student performance. And that's what the assessment of school behavior is all about: making reasonable judgments that lead to better instruction. Sometimes the decisions will strike with great accuracy, and sometimes they will be wide of the mark. The misses do not necessarily reflect a bad professional judgment so much as they indicate the numerous extenuating circumstances that influence learning in the classroom. This is not to say that teacher judgment is simply a trial-and-error gamble. Trials and errors do exist in teaching, as they do in every profession, and the competent teacher makes use of scientific knowledge, insight and experience, and historical wisdom in deciding how to create a better learning environment.

Testing with a Book

What a teacher is trying to assess is the process whereby students gain information and enjoyment from what they read. By observing a given student read books, the teacher has the best opportunity available for examining the operations and procedures he uses, that he has or doesn't have. How to test with a book was described in chapter 1. Added here are two activities that use a book or books from the classroom and offer the teacher a closer look at the way a student processes information. The first requires the selection of three different kinds of passages. Its purpose is to highlight contrasts in the ways a student processes information from one kind of passage to another. Narration, description, explanation, argumentation, and so on are differences in purpose and prose style.

Observing Responses to Contrasting Passages

Observe a student read three different passages (over 500 words long).
Read silently—all three before questions are posed.
Ask questions that start with the broad range and move toward more specificity and more concrete reactions.
Purpose: Analyze how he thinks while he is reading.

Sample Questions

1. Did you approach this article in any special way? How?
2. Do you (did you) organize your thinking to read these articles? How?
3. Were you or are you conscious of the author's organization? What is it? How?
4. How did you decide what was important about the passage?
5. As you read the three passages, were you thinking that they were different in any way—except for their content? How? List the differences noted.
6. Were there any words that caused you to pause? How did you then get their pronunciation or their meaning?

Each passage should be described in terms of its content, the organizational pattern used in its writing, and any other structural features that can be clearly identified, for example, narrative, chronological, direct comparison of characters.

The second technique involves constructing a multipurpose test for a chapter in a book or some other lengthy reading assignment. Similar to the teacher-made tests described earlier, this one uses the subject-matter text for the purpose of seeing how the student makes use of certain aspects of the book to extract the information or to use it for a particular purpose. The strategy is developed through the following stages:

1. Decide on the kinds of procedures or bookthinking operations for which information is desired. For example,

1.1—vocabulary
1.2—parts of the book (table of contents, index, glossary)
1.3—format features (subheads, illustrations, charts)
1.4—comprehension operations (recall, analyze, judge, extend)
1.5—rate of reading (skimming, scanning, words per minute)
1.6—word skills (context, decoding, use of word parts)

2. For a selected chapter or passage, write questions (test items) for each of the procedures to be examined. There should be enough items on each procedure to give the student sufficient opportunities to demonstrate his

ability. Three to five items on each skill or operation are probably a minimum number. Therefore, if ten of the skills above were chosen, the resulting test would have about forty questions in it.

3. When giving the test to the students, its purpose should be explained so they don't think that it is being given to establish a grade. It represents a diagnostic tool that will help the teacher design future work for members of the class.

4. Student answers should be considered satisfactory for a given skill or procedure when they are accurate in 75 to 80 percent of the applicable items. For a skill where only three questions or items are constructed, the teacher should decide whether two out of three is an adequate indication of success in that area. Teacher judgment must be used through this entire process.

5. Discussions or conferences with students about the results of the test should be conducted in terms of the purpose of a set of items. "Harriet, it appears that you are not clear on the use of the table of contents. Look at these four questions and your answers."

SUMMARY

All that has been said in this chapter reinforces the notion that teachers are active decision makers about students and the way they learn. From among the numerous alternative methods for assessing student performance in bookthinking, the teacher must choose those that fit his purposes and his style of working with students. Methods are weak mechanical devices until they are informed with the judgment and insight of an educated and concerned professional teacher.

Analyzing bookthinking behavior involves the teacher in making several important decisions: For example, what aspects of bookthinking should be examined in this class? And how am I going to collect information about student performance? This chapter describes ways in which the teacher is helped to accomplish those important decisions. The two typical categories for gathering student information are discussed—informal and formal observations. Informal techniques include introspection, conferences, problem-solving activities, assignments, oral reading activities, and reciprocal questions. Formal testing and formal observation include normed tests, criterion tests, cloze tests, and teacher-made tests. But guiding and informing all the decisions and the techniques for collecting data is the judgment of the teacher. The chapter emphasizes the need for and the reason teachers should proceed confidently in making the professional decisions they have been educated to make.

DISCUSSION QUESTIONS

1. Under what circumstances can a form like that shown as Question Checklist be used effectively in the classroom?
2. For classroom use what are the advantages and disadvantages of the informal observation techniques described in this chapter?
3. If you had to construct a bookthinking procedures (skills) test for this chapter (or for this book), what would you select and what sample items would you use to test the members of your class?
4. How would you define bookthinking outcomes that you would be looking for in your major teaching area? Or in your minor area?

Suggested Readings

Farr, Roger. *Reading: What Can Be Measured?* ERIC/CRIER Reading Review Series, Newark, Del.: International Reading Association, 1969.

This book is one of a series intended to synthesize broad areas of research for the practitioner. Its major purpose is to explore how tests can provide information about students' reading achievement. Included are an examination of reading skills and a consideration of how well tests provide information useful to instructional planning. In addition, the volume includes a glossary of test-related terms, a guide to tests and measuring devices in reading current at the time of publication, and a list of test publishers.

Harris, Albert J. *How To Increase Reading Ability*, 5th ed., New York: David McKay Company, Inc., 1970.

This volume, which has been in print since 1940 and is now in its fifth revision, provides a comprehensive overview of the reading process, evaluation of reading performance, and development of skills. Of particular interest to secondary teachers are chapters on assessing silent reading, developing comprehension, addressing comprehension problems, and improving reading flexibility. Also included is a graded list of books for remedial reading.

Herndon, James. *The Way It Spozed To Be*, New York: Simon & Schuster, 1968.

This light, easily read account of one teacher's classroom reminds us to be sensitive to a host of cues from the student, some of which have scant resemblance to specific skills. But the teacher was a keen observer and adjusted his instruction to match his philosophy and his analysis of what the kids needed. Not bookthinking specifically, but it is a refreshing view of a teacher making instructional decisions based on his observations of kids in school.

6

Helping Poor Readers

To what extent can a content teacher help to alleviate severe reading difficulty?

What are some problems with which a poor reader might be dealing?

How can poor readers be motivated to gain some experiences with printed materials?

Virtually every teacher has known them, tried to teach them, and wondered what to do for them—adolescents who can't or won't read. There is no single prototype or model to describe them. Their problems may be physical, emotional, social, educational, intellectual, or any combination of these, and often there is too little information available to put together a reasonably complete picture. In any event, the poor reader is usually one in a group of thirty or more who spends perhaps less than an hour a day in a given classroom. The teacher, operating under the pressures of a full schedule and many individual needs to be met, may feel quite inadequate to help these students who apparently cannot read.

The temptation is strong, under these circumstances, to label this type of student (or accept labels bestowed upon him by other teachers) as dummy, lazy, special class material—and then try to ignore him. Other labels that get passed along in school records, such as *dyslexic, reading disabled,* or *learning impaired* imply that the student has some kind of invisible disease that ordinary teachers cannot hope to treat. The teacher may be led to believe that here is a student who will be frustrated or perhaps psychologically damaged by normal work expectations and who therefore must be accommodated in "special ways." Generally, these "special ways" are construed to mean taking it easy on him, smoothing his way, or accepting a low level of performance.

The cumulative effect of this treatment, over the years and in different classes, is that the student gets by without needing to grapple with his reading problem. Since reading ability develops primarily through practice in reading, his deficit increases as he grows older. During the years other students are building the conceptual framework necessary for handling increasingly complex forms of writing, the student who is accepted as a nonreader develops his strategies for getting by. He may also be establishing a personal conviction that he can't read, at least not for school purposes, which is confirmed by the behavior of his teachers. He has been the victim of one of the gravest teacher sins of omission: Nothing was expected of him.

There are many things that the content teacher cannot do for a student who has serious reading deficiencies and at least one very important thing that the teacher *can* do. What he cannot do is erase or make up for the accumulated deficits in the student's reading background. He cannot suddenly change the student's attitude toward reading or toward himself as a reader. He cannot give the student all the individual attention he needs to come to successful grips with his reading problems.

But what the content teacher can do is help to reverse the trend set in the student's former classes, which has given him every reason to believe that reading is not necessary or important or perhaps not possible in his life. The teacher can do this by making reading part of the student's classroom experience. This may require the use of very simplified materials and short assignments or some other adjustment. Some students may even be working at the word-recognition level, learning the written forms of key words in the lesson. But, for reasons given earlier, all students should be regularly required to deal with the written word as a part of learning, and for virtually every student there is a level at which this is possible in the classroom.

In making reading a part of each student's learning experience, no matter how low his level of performance may be, the content teacher is not solving all the problems the student may have. Few miracles will happen by this means alone, although some surprises may come when students blossom under the warmth of positive expectations. Learners with hard-core reading problems should be referred for whatever special services are available in the school. (See chapter 14 on Special Services.) But the content teacher can, at the very least, refrain from reinforcing the student's perception of himself as a nonreader. Beyond that, every successful reading experience will contribute something to the student's conceptual understanding and move him a little further out of the hole into which he has dug himself over years of not reading. If the student is receiving specialized services, these will be greatly enhanced by in-class reading requirements. Ideally, the content teacher will be part of a cooperative effort with a special teacher to reach the student at his level and make reading a regular part of his school life.

DIRECT OBSERVATION:
THE BEST SOURCE
OF INFORMATION

A basic rule that every teacher would do well to adopt is to form his own impressions of a student's performance in addition to consulting other sources of information, such as school records of previous teachers. In this way, the teacher will have his own frame of reference to which to relate what he learns from other sources. In their well-known study, *Pygmalion in the Classroom,* Rosenthal and Jacobson (1968) demonstrated the difference that teacher expectations can make in a student's performance. These expectations are communicated in subtle ways, through body language and attitudes, often below the conscious level of awareness. A teacher who meets a student as a new individual, without the baggage of his past labels, can at least avoid conveying negative attitudes. He can, for the time being, allow the student to present himself in the framework of the present and make a fresh start. Even a beginning teacher should have faith in his ability to evaluate student behavior on the basis of what the student actually does in class. The teacher's own observations are his best source of current information.

It is not a simple matter to distinguish each student from the group early in the school year and view him perceptively. The human mind strives for economy, and it is only natural for teachers to begin to classify their students almost from the beginning as, for example, the bright ones, the lazy ones, the nice-but-mediocre ones, the troublemakers, the silent ones, and so on. Despite the most humanistic of intentions, it is almost impossible to avoid devising such categories when one is dealing with large numbers of people.

To counter this very natural tendency to categorize students, therefore, the teacher needs a system that will ensure an objective and reasonably complete set of observations for each student. Chapter 5, on developing a diagnostic framework for teaching, gives some suggestions for setting up such a system. Other suggestions aimed specifically at identifying the problems of the poor reader are given below.

Assessing Students' Reading
at Four Levels

Keeping in mind that proficient reading entails the ability to process larger and larger units of prose, the teacher can keep track of each student's capabilities at four general levels of prose length and complexity: whole passage (at least a page or more), paragraph, sentence, and word. This approach is conceptualized in Table 6–1. When the student is reading proficiently in the materials assigned he has a broad range of abilities, but if he is not getting beyond lower-level units, the scope of his skills narrows. The best way to use the scheme is to begin at the top and work downward to find out where the student's level of abilities begins.

A student who has difficulty with an entire passage should be observed reading randomly selected paragraphs. If he has trouble with the first two or three of these, he apparently is in difficulty at this level.

If the same student has difficulty with only one paragraph out of several tried, the problem may be one of understanding specific concepts or ideas. From those paragraphs that do give trouble, sentences should be selected at random to see if this is the level at which the student's comprehension breaks down. With problem sentences, vocabulary items should be checked. For most teachers this scheme may be more useful in checklist form, so that a brief record can be kept on each student, as in Figure 6–1.

OTHER SOURCES OF
INFORMATION

In most schools, the student's records will contain at least two types of information: standardized test scores and comments by other teachers. There may also be records of counselor interviews, parent conferences, special examinations, health data, and anything else that at some time might have seemed appropriate to include.

Standardized test results will classify the student according to general intelligence and achievement in specific areas. Tests are frequently used to provide a thumbnail sketch of how the student is doing in particular subjects, producing such glib statements as "he is working below grade level" or "he is not achieving his potential (as indicated by IQ score)."

Test scores may serve a useful function in orienting the teacher to the student's general level of academic functioning. After all, the taking of tests is a basic fact of school life and draws on many of the same skills and strategies that other types of classwork require. However, test scores do not convey the precise information that their numbers may seem to imply. A reading-achievement score that places a student at a 5.3 grade level, for example, does not specify the exact point in the curriculum at which he could

TABLE 6-1
Processing Prose Units

YES		NO
Student can handle reading assignments at this level of difficulty.	A. Can the student process assignment-length passages, demonstrated by: 1. Grasp of main ideas in the text? 2. Understanding of overall structure and relationships among ideas? 3. Ability to give an adequate summary?	Check to see if student is having difficulty at the paragraph level. If not, provide practice in outlining and summarizing.
Student can handle short units of prose but needs practice relating main ideas in paragraphs and understanding relationships among paragraphs.	B. Can the student process paragraphs, demonstrated by: 1. Grasp of topic and main idea? 2. Understanding of reasoning or order of ideas? 3. Ability to paraphrase the main point?	Check to see if student is having trouble at the sentence level. If not, provide practice in identifying main ideas.
Student needs practice relating ideas within paragraphs.	C. Can the student process sentences, demonstrated by: 1. Ability to paraphrase the meaning? 2. Ability to respond to the meaning in a way that shows understanding?	Check to see if the student is having problems with the vocabulary. If not, provide practice in paraphrasing sentences. Provide material with simplified syntax.
Student needs practice understanding sentence meanings and using words in sentences. He may need to attend more closely to relationship words such as prepositions and conjunctions.	D. Can the student process vocabulary, demonstrated by: 1. Ability to give definitions or synonyms? 2. Ability to use words in original sentences?	Provide instructions in vocabulary development. Help student understand key concepts and words associated with them. Provide simplified material with low vocabulary load.

Student Experience and Competence

Student's name _____	Adequate	*Not* *Adequate*
A. Passage-level processing:		
1. Can grasp main ideas of the passage		
2. Understands overall structure		
3. Can give an adequate summary		
B. Paragraph-level processing:		
1. Understands topic and main idea		
2. Has some sense of the order of ideas		
3. Can paraphrase at least the main point		
C. Sentence-level processing:		
1. Can paraphrase the meaning of sentence		
2. Can respond in a way that shows understanding		
D. Word-level processing:		
1. Can give definitions or synonyms		
2. Can use words in original sentences		
Teacher comments: (Include here a brief note about the passage or chapter from which the above observations were made.)		

Figure 6-1. Levels of processing

be placed and begin reading without difficulty (if for no other reason than that there is little uniformity among fifth grades across the nation's schools). In fact, such test results say nothing about his class-related reading, but only his ability to answer the questions given in this test as compared with the performance of other students who have taken the test. In this sense, the test may be said to provide general information about the *product* of reading, but nothing about the *process*.

Informal comments by other teachers that actually describe the student's reading behavior may be very helpful to a teacher who has collected his own descriptive information first. For example, if Mary is found to be having trouble reading sentences even though she seems to understand most of the words in them, her teacher may find it useful to read specific comments from previous teachers who may confirm or supplement this observation. This is also a point to be kept in mind when additions are made to a student's record.

Much less useful are comments expressed in terms that convey judgments rather than descriptions. If a teacher knows from his own observations that a student is in difficulty, he will not be further enlightened by such phrases as "low achiever," "has a learning problem," or "does not pay attention in class." Least useful are lapses into loose labeling—"he may have dyslexia"—and the broad application of tags which may have an aura of scientific certainty but in fact are so variously applied that they have no precise meanings. Since these labels do not describe and do not direct the teacher to verified remedial practices, they are useless. Much worse, they can get in the way of clear observation and lead the teacher to stereotype the student rather than understand him.

OBSERVING STUDENT READING BEHAVIOR: AN INVESTIGATION AND CASE HISTORIES

To investigate more closely ways in which the behaviors of readers can be directly observed, the authors of this text conducted a series of diagnostic observations of high school students identified as nonreaders by their teachers. For this purpose a special set of materials was compiled that provided varying amounts of pictorial and verbal information. These materials were divided into four categories:

I. *High pictorial content:* editorial cartoon; cereal box announcements; place-mat game; comics page; newspaper photograph with a brief legend; pages from a mail-order catalog.

II. *Medium pictorial content:* magazine advertisements in which the basic message is conveyed in the pictures with details in the text; a "Peanuts" story with illustrations on every page; and an article comparing camping stoves, with a picture of each brand discussed.

III. *Low or no pictorial content:* magazine advertisements in which the illustration does not convey the basic message; recipe book; classified-ad section; textbook pages.

IV. *Charts and maps:* automobile comparison chart; herb and spice chart; campus parking map.[1]

Except for the textbook materials, these items were chosen as everyday reading tasks, from which the investigators hoped to find the extent to which students classed as "nonreaders" did try to gain information from printed visual materials outside the school setting and the strategies they were using in doing so. Students were visited individually for a series of

---

[1] The complete study is available from Reading Department, Indiana University, Bloomington, Indiana. Carl B. Smith and S. Smith, "Secondary Nonreaders—Their Performance in Daily-Life Reading," Secondary Research Monograph, 1977.

one-hour interviews which, following an informal conversation between the interview team and the students, were carried out according to the following guidelines:

1. Materials were introduced in a prescribed sequence, one item at a time.
2. The student was not asked specifically to read but simply to tell what each item meant to him. After his initial response, one investigator called his attention to various aspects of the stimulus, both pictorial and verbal, and asked him to comment on this.
3. When it became apparent that the student had reached the limit of his capacity to interpret visual materials, the interview was stopped.

In some instances, the interview team carried out limited tutorial sessions with the student, devising special materials to be tried in his case. In all cases, recommendations were made for ways that teachers in the school could help the student. In addition, after observational data had been collected, the investigators talked with teachers and counselors to learn their insights and conclusions.

From this series of observations, a set of seven case histories was compiled which illustrates a range of different reading problems in combination with as many unique personalities. Indeed, the observers were impressed by the importance of individual personality in the understanding of reading problems. To understand the difficulty, the observers found that they had to understand the person. While we would hesitate to say that these are "typical" case histories, the seven students did represent a variety of problems that any teacher can expect to encounter.

Case Histories

Given here are capsule descriptions of the seven students observed. Complete descriptions of each student are included in Appendix A following this chapter. Presented separately are the interpretations and recommendations given by the investigators for each case. As a class discussion exercise, it might be useful for readers of this book first to read the detailed case histories and decide what they would do for each of the students in a content classroom. When they have responded to each case themselves, they can turn to the section of Appendix A that gives the investigators' analyses.

I. Tony, Grade 11

Described by teachers, parents, and doctors as "dyslexic," Tony was in fact able to use print for his own purposes. Yet, when it came to using textbooks, his symptoms of dyslexia became quite evident. "The lines wavered and I got headaches." Tony's teachers tried to help him by providing nonprint supplements to classroom instruction. Many believed that it would be wrong to expect him to read normal classroom assignments. Tony himself was well aware of the dyslexia label and able to describe his problem in some detail to the investigators. Yet, until he was presented with a history and a science textbook, he demonstrated no problems with reading the other daily-life tasks.

II. Josephine, Grade 9

Josephine had recently arrived with no past records at her present school from a small rural community in a southern state. She was extremely shy and seemed confused about her classes. Her teachers wondered whether she might not be a mentally deficient learner and had the school psychometrist administer a series of tests, which indicated that she had an IQ in the fifties and fifth-grade achievement in spelling and word recognition. The investigators worked with her separately and found that she had the ability to decode almost all material with reasonable fluency, although her comprehension was poor, especially for text materials. However, she was able to understand a one-page story about a teen-age girl.

III. Raymond, Grade 9

Raymond, a cerebral palsied boy in his teens, had considerable difficulty using print although he could comprehend and communicate well using oral language. His school work improved dramatically when he was taught to use a tape recorder to record some answers to homework assignments and an electric typewriter to do required written assignments. For the most part, when he read, he tried to supplement the information on the page with his own ideas as much as possible. It was apparent that keeping his brain and eyes coordinated during reading was difficult for him, and he personally described coordination as a problem. Nevertheless, given time, he was able to read many kinds of material.

IV. Allan, Grade 10

Allan had one consuming interest in life: raising pigeons. Although he had reached the tenth grade without learning even basic sound-spelling patterns and so was an effective illiterate, he now wanted to learn to read so that he could learn more about his hobby/business. He responded with some success to a language-experience approach and also was working with his English teacher using books written for foreign speakers of English (*Moby Dick* with a vocabulary of 2,000 words). He liked receiving special attention and had a mature attitude toward his need for help. However, he often experienced great stress when trying to read.

V. Kathy, Grade 9

Kathy had already decided that she could not solve her reading problems and was planning to quit school as soon as she was sixteen. She was very sensitive to the opinions of her peers and didn't want anyone to know that she was a candidate for special observation. She had little inclination to try various reading tasks, so the investigators could never really tell what she might be able to do had she put forth a full effort. Her frequent absences from school made observation even more difficult. In addition to her passivity in this respect, she was not interested in discussing her learning problems with anyone.

VI. Jeff, Grade 10

Jeff was a friendly and cooperative student who did not, at first, acknowledge any reading problems, although it became evident that he read with comprehension only when material had high intrinsic interest for him. It seemed apparent that he was not able to monitor his own reading for meaning unless he had a specific, personal reason for getting information. His major interest was in cars and motorcycles. He seemed to have the ability to use print, but he was not motivated as a student, only to use print for general learning. In particular, he did not seem to be able to identify concepts or relationships, such as cause and effect. He had had little practice using such abstract operations.

VII. Bobby, Grade 9

Bobby was a quiet, almost nonverbal student with basic reading problems and a great reluctance to participate in any academic venture. He sat quietly in his classroom and avoided the notice of his teachers. After several attempts, the investigators were able to get some dialogue with Bobby on tape and prepare a language-experience transcript for him. This seemed to be the only level at which he could operate: He could, with time, read his own words. It seemed to the investigators that Bobby must have been slipping through his classes with little participation or comprehension. He showed a very limited range of language functioning.

Students like these may appear in any class. Even a student with neurological and physical handicaps may be mainstreamed into the regular curriculum to experience a more typical learning environment. And, of course, there will always be the bluffers, the passive resisters, the bored, the frightened, and the confused.

Your first reaction as a teacher might be to resent the placement of such poor learners in classes with average and superior students where you cannot hope to give them the individual help they need. They may represent the failures and omissions of other teachers, which you may feel you have inherited unjustly. Nevertheless, such students will be as much a fact of your school life as you are of theirs. Just as they will need strategies for dealing with your requirements, you will need ways of dealing with them.

A student who passes through years of school without reading and then is given a textbook in each of five classes is in much the same situation you might be in if suddenly expected to play the harp, speak Russian, or program a computer. Like any activity that requires skill and practice to perform well, proficient reading develops as the result of experience. It is only through considerable reading that the student will reach the point where he can deal with the complex interweaving of concepts and information presented in a textbook.

There is at least as much distance to travel between the alphabet and a high school science text as between the musical scales and an elaborate instrumental composition. Yet no one would expect a teenager or adult who had given up piano lessons at the age of ten to sit down and play the "Moonlight Sonata" with feeling. Without the years of consistent practice needed to become master of his instrument, he cannot be the player he might have been.

The same situation holds true for the poor reader, with one important difference. While one can function reasonably well in life without being able to play Beethoven sonatas or even "Chopsticks," it is a definite handicap not to be able to read. No one is required by law to be a member of an orchestra, where one's musical deficits might suddenly become embarrassingly apparent. But every adolescent, no matter how well or poorly he reads, must sit in classrooms where literacy is the preeminent talent.

This comparison may suggest to you the plight in which poor readers find themselves in school. They have missed a lot of practice in their lives, and some, as the case histories show, must go back nearly to the beginning before they can start to build up their experience as readers. If they are to undertake the tremendous task of making up a deficit of several years, they will need all the help they can get. Most of us can afford the luxury of forgetting about enterprises we lacked the talent, interest, or opportunity to pursue, but not poor readers. If they are permitted to do so, they will pay a heavy price in school and adult life.

HELPING THE POOR READER

Techniques for motivating and guiding students who have difficulty with reading or simply don't like it have been developed by experienced classroom teachers and illustrate the kinds of things that can be done to make reading an interesting experience for all students.

Directed Reading Activities Using High-Interest Materials[2]

This approach can be used with students for whom reading is a low-priority activity. Such students frequently have limited vocabularies as a result of their avoidance of print and give up easily on content materials. The teacher can begin by linking reading to content that has high intrinsic interest for the student and use this connection as a medium for developing strategies that can be applied to textbook reading. Nonfiction magazine articles that present information and special terminology are especially useful for this purpose. For example, a student who enjoys camping and fishing can "study-read" articles in outdoors magazines.

Once an appropriate magazine article has been selected and a warm-up discussion completed, this procedure can be followed:

Vocabulary Instruction

1. Technical vocabulary: Capitalize on the student's expertise on the topic and give him the opportunity to "teach" terms to the teacher. New technical terms that occur in the text should be learned easily.
2. General vocabulary: Other new words can be understood first in the context of the high-interest article and then applied in other contexts. Understanding should be reinforced through an activity such as matching, multiple choice, or sentence completion.

Comprehension Development

The kinds of comprehension activities that can be done might depend on the structure of the article. Examples of these:

STYLE	ACTIVITY
1. Explanation or demonstration	Have the student list major points or steps presented in the article.
2. Narrative style	Design a sequence activity in which events are given in mixed order to be rearranged by the student.
3. Informative style	If the article presents cause-and-effect information, the student could be given results and asked to find or identify the corresponding causes.

[2] Developed by David Knoepfle, Greater Latrobe School System, Latrobe, Pennsylvania.

Comprehension activities should probably be structured in the beginning to provide the student with a skeletal outline with one or two examples already provided for him. Then, gradually, the structure could be removed to allow the student to provide his own structure.

Using Real-Life Reading Materials[3]

Many people do not read books after they have left school, but most class-room instruction still centers on books. Perhaps better results would be achieved for poor readers if teachers asked themselves one pertinent question: "What will my students read when they leave school?" In many cases, people who are not compelled to read books will not do so, although they will still have to deal with road signs, memos, newspapers, job or career instruction, catalogs, and other such utilitarian fare.

In virtually every content area, popular articles, newspaper stories, advertisements, cartoons, and other daily-life printed materials can be found that have some relation to subject matter. Using these for instruction can demonstrate to the student that classroom learning *does* relate to the "real world." In particular, advertisements can be used to teach critical thinking in an area that is important to every consumer. Advertisements present or imply concepts, so the student who examines these for their informative value will be learning to draw inferences as well as to weigh evidence and determine the purposes of writing.

Students can also be taught to analyze the use of words in advertisements, their connotations as well as their "dictionary" meanings. This will place emphasis on understanding language: the use of words and their symbolic content as it affects man's behavior. Using this approach, it should not be difficult for the teacher to individualize the instruction according to the reading abilities of the students while permitting every student to share equally in the substance of what is being done.

Students can also prepare their own advertisements, combining information and persuasion in the way they have seen this done in real advertising. This can be a group activity, or students can present their advertisements for the critical response of the whole class. An advantage for the poor reader is that this approach combines verbal and pictorial information and enables him to make fuller use of his processing strategies.

Using Comics[4]

When a student has reached his mid-teens but still cannot stumble through a primer with success, a major problem is finding materials appropriate for

---

[3] Developed by Lena Mae Scott, Indiana University, Bloomington, Indiana.
[4] Developed by Ann Metlay, University Middle School, Bloomington, Indiana.

him to work with. Comics, however, are enjoyable for all ages and offer possibilities for developing a sense of proper sequencing. For a student with extremely low abilities, the teacher can begin with an oral language approach, letting the student pick a strip from a Sunday comics section and then reading and explaining the action to him. The student then retells the story, while the teacher or a volunteer transcribes his words. For writing experience, the student can then copy the transcript himself. As he gains facility in understanding his own written language, the teacher can scramble sentences for him to restore to proper order using the original comic strip as a guide. Comic strips can also be cut into frames and scrambled for the student to put back into order. Comics can even be related to subject matter as some have historical, scientific or sociological content. While this may not be the teacher's idea of studying for the class, it is far preferable for a student to have some successful experiences with print related to each class than to have no reading practice at all.

Using the Tape Recorder[5]

This approach takes into account the fact that some students simply will not force themselves to read and yet can learn, through success, that the printed word is not as meaningless to them as they had thought. This activity can be used with an entire class or with individual students. The teacher records a suspenseful story related to the subject matter he has been presenting. In history, for example, real events can be adapted, while in science classes a science fiction theme can be used. The taped presentation stops short of the ending, and students must read a handout to learn how the story turns out.

A variation of the approach is to have students provide their own endings, either in discussion or in writing. This activity can be designed so that students apply concepts presented in class. Story endings can be exchanged for reading, comparison, and discussion and then the original ending given for further comparison. This activity can encourage active participation in comprehension, inferential thinking, application of logic, and other critical thinking skills.

The tape recorder, versatile tool that it is, lends itself to another technique, echo reading. The teacher, competent readers from the class, or volunteers read the passages to be read onto tape. Then the poor readers listen to the tape and follow along in their books. The readers should read quite slowly and distinctly, and the poor reader should be encouraged to say the words aloud as he reads along. In that way, the ideas continue to flow; problem words or phrases do not bring the reader to a halt; and the poor reader is gaining valuable practice in the use of print as a means for gathering information.

---

[5] Developed by Lena Mae Scott, Indiana University, Bloomington, Indiana.

Using Whodunits To Motivate
Reading and Writing

Much the same approach—using incomplete stories—can be used with written rather than tape-recorded beginnings. Again, the focus would be on comprehension skills, particularly on making inferences and drawing conclusions. It might also, depending on the whodunit used and the teacher's approach, deveolp skill in literal recall, understanding sequence, and perceiving relationships such as cause and effect.

The whodunit approach, which can be adapted to various content areas, capitalizes on the high interest that adolescents have in mystery stories. By choosing or writing whodunits with elements of humor, such as funny names or improbable circumstances, the teacher can almost ensure success, or at least constructive enjoyment, with this type of activity. Examples of these stories can be found in almost every copy of *Scope* magazine. For the teacher who wants to adapt this approach to his subject matter, they aren't difficult to write:

> Supersleuth was just sitting down to dinner when the phone rang. Third time this week, he thought, going to take the call. Why can't the cops do anything themselves?
>
> Half an hour later, Supersleuth arrived on the scene. The body of Mrs. Hortense Heavybottom, dressed in a black sequined gown, lay sprawled near the open refrigerator door. A thin trickle of blood was running down her right hand. In her left hand was a half-eaten meatball sandwich. In the other hand was a sharp knife, which she had apparently been using to cut slices from a 40-pound cheese in her refrigerator.
>
> Police detectives Sally Forth and Harry Leggett looked puzzled.
>
> "Harry thinks it's suicide." Sally explained, "but I'm not sure. What do you think, SS?"

The student now puts himself in the place of Supersleuth and tries to ask himself pertinent questions. For this story, some examples might be these:

> Did Mrs. Heavybottom kill herself?
> How do you know? (List all the clues.)
> Does it matter that the refrigerator door was open?
> Why do you think Mrs. Heavybottom was dressed in a black sequined gown?
> Can you tell from the story how Mrs. Heavybottom died?

Not all questions lead to relevant information. For example, it does not matter that the refrigerator door was open, and by realizing that not all questions lead to definite answers, students will learn greater flexibility in response to material. Not *everything* is important.

This activity should help students improve their ability to make inferences, read between the lines, and come to conclusions. The strategy should also give them practice in reading for detail. Students can also write their own whodunits and then read each other's work. In this way they will become more aware of the interaction between reader and writer that comprehension entails.

Encouraging a Student To "Graduate" from Word to Phrase and Sentence Processing[6]

No one is highly motivated to perform a task he can't do well, but many students work below their abilities for other motivational reasons. Frequently, students themselves believe that they can't read and easily give up. In such cases, a full page of print appears too formidable to attempt, and the reader might do better if he is given simpler tasks until he has developed more confidence and interest in his ability to comprehend sentence meanings.

A simple technique for doing this is to incorporate words which the student knows but cannot read into phrases and sentences composed otherwise of words that he can read. If the student provides the "new" words himself, he can use the familiar context to assimilate them into his sight vocabulary. For example, if the student uses the word *awl* but cannot read it, he can use the familiar directions from the shop class where the word occurs. "Pick up the _____. Punch a hole with the _____. Use the _____ to mark the leather." And so on. By writing those sentences on the board or on a piece of paper, the teacher or tutor writes the known words first and then slowly fills in and says the new word to be learned.

Other vocabulary for the selection can be developed similarly, also giving the student practice and easing him into more extended reading. When phrases and sentences begin to make sense more easily, two or more sentences can be combined until he is reading short paragraphs. At this point, he should be ready to try simplified text materials, provided he is able to proceed a paragraph at a time, stopping to discuss or mentally summarize the content before he goes on.

Feedback will be very important during this gradual building up of processing strategies. It will take time and encouragement for an adolescent who has ignored print throughout his school years to begin to monitor his own grasp of meaning as he reads. A tutor, even a peer tutor, could add significantly to the chance of success in this technique where careful buildup and constant positive feedback are necessary.

---

[6] Developed by Ann Metlay, University Middle School, Bloomington, Indiana.

Using the Cloze Technique
To Teach Comprehension
Strategies[7]

The cloze procedure involves the selection of a passage appropriate to the student's reading ability and interest and the systematic deletion of words from the text. In restoring the text, students are forced to read actively, paying attention to context clues which are crucial to filling in the missing word.

For the poor reader, cloze activities could be first derived from the reader's own dictated stories, then from materials of interest, and eventually from content material. Selective deletions can be especially helpful in alerting readers to specific kinds of context clues:

1. Verbs: to direct students to deal with the different inflected forms and to watch for signal words and other context effects on the verb form.
2. Other inflected endings (plurals, participles): to help students pay closer attention to required forms and again to context clues.
3. New or difficult vocabulary words: to provide practice with new words, technical terms, or proper names introduced previously.
4. Transition words: to help students appreciate the impact of connectors on the flow of ideas within complex sentences and between sentences.
5. Adjectives and adverbs: to make students aware of the differences in meaning that modifiers and descriptive words can make.

As students become more adept at handling the cloze task, they can design their own cloze exercises and administer them to each other. Discussions about this activity can help students understand what the reader must do to grasp the author's intended meaning, focusing especially on the importance of the whole context in understanding the message. This activity also lends itself to writing practice, as the student may compose his own experience narrative as the basis for constructing the cloze task. Because context is of crucial importance, students will see the importance of clarity and completeness in writing.

Motivating Reading
Through Open Discussion[8]

Book reports have long been standard fare in the English class, but many students regard them as a chore, even when they have enjoyed reading the books. For these students, practice in critical discussion should precede attempts to write about books. They should have the opportunity to discover in a relaxed setting the pleasure of exchanging ideas and viewpoints and of

---

[7] Developed by David Knoepfle, Greater Latrobe School System, Latrobe, Pennsylvania.
[8] Developed by Christine Wherwein, Highland Junior High School, Highland, Indiana.

relating reading to personal experience. To provide this atmosphere, the content teacher (not just in English) can institute book talks—informal discussions about books or articles and the experience of reading them.

The teacher should first demonstrate what a book talk is, by giving one or two himself. In order to be successful, the teacher must choose a book that he is genuinely enthusiastic about, one that is appropriate in both subject matter and difficulty for a particular group of students, and preferably one that contains a passage or two sufficiently brief and intriguing to be read aloud. He should make the presentation as informal as possible, simply "telling about" the book, plot, characters, and whatever else makes it worthwhile. He should not try very hard to sell the book, but mention as he finishes that it is available from him, the library, or wherever. For a more structured approach, the teacher might select books that are available in multiple copies to a group of students. This can be especially important for students easily discouraged by the task of finding books for themselves. The same approach can be used with shorter materials such as interesting magazine articles. When the students have been motivated to read the book or article, they too will want to express their reactions and feelings.

The next step is to encourage students to talk about their own reading, whether the materials are books, articles, newspaper stories, or even something as short as a cartoon. In a relatively short time, book talks and the sharing of reading materials may be a regular part of the class activity. If some students are reluctant to participate, they should be allowed to join in by talking about movies or television programs they have enjoyed rather than be excluded from the discussions entirely. Then, when they are comfortable talking about their experiences with media, everyone should be encouraged to read for further discussions. The informal setting will seem even more relaxed if food is available—a bowl of popcorn or potato chips can set the tone of an informal get-together. Students will learn something about the social value of reading and the pleasure of good conversation.

Some of these ideas may be more practical than others, depending on the situation and opportunity for spending time with individual students. Some techniques work best with small groups. Others might require the cooperation of a reading teacher within the school with time available to spend with students needing intensive help. (Special services for poor readers are discussed in chapter 14.) All these techniques are, however, based on the premise that by some means every student should be involved in reading and given tasks that make reading successful and, it may be hoped, enjoyable.

Basic Guidelines

As in every other teaching problem, helping the poor reader requires the teacher to search continually for the right techniques and the right book for the student who needs help. As much teacher insight is required as scientific knowledge of how young people learn and what books and arrangements have been used successfully in the past. But it would help the teacher make decisions about the poor reader if these basic principles were followed:

1. Find books and practice exercises that are reasonably close to the difficulty level where the student can function. (This is explained extensively in chapters 1 and 12.)
2. When the whole class must use the same book for a particular topic or exercise, the poor reader needs special directions and a reading task different from that for the average student.
3. Because of years of frustration and failure, the poor reader needs additional motivation and immediate success to convince him to try to read.

Study Guides

One of the most direct ways of giving the poor reader specialized help in reading along with the rest of the class is to construct a study guide that leads the student through the chapter or the exercise in a carefully programmed fashion. At each step he accomplishes a relatively easy task and then can proceed to the next one with the sense that he may continue to succeed.

A study guide for the poor reader does the following: (1) it takes him through the vocabulary essential to a minimum understanding of the lesson; (2) it relates concepts to those he already knows; (3) it directs him to photographs and other illustrations in order to answer specific questions; (4) it directs him to specific paragraphs with easy but important questions to answer; and (5) if he is up to it, it gives him a problem to solve that brings the ideas into his own life.

The Cleveland, Ohio, science and English departments worked together in developing study guides for science lessons. Figures 6–2, 6–3, and 6–4 are sample pages from the Cleveland study guides which demonstrate the methodical nature of this type of guide. There are various ways in which the development and use of these guides can be handled. (These issues are discussed in chapters 12 and 13.)

The examples in this chapter show that there is no single reason for poor reading. Environment, lack of language, ineffective teaching, lack of motivation and interest, lack of encouragement, physical and neurological impairment: Any one or a combination of these factors could prevent a student from learning to read well. Whatever the cause, the student shows up in the content class and needs the best thinking and personal attention the content teacher can give. That's the only way that the growth of the sense of failure for these students can be arrested.

SIMPLE MACHINES

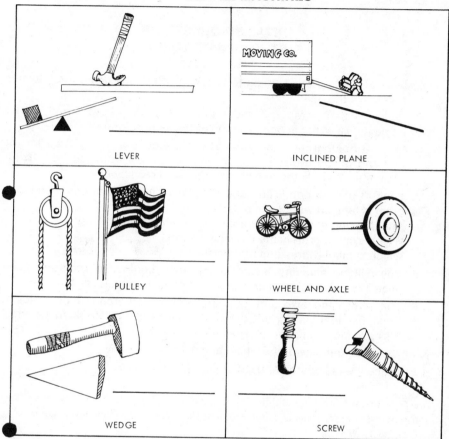

Figure 6-2. From Cleveland Public Schools, Divisions of English and Science, *Science Reading Units II, Project Content-Cognition: Reading*. Cleveland, Ohio, City School District, 1976.

SUMMARY

Many students reach junior and senior high school with real reading deficits resulting from years of avoiding print. While the content teacher can't solve all these students' problems, he can reverse the trend of their earlier years by making reading a part of their experience in his class. He must begin, however, at the student's own level of ability and confidence and build from there. He should also try to put himself in the place of a poor reader by recognizing that every person has areas of gross incompetence which he simply avoids. The poor reader, however, must constantly expose his incompetence as long as he is in school.

PHYSICAL SCIENCE
LEVERS

DAY ONE
WORKSHEET #2

DETAILED QUESTIONS
STUDY GUIDE SHEET
Pages 172–176

1. Look at photograph 1 on page 172. Why is the boy using the hammer to remove the nail?
2. Read the first paragraph under the subheading "Levers and Work" on page 172. What is one meaning of the word *fulcrum*?
3. Look at photograph 2 on page 172. The boy is exerting his effort at one end of the crowbar and feeling resistance from the boy at the other end. What is the meaning of the word *resistance*?
4. Look at photograph 1 on page 174. There are 5 diagrams. Each diagram is labeled with 3 symbols:
   After looking at the photographs, determine the following:
   Which symbol represents the man's effort? ▼ ↑ ■
   Which symbol represents the resistance?
5. You will be studying levers in this unit. Look at photograph 2 on page 175. Why do you think an arm is considered a lever?
6. The wheel and axle and gear are both considered a type of lever. Read the first paragraph under the subheading "Modified Levers." Why are they considered "spinning levers"?
7. Name 2 examples of the wheel and axle.
8. Name 2 ways gears are used in your everyday life.

Figure 6-3. From Cleveland Public Schools, Divisions of English and Science, *Science Reading Units II, Project Content-Cognition: Reading.* Cleveland, Ohio, City School District, 1976.

Not surprisingly, he tends to become adept at avoidance strategies (including dropping out) rather than deal with his embarrassing problem.

The following seven case histories illustrate various kinds of difficulties the poor reader may have and the futility of simply labeling him without taking a close look at his actual responses to printed materials. These are all students who have reached high school without being able to read well enough to use text materials for learning. Suggested solutions for these students' problems are given later in this chapter. The reader is also invited to use this information to make his own prescription for helping students such as these.

Finally, the chapter offers selected strategies that can be used to motivate and guide the poor reader. Besides being useful in them-

PHYSICAL SCIENCE   **DAY FIVE**
LEVERS   **WORKSHEET #1**

CLASSIFICATION AND COMPARISON
STUDY GUIDE QUESTIONS
Pages 174–176

A. Read "Other Types of Levers" on pages 174–175. Answer the following questions:

   1. Look at photograph 1 on page 174. How are the levers in this photograph different from the lever in photograph 2 on page 172?

   2. In a first-class lever the fulcrum is located between the resistance and the effort. Where are the fulcrum, the resistance, and the effort located in
      a. Second type (class) of lever?
      b. Third type (class) of lever?

   3. Look at photograph 1 on page 174.
      a. List the second-class levers.
      b. List the third-class levers.

   4. What class of lever is the human arm?

   5. In which class of lever is the mechanical advantage less than one (1)?

   6. The third-class lever does not multiply force. Of what use is a third-class lever?

   7. Look at photograph 1 on page 174. Tell whether each "machine" is used to gain distance or multiply force.
      a. The man fishing   d. The nut being cracked
      b. The boy shoveling   e. The man using a
      c. The cupboard opening   wheelbarrow

B. Read "Modified Levers" on pages 175–176. Answer the following questions:

   1. How is a "spinning lever" different from the simple lever?

   2. Give three common examples of the wheel and axle that are not mentioned in the reading material.

   3. Of what use are gears?

Figure 6-4. From Cleveland Public Schools, Divisions of English and Science, *Science Reading Units II, Project Content-Cognition: Reading.* Cleveland, Ohio, City School District, 1976.

selves, these ideas should suggest the types of approaches that can be taken with students who can't or won't read.

DISCUSSION QUESTIONS

Read each of the case histories included in the appendix to this chapter. After each, ask yourself the following questions:

1. What are the nature and possible causes of this student's reading problem?
2. What strengths or competencies, if any, could be used as a foundation for developing this student's abilities?
3. What specific strategies might I try in order to provide this student with successful reading experiences?

After you have answered these questions for each student, turn to the authors' analysis of this student's case and compare your conclusions with theirs.

Suggested Readings

Bond, Guy L., and Miles Tinker. *Reading Difficulties: Their Diagnosis and Correction.* New York: Appleton, 1957.

This book provides extensive "textbook" coverage of reading difficulties and remediation and has long been regarded as a standard reference in this area. It is intended for the reading specialist, but chapters on diagnosis, content-area reading and comprehension will be of interest to subject-matter teachers who have students with reading problems.

Harris, Albert J., ed. *Casebook on Reading Disability.* New York: McKay, 1970.

For the teacher seeking an in-depth understanding of severe reading problems, this book is recommended. It presents a collection of sixteen fairly detailed case reports written by specialists in various clinical settings, each of whom worked with the student discussed over an extended period of time. Both diagnosis and remediation are covered. Some technical language is used, but terms are explained and should not prevent the reader from understanding the main features of the case.

Money, John, ed. *The Disabled Reader.* Baltimore: The Johns Hopkins Press, 1966.

This book attempts to cover a wide range of reading problems and teaching methods that may help to ameliorate them. Seventeen contributors discuss many of the traditional issues in reading disability. This book is written for the specialist, but it provides an excellent background for anyone seriously interested in learning about theories underlying practice in treating reading problems.

Smith, Carl B. *Treating Reading Difficulties: The Role of the Principal, Teacher, Specialist, Administrator.* Washington, D.C.: Department of Health, Education, and Welfare, National Center for Education Communication, Catalog No. HE 5.230:30026, Government Printing Office, 1970.

Of special interest to teachers is the third chapter, "Correcting Reading Problems in the Classroom," which discusses diagnosis, techniques for correcting specific problems, and small-group and individualized instruction. This book also provides a perspective on school-wide efforts to deal with reading problems. It is written for the nonspecialist.

Appendix A

Case Histories of Secondary Poor Readers

I. Tony, Grade 11

Tony presented himself as an alert, conversational, and likeable young man with a variety of outside interests and activities. In the third grade, however, a teacher who had taken a course in remedial reading diagnosed him as "dyslexic," and from then on he was considered to have a neurological handicap.

After the diagnosis had been made, Tony's concerned family took him to various doctors for medical confirmation. He was first examined by the family pediatrician, then by other local doctors, and finally by a neurologist in a large city hospital. All tests failed to disclose specific brain malfunctioning, but resulted in prescriptions for various medications over a period of years. By the time he was a sophomore in high school, he was no longer taking medicine or seeing doctors, but the dyslexic diagnosis was still with him.

Tony described his "dyslexia" to the investigators in this way. It was a problem, he said, that took place "in the back of his head" and prevented him from perceiving printed words accurately. It didn't happen with every kind of print, but only with fairly small characters in long passages and was worse on glossy paper. When he tried to read this kind of material, he said, he might see light streaks across it, or the words might appear scrambled or bunched up. This was most likely to happen, he added, with textbooks. He had been told during his elementary years that he might not ever be able to read textbooks successfully as these caused a "disturbance" in his brain and required him to do tricks with his eyes to keep the print steady.

In their examination of Tony, however, the investigators found him capable of reading and explaining all of the daily-life materials with which he was presented during about seven hours of examination. Neither vocabulary nor variations in type size or style seemed to cause him trouble. Without hesitancy, and with good speed and understanding, he attacked each item presented to him, analyzed it, read it, and then explained it to the examiners.

When presented with high school-level textbooks in history and science, his behavior changed. He expressed lack of interest in some of the material. Although he did not demonstrate the perceptual difficulties he claimed were part of his reading problems, there were numerous concepts (words and ideas) that he was not prepared to process or to integrate as he moved ahead in understanding the passage. He did, however, proceed with the reading and gleaned from it ideas related to the passage. His difficulty with many specific concepts seemed to reflect, mainly, his lack of knowledge of and experience with the subject matter. All those years of not reading subject-matter content had deprived him of the concepts needed for an adequate interpretation of secondary-level texts. Further discussion revealed that Tony read novels in the evening before he went to sleep, studied electronics in an adult evening class, used reference materials independently when he needed to find information, and in general could use printed materials in various ways to serve his own needs. He showed the investigators the novel he was currently reading and discussed the plot with them. His responses to all the materials given to him demonstrated an ease and familiarity with using printed information that was quite typical of reasonably competent readers.

The investigators also had the opportunity to talk informally with Tony's mother. She confirmed his story regarding the medical diagnoses, adding that he had always had considerable difficulty reading and seemed to be way behind his grade level, although lately he seemed to be reading more than ever before. She said also that he had read more in the last year than he had ever read previously. She had been told that the "dyslexia" was something that eventually he would grow out of, although he might not ever be able to read dense pages of print such as difficult textbooks.

A talk with Tony's English teacher disclosed that at least one of his teachers was suspicious of the medical documentation in his school folder, although she was not sure exactly how to deal with it. She believed that Tony could read. Other teachers, according to his counselor, flatly accepted the diagnosis of dyslexia and believed that he should not be required to use print as a medium of learning. The counselor herself was not sure what to make of the records and Tony's present classroom performance.

In summary, Tony was an intelligent and active person who used print for a variety of purposes in his personal life but avoided school textbooks, claiming that for neurological reasons he could not read them. His school folder contained medical documentation to back up his arguments. Teachers liked Tony and were willing to work with him so he would not have to read in class. The question is: In what sense, if any, should he be considered a "dyslexic?"

II. Josephine, Grade 9

Josephine, a sixteen-year-old freshman, arrived at her present high school with no records from her previous school. All that was known was that she had attended a school in a small, rural community in a southern state. Eight weeks after enrollment, her counselor still had not received any records from her previous school despite several requests.

Josphine's aura of mystery remained with her as she began to attend the classes to which she was assigned. Her teachers didn't know what to make of her. She talked so little that it was hard to tell whether she understood the work in her classes, but her assignments indicated that she did not. Sometimes her written work consisted simply of copying bits of sentences and paragraphs from a book or putting down numbers apparently at random. Yet, once in her science class, she received the third-highest grade on a test that required recall of chemical formulas, and no one sitting near her did nearly as well.

Generally, though, Josephine's behavior indicated that she was confused about her classwork, and some teachers questioned whether she could read. In an effort to gain some specific information about her abilities, the administration of her school decided to call in the district psychometrist to administer a series of intelligence and achievement tests. At the same time, the authors of the present text were asked to observe her reading behavior and provide supplementary diagnostic data. Actually, the tests were not simply a means of gaining information. The school administration had already decided that Josephine should be placed in a special education program, and the main purpose of the testing was to provide the evidence of poor mental functioning that was necessary to get her into the program. The psychometrist and the investigators worked with Josephine separately and compared their results only after they had drawn their conclusions separately.

Josephine's intelligence test scores were so low that one might wonder how she was able to find her way through the daily school schedule. On the Wechsler Intelligence Scale for Children Revised (WISC-R) she earned a verbal IQ of 57, a performance IQ of 54, and a full-scale IQ of 51. Her performance on the Wide Range Achievement Test (WRAT), however, was considerably higher than one would predict on the basis of the WISC-R results. She earned grade equivalents of 5.4 in word recognition and 5.2 in spelling. As a result of these tests, Josephine was diagnosed as operating in the mentally deficient range of intelligence and recommended for placement in the special education program.

Working with Josephine in two separate sessions, the investigators found evidence of reading ability that also was well beyond the range of functioning suggested in her extremely low intelligence-test scores. She had mastered some of the mechanics of reading and had established at least a basis for further progress. Josephine's handling of everyday print items, which included a magazine advertisement, comic strips, catalog pages, and recipes, indicated that reading was not a part of her normal daily life. She showed some understanding of all the items she was given but her grasp was not complete.

At a second meeting, Josephine read from her physical science and civics textbooks. She decoded readily, but it was apparent that she was not grasping the concepts involved. This seemed to be a problem not only with language but one also related to a lack of experience and previously learned concepts that would enable her to interpret the information. When one of the examiners attempted to restate an introduction to electricity in simpler terms, she still could not understand. That is, she did not seem able to accept certain abstractions, such as the idea of the exchange of energy between molecules, which was meaningless in terms of her concrete experiences with electricity.

Her inability to deal with such abstract concepts was also apparent when she read her civics text. She was able, in this case, to understand an orally restated discussion of suburbs. But her experience with large cities and their surrounding communities was apparently so limited that her understanding was not the same as that of a more experienced adolescent. When asked to state the meaning of something she had read, Josephine resorted often to reading fragments from the text, another indication that she had difficulty processing the meaning. She had learned to rely heavily on her decoding strategies as evidence of reading and apparently had had little practice in expressing ideas in her own words.

Josephine read a five-page story with little comprehension but did better with a one-page story, written by one of the examiners, about a teen-age girl living in the country. In the latter story, the girl is experiencing a mild conflict with her mother and finds solace in the company of a girl friend her own age. Although she got some of the details wrong in the retelling, Josephine grasped the plot and understood that it was "about" the importance of friendship. When asked to tell what she thought happened next, she replied that "the girl went back home and tried to be real sweet to her mother," which was a plausible prediction.

In summary, Josephine had fairly well-developed decoding skills, especially for a student with her apparent difficulties in school. She had a lot of trouble grasping concepts and discussing content in her own words. As an individual, she was shy and anxious, but she did not present the appearance of having the extreme mental retardation indicated by her intelligence-test scores. Nevertheless, she was labeled "mentally deficient" primarily on the basis of those scores.

III. Raymond, Grade 11

At the time of the team's observation, Raymond was a seventeen-year-old cerebral palsied boy attending a public school for the handicapped in a large city. He had difficulty with any task that required fine motor coordination and, as he himself put it, trouble getting his eyes and brain to work together. Throughout most of his time in school he had managed to avoid reading, although he had developed normal oral language facility and could gain much information through listening.

There was no reading program per se at Raymond's school although the majority of students there (grades one through twelve) could be presumed to have reading problems. Raymond began learning basic decoding skills at the age of ten from a volunteer tutor and progressed in time to where he could read at a fourth- or fifth-grade level, though slowly and with considerable effort. From casual observation it appeared that he had difficulty keeping his eyes correctly focused on a page of print. He frequently looked upwards and lost his place, resulting in long pauses during which it seemed his mind was elsewhere. When reading silently, he would sit and study the page, sometimes moving his lips or talking softly to himself, but his eye movements did not indicate a forward, linear progression. After a time, if asked, he could report some of the information in a short section, making use of whatever pictorial cues might be present and frequently elaborating on his own rather than actually reporting what he had read, a kind of imitation of reading.

In short, Raymond's reading behavior was quite perplexing. He seemed to have all the necessary skills for reading—decoding, context utilization, construction of meaning from connected discourse—yet he couldn't put them together well enough to get beyond the point where reading was an intolerable chore. He continued to demonstrate excellent speaking and listening abilities while literacy skills dragged. At school he did little work. His handwriting was slow, laborious, and virtually illegible. A paragraph of simple statements was the most he could produce, a record which did more to conceal his abilities than to reveal them.

When he was about fifteen, his tutor taught him to type on an electric typewriter, given to him by his parents, and worked out with the boy a method by a which he taped oral essays on a cassette recorder and then transcribed these on the typewriter. This method enabled Raymond to make the most of his oral language abilities and avoid the tremendous effort of writing by hand. As a result, his response to school assignments improved greatly and he began to edit his tapes as he learned various conventions of written language. His reading improved somewhat too, partly because he was also using the tape recorder to practice. But he continued to prefer aural to visual means of gaining information. What improved even more, however, was his ability to seem to be reading while he composed his own version of the text.

Raymond spends a lot of time talking on his CB radio, through which he is known to the world (see chapter 7 of this book) as Circle City Baretta. This activity is significant because it exemplifies his well-developed interest and facility in oral communications. He has acquired the CB lingo, has established many regular contacts, and in this way has built up a circle of friends in the outside community to which otherwise he would have little access because of his handicap.

Raymond dealt with the materials presented to him in a sporadic way, reading bits and pieces and putting together his own version of these. He had best success with a catalog page showing digital watches, combining the verbal and the pictured information on a chosen watch quite logically. He made little sense, however, on items that were not of interest to him.

The last item he read was a transcript he had typed himself from a tape made several weeks earlier. In doing this he read in a fashion that was quite typical for him, taking phrases in bursts, then pausing for long periods, frequently distracted by his own typing mistakes and especially by corrections penned in by his tutor. As soon as the session was finished he was back on the CB again, contacting his friend.

In summary, Raymond is a young man with documented brain damage that has affected all of his physical functioning and makes reading a difficult and fatiguing experience for him. He has learned most of the basic skills associated with reading but cannot read fluently. He has a strong preference for other forms of information, especially aural, and tries to avoid reading by substituting what he knows for what is on the page. Nevertheless, he has demonstrated that he has the ability to learn.

IV. Allan, Grade 10

Allan was recommended for observation by his English teacher who had been helping Allan on an individual basis in response to his desire to learn to read. He presented himself as a good-humored, friendly, independent person who conversed easily with adults. He described at length his hobby of raising pigeons, which he had turned into a moderately successful business. He also helped his father raise rabbits and ducks and so was making a significant contribution to the family.

Although he had never warmed up to rabbits or ducks, Allan talked about pigeons with real affection, considering them to be the most beautiful and intelligent of birds. He wanted to learn to read so that he could read about pigeons. Sometimes his talk merged into fantasy as when the size of his flock grew suddenly into the thousands, or individual birds assumed weights of twenty-five or fifty pounds. But essentially he was describing a real situation and was knowledgeable in many aspects of pigeon husbandry.

At the first of several sessions the investigators spent with Allan, he was asked to look at materials that had a high percentage of information presented in nonverbal form. His response generally was to talk about the materials rather than try to interpret them. That is, he drew associations from the materials to his own experience and talked about that. This observation gives some idea of how Allan dealt with the everyday reading tasks that are a part of most adults' lives. For the most part, he didn't deal with them at all. He had developed workable alternate strategies for gaining information that enabled him to avoid printed language.

Having determined that Allan was in fact virtually unable to read, the investigators tried a language-experience approach to help him associate oral and written language. One team member engaged him in a discussion about pigeon raising, to which Allan contributed the bulk of the dialog, and transcribed the conversation from a tape recording. This was then used for reading practice. When asked to read passages of connected discourse, even when it was language he had produced himself, Allan attacked each word separately. For the most part he relied upon rather poorly developed sound-letter decoding techniques, which failed him more often than they served. He frequently confused common words like *who* and *how* or *that* and *what*. After he had gone over words separately, however, he could go back and read a sentence as a unit. He had no strategies for using context information. But, because he had produced the text himself, he could be pressed to use meaning as well as decoding cues.

Allan was under an obvious physical strain while reading. After a short time he would begin to try avoidance techniques, such as starting a conversation that would divert attention from reading or going into lengthy explanations of a point. Sometimes he would stand up and walk around while he held the transcript, and once he stretched out flat on his back over three desk tops and held it over his head.

Despite his difficulties, however, Allan had many things going for him. One was that he was making an effort to find meaning by relating materials to his own experiences. He expressed judgments freely, showing a willingness to respond critically. Another strong factor in his favor was that he wanted to learn and was optimistic about his progress. He was more concerned with his successes than with his failures and frequently congratulated himself when his reading went a little more smoothly than usual. He had a mature attitude toward receiving help and worked willingly with student tutors as well as with his teacher. And, of course, he was motivated by his interest in pigeons.

V. Kathy, Grade 9

Kathy's teachers were eager to have the investigators work with her because she had expressed her intention of quitting school as soon as she was sixteen, which would be during the current school year. She was discouraged by her inability to read and also very embarrassed about it. Kathy was an attractive girl with a somewhat retiring but sociable personality, obviously interested in being liked and accepted by others. Her difficulties in school were detracting from her positive image of herself, and she wanted to get away from the scene of her persistent failures.

Kathy's anxiety about her reading problem made it difficult to help her. One of the first problems was finding a place private enough for her to feel comfortable. During the first session, a group of students unexpectedly walked through the area where she was being interviewed and Kathy literally cringed, put her hands over her head and cried, "Oh no! Get me out of here." While talking with the examiners, she was friendly and cooperative, yet could not openly discuss her academic problems or offer any insights from her own point of view. Rather, she said as little on this subject as possible as if hoping to diminish the importance of this aspect of her life. She did express a wish to receive help and at first said nothing about her intention of leaving school. But she did not convey a great amount of conviction concerning her willingness to attack her problems.

Another problem the investigators encountered working with Kathy was her frequent absences from school. She seemed to be well along in the process of dropping out. Over a period of several weeks, during which the team visited her school once or twice weekly, they met with her only three times, once for a partial period. Because she worked slowly, this discontinuity and small amount of total time made it difficult to proceed very far in the diagnosis.

Kathy proved to be passive in her responses to most of the materials presented to her. She was most successful with a catalog page showing items of jewelry, indicating some previous experience in using catalogs. For the most part, however, it was apparent that reading was not a part of her everyday life and definitely not something she was comfortable undertaking before an audience. Her general strategy was to attempt to apply decoding techniques from the beginning of a passage as a way of simply getting through the material. She had no organized approach to the materials, no way of assessing what an item was before she attempted to read it. Unfortunately, her decoding skills and sight word vocabulary were so poor that this approach could not get her through most of the items presented to her.

Her evident embarrassment over her poor reading caused her to avoid any display that might require her to stumble around in front of other people. Understandably, when one investigator asked her if she would be willing to dictate stories of her own and read them back to a peer or to a tutor, she shook her head—negative. It was then that she revealed her plans to quit school and take a job in a print shop starting the next summer. She had learned the previous summer to operate a small multilith machine, had a job that started her one dollar above the minimum hourly wage, and was promised that she could double that rate within a two-year period. "I enjoy it, and I can do it well," she smiled.

In summary, she had some partially developed skills which might have provided a basis for improvement, but she seemed to have little energy or motivation for the task. Her reading deficit had brought her to the point where she no longer wanted to try to learn in school.

VI. Jeff, Grade 10

Jeff met with the investigators for only two sessions, but, unlike Kathy, accomplished enough in these meetings to provide the team with at least a general impression of his reading behavior. He had been referred by his English teacher as having difficulty with class-related reading, although he himself did not acknowledge such difficulties.

Jeff talked easily though rather briefly with the examiners before his sessions began. He listened with interest to an explanation of the diagnostic method being used and expressed his willingness to partipiate. His main interest was in cars and motorcycles, and he said he had one of each which he worked on himself, locating and installing parts. His favorite class was shop where he was learning woodworking, drafting, working with plastics, and silkscreening. Although he felt able to do school work, he later mentioned both science and social studies as being hard subjects for him. He said he liked English second best because it was the easiest. He had with him a paperback novel received in his English class, but he hadn't started to read it yet and knew little about it.

When Jeff began looking at the materials in the diagnostic set, he proved able to respond to some high-pictorial items with normal comprehension. However, he was not able to make sense by himself of many of the more complex items. When probed with questions and directed to specific parts of the copy, he was able to gain some understanding of the materials that gave him difficulty, but apparently he would not have persisted on his own. He seemed to be able to deal with reading of this type if the content was familiar and of interest to him but to lack strategies for approaching unfamiliar tasks.

At the beginning of the second session, Jeff saw a stack of *Time* magazines in the room and suggested using one of these. This suggestion demonstrated that he understood the nature of the diagnostic process and was interested in helping it along. He first selected an advertisement for a Chevrolet Nova (the kind of car he owns) and gave a fair accounting of the information in it, although he did not systematically review everything mentioned in the ad. His second selection was an article on various rock musicians, and he was able to restate some items from it but in a hit-or-miss way, which did not demonstrate an overall understanding of the article. Textbook passages presented considerable difficulty. He had trouble with a number of words and could not explain the concepts of procedures he read in a general science text. It became apparent that he had difficulty processing connected prose and acquiring concepts. He could identify topics and tried, to some extent, to reason out his own connections. But the effort was not particularly successful.

Jeff then read aloud a part of the text describing the first moon landing, stopping after each paragraph to restate what he had read. After considerable difficulty with the first paragraph, his retelling of each succeeding paragraph improved in that it became more elaborate and complete. Vocabulary, both technical and long nontechnical words, seemed to cause him great difficulty. In his mathematics text, he had little comprehension of story problems. He did not really understand what the problem was asking for or apply reasoning to it. In another instance, he read the numeral 400,000 as "four million thousand" without reacting to the incongruity of the number.

In general, it seemed that Jeff had some basic reading skills but was uncritical with regard to whether he was deriving sensible meaning from what he read. He seemed equally satisfied whether he had understood something or not and gave up easily when material seemed difficult. Yet he could read some items directly related to his personal interest without great difficulty.

VII. Bobby, Grade 9

Bobby, a fourteen-year-old freshman, could be described as a young man who had learned to use passive resistance as a chief tactic in his school life. He endured the presence of the examiners in much the same fashion as he must have endured the many classes he had sat through in his lifetime: by sitting quietly and letting others do the talking.

According to his counselor, Bobby was the youngest of eight children, all the rest of whom were girls. Although the examiners knew little else of his home background, it was impossible to resist speculating on what life might have been like for a small boy with seven older sisters, all vying to help him and tell him how to manage his tasks. For whatever reason, his capacity for response and verbal communications seemed to be severely limited. When he did talk to the examiners, almost always in response to direct questions, his face was impassive and his voice so low as to be virtually inaudible. Like Kathy, he seemed to be very uncomfortable about being singled out for this kind of attention.

Although Bobby did eventually demonstrate that he had some ability to communicate with words, he never relaxed enough to speak freely with the examiners or volunteer comments of his own. In several sessions, he never went beyond answering direct questions or giving information that was specifically called for. In this sense he was a nonreinforcing individual who wore down the enthusiasm of his interviewers rather quickly. By contributing no effort of his own to the interaction, he made the other person do all the work. It could be inferred that this avoidance strategy was one he had used successfully in school, resisting efforts to reach him without committing punishable acts. He probably became, in the eyes of his teachers, a neutral entity —a student who neither participated in nor disrupted the class.

Bobby did not demonstrate any ability to deal with the materials presented during the diagnostic sessions. When asked what an item meant to him, he invariably mumbled, "I don't know." The examiners then concentrated their efforts on trying to determine whether Bobby's oral language skills were as deficient as they had initially seemed to be. To do this, they used a language-experience approach, getting Bobby to record some discussion of his own. The topic was hunting, the only personal interest he had disclosed.

It was not easy getting Bobby to talk. The first attempt to do so was a failure as Bobby murmured so softly that his words, few as they were, were unintelligible on the tape. On the next try, he produced three or four audible sentences in a dialogue with one of the examiners, all of them answers to questions. When these were transcribed, however, he had great difficulty trying to read back his own words although the examiner read his own part—the questions.

In a later taping session, Bobby surprised the examiners by elaborating his responses in a way that seemed uncharacteristic in comparison with his performance so far. The examiner working with him asked him to describe the small town he lived in as if to a newcomer, and he began naming the various businesses and where they were in relation to each other, producing a fairly complete roster of the stores, restaurants, and service stations in the central part of town. Bobby revealed this unexpected willingness and ability to express himself verbally when he could describe something concrete that provided its own structure. His language became more fluent when he could connect it with definite physical clues in the environment. Moreover, when he listened to the tape he responded to it, filling in an occasional pause where he had groped for words.

In general, though, he seemed to be unaccustomed to talking beyond making the most cryptic of responses and had difficulty thinking of things to say. Even when he was describing the business section of his home town, he could not always think of the right names for some businesses. For example, he didn't know what to call a place where people worked on the bodies of cars. It was also noted that while Bobby could report facts he resisted giving opinions or rendering judgments. His customary response to any question that called for his own thoughts on something was "I don't know," a phrase which seemed to constitute the bulk of his conversation. He had no inclination to render a personal response.

Bobby continued to have difficulty reading his own transcripts. He had an extremely low sight-word vocabulary and tended to forget a word he had seen only a line or two before. He made no use of context cues even though he had produced the context himself. When he encountered difficulty, he simply stopped and waited, creating a vacuum of silence that the examiner felt almost compelled to fill. It was his usual technique of tapping the energies of others rather than attacking a problem himself. He did not do this out of design or with a calculated intention of manipulating others. It was rather that he felt he lacked the resources to deal with written language on his own and had learned to depend heavily on others.

To summarize, Bobby seemed to have very poorly developed oral language skills for a student his age and even less ability to deal with the printed language. He did not participate in his classes and had invested little energy of his own in the remediation of his language/learning problems. To make matters worse, he was difficult to work with because his strategy of passive resistance worked so well. Yet he had demonstrated some response to the dictation-transcription techniques tried by the examining team.

Appendix B

Case Histories: Interpretations and Recommendations

I. Tony

Tony, diagnosed in the third grade as dyslexic, was judged by the investigators to be an alert and intelligent teen-ager who did not have much interest in certain academic subjects and therefore experienced difficulty with the reading. It was to his advantage, of course, that his lack of background and motivation to read certain types of subject matter could be construed as dyslexia. His school folder contained enough medical and parental documentation of neurological deficits to convince his teachers that Tony, though obviously bright, could not read and therefore could not be expected to handle textbook assignments. In this way, school work did not interfere greatly with his outside interests, which included woodworking, carpentry, and CB radio as well as electronics. Although occasionally an individual teacher might challenge his claim to dyslexia, this never got into his school record. So, in general, he was able to pass as a certified nonreader.

Tony did, however, have a reading problem. Because he had not read extensively in textbooks, especially those with historical, scientific, or historical-literature content, he had not built up the set of concepts and related vocabulary he needed for fluent reading in these subjects. He was clearly bright enough and had the basic skills to do so, but his success in avoiding such texts had created a deficit that he now must work to overcome. What he needed to do was read more broadly and extensively to build those concepts and vocabulary in the neglected areas. It was largely a matter of self-discipline. Teachers could help by providing books with an easier vocabulary and a light concept load. Teacher and peer tutoring would also help, but the main emphasis should be placed on reading itself. By and large, it was up to Tony.

The next logical step for Tony was for him to acknowledge that his reading problems were motivational rather than physiological and could be dealt with. He would have to work to broaden his interests or at least accept as a fact of school life that he must read some things that were not personally interesting or immediately applicable to his daily life. He acknowledged this necessity in a final interview.

At this point in his development, there could be no substitute for considerable practice in reading. He possessed the basic organizational skills and mental operations needed to deal with expository writing. He also had sufficient word-analysis strategies to be able to develop further through practice rather than specific skill instructions. Tony's own habit of reading for pleasure was invaluable and needed encouragement. Far from being viewed as a dyslexic, he should be viewed as an active reader with no limit to his potential for using print in any form. Most important, he needed to gain this perception of himself.

Tony's case illustrates rather dramatically the impact that words and medical documentation can have. Doctors, parents, teachers (and Tony himself) were willing to regard him as dyslexic although reading was an important part of his life. As a result, he accumulated a conceptual deficit in some subjects that created a real reading problem, although one of a different sort from that implied in the dyslexia label.

II. Josephine

Josephine's case history demonstrates how much divergence can occur between a diagnosis based on personal observation of behavior and a battery of standardized test scores. In this instance, an adolescent girl was diagnosed as trainable mentally retarded, indicating inability to do any kind of academic work although she could read some materials with understanding.

Josephine's reading behavior, while not spectacular, belied the extremely low rating of her intelligence derived from her standardized test scores. Although she showed little ability to deal with ideas or abstractions, she could relate to material that was sufficiently concrete in terms of her own experiences. It was recommended that she be given reading materials related to concrete situations and tasks that were personally relevant. Her well-developed decoding abilities showed that she had grasped the relationship between oral and written language, at least at the sound-letter level. If she could be encouraged to restate content in her own words, she might continue her development in reading to higher levels of comprehension. Language experience (dictation-transcription) was also recommended as a way of developing her ability to understand connected discourse.

As it happened, Josephine was assigned to a special education program which involved her in work-study experiences that proved to be well suited to her abilities. It is unfortunate, however, that she had to be labeled as mentally deficient to get into such a program. This label is now part of her school records and will not easily be overcome by other kinds of documentation of her actual abilities.

III. Raymond

This case history describes a student classified as physically handicapped and placed in a special education program where he was accommodated as a nonachiever rather than helped to develop the intellectual strengths he in fact possessed. Instead of being helped to master tools that would enable him to compensate for his perceptual and motor problems, he remained at a very low level of functioning in a more-or-less traditionally oriented curriculum until he developed certain skills on his own with outside assistance.

Raymond easily passed as a nonreader because in fact he did not read unless required to. This was partly because he was satisfied with the information he got from other sources. A good example of this was his response to the machine in the motorcycle ad, which he was satisfied to call a Honda, because that is the most common make, and he wasn't particularly interested in motorcycles anyway.

Raymond's reading behavior is tied into his overall strategy of living in which he must, by necessity, practice a strict economy of effort. He lives a prescribed kind of existence in which a great amount of time is absorbed in a daily routine, so not much of his day is open for personal interests. His main outlet is through social contacts, which as we have seen he has developed on his own through CB activities. It is as if he had made his own assessment of his situation and possibilities and realized where investment of his time would reap the greatest personal gain.

This is not to say, of course, that Raymond should not be encouraged and helped to read better and more fluently. Printed language, however, will probably never play as important a role in his life as it does in most people's. In Raymond's case, the development of literacy skills should be related to oral language, which is why the use of the tape recorder has proved so successful. Another clue that can be inferred from his personal preferences is that he seeks opportunities to express himself, and this may be especially important for an adolescent who has had limited social experiences.

It is unfortunate that reading services are not available in Raymond's school for a number of reasons. He would benefit from consistent, guided practice that did not subtract from his personal time. Also, because there is some physical basis for his difficulty with print, a school designed for the handicapped might be expected to provide facilities to improve his condition. The problem of motivation might also be addressed in the school setting, where he is most likely to see the need for using printed materials.

IV. Allan

This case history describes a student who called attention to his own reading deficiencies at the age of sixteen and received help. Although the full details of his educational history are not known, it is evident that he reached his sophomore year in high school without acquiring even minimal reading skills. Apparently he was passed from grade to grade without being required to read or receiving special attention. Allan escaped labeling, but he also missed out on the individual attention that might have helped him develop reading abilities much earlier in life.

Allan had had a number of personal characteristics that greatly increased his chances of learning to read, even though he was virtually starting from scratch at the age of sixteen. One of the most important of these was that he viewed himself in his own terms and was not greatly concerned with peer approval or teacher judgments. His case illustrates the importance of personality in learning.

Because of Allan's high level of motivation, coupled with his interest in learning more about raising birds, the investigating team spent additional time with him trying out strategies suggested by their analysis of his readings. From these, specific recommendations could be derived.

1. Use language experience to reinforce the relationship between oral and written language: As part of the strategy lessons, Allan and one of the examiners taped a conversation regarding the raising of pigeons, which was then typed up for him to read. Since he had produced the vocabulary and sentences himself, he could be pressed to

provide meaning as he read. Knowing the subject enabled him to read with reasonable fluency.

2. Use writing to reinforce word-attack skills and further strengthen the association between oral and written language: The same tape was used to provide writing and encoding experience. Allan listened to sentences on his tape, then tried to write what he had said. The written sentences were always shortened versions of the original statements, but he was able to render oral language into written form, sometimes with help from the examiner. The writing itself provided the opportunity for impromptu lessons on encoding strategies that would also be useful in decoding.

3. Read simplified material on a subject of high interest: Some information on pigeons from the *Encyclopaedia Britannica* was rewritten in simplified form. Allan read this about as well as he had read his own transcription and was interested in keeping the copy prepared for him. He reacted critically, denying its factuality from time to time, which was a good sign. He was processing material, not just mechanically decoding it. In preparing this kind of material, the writer should try to do the following:

   a. Restrict the vocabulary and preteach some items.
   b. Repeat key words several times.
   c. Use simpler sentence structures and very gradually increase their complexity.

4. Read into the tape recorder as a way of reinforcing the association between oral and written language: Allan read the pigeon material into the tape recorder, controlling the microphone himself. When he had difficulty with a word, he turned off the recorder, figured out the word, and then continued taping his reading. The result was a tape that sounded fairly smooth (at least compared to his usual reading performance), and Allan was pleased when he heard it. Some practice of this kind with the tape recorder would be beneficial as a confidence builder.

V. Kathy

As her case history suggests, Kathy was already well along the way toward dropping out of the educational process by the time the investigative team met her. Her level of commitment was by that time so low that only a well-organized, all-out effort to make learning a positive experience would bring her back to active participation. What she really needed was an individualized program that combined counseling, tutoring, and a structured setting in which she could proceed at her own rate without risk of failure. Because of her sensitivity to peer judgments, she would probably do best in an alternative program in which her classmates would be receiving the same kind of special attention. Because she had failed so far to find personal significance in academic work, she might also benefit from a work-study arrangement that tied school learning in with vocational preparation.

Within such a setting, Kathy could be guided through a basic skills program that would help her to develop the organization needed to become an independent learner. At the same time, counseling could help her to clarify her view of her future and set reasonable goals. At this point in her schooling, Kathy needed structure, a clearly defined plan for progress, and continuous reinforcement. At the same time, she needed to be able to relate personally to what she was doing and grow in self-esteem.

Her community did not provide such a complement of services. However, Kathy is a good example of the type of student who quietly withdraws from a standard curriculum, virtually disappearing before the eyes of her teachers. Kathy's case provides a strong argument for flexible, imaginative programming that allows students to select alternate routes to future goals.

In a school where such programming is not available, Kathy could still be helped by a cooperative effort among her teachers to extend as much individual attention and guidance as the school day would allow. She should receive structured assignments with regular but easy reading tasks, perhaps beginning with vocabulary development. In addition, a personal interaction approach that would encourage her to verbalize her perceptions of herself and her future would be beneficial both for developing language abilities and helping her gain some insights into her school experience. Conferences with Kathy and her parents regarding her attendance problems would also be necessary.

Perhaps if enough adults in Kathy's life were to join in the effort of reversing her present drift away from school, she would find that formal education really could have value for her. The one thing that impressed her and pleased her was that her English teacher was concerned enough to ask someone to talk to her about improving her reading skills. "No one ever did that before," she said.

VI. Jeff

Jeff had some strategies for dealing with schoolwork and a willingness to try, although it seemed unlikely that he was getting much out of his school-related reading. Before he could be expected to process whole passages of expository prose on his own, he needed to work at the word-and-sentence level of meaning. He needed practice in grasping single concepts before trying to relate concepts to each other in more complex writing.

Jeff showed a strong tendency to focus on particular details without grasping the overall form or purpose of what he was reading. This could be why he had trouble developing a framework for problem solving, as demonstrated by his inability to do a simple story problem in his mathematics text. An inability to grasp the structural aspects of a problem or written passage makes it difficult for the student to conceptualize the general significance of what he reads and therefore to make sense of the details. Jeff needed practice in perceiving the structural characteristics of what he was reading. This practice might be in the form of outlining, identifying topic sentences in paragraphs, and observing text cues to organization, such as chapter titles and subheadings.

Jeff should be able to use the reading skills he has already developed if he is provided with texts that have a low vocabulary load and repetition of key terms. He would also benefit from practice in restating meanings in his own words, beginning at the sentence level and proceeding from there to longer units of prose. This would require him to become more active in deriving sense from connected prose. Because he was inclined to be uncritical in this regard and willing to give up when material was difficult, some attention to the development of a self-monitoring system would help.

Worksheets that would structure his reading responses and require him to state concepts completely and in his own words were also recommended. Writing practice would also help to strengthen his decoding skills, which readily broke down when he encountered complex words. Individual or small-group tutoring, in which he was asked to explain concepts orally, would provide good practice. Also it is especially useful for students like Jeff to have an overview of material before they attempt new reading. He would benefit from prior discussion of major concepts and, of course, instruction in the vocabulary of the text.

Jeff's attitude was cooperative and friendly, and he had already developed some cognitive strategies for dealing with material of personal interest. His progress in school would depend largely on whether this motivation could be extended to include class-related reading. And this in turn would depend on whether he could develop specific strategies for dealing with this kind of material on his own.

VII. Bobby

Bobby appeared to be a student very much in need of special services in reading. It is doubtful that he could perform in any academic classes until he had worked intensively on language development and general communication skills. Only in this way could he be brought to a point where he would give up his present strategy of nonparticipation.

The dictation-transcription approach appeared to be making some changes in Bobby's behavior even during the limited time he spent working with the investigators. It was recommended, therefore, that Bobby continue this activity on a regular basis, perhaps as a part of his work in English.

Since oral language abilities must be the basis for developing reading skills, Bobby needed to be encouraged to talk more in other ways too. One way of doing this would be to allow him to tape record rather than write some of his outside assignments. This approach, which provides some privacy along with practice in oral expression, would probably be much more successful than expecting Bobby to talk in class. At the same time, involvement in small-group projects, preferably with friends, might encourage him to interact in a natural way within the classroom.

Bobby could also be teamed with another low-achieving student with whom he felt comfortable and a tutor who might encourage dialogue between the two students. In this way he could not rely on the other student to fill in his gaps of communication. The situation might be set up so that the students explained concepts presented in class to each other and practiced with word lists or simplified reading materials. The tutor would have to be able to direct a dialogue without becoming too involved in it himself, mainly by asking questions without providing answers. Tape recording these sessions would provide students with feedback and, it might be hoped, increase their interest in the activity.

Along with a strong program for developing oral language, reading tasks could be introduced as appropriate. For example, a discussion of a lesson could be preceded by vocabulary instruction. Tapes, of course, could be used for making transcripts to be read. Short and simplified explanations of single concepts could be substituted for more complex textbook assignments.

Because of his introversion and lack of self-confidence, Bobby might also benefit from a programmed-learning approach to basic skill building. Such materials systematize learning and enable slow learners to work things out for themselves without exposing their deficiencies to classmates. Such an approach would not be sufficient by itself because Bobby's need is to develop his ability to express himself, but it could be a valuable supplement to other language-centered approaches.

Left to his own devices, Bobby would probably continue to give his teachers the silent treatment in class and, like Kathy, gradually drop out of the educational process. With help, however, and the preservation of his dignity, he could be helped in many ways to become a more communicative individual. This would give him the foundation he needed to develop independent reading abilities.

part 3

Strategies for Coping with Books

7

Vocabulary Development and Wordthinking

What is wordthinking?

What is the relationship between reading and vocabulary development?

How can the teacher incorporate vocabulary growth into content learning?

Language develops in response to two basic needs: the need to identify socially with other people and the need to think and communicate as an individual. For example, a cerebral-palsied but intellectually alert teen-ager, known to the world as Circle City Baretta, sits by his citizens band (CB) radio unit and talks to various friends in the community at large: Papercutter, Munchkin, Matchbox, Cinderella, and Purple Demon to name a few. He presses the button on the microphone and cuts into miscellaneous sounds on the channel, calling for "break one one" and then "break one two" as he changes channels, identifying himself by his "handle" (Circle City Baretta) until he finally gets a response. It's from "the Hustler." They exchange information on their "ten-twenty" (locations), the quality of their "copy" (reception), and how well they "modulate" (are able to understand each other). When the exchange is finished, C. C. Baretta signs off by saying, "ten-forty there, Mr. Hustler. Pleasure. Greetings to you there guy. Mercy. Keep the shiny side up and the greasy side down. One Circle City Baretta said that, and I'm gone."

In this conversation, C. C. Baretta is not so much communicating a message as using words to make contact with other members of a group with which he has identified. Everything he said was predictable from a knowledge of CB lingo. For him, an electronic transmitter plus a certain assortment of terms have provided a channel between his home and the outside world. Despite physical problems that make reading difficult, he has, in a short period of time, acquired an entirely new vocabulary which constitutes a special area of expertise that people outside the CB culture may not readily understand. In this way, words have increased the sense of personal identity that distinguishes him as a unique individual.

This new sense of identity becomes apparent when he explains his CB activities to people—like the authors of this book—who aren't members of the CB culture. And he enjoys doing this, too. In conversations with us, he tries to *bridge* a difference in understanding. For this purpose, he uses a different kind of language so that we can understand. Now he becomes deliberate in his choice of words, patient with us as listeners, and willing to go back over a point in different words if necessary. As he puts it, he uses "regular" English. In the course of this discussion, moreover, he relates his CB activities to other topics and even considers the subject of communications in general. For example, he comments on the role of communications in the generation gap, and wonders about the relationship between drug use and lack of communication. One idea leads to another, and there is no limit to where the conversation may lead.

At this point, it is clear, he is using language as something more than a prescribed code for contacting other members of a particular group. Now language has become a tool for exploring his own thoughts and relating ideas. In both of these uses of language—relating personally to others and developing his own thoughts—words are very important resources.

WORDTHINKING

Earlier in this book, we introduced the concept of *bookthinking* to describe the kind of interaction that occurs between a reader and a book. Now we present the term *wordthinking* to suggest the importance of words and word concepts to the thinking processes of the individual.

A word that a person can both understand and use is a valued possession, something that can't be worn out, taken away, or lost except through drastic circumstances. The more kinds of words a person has at his disposal, the better equipped he is to adapt to different situations that call for language. From the earliest stages of language acquisition, children understand this. The teacher's task, then, is not so much to promote a natural human interest in words as to exploit it fully in the classroom.

Words imply meaning and meaning is the core of language. But meaning does not reside in definitions. Rather, meanings are formulated in the minds of individuals in response to particular words and the associations they arouse. In the process of understanding, one creates his own semantic context from what he knows and feels; it is within this largely personal framework that he interprets the meaning of any piece of language.

For example, the famous linguist Noam Chomsky made up the following sentence, which was supposed to be meaningless although syntactically correct:

Colorless green ideas sleep furiously.

But is this sentence meaningless? Only when looked at in a strictly logical way. The sentence contains a contradiction (*colorless* contradicts *green*); it assigns sensory properties to an abstraction (an idea cannot be colored or uncolored); and it uses a modifier incongruously (sleep cannot be done furiously).

But no sooner is one told that a sentence is semantically impossible than he begins to find an acceptable meaning for it. This is because the word-conscious individual is not to be stopped by apparent contradictions of meanings or the constraints of ordinary usage. "Colorless green ideas" could very well describe the sense of a peculiar dream, and the fact that they "sleep furiously" follows quite sensibly from this beginning. The phrase expresses the restless, urgent experience of sleep when one is dreaming in a vivid, puzzling way. The sentence might be considered impressionistic or poetic, but it is no less meaningful for that. The mind is not always so responsive to new words or word combinations, however. If the reader has no context for it, it will not fit into his universe of thought. Then planned learning must take place.

Can Adolescents Develop a Philosophy of Wordthinking?

The extent of a student's interest in expanding his vocabulary will depend upon his need for new words, and this in turn depends upon the opportunity he has to express himself for various purposes. By the time of adolescence, thinking and language have become closely associated. The individual has developed what the Russian psychologist Vygotsky called "verbal thought" and "rational speech." Because words represent concepts, they provide a means for thought, a fact an adolescent can appreciate if he is not afraid of making mistakes or differentiating himself unfavorably in the eyes of an important peer group.

As the example at the beginning of this chapter illustrates, it is important to differentiate between using language to identify with groups and using it to individualize thought. By learning to adapt language to different situations, students increase their need for a flexible vocabulary and wide range of word concepts. This need will motivate them to pick up vocabulary items as the opportunity arises. Through vocabulary expansion, the language acquisition process goes on through life.

What Is the Relationship Between Reading and Vocabulary Development?

Obviously this relationship is very close, because, by the time a student reaches middle school, print is his primary source of new words. In fact, at this point written language begins to be clearly differentiated from spoken language by its use of a more varied and increasingly sophisticated vocabulary. But while the study of classroom subjects provides a principal source of new words, reading cannot always be subordinated to this purpose. In the reading of connected discourse, there are times when an unknown word disrupts the process of constructing meaning. Then the student should be encouraged to deal with it in context rather than as an object of learning in itself. The relationship between words and the larger discourse of which they are a part continually poses the question, which is the end and which the means?

There are two ways of looking at the relationship between reading and vocabulary development:

1. Reading can be used as a means for acquiring new words in the formation of an increasingly versatile and precise vocabulary.
2. Knowledge of words and how they function in context can be used to derive meaning from connected discourse without undue interruption.

While these two goals can be differentiated, they are complementary and mutually reinforcing. The distinction is useful, however, because it helps to point out that two sets of strategies are involved and that readers are constantly switching between the two.

READING AS A MEANS OF ACQUIRING NEW WORDS

One can say that there are two essential kinds of vocabulary to be learned in content reading:

1. Word concepts that are presented as an essential part of the lesson content, sometimes identified as technical words.

2. A less-specialized assortment of words that are not common in the reader's speaking vocabulary.

There are well over a million words in English of which nearly half belong to special fields. This means that there are a lot of special concepts to be learned in content areas and a lot of distinctions to be made among near synonyms.

An important characteristic of special terms is that they usually have fairly reliable definitions and specific applications. Other words, however, depend more on particular contexts. While technical terms and basic concepts can often be grasped from a formal definition and examples of application, other words must be noted in a variety of contexts before the learner begins to develop some confidence in using them.

To appreciate the burden that nonspecialized but unfamiliar words can place on reading, consider the following paragraph from a short story anthologized in a secondary literature text:

> When they asked Boaz why he had not told what he knew as to the identity of that <u>fugitive</u> in the night, he seemed to find it hard to say exactly. How could a man of no education define for them his own but half-defined <u>misgivings</u> about the Law, his sense of <u>oppression</u>, constraint, and <u>awe</u>, of being on the defensive, even, in an <u>abject</u> way, his <u>skepticism?</u> About his wanting, come what might, to "keep clear of the Law"?[1]

If a young reader tried to look up every underlined word in this passage, his sense of the meaning would probably be destroyed. And yet the context is really too slight to provide clues for all the meanings juxtaposed here. An entire story written at this level would tax the resources of even a sophisticated reader. Teachers should be alert to the relationship between context clues and conceptual load and realize that some inexperienced readers may not be able to handle passage in which the supporting context is not ample and strong.

Using Context Analysis

In most prose, however, there is a reasonable balance between unusual vocabulary items and supporting context. Therefore, context analysis is a very basic activity in reading. Indeed, one may say that reading connected discourse is an exercise in context analysis.

Contexts provide various kinds of information, and most of the time this is confined to one particular meaning or use of a term. Therefore, context cues are mainly helpful for maintaining the flow of meaning so that reading

---

[1] From Wilbur Daniel Steele, "Footfalls," in *Exploring Life through Literature* (Chicago: Scott, Foresman, 1964), p. 30.

can be a continuous process. Building up word meanings through context is a gradual inductive process that occurs over a long time.

Because of its importance in the reading process, context analysis should be taught. Among the various ways that context can reveal meaning are these:

1. Actual definition given right after a new word is introduced:

Students of language have long been interested in *aphasia*, a total or partial loss of the ability to use or understand language. Since this condition is usually caused by physical injury to the brain, it gives indirect evidence of how the brain processes language.

2. Example of how a concept is applied:

There was good reason to call him a *compulsive* person. He possessed seven suits, one for each day of the week, which he always wore in proper sequence. He always washed his hands before starting any new activity, even if it was merely changing from one batch of paperwork to another. In the evening, before beginning his invariable meal of meat, salad, potato, roll and sherbet, he never failed to polish his silverware with his napkin.

3. Synonym or restatement in other words:

She had developed a fondness for *abstract* thoughts, a love of ideas rather than things. This tendency often made her seem out of touch with the real world.

4. Additional information that allows inference (sometimes difficult to distinguish from examples):

The *neurasthenic* individual will eventually wear out the patience of family and friends because of his excessive, unrelenting negativism. His chronic fatigue, hopelessness, and search for physical ailments make him seem listless, morbid, and self-centered. This method of dealing with unresolved conflicts is unproductive and makes the individual's problems progressively worse.

5. Extended discussion of a concept, often with the intent of establishing a particular meaning for it. This might be given in combination with formal definition.

In 1965, in an article in *Horizon*, I coined the term "future shock" to describe the shattering stress and disorientation that we induce in individuals by subjecting them to too much change in too short a time. Fascinated by this concept, I spent the next five years visiting scores of universities, research centers, laboratories, and government agencies, reading countless articles and scientific papers and interviewing literally hundreds of experts on different aspects of change, coping behavior and the future. . . . I came away from this experience with two disturbing convictions:

First it became clear that future shock is no longer a distantly potential danger, but a real sickness from which increasingly large numbers already suffer.

This psycho-biological condition can be described in medical and psychiatric terms. It is the disease of change.

Second, I gradually came to be appalled by how little is actually known about adaptivity, either by those who call for and create vast changes in our society, or by those who supposedly prepare us to cope with those changes.[2]

By various means, teachers can help students become aware of how context works in disclosing meanings. Their own texts can be analyzed for these various ways of presenting meanings contextually, and the need to infer connections can be brought to the student's attention. Students themselves can find concepts presented in different ways. For example, an assignment might ask a student to find a word that is formally defined in the text, one that is defined by example or additional information, and one that is defined by restatement. As a writing assignment, a student can extend a formal definition into a discussion, gaining contextual awareness through the design of a context. These suggestions are directed not only to the English teacher but to all subject teachers who must help students understand and use the language of their texts.

Applications

What context clues are available for determining the meanings of these terms?[3]

1. Static, adapt

Governments are not static, unchanging things. They are constantly undergoing change to fit new social and economic conditions. Because governments are made of up human beings they too are alive, and like all living things governments must grow and adapt to change. Any living organism that is unable to adapt itself to changes in its environment cannot survive, and so it is with political systems.[3]

2. Evolution, evolutionary change, evolve

Sometimes change occurs slowly, gradually, through evolution. The readings have demonstrated some ways in which governments and laws can evolve over many years. Old kinds die and their younger, often more ambitious successors institute new ideas. Weak leaders are succeeded by strong ones like the Greek Solon who set Athenian government on a different course. In other examples, weak or corrupt kings are confronted by their subjects and forced

[2] From Alvin Toffler, *Future Shock* (New York: Random House, 1970).

[3] Examples 1–3 are from David Weitzman and Richard E. Gross, *The Human Experience*, World Cultural Series (Boston: Houghton Mifflin, 1974). Example 4 is from William Fiedler, ed., *Inquiring About Technology: Studies in Economics and Technology*, Holt Databank System (New York: Holt, Rinehart and Winston, 1972). Example 5 is from Stanley Wolfe et al., *Concepts and Challenges in Science*, Vol. 1 (Fairfield, N.J.: CEBCO PFLAUM, Standard Publishing, 1975).

to make changes. The barons' revolt did not create Parliament, but it did take a big step in setting down rules for an advisory body to the king. From this a parliamentary form of government evolved.

3. Revolution

But sometimes political change occurs swiftly, like a great wind suddenly sweeping away one form of government and replacing it with another. At times like these, when people are impatient for change or some disaster forces the change to happen, a new government comes about through revolution. Revolution is characterized by quick, complete, and total change.

4. Technology

Watt's invention was based on Newcomen's steam engine. It also built on earlier inventions and discoveries that made up man's technology. Watt's knowledge of tools and machines driven by human, animal, water, and wind power helped him when he invented his steam engine.

5. Suspension, particles

Fill a graduated cylinder with water. Add some sand, some clay, and some copper sulfate to the water. Shake the cylinder so that everything mixes together. A cloudy mixture forms. This is a suspension. Allow the suspension to stand. After several minutes, the sand settles to the bottom. By the next morning, the clay has settled to the bottom. The particles of sand are much larger and heavier than the particles of clay. The heavier particles of sand settle faster than the lighter particles of clay. The copper sulfate does not settle at all. It is dissolved in the water.

Inference in Context Analysis

Deriving meaning for words from context is really practice in inference. Inference entails understanding what is implied as well as what is stated. When a reader infers information beyond what is given, he is drawing conclusions of his own. Certain features of inference can be brought to a student's attention. Consider the following passage and how you might infer the meanings of the underlined words.

Formal attempts to impose one dialect as standard on all the speakers of a language are usually <u>superfluous,</u> because the conditions that make it desirable—closer communication and greater economic and political interdependence, are already at work in informal ways to bring about a kind of standardization. As speakers of different dialects are thrown together, they absorb more and more from one another where doing so enriches their communication and discard more and more of their <u>idiosyncrasies</u> where doing the opposite would interfere with it.

Yet for various reasons and in numerous places people have felt that attaining a standard by unpremeditated accommodation would be too slow a process, and reformers and would-be reformers, official and unofficial, have stepped in. The impulse may come from a <u>burgeoning</u> nationalism that seeks identity in a common language, or from a centralization of government with the rising need to communicate with all citizens quickly and efficiently, or from a technological or commercial interdependence that must no longer be hobbled by a division of tongues.[4]

What cues are available from context for understanding each of these words, and how do these cues call for inference on the part of the reader?

Superfluous

We are told that certain conditions already exist from which we infer that certain other measures are unnecessary. We are also shown ways in which dialect standardization comes about, from which we infer this is done naturally, so there is no need to make formal efforts. From this inferred information we can say that superfluous means "unnecessary" in this passage.

Idiosyncrasies

We are told that these are what get discarded as people begin to communicate across dialect groups. From this we can infer that idiosyncrasies make dialects unintelligible to nonspeakers. We are also told that not discarding them would make communication difficult, which confirms the above inference. From this inferred information, we can say that idiosyncrasies in this passage means expressions that only speakers of a particular dialect can understand. (Note that this is not a general definition of the word, just an interpretation of its meaning in this context.)

Unpremeditated

The transition word at the beginning of this paragraph, yet, tells us that there is a relationship of contrast. Therefore, we can infer that the phrase "unpremeditated accommodation" refers back to the process described in the preceding paragraph. If this is so, the process defines the phrase. We can infer that unpremeditated in this context means "natural" or "informal." Again, this is not a general definition of the term, but one that works in this particular context.

Burgeoning

Unlike the other words discussed so far, this one has no specific restatement in the passage, so that inference here is more dependent on logic than on gathering clues from other things said. The person might ask himself the question, What kind of nationalism would seek identity in a common language? If he understands that here nationalism means seeking identity with one's nation instead of a smaller unit such as community or family, then he might conclude that the more nationalism there is, the more need there is for a common language. So burgeoning can be inferred to mean "increasing."

Hobbled

From the context, we learn that a division of tongues should not be allowed to hobble interdependence. Since this is offered as something to avoid, one can ask what shouldn't be done to people's need for each other, and the

---

[4] From Dwight Bolinger, *Aspects of Language* (New York: Harcourt Brace Jovanovich, 1968), p. 282.

answer might then be that unnecessary difficulties should not be attached to it. Thus, the inferred meaning of the word <u>hobbled</u> here is "handicapped" or "made difficult."

Inference is useful for working out what a word means in a particular context. The student may not yet have a full understanding of the term or be ready to generalize it to other contexts or use it himself. But he has used his own thinking to work out the meaning of the term in a particular instance, and this is more useful to him than simply looking it up in a dictionary.

This kind of practice could be carried on through a combination of writing and discussion. Students might be given a passage with certain words underlined and sheets of paper with places to write in definitions that they can infer from the context. Then in group discussion, students can compare the reasoning by which they arrived at their definitions. Again, this is practice that can be geared to the student's level of reading ability. A logical follow-up for this kind of practice would be for the teacher to present other contexts that cast the word in a slightly different light, extending its application while the common denominator of meaning is inferred. After the teacher has provided a model for amplifying the meaning of a word, individual students could volunteer to write similar passages for other words. The following illustrates the essential ingredients of a lesson in word analysis.

Word Analysis

A valuable supplement to context analysis is the ability to recognize the meanings of word parts. Word analysis, which enables the reader to identify the components of a complex word, is especially useful for speakers of English. English is distinguished by having an exceptionally large number of words derived from other languages, notably Greek, Latin, and French, itself a derivative from Latin. Consequently, complex words tend to be qualitatively different from simple, very common words. This heritage also gives the English language an interesting etymological history that can reveal relationships among words that one might never guess from their modern representations.

An interesting feature of any language is its adaptability to change as knowledge grows. To accommodate such growth, existing elements are put together to form logical compounds, a practice common in today's world of rapid technological change. Despite reservations by some traditionalists, this is a legitimate activity for anyone, provided that three conditions are met: The compound must be (a) logical, (b) understandable, and (c) necessary in that no other word already exists to express the concept. One might even say that this is the learned community's version of slang—coined expressions to communicate understandings shared within a specific group.

Worksheet

Passage

The fundamental causes of poverty are numerous, complex, and inter-related. Perhaps the most important of all is lack of a good education. It has been said that "Ignorance is the handmaiden of poverty." With-out education, one cannot easily overcome race and sex discrimination or escape from a low economic level.*

What definition for <u>interrelated</u> can you infer?

_____

_____

_____

Following discussion of this exercise, additional contexts could help to confirm and extend the meaning of interrelate:

1. The <u>interrelationship</u> between man and his environment is a basic fact of human existence. No matter how intelligent man becomes, or how technologically able, he still needs to get energy from the sun, food from the earth, and oxygen from the air. At the same time, his actions affect the environment and make it more or less productive for his needs.

2. My interests and yours are <u>interrelated</u>. You need something from me, and I need something from you. Therefore, if something happens to me, you also will lose, and vice versa. In view of this obvious <u>inter-relationship</u>, let's stop wasting time and energy on foolish competitions.

* Adapted from William E. Dunwiddie, *Problems of Democracy* (Lexington, Mass.: Ginn & Co., 1970), pp. 344–345.

The main difference is that technical terms coined in this way represent con-cepts important to the world at large and are more easily accepted into the general community. Hence, they are viewed as "legitimate."

Word analysis and its companion activity, word coining, are powerful tools for increasing word consciousness and developing an independent approach to unfamiliar terms. While this general strategy has limitations, it creates an awareness of the nature of words that is important for long-range vocabulary development.

It should be understood that word analysis is more like translation than definition. Most teachers at some time, for example, have been informed that the "meaning" of the word *education* is "a leading out from" or some similar translation from its Latin elements. This is not a definition of the word as it is used now but an analysis of its parts that leads to some sense of its logic. Word analysis should not be confused with finding a word's meaning, but it is a useful technique in combination with the use of context clues.

Nevertheless, word analysis can be a valuable strategy, especially for ongoing vocabulary development. Students can learn that the "fancy, two-dollar" words that writers are so fond of using are really just combinations of shorter words. To teach word analysis, the teacher needs a comprehensive list of word elements, and one has been provided in the appendix of this chapter. Here word elements are classified into seven major categories of meaning, or semantic categories. These categories reflect some of the basic areas of human knowledge. Hence, they bear some relationship to the content fields. A brief summary of this classification is given here.

I. *Human and Human Experience:* This is by far the largest category of all, because we humans are mainly interested in ourselves. Also, human experience is so varied and complex that we need a lot of words for it. This major category has been divided into eight subcategories:

A. *Humankind:* These are elements for different kinds of people: men, women, and mankind. Examples are *gyn,* the Greek element meaning "woman," and *homi,* the Latin element meaning "man."

B. *Human relationships and organization:* These word elements refer to people in groups and their social or political structures. They include *gam,* the Greek element meaning "marriage," *ped* the Greek element meaning "child," and *urb,* the Latin element meaning "city."

C. *Thinking and communication:* These very important human activities are reflected in many word elements. We humans have long been concerned with our thought processes and the way we express ourselves. Some examples are *gnos,* the Greek element meaning "to know," *loc,* the Latin element meaning "to speak," and *psych,* Greek for "mind" or "soul."

D. *Values and emotions:* These elements help people express how they feel about things. Love and hate, fear and attraction—these are important human experiences and therefore a significant part of language. Examples include *bene* and *mal,* Latin terms for "good" and "bad," *pseudo,* the Greek element for "false," and *sanct,* Latin for "holy."

E. *Parts of the body:* Classical names for the parts of the human body have become embedded in our language in many ways. Examples are *brach,* Latin for "arm," *dactyl,* Greek for "finger," *hem,* Latin and Greek for "blood," and *som,* Greek for "body."

F. *Physical and sensory experience:* This category of elements is closely related to the last but involves bodily sensations: pain, fatigue, pleasure, and of course the impressions of the five senses. Examples include the Greek element *alg,* meaning "pain," the Latin element *lum,* meaning "light," and Latin *tang* for "touch."

G. *Actions:* Much of what we say is about what we do, and there are many common elements in the category of human actions. Some of these are *cap*, a Latin root meaning "make," *mis*, a Latin root meaning "send," and *tax* or *tact*, Greek for "arrange."

H. *Objects of human manufacture:* The artifacts we create are the materials of our culture and an important part of experience and language. Examples include *eco*, Latin for "house" or "habitat," *lib(r)*, Latin for "book," and *tech*, Greek for "craft."

II. *Animal life and animal characteristics:* This is also an important major category, especially in the life sciences. Included are names of animals, such as the Greek *echin* for "hedgehog"; the names of animal body parts (when these are not also human body parts), such as Latin *caud* for "tail"; and other characteristics, such as Latin *respiro*, indicating "breath."

III. *Plant life and plant characteristics:* This group is a complement to the last and also important in the life sciences. Examples are *agr(i)*, a Latin element meaning "field," *phyl*, Greek for "leaf," and *pom*, Latin for "fruit."

IV. *Other natural phenomena:* After people, animals, and plants, there are still a few things to account for in nature, such as minerals, climate, and the universe. These elements are included in this category and include *glac*, Latin for "ice," *lun*, Latin for "moon," and *potum*, Greek for "river."

V. *Colors:* Many elements describing attributes are derived from terms for various colors. Some fairly common ones are *alb*, Latin for "white," and *chlor*, Greek for "green."

VI. *Numbers, quantity, measurement, and comparison:* These elements help people talk about concepts of amount and measurement. They are common in most fields and form an important part of everyday speech. Examples include *equi*, the Latin term for "equal," *micr*, the Greek element for "small," and *poly*, Latin for "many."

VII. *Time and space concepts (including form):* This category includes many relationship terms in English, including prepositional expression. Place relationships alone form a fairly large subcategory. Examples from these two subcategories include Greek *chron*, meaning "time," Latin *contra*, for "against," and Latin *ipsi*, for "the same side."

THE MOST COMMON ROOTS

While the number of borrowed roots in our language is seemingly endless, certain roots are particularly common and will be encountered again and again. Many short lists of common word elements are available. One especially useful list identifies fourteen "master words" (Table 7–1), which contain prefix and stem elements found in more than 14,000 relatively common words, or in an estimated 100,000 common and special terms.

These roots, as mentioned earlier, appear in a variety of forms. Therefore, they might not be immediately recognizable. Some of the variations are illustrated in the following groups of words derived from the common roots:

TABLE 7-1
Master Words[a]

WORDS	PREFIX	COMMON MEANING	ROOT	COMMON MEANING
1. precept	pre-	(before)	capare	(take, seize)
2. detain	de-	(away, from)	tenere	(have, hold)
3. intermittent	inter-	(between)	mittere	(send)
4. offer	ob-	(against)	ferre	(bear, carry)
5. insist	in-	(into)	stare	(stand)
6. monograph	mono-	(alone, one)	graphein	(write)
7. epilogue	epi-	(upon)	legain	(say, study of)
8. aspect	ad-	(to, towards)	specere	(see)
9. uncomplicated	un-	(not)	plicare	(fold)
	com-	(together with)		
10. nonextended	non-	(not)	tendere	(stretch)
	ex-	(out of)		
11. reproduction	re-	(back, again)	ducere	(lead)
	pro-	(forward)		
12. indisposed	in-	(not)	ponere	(put, place)
	dis-	(apart, from)		
13. oversufficient	over-	(above)	facere	(make, do)
	sub-	(under)		
14. mistranscribe	mis-	(wrong)	scribere	(write)
	trans-	(across, beyond)		

[a] From James I. Brown, *Programmed Vocabulary*. Chicago: Lyons and Carnahan, 1965, pp. 3–4.

1. *capare* (take, seize)
   capable, capacity, capacious, caption, captive, capture, accept, anticipate, conceive, except, inception, occupy, perceive, precept, receive, susceptible.
2. *tenere* (have, hold)
   tenable, tenacious, tenant, tenet, tennis, tenor, tenure, abstain, contain, detain, entertain, continue.
3. *mittere* (send)
   mass, mess, message, missile, mission, missive, admit, commit, compromise, dismiss, emit, omit, permit, submit, premise, promise, surmise.
4. *ferre* (bear, carry)
   fertile, confer, defer, infer, prefer, refer, suffer, differ, vociferate, metaphor, periphery, euphoria.
5. *stare* (stand)
   stage, stance, stanza, status, arrest, circumstance, constant, constitute, contrast, distant, extant, instant, institute, obstacle, obstetric, substance, superstition.

6. *graphein* (write)
   graffiti, grammar, graph, diagram, epigram, paragraph, program, topography.
7. *legain* (say, study, collect)
   lecture, legend, legible, legion, collect, diligent, elect, elegant, intelligent, neglect, prelect, sacrilege, lexicon, catalogue, dialogue.
8. *specere* (see)
   specimen, specious, spectacle, spectrum, speculate, speculum, aspect, auspices, prospect, suspect, circumspect, conspicuous, despise, expect, perspective, respite.
9. *plicare* (fold)
   plait, pliant, ply, apply, complicate, deploy, display, employ, explicate, implicate, replicate, supplicate.
10. *tendere* (stretch)
    tend, tender, tendon, tense, tent, attend, extend, ostensible, pretend.
11. *ducere* (lead)
    dock, duchess, duke, duct, ductile, abduce, adduce, conduct, introduce, redoubt, subdue, educate.
12. *ponere* (put, place)
    apposition, composite, composition, compound, deposit, depose, position, positive, post, posture, preposition.
13. *facere* (make, do)
    fact, faction, fashion, feasible, fetish, affair, affect, amplify, artifact, beneficience, counterfeit, defeat, defect, edifice, facsimile, forfeit, infect, justify, manufacture, proficience, sacrifice, suffice, profit.
14. *scribere* (write)
    scribble, scribe, script, ascribe, circumscribe, conscript, manuscript, prescribe, subscribe, transcribe.

Word analysis skills combined with context clues can enable a student to handle an unknown word without interrupting the flow of meaning as he reads. Knowledge of word components can give enough insight into a word to make contextual clues helpful. Thus a "precarious situation" can be interpreted as one calling for prayer, hence, uncertain. Or a monkey's "prehensile tail" can be understood as a tail useful for holding onto limbs. A "contingent circumstance" is seen to be a circumstance touching something else and therefore a condition to be taken into account.

Definition

Besides context clues and word analysis, a third common way of dealing with unfamiliar terms is definition. As was pointed out earlier, some words lend themselves better to formal definition than others because they are linked to fairly precise concepts. Other words require a more equal interplay between definition and use in various contexts. A third class of words can also be distinguished. These are words that are familiar to most readers but cannot be usefully defined at all, except in particular contexts, because they are used in so many ways. Examples of these are *freedom, justice,* and *patriotic.* They have to be defined virtually every time they are encountered by careful attention to the way the writer is using them. It is their function to express personal values, not objectified concepts.

This discussion suggests that it is useful to think of words on a continuum of formal definability, as in Table 7–2. (Only nouns are given as examples, but the principle extends to verbs and modifiers as well.)

Considering words in this dimension suggests that a variety of approaches must be taken to the task of helping students develop an active vocabulary from content reading. Words that are highly definable can be taught as formal concepts. But as words tend to fall at the middle of the continuum, they must be placed in a variety of contexts, including contexts constructed by the student himself, and in most instances he will require a number of exposures and opportunities for practice before he develops confidence in his grasp of the word. Words that fall towards the low-definability end of the continuum merit special attention because they are potentially confusing. Both in reading and in writing, the student should be aware of the importance of adequate explanation and clear context when these terms are used.

Application

Using the categories of definability given above, place each of the following terms in an appropriate category. Ask yourself this question: To what extent does the term rely on a particular context in addition to a formal definition?

1.____foot   11.____datum
2.____ooze   12.____par excellence
3.____calque   13.____tiffany
4.____northland   14.____paresis
5.____verity   15.____concurrent
6.____efface   16.____transistor
7.____stalemate   17.____thryrotropin
8.____foresight   18.____withershins
9.____democratic   19.____exacerbate
10.____zinc   20.____liberty

There are no absolute designations for these, so be prepared to explain the reasons for your choice in class discussion. Also, as a hint, if you had to look up a word and still weren't sure of its meaning or how it is used, this is a good indication of the importance of context for that word.

TABLE 7-2
Continuum of Formal Word Definability

DEGREE OF FORMAL DEFINABILITY	EXAMPLE
High formal definability: words that are linked to single, precise concepts. Within a subject area, an effort is made to maintain a specific conceptual reference. The words constitute the special vocabularies of specific subject fields.	phoneme, biosphere, onomatopoeia, leucocyte, parallelopiped, syllogism
Moderately high formal definability: words that are linked to established concepts but in usage have become generalized so that alternate meanings are possible, although much specificity remains.	ecology, grammar, environment, analogy, hallucination, perception
Moderate formal definability: words that have become generalized through application to a variety of contexts so that, while formal definition is helpful, it must always be considered in relation to specific usage. Most abstract, nontechnical words fall into this category.	compensation, immanence, exigency, insight, concept, corollary, probity
Low formal definability: words that are commonly used and readily recognized but have developed so many alternate meanings through widespread usage that context is far more useful than formal definition for determining meaning.	economy, discrimination, society, experiment, objectivity, significance, operation
Nil formal definability: greatly used words that always serve the particular purpose of a user or represent one of several sets of values. At this extreme, it can be said that no word has the same meaning twice and cannot be meaningfully considered apart from a particular context.	love, freedom, authority, patriotism, courage, happiness, disloyalty

ANALYZING A TEXT
AND PRETEACHING
DEFINABLE CONCEPTS

Most textbooks provide a vocabulary learning section in each chapter or lesson. Also, a text may feature a glossary, which provides an overview of definable concepts. In addition to these aids, the teacher should go through a reading assignment to find additional terms which have not been covered in the vocabulary or which seem to assume knowledge from some other part of the book. All words gathered in this analysis should be listed for the students and pretaught, so the student has a grasp of the words' meaning and pronunciation when he encounters them in the text. Sometimes pronunciation is very important to a student. It is difficult to grasp a new word as a piece of language unless one can confidently assign a pronunciation to it.

The general pattern for presenting a highly definable word concept is to give a formal definition and several (at least three) examples of how the concept is used or applied. Even for words of high definability, the concept will have to be learned over a period of time. The definition is simply a starting point. A presentation of the term *photosynthesis,* then, might look like this:

Word concept: photo-synthesis

Word analysis: putting together with light energy

Formal definition: a process in green plants by which light energy (from the sun) is used to convert water, carbon dioxide, and minerals into oxygen and organic compounds, especially carbohydrates. Through photosynthesis, plants make the energy of the sun available to animals, including man.

Examples or applications

1. Growth, repair, and reproduction are functions of life that could not go on without the chemical energy stored in green plants.
2. By examining the food chain, we can see how all forms of nourishment used by man began as sunlight absorbed in the chlorophyll of green plants.
3. At an earlier time in the earth's history, there was an abundance of carbon dioxide. This increased the amount of photosynthesis and produced an abundance of green plants, which were eventually converted into the fossil fuels we depend upon now for energy.

From this beginning, students can be encouraged to add their own examples of how photosynthesis works in their lives. These can be as simple as the observation of a growing houseplant, the realization that cows eat our grass for us, or a grasp of the dynamics of a terrarium. Or they can be as complex as an understanding of how algae affect the oxygen supply of a lake and therefore its whole ecology. As students use their definition of a concept to collect examples of how the concept applies, they will be learning the definition at increasingly deeper levels of understanding. For words that define basic concepts in a content area, a record-keeping system that enables a student to work on his own definition by expanding his application of the term can be very helpful. The teacher can provide prepared sheets or large note cards on which students enter the information in prescribed form as it is presented in class, with space for additional notes later:

Word concept _____

Formal definition _____

_____

_____

_____

Examples and application _____

_____

_____

_____

Students can keep their reference notebooks or card files throughout the year and should be encouraged to add new information or examples of uses at any time.

The formal definition, however, might not alone convey much real understanding without the accompanying examples. Consider how much this definition of the technical term *morpheme* is aided by the examples that follow it:

1. Some morphemes function as words: most prepositions and articles are single morphemes—of, at, by, in, out, down, up.
2. Some morphemes function as parts of words. These are called *bound* if they function only as parts of words and *free* if they can also function alone:

   Words composed of two free morphemes:
       in/to   text/book
       can/not   class/room
   Words composed of one bound and one free morpheme:
       un/lock (bound + free)
       judg/ment (free + bound)
   Words composed of two bound morphemes:
       morph/eme   con/cept

To make an application to this chapter, morphemes are what were called "word elements" in the discussion of word analysis. They are the prefixes, roots, and suffixes of complex words.

Letting Students Identify Words
That Give Difficulty

While the teacher can identify major concepts that should be taught as part of content instruction, it is not always eays to know what other terms might be giving students trouble. A college student will often take for granted vocabulary items that are quite unfamiliar to young readers. One beginning teacher we know antagonized an entire class of high school juniors by expecting them to know the word "ambiguous." Another young man found that some high school students couldn't deal with the word "relationship." To avoid such lapses of communication, you might have a small team of students, probably no more than three at a time, go through a text assignment in advance to pick out words they don't understand. This will provide some insight into how the text appears to the class and enable the teacher to smooth out some potential wrinkles in advance. The role of team members should be circulated among all students in the class, and each new team should have at least one member with relatively low reading ability.

DICTIONARIES
AND ENCYCLOPEDIAS

A discussion of definition as a device for word and concept development would not be complete without some mention of the use of dictionaries and encyclopedias. Because these are the source books most readily available to students for independent use, teachers might spend some time discussing these as supplements to the classroom texts. A very useful exercise is comparing definitions. In addition to his own presentation and the definition of a term given in the text, a teacher can duplicate definitions found in a standard dictionary and an adult-level encyclopedia, for example, the *Micropaedia* section of *Encyclopaedia Britannica III*. The differences among the four sources of definition will probably be as follows:

1. *Teacher's presentation*:   This should be strong on application of the concept in ways most meaningful to the student. The teacher has the advantage of being able to go on explaining and applying a concept for as long as students seem to need it.

2. *Textbook definition*:   This will be written at a level intended for student consumption and integrated into an explanatory context. By the time a student encounters a word concept in reading, hopefully, he will be familiar enough with it to use it as an aid in understanding the context as well as vice versa.

3. *Dictionary definition*:   This is the source the student shares with the world at large, and it may seem cryptic in comparison with the more fully developed and contextually rich explanations given in class. However,

the dictionary does give the advantage of multiple word uses and information on word analysis. A useful exercise for students would be to look up a term in the dictionary after they have learned it through class discussion and reading to see what new perspective on the word the dictionary can provide.

4. *Encyclopedia*: Besides giving a more complete discussion of a word concept than a dictionary, the encyclopedia will usually break it down into subtopics that also define its range of application and significance. For example, the *Micropaedia* discussion of *photosynthesis* in *Britannica III* provides forty subtopics with references to other parts of the encyclopedia, including such items as agricultural needs and adjustments, aquatic ecosystem productivity factors, chlorophyll types and properties, and life cycles of plants.

This comparative technique, which can be done by students themselves as well as by the teacher, will help to develop an understanding of how these standard reference works are useful aids in specific content fields.

Application

Select a special term from your content area and prepare a presentation of the concept which includes a formal definition and at least three examples. Then look up the term in a textbook, a dictionary, and an encyclopedia and compare those three treatments of the term with your own.

A STRATEGY FOR DEALING WITH NEW WORDS

To summarize what has been said in this chapter so far, the following strategy for dealing with new words can be taught:

1. First, try to figure out the meaning of the word from the context. What clues, such as restatement, definition, examples, or applications, have been given?
2. If context alone does not give sufficient information, look at the parts of the word to see what clues are there. Word analysis along with context clues provides a powerful tool for understanding.
3. If the meaning of a word still is not clear, or if confirmation is sought, look up the word in a dictionary. Then look again at context and word parts. Relate the dictionary information to the way the word is used in the specific context.

4. Use these three techniques together. They are mutually reinforcing. To really understand and incorporate a word into one's vocabulary, one needs to understand its usage, its components, *and* its formal definition.

ACTIVE VOCABULARY DEVELOPMENT AS A FOUNDATION FOR READING

Now we will briefly turn the coin over to consider how a focus on vocabulary development per se can strengthen reading. It has been pointed out that a large number of words in English—some half million—are special terms, related to particular content fields. Each field has its own vocabulary. If students are to learn independently in any content area, they must have the basic vocabulary and an understanding of key word parts for that subject. The teacher should always keep in mind that his goals for students extend beyond their reading of particular materials. The teacher's long-range goal is to get students ready to read content materials on their own. Therefore, it is important for teachers in every subject area to provide some vocabulary development for its own sake.

Because word acquisition is a gradual process, it is better to spend a few minutes daily or at regular intervals on word awareness rather than try to accomplish a lot in a single unit. Many of the strategies already discussed would contribute to a consistent, year-long focus on building a word stock. These can become a regular part of instruction. Following are some further suggestions for brief activities that will help students develop their understanding of words.

1. *Individual card files for content-related concepts*:   Using a format similar to that presented earlier in this chapter, prepare cards for students to use to record and keep notes on new concepts. The information recorded should include (1) analysis of the term, (2) brief formal definition, and (3) examples of how the concept is applied. In addition, space for further examples should be provided. The same format can be adapted to notebook form if this is more convenient.

2. *Use the word-component list at the end of this chapter (or one developed specifically for your content area) for "word translations."*

Provide a list of unusual words in your subject field and have students "translate" them as shown below. Make sure that all needed elements are on the list you provide.

Science

brachiopod	arm-footed
multiramose	many-branched
platycephalous	flat-headed

Social science

matronym	name derived from the mother's family
pentarchy	rule by five
psychopathology	mental illness

Mathematics

orthotectic	making straight
epicycloid	circular form beside a circle
hemispheroid	half circular

English

polysemia	having many meanings
palindrome	running backwards
oxymoron	sharp and dull at the same time; opposite

Working in the other direction, provide students with a list of word elements and some descriptive phrases such as the following:

yellow-colored	xanthrochromatic
rock-inhabiting	saxicolous
causing redness	rubifacient
turning toward the sun	heliotropic
having three sides	trilateral
fear of bees	apiphobia

All of these have actual scientific terms, and students can compare their own constructions with the conventional terms. This might lead to discussion of the nature of language evolution and how language can be adapted to specific purposes. In this exercise, one is getting at the relationship between thought and language.

3. *Finding related words*: To help students develop a familiarity with words derived from Latin and Greek that commonly occur in print, the class can occasionally spend a few minutes finding words related through possession of a common root. Examples are the fourteen roots cited as "most common" earlier in this chapter, for which a number of derived terms are given. Using these and other examples, have students come up with examples of their own.

    a. The word *distract* contains an element derived from the Latin word *trahere*, meaning "to draw or pull." What other words can you think of that contain this element?

    b. The Latin word *intra* means "within." Can you think of at least three words that contain this element? What is the difference between *intra* and *inter*? Think of three words that contain the element *inter*.

    c. Two commonly used Greek elements are *hyper*, meaning above, and *hypo*, meaning beneath. What words can you think for each of these elements? What is the difference between a person who is hyperactive and one who is hypoactive? What other contrasts like this can you think of?

4. *Deriving definitions from context*:   Have the students read a prepared passage to derive a definition for a specified term, and then have them write the definition in their own words:

> What is the meaning of the term *ecosystems*?

> More complete accounts can be given of interactions within smaller and simpler ecosystems than for the entire ecosphere. There is a certain arbitrariness in delineating ecosystems within the larger ecosphere, but if the arbitrariness is kept in mind, extremely useful analyses can be made. One can ask questions about the overall behavior of such an ecosystem as a pond, a forest, an island, or a desert. One may set up artificial or model systems for their general interest or for their relevance to the problems of such *man-made* ecosystems as an isolated space capsule. In each system one can investigate the balance sheet of input and output of energy and material, the nature of the flow of energy and material through the system, and the effect of variation of one living component upon others.[5]

> Definition: _____

> _____

> _____

5. *Choosing synonyms*:   This is a common format for vocabulary development, but it is possible to build in some variations that give the lesson a new twist. For example, among the terms from which the student picks the synonym can be pairs of antonyms, so that in discussion the meanings of the selection words are also reinforced:

> An *exigent* matter is one that is (a) peripheral, (b) central, (c) urgent, (d) unimportant.

A challenging exercise can be provided if students are asked to pick the best of near synonyms:

> An *obsequious* person is one who is (a) fawning, (b) parasitic, (c) menial, (d) inferior.

Here the student is called upon to make distinctions among terms that could all be associated with the target word although they have varying degrees of actual overlap.

A third variation on the conventional synonym choice format might be to have students choose from among paraphrases rather than one-word replacements. This can make them aware of *descriptions* of word meanings and encourage self-made definitions:

> A *concomitant* event is one that (a) happens just after another event, (b)

---

[5] From Clifford Grobstein, *The Strategy of Life* (San Francisco: Freeman, 1964), p. 30.

happens at the same time as another event, (c) happens just before another event, (d) happens in place of another event.

6. *Finding the right word*:   This exercise will also encourage students to make distinctions, this time among words that are frequently confused. Have students find the incorrect word in specially constructed sentences, write the correct word above it, and then use the original word in a sentence that demonstrates its correct application:

The doctor administered an *anecdote* to the patient who had swallowed poison.

_____

_____

_____

_____

The speaker tried to *illicit* comments from the audience, but to no avail.

_____

_____

_____

_____

The neighborhood was unhappy because the woman allowed her dog to *illuminate* on other people's lawns.

_____

_____

_____

_____

7. *Analogies*:   This is a format common in standardized academic tests and so will provide useful practice for students who will eventually take SAT or similar placement examinations:

philologist : language :: _____ : _____.
(a) ornithologist : birds, (b) botanist : animals, (c) biologist : cells, (d) pediatrician : feet.
rectangle : oval :: _____ : _____.
(a) acre : rod, (b) cube : sphere, (c) square : circle, (d) hexagon : pentagon, (e) sphere : cube.
implicit : explicit :: _____ : _____.
(a) suggestion : recommendation, (b) state : hint, (c) innuendo : assertion, (d) allusion : insinuation, (e) indirect : devious.[6]

8. *Sentence completion*:   This is another format frequently encountered

---

[6] From *Graduate Record Examination: Preparation for Graduate Record Examination Aptitude Test*, rev. ed. (Chicago: Henry Regnery, 1973).

in standardized tests. In addition, this kind of practice provides considerable interaction with context and leads students to consider meanings of words in terms of each other.

> History tells us that Demosthenes made several long speeches warning the Greeks against Philip of Macedon. Since these _____ were strongly worded, personal in value, and full of abuse, a new word, _____, has passed over into our language. (a) speeches, demonstration, (b) invectives, geriatrics, (c) outbursts, genocide, (d) peaens, acrimonious, (e) declamations, philippics.
>
> As often happens with those who rule by emotion rather than by reason, their discussion soon retrogressed from _____ to _____.
> (a) argument, controversy, (b) consideration, rationalization, (c) disagreement, altercation, (d) dispute, disagreement, (e) squabbling, wrangling.[7]
>
>   (Taken from source cited above)

9. *Fitting actions to attributes*:   Ordinarily, people respond to words rather than try to define them or specify meanings in other ways. This exercise enables the student to demonstrate his understanding of words by choosing an appropriate response.

> If you were studying at the library and the person next to you became *loquacious*, what might you do?
> a. Ask him to move his books from your part of the table.
> b. Ask him to stop making noise.
> c. Ask him if there is anything you can do to help.
> d. Ask him to sit still.
>
> If someone asked you to give a *retrospective* account of an event, what would you do?
> a. Make up a story and tell it as if it were real.
> b. Describe something you observed at an earlier time.
> c. Predict something that is going to happen in the future.
> d. Give your own opinion while describing an event.
>
> If you were asked to draw an *epicycloid*, what would it most likely resemble?
> a. The sun
> b. The moon
> c. A rock
> d. A pear

10. *Relying on context alone*:   Sometimes it helps to have faith that the meaning of unfamiliar words will become clearer as one reads on. To help students realize that context alone might disclose meaning, provide passages that contain enough information about certain key words that students can infer the terms. One passage that develops the meaning of a single important concept can help the student to focus on meaning in con-

---

[7] From *Graduate Record Examination: Preparation for Graduate Record Examination Aptitude Test*, rev. ed. (Chicago: Henry Regnery, 1973).

text. A list of choices might be given with the passage if the teacher thinks this is necessary.

There is a constant flow of energy and materials into, through, and out of the _____. Nevertheless, the _____ persists as a whole, despite the continual turnover of the materials which compose it. At successive times the _____ may look the same, and it may contain the same numbers and kinds of organisms, cells, molecules, and atoms. But the individual components are not the same ones; some have moved out or have broken down, and others have moved in or have been newly formed. The materials and units are constantly undergoing turnover; the substance of the _____ is in constant flux. Components at each level are appearing and disappearing, but continuity of properties is preserved nonetheless. Like a candle flame, or a waterfall, the _____ endures desipte the change of its components.[8]

What word will fit into all these blanks?

    a. universe   d. solar system
    b. earth   e. biomass
    c. biosphere   f. ecosystem

Vocabulary Development through Writing

Another way of encouraging active use of words is, of course, writing, and students should be encouraged to use a wide variety of words in writing even at the risk of inelegance or incorrectness. Many persons with a well-developed writing style report a period in adolescence when they became outrageously "sesquipedalianistic," seeking the learned or esoteric phrase often at the expense of meaning. Teachers should view such tendencies as trial-and-error behavior, the best means for permanent learning. Like any other phase of learning, of course, it should be temporary, and students should be guided away from a fixation on words per se. Nevertheless, the student who is encouraged to try new words will be the one who eventually develops the most versatile vocabulary. The distance between a so-called recognition and an active vocabulary can be reduced by experimentation with words.

To encourage students with a bent for such experimentation, the classroom should contain a library of "word books," dictionaries, and other reference works that help in the search for new ways of saying things. Students should also be encouraged to own their own dictionaries. The publication of such books in paperback editions makes this a plausible suggestion. Below is a brief review of some of the most common word-finding books (other than dictionaries) issued in paperback.

Students may also wish to undertake vocabulary development on their

---

[8] From Clifford Grobstein, *The Strategy of Life* (San Francisco: Freeman, 1964), p. 53.

own, and, again, a number of paperback books are available for this purpose. Some of these are also listed. Finally, the classroom might stock some of the "special" dictionaries available, dictionaries that get at certain aspects of language such as strange words or slang, and these also are reviewed. Such books provide good resources for the teacher too. They contain many suggestions for brief vocabulary exercises that can be adapted to specific content material.

SUMMARY

Words represent concepts and so are a primary feature of language in most people's minds. Adolescents can be encouraged to extend their natural interest in words into a variety of areas and communication. They can learn how words increase their flexibility as speakers, writers, and thinkers. We call this "wordthinking."

This chapter examines the relationship between vocabulary development and reading in two ways. First, reading can be a way of acquiring new words in the development of an increasingly versatile and precise personal vocabulary. And second, knowledge of words can increase fluency and comprehension in reading. This chapter presents concrete illustrations of both ways of looking at words and many practical suggestions for teaching vocabulary development. Techniques discussed include making use of context cues, using word analysis, and using dictionaries. These three basic strategies are most effective when used together, but different words and contexts call for diffrent emphases. Words are more or less "definable" to the extent that they depend upon a larger context for full meaning. A scale of formal definability is given to help the teacher become more aware of this aspect of word comprehension.

Aids appended to the text include a review of paperback word books and a listing of special dictionaries. Also a guide to word elements, grouped into semantic categories, is given.

[Discussion questions were systematically interspersed in the text of this chapter and so none are provided here.]

Appendix A

Review of Word Books

*Paperback Aids for Finding Synonyms, Related Words,
Alternate Expressions*

Devlin, Joseph. *A Dictionary of Synonyms and Antonyms.* New York: Popular
Library, 1961.

A dictionary format is used. For each word entry, there is a list of synonyms
followed by a list of antonyms. Over 1,000 main entries are included. In addition, there is a section on word formation, which includes lists of Latin and
Greek prefixes and suffixes, and Greek, Latin, and Old English roots and
derivatives. Also there is a list of the 5,000 words most commonly mispronounced.

Dutch, Robert A., ed. *The Original Roget's Thesaurus of Words and Phrases.* New
York: Dell, 1962.

As described in the preface, this is "a collection of synonyms on a grand
scale." This edition is called original because it preserves Roget's original
system of classification, which groups words into six broad categories: abstract relations, space, material world, intellect, volition, and sentient and
moral powers. These are further subcategorized, and the entire classification
system is presented in a tabular synopsis that is itself twenty pages long.
Following the actual classification is an index of words in alphabetical order
with snyopses that are referenced to the main corpus of word categories.
Although some find this complex organization difficult to get used to, this is
the most comprehensive word reference book and is recommended over dictionary formats for persons seriously interested in finding words.

The Merriam-Webster Pocket Dictionary of Synonyms. New York: Pocket Books,
1972.

This book attempts to combine dictionary and thesaurus features. It discusses
a concept and gives synonyms. Each article begins with a list of related words
to be discriminated, the first word being the most general in application or
most central in meaning. Brief discussion of the area of meaning in which
the group is to be compared is followed by discussion and illustration of
each word in the list. Antonyms and cross-references to words that develop
particular meanings of a more general word are also given.

Moorehead, Albert H., ed. *Roget's College Thesaurus in Dictionary Form.* New
York: New American Library (Signet), 1962.

This book combines dictionary and thesaurus functions. That is, it uses a
dictionary format and defines by giving synonyms. Some antonyms and cross-
references are included in main entries. The introductory discussion by Laird
is discursive but interesting.

Pei, Mario, and Salvatore Romondino. *Dictionary of Foreign Terms.* New York:
Dell, Laurel Edition, 1974.

This book lists widely used and encountered terms and phrases from French,
Spanish, Italian, German, Latin, Greek, Russian, Sanskrit, Hebrew, Arabic,
and other languages. Information on meaning, history, and pronunciation of
the term is given. A pronunciation key is included.

Paperback Books on Vocabulary Improvement

Funk, Peter. *It Pays to Increase Your Word Power*. New York: Bantam Books, 1970.

As the title indicates, this book is based on the *Reader's Digest* feature. The author suggests that a chapter be covered each week with monthly review. Each chapter begins with a brief introductory statement, followed by a multiple-choice quiz on twenty words and a brief definition of each word and two examples of its use in sentences. Further practice exercises for using the words are provided. The chapters do not indicate a division by topics or types of words. The book contains fifteen chapters. A "refresher quiz" and index of all words presented are provided at the end.

Funk, Wilfred. *Six Weeks to Words of Power*. New York: Pocket Books, 1955.

This book is also divided into weekly lessons. The first two weeks concentrate on verbs, the second two weeks on nouns, and the last two weeks on modifiers. These parts of speech are subcategorized semantically, for example, "Verbs that Deal with Human Traits," "Verbs of Energy," "Nouns of Unusual Power," "Nouns of Shame and Shameful Acts," "Adjectives that Suggest Strength." Each chapter includes examples and definitions of the category of words that are being discussed, and exercises are given so that students have the opportunity to practice their use.

Funk, Wilfred, and Norman Lewis. *Thirty Days to a More Powerful Vocabulary*. Rev. ed. New York: Pocket Books, 1971.

This book outlines activities for fifteen minutes each day. Roughly, on each day the reader devotes himself to a particular category of words, e.g., "Words for Mature Minds," "Words for Human Traits," "Words That End in 'ology.' " Interspersed are quizzes and tests. Words are given in sentence contexts.

Nurnberg, Maxwell, and Morris Rosenblum. *How to Build a Better Vocabulary*. New York: Popular Library, 1961.

According to the authors, the format of this book attempts to build up a solid method for acquiring words (opposed to "hit-or-miss" word lists). The first part deals with word analysis and words in context. Part Two deals with words commonly misused or confused with other words. Included here are a section on pronunciation and spelling and a review of desk dictionaries. Part Three deals with slang, archaic words, foreign words, and words derived from names. Part Four features a section on preparing for vocabulary tests on academic and professional examinations, including eighty practice quizzes with answers and a list of 1,000 words likely to appear on such exams.

Pei, Mario. *The Families of Words*. New York: St. Martin's Press, 1962.

This is more of a scholar's book, which contains a very thorough treatment of word relationships. Word connections are traced back to their origins in Indo-European, the protolanguage from which Latin, Greek, and English were derived. Thus, this reference enables the reader to find relationships among elements of various languages that contribute to an estimated 600,000-word vocabulary in modern English.

Special Dictionaries and Wordbooks

Asimov, Isaac. *Words of Science and the History Behind Them.* Boston: Houghton Mifflin, 1959.

———. *More Words of Science,* Houghton Mifflin, 1972.

The first book explains the derivation and use of about 1,500 words in science from such simple terms as *oil, cell,* and *line* to unusual ones like *archeozoic* and *elasmobranchii.* Words are discussed in 250 page-long essays, one for each key concept, which include the history and etymology of the term, its present application, and its relationship to other words. The second book reflects the increase in scientific terms between 1959 and 1972 and the new significance that has become attached to some older terms such as *pollution.* Both books are completely indexed. Explanations are written in a readable, narrative style. Other word books by Asimov include *Words from the Myths, Words in Genesis, Words on the Map, Words from Exodus,* and *Words from History.*

Bernstein, Theodore. *The Reverse Dictionary.* New York: Quadrangle/New York Times, 1976.

This book claims to enable the reader to go from meanings to words. Actually, it is more a way of going from common language to esoteric words and phrases, and in this sense it is good for finding technical terms or little-used names. It can also help a person reduce a phrase to a word.

Examples: following in time: *subsequent.* Sound caused by the hitting of one body against another: *percussion.* Sound transmitting system used under water: *sonar.* There is also an index of target words so one can go from word to meaning.

Byrne, Josefa Heifetz. *Mrs. Byrne's Dictionary of Unusual, Obscure and Preposterous Words.* Secaucus, N.J.: University Books, Inc., 1974.

In the author's words, this book contains "6,000 of the weirdest words in the English Language." It also contains words with an "odd mixture of meanings." Only brief definitions are given; no information on background or etymologies is provided.

Examples: hunkerousness: opposition to progress, old-fogeyism. Bletonism: alleged ability to perceive an underground water supply. Savate: fighting with the feet.

Urdang, Laurance, ed. *The New York Times' Everyday Reader's Dictionary of Misunderstood, Misused, Mispronounced Words.* New York: Quadrangle/The New York Times, 1972.

The purpose of this book is to list very obscure words, for example, obsecrate, neoteric, nugatory, fuliginous, lestobiosis, oscitant, and reinfleur. These are words that are not likely to be found in small dictionaries, although most can be found in more comprehensive dictionaries. These are mainly words that might be encountered in print or high-level conversation.

Partridge, Eric, ed. *The Macmillan Dictionary of Historical Slang.* Abridged by Jacqueline Simpson. New York: Macmillan, 1974.

This is an abridgment of the 1961 edition of Partridge's *A Dictionary of Slang and Unconventional English.* It contains only words and expressions already in use before World War I. Nearly 50,000 entries are given. Approximate date of origin and etymology are provided for each word, along with quotations and a note of the milieu in which the expression arose. Entries go back as far as the seventeenth century and provide an interesting angle on social history.

Wentworth, Harold, and Stuart Berg Flexner, eds. *The Dictionary of American Slang.* New York: Thomas Y. Crowell, 1975.

This book contains more than 22,000 entries with definitions, including 2,000 in the new supplement which reflect such recent social developments as the Watergate affair, the women's movement, and changing sexual values. Also included is a list of suffixes commonly used to coin new terms. (This book could inspire some word-conscious students to produce supplements of their own.)

Partridge, Eric. *Origins: A Short Etymological Dictionary of Modern English.* New York: Macmillan, 1958.

Patridge traces the etymological histories of 12,000 words. In addition, etymological lists of prefixes, suffixes, and compound-forming elements are provided. The style is especially readable for a dictionary of this kind.

Onions, C. T., ed. *The Oxford Dictionary of Engilsh Etylomology.* London: Oxford University Press, 1966.

This book contains 24,000 main entries. For each entry, pronunciation, present-day meaning, date of its first record in English, chronology of the development of its meanings, and earliest form in English are given.

Williams, Raymond. *Keywords: A Vocabulary of Culture and Society.* London: Oxford University Press, 1976.

This examination of certain kinds of words traces the history 155 words in the English language, identified as "keywords," showing how meanings have gradually changed or expanded over time. Each entry is an essay. Williams discusses the changes in thinking reflected by meaning shifts. He is interested in the interactions of words, concepts, and experiences. In a series of connected essays, he discusses the language of cultural transformation. Words chosen are those which presumably embody social and political attitudes, patterns, and prejudices—for example, *alienation, capitalism, democracy, equality, ideology, labor, nature, realism, society.*

Appendix B

Word Combining Elements by Semantic Categories

I. Humans and human experience

    A. Humankind

       andr(o) (Greek): mankind or man the male: androgenous, polyandry, androecium

       anthrop (Greek): man, human being: anthropology, anthropomorphis

       femino (Latin): female, feminine

       gyn (Greek): woman: misogyny, gynarchy, gynoecium

       homi (Latin): man: homicide, hominoid

seni (Latin): old man: senile, senior, senescent
vir (Latin): man: virile, virtue, virtual

B. Human relationships and organization
   aut(h) (Greek): of, by, for oneself: auto, autistic, automatic
   col, cul (Latin): inhabit, settlement: colony, colonial, saxicolous
   demo (Greek): race, nation: ethnic, ethnology
   eth(o) (Greek): custom: ethos, ethology, ethic
   fil (Latin): son: affiliation, filial
   frat (Latin): brother: fraternity, fraternize
   gam (Greek): marriage: monogamy, polygamy
   gen (Greek): birth, race, kind: genetics, generic, generate
   her(ed) (Latin): heir: inherit, hereditary
   matr (Latin): mother: matrix, matriarchal
   metro (Greek): mother: metropolitan, Demeter
   nat (Latin): birth: natal, native, nation
   ped(o) (Greek): child: pediatrician, pedogogy
   phyl(o) (Greek): tribe, racial stock: phylum, phylogeny, phyle
   pol (Greek): city: politics, policy
   soror (Latin): sister: sorority, sororate
   sui (Latin): oneself, one's own: suicide, sui generis
   urb (Latin): city: urban, urbane

C. Cognition and communication
   cred (Latin): trust or believe: incredible, credibility
   cog (Latin): think actively: recognize, cognition
   dic (Latin): speak: dictate, contradict
   dox (Greek): opinion, body of opinion: orthodox, doxology
   etym(o) (Greek): truth, establish with truth: etymology, etymon
   gnos (Greek): know: diagnose, agnostic, gnosis
   gram (Greek): letter, writing: telegram, grammar
   graph (Greek): writing: graphic, autograph
   ideo (Greek): idea: ideology, ideogram
   juris (Latin): law: jurisprudence, jury, adjudicate
   lal(ia): (Greek): talk, chatter: echolalia
   leg (Latin): law: legislate, legitimate, legacy
   lex (Greek): speech, word: dyslexia, lexicon
   lit, let (Latin): letter: literate, literary
   loc, loque (Latin): speak: eloquent, loquacious
   log (Greek): word, discourse: dialogue, logic
   math (Greek): learning: mathematics
   ment (Latin): mind: mental, temperament
   mnemo (Greek): memory: mnemonics, amnesia
   nom (Latin): name: nominate, nominal
   onym (Greek): name: synonym, pseudonym
   phem, phas (Greek): speak: aphasia, euphemism
   phras (Greek): way of speaking: paraphrase, phraseology
   phren (Greek): mind or heart: phrenology, schizophrenic
   psych (Greek): mind, soul: psychology, psychical

scrib, scrip (Latin): write: describe, scripture
sem (Greek): sign, meaning: semantics, semiotics
soph (Greek): wise: sophisticated, sophomore
verb (Latin): word: verbal, verbiage
ver (Latin): true: verify, veridical
voc (Latin): voice: vocal, vociferate

D. Values and emotion
   arch (Latin): chief, principal: hierarchy, monarchy, archbishop
   belli (Latin): war, warlike: belligerent, bellicose
   bene (Latin): well, good: benevolent, benefit
   calli (Greek): beauty: calligraphy, calisthenics
   dys (Greek): badly, ill, disturbed: dysfunction, dyslexia
   eu (Greek): well, good: euphoria, euphemism
   felic (Latin): happy: felicity
   hed (Greek): pleasant: hedonism
   hier (Greek): holy, sacred: hierarchy, hieroglyphic
   idio (Greek): private, peculiar: idiosyncrasy, idiom
   latr (Greek): worship: idolatry, bibliolatry
   leni (Latin): soft, mild: lenient
   libr(o) (Latin): free: liberation, liberal
   mal (Latin): bad, evil: malevolent, malice, malign
   man, manc, mant (Greek): prophecy, madness: necromancy
   mis (Greek): hatred: misanthropy, misogyny
   miser (Latin): feel pity, be wretched: miserable
   moro (Greek) stupid, foolish: moron, sophomore
   paci (Latin): peace: pacific, pacify
   pen(u) (Greek): dearth, poverty: penury
   phil (Greek): love: philosophy, bibliophile, philanthropy
   phob (Greek): fear: claustrophobia, photophobia
   priv (Latin): private: privilege, deprivation, privacy
   pseudo (Greek): false: pseudopod, pseudonym
   quasi (Latin): apparently: quasihistorical
   sanct (Latin): holy: sanctuary, sanctimonious
   sol (Latin): alone, solitude, soliloquy
   tel (Greek): complete, perfect: teleology, telophase
   thauma (Greek): wondeful thing: thaumatology (study of miracles)
   theo (Greek): god: theology, theism
   val (Latin): well, good: value, equivalent, valence

E. Parts of the body
   arthr (Greek): joint: arthritis
   aur (Latin): ear: aural, auricle
   brach (Latin): arm: brachiopod, brachiosaurus
   card (Greek): heart: cardiology, endocardium
   cephal (Greek): head: cephalograph, encephalitis
   cerebr (Latin): brain: cerebral, cerebellum
   cost (Latin): rib: intercostal
   crani (Greek): skull: cranium

dactyl (Greek): finger: dactyl (the metrical foot＿＿ ∪∪ of the pointing finger)

dent (Latin): tooth: dental, dentrifrice

derm (Greek): skin: dermatologist, taxidermy

dextr (Greek): right hand: ambidextrous, dexterity

digit (Latin): finger or toe: digital, digit

dors (Latin): back: dorsal

femor (Latin): thigh: femur, femoral

gastr (Greek): stomach: gastronomy, gastric

genu (Latin): knee: genuflect

gingiv (Latin): gums: gingivitis, gingival

glos, glot (Greek): tongue: gloss, polyglot

gnath (Greek): jaw: prognathus (-gnatha in zoological class names)

guttur (Latin): throat: guttural

hem, haem, emia (Latin and Greek): blood: hemorrhage, anemia

hepat (Greek): liver: hepatitis

humer (Latin): shoulder: humerus, humeral

hyster (Greek): womb: hysteria

labio (Latin): lip: labial

lingu (Latin): tongue: lingual, linguistics

mamm (Latin): breast: mammal, mammary

manu (Latin): hand: manual, manipulate

mas(t) (Greek): breast: mastoid, mastodon

maxilli (Latin): jawbone (lower): maxilla

nephr (Greek): kidney: nephritis

neur (Greek): nerve: neurology, neuron

ocul (Latin): eye: oculist, ocular

odon (Greek): tooth: orthodontist, mastodon

op, ops, opt (Greek): eye: optometry, cyclops, myopic

ori, ora (Latin): mouth: oral, orifice

oss (Latin): bone: ossify, osteopathy

palp (Latin): palm of the hand: palpable, palpitate

pectori (Latin): chest: pectoral

ped (Latin): foot: pedal, centipede

phleb (Greek): vein: phlebitis

pil (Latin): hair: depilatory, piliferous

pleur (Greek): rib, side: pleurisy

pod (Greek): foot: podiam, platypodia

ren (Latin): kidney: renal, reniform

scel (Greek): leg: isoceles, skeleton

som (Greek): body: psychosomatic, somatology (study of human body types)

stern (Greek): chest: sternum

stom (Greek): mouth: cyclostomate (round mouthed), cryptostomata (order of animals with hidden mouths)

tal (Latin): heel, ankle: talon, taligrade (walking mostly on the heels)

tars (Latin): ankle: tarsus, tarsal

ventr (Latin): belly: ventriloquist, ventricle

viscer (Latin): internal organ: visceral, visceromotor

F. Physical and sensory experience
   acou (Greek): hearing: acoustic, dysacousia
   alg (Greek): pain: analgesic, neuralgia
   asthen (Greek): weakness: neurasthenia, asthenosphere
   audi (Latin): hearing: audible, audience
   cal (Latin): warm, heart: calorie, calorimeter
   cry (Greek): icy, cold: cryogenics, crystal
   dur (Latin): hard: dour, duress, endure
   ger (Greek): old age: geriatric, gerontology
   gluc, glyc (Greek): sweet: glucose, glycerol
   hebe (Greek): youth, puberty: hebephrenia
   hypn (Greek): sleep: hypnosis
   kine (Greek): movement: kinetic, cinema
   lamp (Greek): brightness, shining: lamp, lantern
   leps (Greek): seizure: epilepsy, catalepsis
   luci, lux (Latin): light: lucid, elucidate
   lum (Latin): light: illuminate, luminous
   morb (Latin): disease: morbid, morbific
   narco (Greek): numbness, torpor: narcotics, narcolepsy
   noc, nox (Latin): hurt: noxious, obnoxious
   obtus (Latin): blunt: obtuse
   orama (Greek) sight or view: panorama, cinerama
   path (Greek): suffering: pathology, telepathy, psychopath
   peno (Latin): pain, punishment: penal, pain, penology
   perspect (Latin): look through: perspectus, perspicuity
   pest (Latin): plague: pestilence, pestiferous
   phag (Latin): eat: phagocyte, sarcophagus
   phan (Greek): appearing like: cellophane, diaphanous, phantom
   phon (Greek): sound: phonics, telephone, phonology
   phos, phot (Greek): light: phosphorus, phosphorescence
   pleg (Greek): stroke, paraplepsis: paraplegic, plegometer
   san (Latin): health: sanitary, sanatorium
   sapor (Latin): taste: saporific, savor
   schis, schiz (Greek): split: schism, schizoid
   scope (Greek): regard or view: telescope, microscopic
   sens (Latin): feel, perceive, sensitive, sensory
   seps, sept (Greek): putrefaction of bodily part: septic, antiseptic
   sic (Latin): dry: desiccate
   somn (Latin): sleep: somnambulist, insomnia
   son (Latin): sound: sonic, sonnet, sonorous
   spect (Latin): appear: aspect, speculate
   stas, stat (Greek): stoppage, stand: homeostasis, status
   stere(o) (Greek): hard, solid: stereophonic, stereotype
   tact (Latin): touch: tactile, tactometer
   tang (Latin): touch: tangible, tangent
   ten (Greek): stretch: tension, tendon
   thana (Greek): death, euthanasia, thanatopsis
   therm (Greek): heat: thermos, thermometer

ton (Greek): sound, stretching: intonation, tone, tonic
traum (Greek): wound: trauma, traumatic

G. Actions

ambulo (Latin): walk, ambulatory, perambulate
bol (Latin): throw, cast, stroke: parabola, parable
cid (Latin): kill: homicide, insecticide
clas (Greek): break, fracture, iconoclast, clash
claustra, cloistr (Latin): enclose, close: claustrophobia, cloister
cras (Greek): mix: idiosyncrasy
drom (Greek): run, a course: hippodrome, dromedary
duc (Latin): lead: induce, education
fac, fic, fect (Latin): make: factory, artifact, artificial
fer (Latin): bear, produce: conifer, efferent, different
fin (Latin): end, limit: final, infinite, confinement
flec, flex(Latin): bend: flexible, reflex, reflect
flu (Latin): flow: fluent, ffluorescent, superfluous
frac, frag, frang, fring (Latin): break, fragment: fracture, frangible, infringement
fug (Latin): put to flight: fugitive, centrifugal
ger, ges (Latin): bear, carry: belligerent, armiger
glom (Latin): aggregate, compact: conglomerate, agglomeration
grad, gred, gres (Latin): step, walk: gradient, digress, ingredient
ia(t) (Greek): heal, cure: psychiatric, hypochondria
ject (Latin): throw, cast: trajectory, conjecture, inject
junct (Latin): join: juncture, conjunction, adjunct
klept (Greek): steal: kleptomania, biblioklept (book thief)
lect (Greek): choose: collect, elect, select
leg (Latin): gather, read: college, legend, legion
lys, lyz, lyt (Greek): free, dissolve: analyze, electrolyte, catalyst
misce (Latin): mix: miscellaneous, miscegenation
mis, mit (Latin): send: mission, commit, omission
mot, mob, mov (Latin): move: automotive, mobile, motive
mut (Latin): changes: mutation, immutable
nost (Greek): return: nostalgia
nutr, nurt (Latin): nourish: nutrient, nurture
plec, plex, plic (Latin): fold: complex, replicate
prehen, pren, preg, pris (Latin): grasp: comprehend, comprise, prehensible, impregnable
rupt (Latin): break: interrupt, rapture
tax, tact (Greek): arrange: taxonomy, syntax
tech, tect (Greek): build: technology, architect
thes, thet (Greek): set, establish: thesis, thesaurus, parenthetical
tom (Greek): cut, section: lobotomy, anatomy
tor(s) (Latin): twist: torsion, torque
trop (Greek): turn: entropy, tropism, tropical
turb (Latin): spin: turbine, disturb
ut, us (Latin): use: utility, usury, abuse
ver (Latin): turn: vertical, vertex, adverse

H. Objects of human manufacture

acu (Latin) : needle: acute, acupuncture

ax (Latin and Greek) : axle: axis, axiom

biblio (Greek) : book: bibliography

cart (Latin) : map or chart: cartography, cartoon, cartridge

cruc (Latin) : cross: crucible, crucifix, cruciform

eco (Latin) : house or habitat: ecology, ecosystem, economy

fil (Latin) : thread: filigree, filament

icon (Greek) : image: iconography, iconoclasm

idol (Greek) : image: idolatry, idolize

lab (Greek) : implement, instrument: astrolabe

lib(r) : (Latin) : book: library, libel

lucr (Latin) : monetary gain: lucrative, lucre

mur (Latin) wall: immure, mural, extramural

nau(t) (Greek) : ship: nautical, naval

nod (Latin) : knot: nodule, node

ole (Latin) : oil: oleomargarine, oleiferous

pharmaco (Greek) : drug, medicine: pharmacy, phamaceutical

rei (Latin) : thing: reify

rot, rod (Latin) : wheel: rotary, rotund, rodeo

stip (Latin) rod or post: stipule, stipulate

strat (Latin) : covering: stratosphere, stratum

tox (Greek) : bow or arrow, hence poison: toxic, toxicology

zyg (Greek) : yoke or crossbar: zygote, homozygous

II. Animal life and animal characteristics (see also parts of the human body.)

ali (Latin) : wing: aliform

angi (Greek) : seed, blood, lymph vessel: angiogram, angiocarpores

anim (Latin) : life, soul: animal, inanimate

api (Latin) : bee: apiary, apiculture

arct (Greek) : bear: arcturus, arctic

bio, bia (Greek) : life, living organism: biology, amphibious, aerobia

blast (Greek) : formative cell: blastula, blastoderm

capilli (Latin) : hair: capillary, capilliform

carn (Latin) : flesh: carnivore, carnal

caud (Latin) : tail: caudal, caudodorsal

cer (Greek) : horn: rhinoceros

cochl (Latin) : snail: chochlia, cockle

coel (Greek) : bodily cavity, cell: coeloblastic, neurocoele

corn (Latin) : horn: unicorn, cornucopia, cornulite

corp (Latin) : body: corporal, corpus

echin (Greek) : hedgehog: echinocactus, echinocrome

faun (Latin) : animal: fauna, faunology

feli (Latin) : cat: feline

fung (Greek) : sponge: fungus, fungillis

galact (Greek) : milk: galaxy, galactic

galli (Latin) : fowl: galliformes

gangl (Greek): swelling, excrescence: nerve center: ganglion, ganglio-
cyte

gon(y) (Greek): germ cell: gonad, ontogony
gymn (Greek): naked: gynospore, gymnasium
hipp (Greek): horse: hippopotamus, hippodrome
hirsut (Latin): hair: hirsute
hist (Greek): tissue: histology, histolysis
hymen (Greek): membrane, marriage: hymenoptera, hymeneal, hymn
ichthy (Greek): fish: ichthyologist, ichthyosaurus
lact (Latin): milk: lactate, lactose, lettuce
leon (Latin): lion: leonine
lip (Greek): fat: lipid
lepor (Latin): hare: lepori-form
lup (Latin): wolf: lupus
lyco (Greek): wolf: lycanthropy, lycopod
mel(li) (Greek): honey: mellifluous, mellivorous
mening (Latin): membrane: meninges, meningitis
myel (Greek): marrow, myelitis, myelin
odo(n) (Greek): tooth: mastodon, macrodontia
onych (Greek): nail, claw
oo, ooph, ooth, ov (Greek): egg: ovary, ooviporous, oval
orni (Greek): bird: ornithologist
penni, pinni (Latin): feather: pinnate, pinniform
pisci (Latin): fish: pisciculture
pithec (Latin): ape: pithecanthropus, pithecological
pneu (Greek): breath: pneumatic, pneumonia
por (Greek): pore: porous, blastopore
proli (Latin): offspring: proliferate, prolific
pter (Greek): feather: pterodactyl, ornithopteris
respiro (Latin): breathe: respiratory, respirometer
rhin (Latin): snout, nose: rhinoceros, platyrhine
rostr (Latin): beak: rostrum, rostriform
sarc (Greek): flesh: sacrophagus, sarcasm
saur (Greek): lizard: dinosaur, sauria, Brontosaurus
serrat (Latin): saw-toothed: serrate, serrato-dentate
spir (Latin): air-hold: spiricle, inspire, spirometer
taur (Greek): bull: taurus, tauromachy
thromb (Greek): clot, lump: thrombosis
ur (Greek): tail: brachyurous
urs (Latin): bear: ursine, ursiform
vacci (Latin): cow: vaccinate, vaquero
vit, viv (Latin): life: vital, survive, convivial
vor (Latin): devour: voracious, herbivorous
zoo (Greek): animal: zoology, protozoa

III. Plant life and plant characteristics
acanth (Greek): spiny flower: acanthus
acini (Latin): grape or grape stone: acinose
agri(i) (Latin): field: agriculture, agronomy
anth (Greek): flower: anthology, monanthous
arbor (Latin): tree: arbor, arboreal

bacci (Latin): berry: bacciferous, baccivorous
carp (Latin): fruit: carpophagous, endocarp
cort (Latin): bark: cortex, cortical
flor (Latin): flower: floriculture, uniflorous
fol (Latin): leaf: foliage, folio
frond (Latin): leafy branch: frond, frondose, frondescent
fruct, frug (Latin): fruit, fructify, frugivorous
gem (Latin): bud: ingeminate, gemifer
gran (Latin): grain: granule, granary
herb (Latin): grass: herbiferous, herbal
hort (Latin): garden: horticulture
hyl (Greek): wood: hylogeny, hylomorphism
lem, lep (Greek): rind, husk: lepidoptera, neurilemma
myc (Greek): fungus: mycetes, mycology
phyl (Greek): leaf: chlorophyll, phyllotaxy
phyt (Latin): plant: zoophyte, sporophytic
pom (Latin): fruit: pomegranate, pomiculture
radi (Latin): root: radical, eradicate
ram (Latin): branch: ramification, ramose
rhiz (Greek): root: rhizoid, rhizome
silv, sylv (Latin): forest: sylvan, silviculture
spin (Latin): thorn: spinose, spinifex
spor (Greek): seed: sporangium, sporicide, microspore
uvi (Latin): grape: uvula

IV. Minerals and other natural phenomena
abys (Latin): depths of the sea: abyss, abysmal
aer (Greek and Latin): air, gas: aerify, aerate
ast (Greek): star: astral, disaster, astronomy
bulli (Latin): bubble: ebullient
calc (Latin): lime or calcium: calcium, calcareous
chalc (Greek): copper: leucocalcite, chalcolithic
chrys (Greek): gold: chrysanthemum, chrysalis
combu(s) (Latin): burn: combustible, combustion
fer (Latin): iron: ferrous, ferromagnetic, ferrite
flu (Latin): flow, river: fluent, influence, fluid
fum (Latin): smoke: fumigate, perfume
gem (Latin): precious stone (derived from "bud"): gemmology
geo (Greek): earth: geology, geometry
glac (Latin): ice: glacier, glacial, glacification
hal (Greek): salt: halibios, halite
heli (Greek): sun: helium, heliotrope
humi (Latin): moisture: humidity, humid
hyal (Greek): transparent stone, glass: hyaline
hydro, hygro (Greek): water: hydraulic, hydrogen, hygrometer
lapi (Latin): stone: lapidary, lapidicolous, dilapidate
limn (Greek): pool, marshy lake: limnology, limnobiology
lit, lith (Greek): stone: monolith, lithograph
lun(a): (Latin): moon: lunar, lunacy

mar, mer (Latin): sea: maritime, marinade, mermaid
meth (Greek) wood spirit: methyl, methylene
mont (Latin): mountain: paramount, insurmountable, Montana
mund (Latin): world: mundane
nebal, nimb (Latin): mist, cloud: nebulous, nebula, nimbus
ombr (Latin): shower, rain: ombrifuge, ombrometer
ond, und (Latin): wave: ondoscope, inundate, redundant
pelag (Gree): sea: archipelago
petr (Latin): rock: petroleum, petrology
potum (Greek): river: hippopotamus, Mesopotamia
pyr (Greek): fire: pyre, pyrotechnics
sax, sac (Latin): rock: saxicolous, saxifragous
seism (Greek): earthquake: seismology, seismometer
silic (Latin): flint: silicon, siliceous
sol (Latin): sun: solar, solarium, solstice
stell (Latin): star: constellation, stellar
terr (Latin): earth: terrarium, terrestrial, interment
umbr (Latin): shade: umbrella, umbrage
und (Latin): wave: inundate, undulate
vent (Latin): wind: ventifact, ventilate
vitr (Latin): glass: vitreous, vitriol

V. Colors
alb (Latin): white: albino, albumin
chlor (Greek): green: chlorophyll, chloroplast
chrom (Greek): color: chromatic, chromosome, monochrome
chrys (Greek): gold: chrysalis, chrysolite
cyan (Greek): blue: cyanide, cyanosis
eryth (Greek): red: erythrocyte
flav (Latin): yellow
fusc (Latin): tawn, dark colored: obfuscate
glauc (Greek): silvery, bluish grey: glaucoma
lur, lut (Latin): orange-yellow: lurid
mel (Greek): black: Melanesia
poli (Greek): grey, pale: poliomyelitis
porphr (Greek): purple: porphyry, porphyrogenite
purpur (Latin): purple
rub (Latin): red: ruby, rubefacient
virid, verd (Latin): green: verdure, verdant
xanth (Greek): yellow: xanthos, xanthine

VI. Number, quantity, measurement, and comparison
bi (Latin): two: bifurcation, bicentennial
bar (Greek): heavy: baritone, barometer
brach (Greek): short: amphibrach, brachycephalic
cent (Latin): hundred: centigrade, centenary
dec (Greek): ten: decade, decathlon
deci (Latin): a tenth of: decimal, decimate
demi (French): half: demigod, demitune

deutero (Greek): second: Deuteronomy, deuterium
dipl (Greek): twofold: diploid, diploma
di(s) (Latin): in two, apart: diverge, digress
dodec (Greek): twelve: dodecahedron
dyn (Greek): unit of power: dynamic, dyne
equi (Latin): equal: equilateral, equilibrium, equinox
fissi (Latin): cleft, divided; fissure, fashion
gram (Greek): unit of weight: centigram, kilogram
grav (Latin): heavy; gravity, grave
hapl (Greek): single: haploid
hec, hect (Greek): hundred: hecatomped, hectowatt
hemi (Greek): half: hemisphere, hemiplegia
hept (Greek): seven: heptagon, heptometer
heter (Greek): other: heteronym, heterodox
hex (Greek): six: hexagon, hexapod
hol (Greek): whole: holocaust, holistic
hom (Latin): same: homeopathy, homologous, homonym
kilo (Greek): thousand: kilogram, kilowatt
logarith (Latin): an account, indicator of number: logarithm
magn (Latin): great: magnitude, magnanimous
meg (Greek): great: megapower, megalomania
mer (Greek): fraction, part: polymer, isomeric, meroplankton
metr (Greek): measure: metric, meter, geometry
micr (Greek): small: microcosm, microscope
mill (Latin): thousand: millipede, milligram, mile
mon (Latin): alone, one: monastery, monogamy, monopoly
mult (Latin): much, many: multisyllabic, multiple, multifarious
myri (Greek): ten thousand, many: myriad
nov (Latin): nine: November, novenniel
oct (Greek): eight: octagon, octopus
omni (Latin): all: omnipotent, omnifarious, omniscient
pan (Greek): all: panacea, pandemonium
pari (Latin): equal: parity, paratyphoid
pauci (Latin): few: paucity
pene (Latin): almost: peninsula
pent (Greek): five: pentagon, pentometer
pleni (Latin): full: plenitude, plenipotentiary
pluri (Latin): several, many: plural, plurality, plus
poly (Latin): many: polygamy, polygraph, polychromatic
ponder (Latin): weight: ponderous, ponder
prim (Latin): first: primitive, primogeniture
prot (Greek): first: prototype, protocol
quad (Latin): four: quadrangle, quadruped
quint (Latin): five: quintet, quintessence
sesqui (Latin): one and a half: sesquipedalian, sesquicentennial
sex (Latin): sextet, sextant
tenu (Latin): thin: tenuous, attenuate
tetr (Greek) four: tetralogy, tetrahedron

tot (Latin): whole: total, factotum, totalitarian
tri (Latin): three: trilogy, triple
uni (Latin): one: unilateral, unify, universe

VII. Time and space concepts (including form)
   A. Time
       anni, enni (Latin) year: annual, centennial
       chron (Greek): time: chronology, chronometer, chronosynclastic
          infundibula
       eval (Latin): age: medieval, primeval
       horo (Greek): hour: horoscope
       mester (Greek): six months: semester
       neo (Greek): new: neonate, neologism
       nov (Latin): new: innovate, novelty, novitiate
       nox, noct (Latin): night: nocturnal, equinox
       pre (Latin): before: prenatal, preface
       post (Latin): after: posterior, posthumous
       telo (Greek): last, final: teleology, telophase

   B. Space, form
       acr (Greek): top, farthest point: acrobat, acrostic, acrophobia
       ante (Latin): before: anterior, anticipate
       apec, apex (Latin): summit: apical, apex
       cap(a) (Greek): downward: cataclysm, catharsis
       circum (Latin): around: circumvent, circumference
       com, con, col (Latin): with, together: committee, connect, collide
       contr (Latin): against: contradict, counterculture
       cyclo (Greek): circular: encyclopedia, cyclotron
       dia (Greek): across, through: diameter, diachronic
       ec (Greek): off, away from: eccentric, ecstasy
       endo (Greek): within: endogenous, endomorph
       entr (Latin): between, among: entrench, entrails
       epi (Greek): upon, besides: epigram, epiphyte, epilogue
       exo (Greek): outside: exotic, exodus, exogamy
       extra (Latin): outside: extract, extracellular
       gon (Greek): angle: polygon
       gyro (Greek): circle: gyroscope, gyrate
       hedr (Greek): seat, base: cathedral, polyhedron
       heli (Greek): spiral: helix, helicopter
       hyper (Greek): over, above: hyperkinetic, hyperbole
       hypo (Greek): beneath: hypodermic, hypoactive
       infra, infer (Latin): below, beneath: inferior, infrared
       inter (Latin): between, among: interdict, intercollegiate
       intra (Latin): within: intramural, intravenous
       intro (Latin): inwards: introduce, introvert
       ipsi (Latin): same side: ipsilateral
       juxta (Latin): next to, close: juxtapose
       iat (Latin): side, wide: latitude, lateral
       lim (Latin): boundary: limit, eliminate, subliminal

lox (Latin): place: locomotive, allocate
med (Latin): middle: medium, intermediary
mes (Greek): middle: mesentery, Mesopotamia, mesolite
meta (Greek): along with, after: metaphysics, metamorphosis
morph (Greek): form: morphology, amorphous
ob (Latin): toward, facing, against: obverse, obstruct
orth (Greek): straight: orthodox, orthodontist
pali(n) (Greek): backwards, again: palindrome, palingenesis
para (Greek): alongside: paradigm, paradox, parallel
per (Latin): through: permeate, percolate
peri (Greek): all around: periscope, perimeter, peritoneum
pro (Greek and Latin): before: progress, prohibit, prophage
pros (Greek): toward, near: poselyte, prosody
retro (Latin): backward: retrospect, retrograde
schem (Greek): shape or form: scheme, schematic
sinu (Latin): concave, curved surface: sinuous, sinus, sinusoid
spher (Latin): round: sphere, spherical
spir (Greek): coil: spiral, spirochete
sub (Latin): under: subliminal, substandard
super, supra (Latin): above, higher than, greater than: superstructure,
    supramolecular
syn (Latin): along or together: synthesis, synergism
termin (Latin): boundary: terminate, interminable
top (Greek): place: topography, topic, topiary
trans (Greek): through: transduce, intransigent
troch (Greek): round, circular: trochlea, trochoid
ultra (Latin): beyond: ultracentrifuge, ultramarine
via (Latin): way: viaduct, viable

8

Comprehension Strategies

How can comprehension be labeled for daily instruction?

What kinds of question-asking techniques promote understanding and learning?

It is said that a famous scientist's wife once remarked of her husband, "I can understand his words but not his sentences." Many students seem to have the same experience with their textbooks. They can read the words, but the meanings of sentences and paragraphs elude them. Or some might seem to understand well enough as they are reading along but find that they have very hazy recall of the content when they are through. Or, finally, some might be able to recall specific details of material they have read but be unable to see its overall structure and purpose. These are all basic problems of comprehension.

MEANING OF COMPREHENSION

What does it mean to comprehend? Philosophers have struggled with this question; so must all teachers. Getting the student to comprehend is the most fundamental task of teaching, and yet it seems difficult to say exactly what we mean by this word. Generally, however, we can assume that comprehension entails *understanding* something, *retaining* its meaning, and being able to *use* or *apply* the material appropriately.

When we speak of understanding, it is important to realize that meaning is not a property of written materials themselves. It is something constructed in the mind: first in the mind of the writer and then in the mind of the reader. When a reader comprehends, he is able to grasp the message conveyed by the writer and relate it to what he already knows. This process is very complex in most content-area reading where the reader must go beyond individual words and sentences and deal with a stream of incoming concepts and information, page by page. If he can't "put it together" in a holistic sense, he isn't comprehending.

Memory

Once material is understood, it must be stored in a form accessible for future retrieval. This can be a problem, because the nature of memory is such that specifics tend to fade quickly away while generalities remain. Thus it is very important that comprehension involve a grasp of the structure and main implications of what is read. In most cases, this is the kind of content that can actually be retained, along with information concerning where to find details if they are needed.

Current research in cognition is establishing the notion that all new learning must be related to what the person already knows. That is, one must interpret material within a framework of one's own knowledge and experience. If one does not do this, it is unlikely that much significant learning will take place. That is why memorizing content solely for the purpose of answering questions on a test is usually not a productive enterprise. Therefore, we must say that comprehension includes the ability to relate material to a personal framework of knowledge and to apply concepts to new situations.

Perhaps a good operational concept of comprehension is this:

Comprehension entails putting together the message of the text with what the reader already knows, retaining this product in a form accessible to recall, and being able to use it in constructive thinking.

Usually the teacher will have two major concerns regarding the student's comprehension: (1) Has the student adequately grasped the main elements and structure of the writer's message? and (2) Can he respond to the message in his own terms? There two questions imply a two-way process of communication. Bookthinking *is* this kind of communication: the reader "listening" to what the text has to say and then "answering" with ideas of his own. The communications aspect of bookthinking suggests a basic ground plan for comprehension that the student can learn to apply. A pattern for discussion can follow these lines: First talk about the writer's purpose, then discuss what he wrote to convey this purpose, and then ask the students to respond to it on their own terms. Or, alternatively, begin with the student's response and go from this to an examination of what the writer's intentions seem to be. If a pattern that includes these elements is followed regularly, students will become accustomed to dealing with material in these terms, and they will have a basic strategy for approaching content reading.

Response to Writing

Writing differs, however, in the extent to which it requires close attention to the text or encourages more open response. We can usually assume, for example, that a scientific concept must be learned as it is given before it can be accurately applied, while creative literature invites personal interpretation. For any kind of material, the reader must do his own thinking—drawing inferences and making associations beyond the text—if real learning is to occur. But the reader must learn to adjust to the demands of the text.

A common way of conceptualizing the act of comprehension is to think of it as having three "levels": literal, inferential, and elaborative. As is discussed in chapter 2, this is really a way of sorting out the kinds of responses students might make to what they read and a basis for the teacher to use in formulating different kinds of questions. Typical Henry, you will recall, was asked only the most trivial of literal-level questions, while his more fortunate classmates got to give interesting elaborative answers that did not reveal whether or not they remembered the color of the dog's eyes. Questions on any level, of course, need not and should not be trivial. But students should have the opportunity to practice answers of all kinds—those asking for specific recall, which will help them attend to details, and those eliciting personal response, which will help them find relationships in what they read.

"Levels" of Comprehension?

In describing comprehension activities, many student books categorize them into "levels," usually three, such as literal, inferential, and elaborative. Different authors use different labels, but they have a similar intention, that of reminding teachers and students to seek out various kinds of information. The three categories, irrespective of their labels, focus on the types of information to be generated rather than describe the thinking operations that a reader uses. (Chapter 2 discusses different thinking operations.) In deference to student skill texts and therefore to direct applicability of comprehension strategies, "levels" of comprehension are described here according to the information sought and its explicitness in the printed text, thus the categories: *literal inferential, elaborative.*

Literal

At this level, students can paraphrase meanings given explicitly in the text. They can recall specific items of information and answer questions derived from the material itself. Literal recall can be sparse and unconnected or it can be detailed, but it does not by itself reveal the reader's own mental organization of the specific items he has picked up. Also it does not reveal the depth of his understanding of concepts or whether he would be able to transfer his understanding to other contexts. The emphasis is primarily upon immediate grasp of the material and memory for specific details.

Some Literal Thinking Operations

1. Understanding words, particularly word concepts taught as part of content instruction or vocabulary development.
2. Understanding sentences and sentence relationships, including types of subordination. Showing ability to follow fairly complex sentence structures.
3. Recognizing explicit sequences in passages of connected discourse, for example, order in time, order in space, and stated cause-and-effect sequences.
4. Relating to graphics; combining written with other visual materials.
5. Retaining information necessary for performing specific tasks, such as identification and classification of specimens, interpretation of laboratory results, or analysis of language structures.
6. Following directions so that a task or project is done correctly.
7. Describing a process or procedure in one's own words.
8. Recalling specific content sufficient for a retelling that includes salient information.

Inferential

At this level, the reader derives some kind of organization from the material and seeks out ideas as well as specific items of information. Items are related to each other and additional ones are inferred. The question is frequently asked or implied, "What does the writer *mean* by this?" The reader deals with the material in an active way, seeking answers to cognitive questions, and expression becomes an important adjunct to comprehension. Hence the emphasis is on finding a relationship between what is given and what is known.

Some Inferential Operations

1. Identifying the main idea(s) of a paragraph or other unit of prose.
2. Identifying patterns or organization of paragraphs or larger units.

3. Making comparisons and contrasts; understanding relationships based on comparison/contrast structures.
4. Recognizing implicit cause-and-effect relationships.
5. Distinguishing correlative from casual relationships.
6. Understanding hierarchical relationships.
7. Selecting salient points for adequate summary (showing more grasp of underlying organizational patterns than would be the case at the concrete level of recall).
8. Inferring implicit information and concepts.
9. Responding to questions in the text.
10. Distinguishing between relevant and irrelevant information in relationship to selected points or arguments.
11. Evaluating support for assertions.
12. Distinguishing between objective and subjective information (fact vs. opinion).
13. Judging authenticity, completeness, and logical adequacy of information.
14. Recognizing elements of style including tone, sentence patterns, direct and indirect modes of expression, and so forth.
15. Deriving meaning from figurative and symbolic language (metaphorical reasoning).
16. Recognizing the author's point of view and underlying purpose; detecting the author's bias.
17. Predicting outcomes and solutions; problem solving.
18. Comparing material from different texts.

Elaborative

At this level, understanding stimulates new thought processes, enabling the reader to make far-reaching connections or produce original ideas. Expression is very important in the development of elaborative thinking, as the reader has in effect embarked upon his own line of thinking which he must work out. In elaborative thinking, the emphasis is on creating ideas of one's own.

Some Elaborative Operations

1. Fitting information and concepts into an overall structure of the content area and altering the structure as learning proceeds.
2. Forming an organized system for maintaining information and concepts for future use.
3. Applying information and concepts in the development of personal values.
4. Formulating questions and ideas that go beyond the information, inferences, and concepts in the text; formulating hypotheses and theories for further investigation.
5. Relating information and concepts from different content areas.
6. Making use of textual materials as models or inspiration for original work.

These ways of responding do not represent alternative styles of thinking or steps in building comprehension. In fact, "levels" is a poor term because it suggests a hierarchy, but the most important point to remember is that these modes of understanding are integrated and must work together. Consider, for example, the following passage from a high school English text:

What Is a Symbol?

You are probably familiar with the story about the little boy who asked his father, "Where do I come from?" The father nervously launched into a full explanation of the birds and the bees. When he had finished, he asked his son if there were any further questions. "Yes," the boy replied. "My friend Charley told me he comes from Pittsburgh, and I still want to know where *I* come from."

In other words, there are many different ways of answering a question, and some questions lend themselves to answers of different levels of maturity. The question which is the title of this chapter is of that kind. Perhaps you faced it when you were in the seventh grade and answered it to your own satisfaction. But that is not the end of the matter. You are facing it again here because it is the kind of question that produces for you a different answer each time you ask it and a wiser answer as you become wiser. You are also facing it here because the question, "What is communication?" doubtless required some of you to talk about symbols and symbolism. In this chapter, you will explore in different ways the meanings of the word "symbol." In doing so, you will need to draw on much of what you know of communication and your own culture.[1]

This introduction to a discussion on symbolism begins with a little story that could stand by itself as a humorous anecdote. Because of its position between a question and more writing, however, the reader is likely to suppose that the writer is telling it in order to make a further point. This supposition is not stated in the text. The reader supplies it, and it sets up an expectancy for what will come next: an explanation of the point raised in the initial question. Thus the reader is thinking critically as he reads the words of the writer. He could just read the story and think nothing further about it, but only if he is oblivious to certain cues. All the information in a passage is not contained in the words and sentences of the writer. Much is conveyed in other kinds of cues, such as subheadings, arrangement of material on the page, marginal notes, pictures, and all the subleties of written style and tone. We can talk about what is stated explicitly and what isn't, but in the reader's mind, both kinds of information are integrated.

Suppose, however, that the story is being read by our old friend, Typical Henry, who has reached high school believing that he must collect small details to "prove" that he has read something. *His* literal reading may

---

[1] From Niel Postman, *Language and Reality* (New York: Holt, Rinehart and Winston, 1966), p. 6.

not be integrated with inferential thinking. He might stash away the question asked at the beginning, note the relationship between the two speakers, and of course remember that the friend's name was Charley and that he came from Pittsburgh. One hopes that not even Henry is in this much trouble, but if he is, it is probably because he has learned that reading is for memorizing, not thinking. He believes that he must focus on the literal meaning so rigidly that he locks out his own thoughts. In this circumstance, it is unlikely that he will proceed much further in the assignment. By the time he has reached high school, understandably, he has had enough of trivia and potential humiliation. It is much better for him to let the teacher know how he feels by simply not reading the text.

Now consider another passage, this one from an eighth-grade science text:

Looking Inside Your Eye

Just behind the pupil is the lens of your eye. The lens causes the incoming light to bend so that it comes together or focuses at a point. The light is focused on the pigment at the back of your eye. The pigment is contained in cells that form the inner lining of the back of your eye. This lining is called the retina, and it is about the size and thickness of a postage stamp.

Your eyeball is not empty. It is filled with liquid. In front of the lens, there is a watery fluid. The rest of the interior of the eye is filled with a jelly-like fluid. The pressure of these fluids helps the eye keep its shape. Like the cornea and lens, these fluids help to bend the incoming light so it comes to a focus at your retina.

The pigment in the cells of your retina captures the incoming light. There are two types of pigment-filled cells in the retina, cones and rods. Each is named for its shape. The rods are sensitive to dim light. The cones are insensitive to dim light but work well in bright light. Cones gives you color vision.

Biologists believe that there are three types of cones. Each type of cone probably responds to light of every color, but to different degrees. Probably one type is most sensitive to red light, another to blue, and another to green. When you look at a particular color, a combination of signals is sent to the brain from the cells in the retina. The brain interprets this combination as a particular color.[2]

This passage, we will assume, is being read by Henry's bright little sister, Angela, who always got to answer the "what do you think" questions but never had to be concerned with details. When she encounters this kind of material, she might not know what to think, except perhaps that this is a bunch of facts that tell her more about eyeballs than she cares to know. Of course, since Angela is bright and used to getting along with teachers,

---

[2] From Roy A. Gallant and Isaac Asimov, *Ginn Science Program*, Advanced Level (Lexington, Mass.: Ginn & Company, 1975), p. 202.

she can probably memorize details too. But her critical thinking will be along the lines of "what should I remember for the test." If so, she is not much better off than Henry, for her critical and literal thinking are not integrated.

How would you integrate your literal, critical, and elaborative thinking in response to this passage, assuming that you do not have a developed interest in the structure of the eye or the dynamics of light perception? Of course, you have already passed your eighth-grade science course so this is an academic question, but, still, it might be nice to have an understanding of these things since vision is such an important part of experience. That is the clue to the answer. You have to stop and think about your own experience and realize the amazing sensitivity of your eyes and how much you depend on that faculty before you can begin to wonder about and appreciate the intricate mechanims of sight. Then a text that seems bound, at first glance, to a literal level of understanding begins to involve critical and elaborative thinking as well. Consider the following questions that might be asked in connection with this text:

1. What is the retina of the eye, and what is its purpose?
2. What are cones and how do they function?
3. How does amount of light affect preception of color?
4. Observe a scene from a particular window at three times of the day, say midmorning, early evening, and night. What differences can you describe?

Which of these questions do you think should be asked first? Should one begin by asking students to concentrate on the details of the anatomy of the eye, or have them use their own eyes in directed observation? Sometimes it is necessary to tap into elaborative thinking before getting down to specific details. Indeed, this may be the rule, for elaborative thinking will arouse the student's awareness of what he already knows and prepare him for a new set of factual information.

Angela is also taking a math class in which she always gets good grades, although she doesn't like it much in comparison to English, her favorite subject. Let's look at a page from her math text (Figure 8–1). This text, it seems, asks only that the reader understand the directions well enough to apply them, and that is what Angela does very well.

But when she does her math homework, she always listens to the radio or watches television at the same time, because she doesn't have to think that much about what she's doing as she applies the instructions. Apart from her homework techniques, however, she could be given something to think about in class, and this might even raise her opinion of geometry. Besides asking for definitions of a quadrilateral, a parallelogram, and a median, her teacher might ask questions like these:

Why is precision important in making these kinds of tests?
What is the relationship between the *shape* of something and its *area*?

Pictures and examples can often be used to decide if a statement is reasonable.

In triangle ABC each of the segments AX, BY, CZ connects the midpoint of one side with the opposite vertex. These segments are the medians of the triangle.

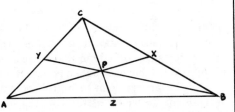

1. In the triangle, the medians intersect at a single point P. Do you think that in any triangle, the medians meet at a single point?

2. Copy the four triangles below on a sheet of paper.

  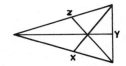 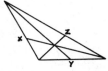

3. Points X, Y, and Z are the midpoints of the sides of the triangles. Draw the three medians of each triangle.

4. In each case do the three medians intersect at a single point?

5. Draw several other triangles of different sizes and shapes. Locate the midpoints of the sides. Then draw the medians.

6. Do the medians of each triangle you drew for exercise 5 meet at a single point? In geometry, it is possible to prove the following statement: the three medians of any triangle meet at a single point.

Figure 8-1. From Donovan A. Johnson, Viggo P. Hansen, Wayne H. Peterson, Jesse A. Rudnick, Ray Cleveland, and L. Carey Bolster, *Applications in Mathematics Course B: Decision Making* (Glenview, Ill.: Scott, Foresman, 1974, pp. 10–11).

Why are rooms generally rectangles instead of some other shape?
When do you see triangles in real life?
Can you figure out a quick way to convert a parallelogram into a rectangle?
If you are told that a house has 3,000 square feet, how do you visualize this?

If Angela can start relating the lines she is drawing on graph paper to real space and boundaries as she experiences them, she will be able to integrate literal, critical, and elaborative levels of thinking, even when she is doing math.

Now let us return to Henry for another scenario in the world of textbook reading. Being typical, Henry has to take a course in American government, and here is a passage from the assignment he didn't read for today:

Public Opinion

What is public opinion, and how does it affect our lives? We should consider this question, because many claims are made in the name of public opinion. We are asked to assume that there is such a phenomenon as public opinion and that it influences public policy. But what is it?

The papers seem to be full of public opinion. An editorial, claiming to represent the views of the common man, speaks out against a law or situation. A group organizes to lobby against a proposed bill, again claiming to represent the majority opinion.

The term "public opinion," however, cannot easily be defined. Its definition is difficult to pin down. This is true because it is not easy to say *who* it is that expresses the opinion of the public. In fact, we may not easily define exactly who the public is.

Not everyone has an opinion on every issue. A motorist, for example, might have much to say about the operation of road-cleaning services during a winter storm but have little concern about the salaries of the road-maintenance workers. Does this person become a part of the "public" only when he has an opinion? And when he does, how is this opinion expressed? through voting? through letters to the editor or to his congressman? through complaining to his neighbor?

The vast majority of citizens will never write a letter to a public official or news medium, and many voters stay away from the polls. Who then really speaks for the mass of citizens in instances of "public opinion?" Or in what other ways does public opinion make itself felt?

This is a well-written text in a style that corresponds with its rather complex subject matter, and it regularly directs the reader to consult his own experience. But it is not hard to see why Henry keeps his government book permanently stored in his locker. This passage isn't giving factual information at all, only asking a lot of questions that imply there are no facts to be had. Henry can handle this kind of situation in real life but not in a book. After all, books contain items to remember, if you have time for it, but this one seems to be asking the reader to supply all the answers. All this book says is that it doesn't know the answers to its own questions.

So Henry has spent the previous evening working with his friend on a car, talking about the fifty-five-mile speed limit and how stupid it is because no one observes it. It did not occur to him at the time that he was discussing an issue of public opinion and how it makes itself known. And in class today he keeps his mouth shut, because he doesn't have any answers from the book to contribute. He doesn't know that the usual kind of thinking he does has anything to do with books.

There is one class that Henry likes, however, and that is shop. There are many reasons for this, not the least of which is that instead of asking questions to determine what a student knows, the teachers looks at his work. Yet there is reading in shop, too, and the teacher expects the students to understand and apply the explanations given in the text. Realizing that he needs the information it provides, Henry brings his book to class and consults it as he works. This is the kind of reading he does:

Unit 47. Preparing Wood for Finishing

A smooth, final finish depends upon complete sanding of all visible parts. The project should be sandpapered thoroughly even though the parts were sanded before they were assembled.

Sandpaper is the abrasive material most often used on wood. The grit on the paper looks like sand, but the substance is actually crushed flint or quartz of gray-tan color. Garnet paper, reddish in color, lasts longer than flint paper. Emery cloth is tough and black in color.

Abrasive papers and cloth are graded from fine to coarse. The table below lists the grit and number classifications of the three types of abrasives discussed in this unit.

Preparing the Surface

1. Inspect all board surfaces to see that planer marks have been removed with the plane or scraper.
2. Remove all traces of glue, especially around the joints.
3. Moisten any dents (depressions) in the wood if the fiber has not been broken. Let the wood dry naturally.
4. Fill small knots, holes, and cracks by pressing in colored wood plastic or wood dough. Select the color that will match the wood when it is finished.
5. Smooth the hardened wood plastic to the wood surface. Use abrasive paper.[3]

Why is Henry suddenly willing and able to read? Because he knows what the writer is trying to get across and he knows what to do with it. He is able to think literally, critically, and elaboratively all at once and could probably discuss the following questions intelligently without even realizing that he was "giving answers."

On what basis would you select the type and grade of abrasive material to prepare a wood surface?

Why is it better to use a sanding block instead of just the paper by itself?

How would you determine when a surface had been sufficiently prepared?

How will the finished product reflect the amount of work put into this stage of preparation?

---

[3] From Chris H. Gone and John L. Feiner, *General Shop*, 4th ed. (New York: McGraw-Hill, 1969), pp. 184–185.

As these passages from the lives of Typical Henry and Bright Angela suggest, priorities of emphasis are constantly changing and the student must become accustomed to the need to adjust to different purposes in reading. The teacher can help by being aware of the nature and demands of the reading material.

WHAT IS THE RELATIONSHIP BETWEEN THE TEACHER'S QUESTIONING STRATEGIES AND STUDENT LEARNING?

Comprehension analysis is, primarily, a guide for formulating questions. Learning proceeds through the art of questioning, and no single aspect of teacher behavior is as important as the ability to pose purposeful questions, unless it is the related art of listening to answers. Like any other form of verbal expression, students' answers represent various levels of thinking, and the teacher must understand not only what the student has said in response to a question but also why he has responded in this way.

Two aspects of the use of questions will be discussed below: (1) question asking as an instructional strategy and (2) student questioning as a learning activity. In this discussion, it should be kept in mind that it might take considerable exposure and practice for students to become able to use questions effectively as learning devices. Also, as a general rule, the emphasis should be on developing complete answers to a few good questions rather than brief answers to many questions, although this is a choice of emphasis to be determined by specific instructional objectives.

Question Asking as an Instructional Strategy

One important effect of questions is that they tend to direct students' attention either toward the text itself or beyond it to their own thinking, a distinction for which Guilford's concepts of "convergent" and "divergent" thinking are very useful. In convergent thinking the individual focuses his attention on specific material and gets answers from the text, while in divergent thinking he goes beyond the material to develop answers that are not text-dependent. Textual material itself will tend to draw the reader in one direction or the other.

For example, an explanation of the atomic model in a physics text will require careful attention to the text with little basis for reflection on one's own. It is difficult, to say the least, to relate the activity of molecules to personal experience or to evaluate the concepts being presented. On the other hand, a discussion of the causes of poverty in a social studies text will call for individual response. The student is expected to relate this material to his knowledge about people and society. What he is being given are broad generalizations, subject to question, rather than scientifically verified facts.

When a text pulls strongly in one direction, toward either literal comprehension or a personally elaborated response, the teacher can choose whether to even the balance or to reinforce the tendency of the text. For example, to balance the highly factual content of the explanation of molecules, the teacher might ask the students to consider the basic role of electrical energy in the dynamics of life. Or, to balance the tendency to respond personally to the statements made in the discussion of causes of poverty, the teacher might ask students to examine the evidence given by the author for his generalizations and the strength of his reasoning. By calling for divergent thinking when the text demands careful attention, and convergent thinking when one springs too easily off into his own universe of opinions, the teacher can provide the balance between literal and intepretive reading that is the basis of effective study.

When a passage is primarily informational, teacher questions can help the students construct an overall framework for keeping the information in some kind of meaningful arrangement. For example, a history text might present a brief account of the main events involved in the establishment of the Oregon territory, spanning a period of about twenty-five years. Two relationships are important here: the sequence of events over time, and the cause-and-effect relationships that led from one event to the next. The student might first be asked to make a time line of significant events that would help him to summarize the main points in chronological order. To get at causal relationships, the teacher should provide a series of "why" questions, for example, "Why did Russia and Spain give up their claims on the Oregon territory?" and "What caused the increase in immigration to Oregon?" If the text is strictly informational, the student may have to infer his own answers to these questions or check other sources for more complete answers. Class discussion and writing would focus on fitting this interpretation of why certain events were taking place into a larger, developing view of history, as well as on the process of finding things out and keeping some kind of records. The questions used here, then, would lead the student beyond a simple accounting of events to a deeper understanding of why things happened as they did.

Sometimes questions in the text itself will help the student relate his own thinking to information. An explanation of the action of DNA molecules in directing cell specialization, for example, might ask the reader to consider why toes are different from ears, even though all cells in the body contain the same chromosomal material, or why damaged tissue replaces itself with the appropriate kinds of cells. These are, in fact, the same kinds of questions that have led scientists to an increasingly accurate knowledge of how the body maintains itself. In fact, scientists are still asking these kinds of questions.

For this kind of material, the teacher's questions should focus on both literal and inferential levels of thinking. While the questions in the text place the student in the position of the scientist hoping to discover new knowledge, the teacher will want to make sure that students understand key terms. If they understand the components of the explanation, they should be able to retell it in their own words. The explanation itself centers on certain cause-and-effect relationships. At the inferential level, the student should be guided to formulate his own understanding of the process described so that he can state it and respond to the question posed in the text. Among the latter may be questions concerning how this understanding will benefit human welfare and how models help to advance knowledge of real events. These questions help the student understand how the scientific mind works.

Through questions, the teacher can also lead the student to an examination of his own thought processes. For example, an explanation of the structural characteristics of verbs in an English text might begin with an "attention-getter"—a story of a traveler in a foreign country who must learn the local driving rules too. But the reader may have to get through several paragraphs to reach the actual topic of discussion, and many things can happen to him en route. Perhaps he gets interested in the prospect of traveling in a foreign country and loses interest when he gets to verbs. Perhaps he fails to see the relevance of the introduction to the topic at hand and is confused by the indirect beginning. Perhaps he dislikes (or likes) the subterfuge of this kind of approach. Whatever his feeling, the teacher can first find out the nature of his response to a particular passage and then help him see what the author had in mind. Questions can also set up a discussion as to the effectiveness of the kind of attention-getting devices used by writers— quite appropriate for an English class. Questions that lead the student to examine his own responses are especially useful in getting him to pose questions himself.

Helping Students To Become Question Askers

Students should learn how to ask questions as well as how to answer them. Some assignments should call for the formulation of questions that go beyond the materials read and discussed. For example, the explanation and instructions for an experiment would lead naturally to a series of questions. The teacher can make the formulation of questions a part of the whole experimental procedure, which is a way of getting them started in hypothesis formation.

Students can also direct questions to each other or to the class in discussions, and for this purpose some instruction in questioning techniques will be useful. Students as well as teachers can make use of the convergent/

divergent dichotomy, focusing deliberately on textual recall and inference at first, and then asking questions that call for extension of material. A social studies text explanation of past cultures, for example, would lend itself to this approach very well. Students could first focus on the particular characteristics of the culture being studied, and then ask comparable questions about their own times. The ancient Lapps settled in many different nations, yet retained their identity as a single society or culture. Are there examples of this pattern in today's world? The Lapp culture was characterized by common religious beliefs and common language. How are modern cultures characterized? The Lapp culture survived over many generations. Are cultures as durable today? Students can learn to project questions into a text and then extend implications of a text outward. In so doing they are learning a basic pattern for critical response that combines the message of the text with the reader's own thinking.

Models for Teacher Questioning

Guszak (1967) studied the characteristics of teacher questions on student responses during instruction. He recorded question-response exchanges in several classrooms and compiled a useful classification of types of teacher questions:

Recognition	Asking students to locate information in the text.
Recall	Asking students to recall information in the text.
Conjecture	Asking students to anticipate what might happen given some information.
Explanation	Asking students to infer reasons, conclusions, and main ideas.
Evaluation	Asking students to render a judgment of worth, acceptability, or probability.

He found that a large majority (70 percent) of teachers' questions centered on recognition and recall, resulting in what he felt was an insufficiency of opportunity for critical response.

Other writers have provided taxonomies which enable the teacher to classify and vary the kinds of questions asked in class. Two of the best known of these are Bloom's taxonomy of educational objectives in the cognitive domain (1955) and Barrett's taxonomy of both cognitive and affective aspects of comprehension (1970). These are summarized here as guidelines for teacher questioning. Like Guszak's categories, they trace the same contours of literal, inferential, and elaborative "levels" discussed above. The teacher may, however, find one particular organization especially adaptable to his purposes.

Barrett's Taxonomy

Recognition	Asking the student to locate details, main ideas, or particular relationships, all as stated in the text.
Recall	Asking the student to produce these responses from memory.

Reorganization	Asking the student to analyze or synthesize information given, that is, to perceive the structure or put together elements from different parts of the text.
Inference	Asking the student to bring in his own intuition and personal experience to extend the meaning of the text.
Evaluation	Asking the student to judge a writer's ideas.
Appreciation	Asking the student to respond emotionally to the aesthetic or psychological implications of the text, that is, to express how he feels as well as what he thinks.

Bloom's Taxonomy

Knowledge	Asking the student to identify or restate items given in the text.
Comprehension	Asking the student to indicate his understanding of the material and his ability to draw further inferences from what is explicitly stated.
Application	Asking the student to apply concepts and ideas to new situations, that is, to use information.
Analysis	Asking the student to find the structure of ideas in the text, to break down explanations into stages or constitutent processes.
Synthesis	Asking the student to bring together information from various sources, including his own knowledge and experience, and construct something of his own.
Evaluation	Asking the student to judge the quality and worth of material.

A fairly simple way to conceptualize the comprehension process, and the relationship of teacher questions to it, is to think of the text as a center line, representing literal comprehension (Figure 8–2). Above this line is a "region" we will call elaboration, and below it is a "region" we will call inference. The reader goes above or beyond the text when he is elaborating ideas and below or into the text when he is drawing inferences. In most reading, thinking will follow a wave-like progression as the reader alternately rides along with the text, delves between the lines, or goes beyond it into associations of his own. As Figure 8–2 shows, this model can be related to the models of other writers discussed above.

Some texts, say instructions for assembling a bicycle, call for close adherence to the literal level. It is annoying to have to make inferences while following directions, and flights of fancy seldom contribute to the successful completion of the task. Reading a poem, on the other hand, calls for personal associations along with careful, between-the-lines reading of the text. One can "tip" the diagram, then, and say that, with some types of material, departures from the text are restricted, while, for other types, the departures can go very far beyond the text or very deeply into it.

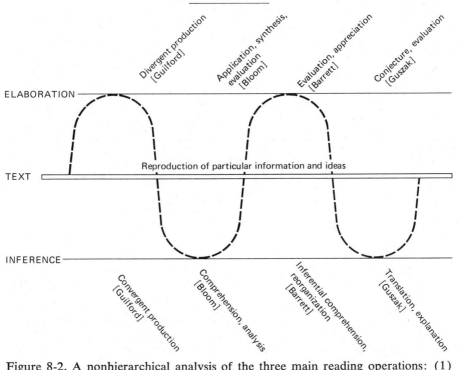

Figure 8-2. A nonhierarchical analysis of the three main reading operations: (1) text recognition and recall, (2) inference or reading for implied as well as given information, and (3) elaboration, or making connections with information outside the text. The text itself is the center line. The reader, however, is constantly going "into" the text (drawing inferences) or "beyond" it (consulting his own store of knowledge).

The diagram in Figure 8–3 suggests that different materials call for different kinds of responses, and different questions. One would hope that this way of conceptualizing the reading process in relation to various kinds of materials will help the teacher guide students through questions to the most appropriate kinds of responses.

What About the Student Who Can't or Won't?

Perhaps at this point you are still worrying about Henry, because he is in your class and you don't happen to teach shop. Of course, he may soon be earning more than you do as an auto mechanic or construction worker, but that doesn't solve your problem now as a content teacher. It is at this point that textbooks like this one tend to get vague, because Henry makes us all uncomfortable and maybe sour enough to say it's only because he didn't

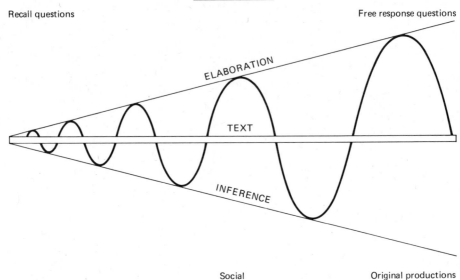

Recall questions

Free response questions

ELABORATION

TEXT

INFERENCE

| Terminology | Mathematics | Science reporting | Science concepts | Social science concepts | Literary essays | Fiction | Poetry | Original productions based on reading (discussion, writing) |

Figure 8-3. The inference and elaboration lines are tipped to show that sometimes reading remains very close to the given text and sometimes calls for fuller exercise of other cognitive operations. Purposes set for reading will help to determine whether the student adheres closely to text information or engages more freely in inference and elaboration.

learn phonics in the first grade. But we have discovered a secret about Henry which he has managed to conceal rather successfully from his English and social studies teachers. He can read his shop text. Maybe we should ask what it is his shop teacher is doing right that his other teachers can make use of.

1. In shop, the reading is linked to a concrete task that makes the purpose of the text clear.
2. Henry is not being asked to learn the material for its own sake but rather to be able to use it as a reference.
3. Therefore, the focus is on the outcome of reading, not on the act itself, which allows reading to be experienced as a natural language process.

In shop, Henry can forget the negative concept of reading he associates with books in other classes.

For students who can but won't, the teacher should try to reduce the pressure by placing emphasis on outcomes rather than on reading itself. Like the shop teacher, he should get these students involved in "hands on" projects for which reading is a useful adjunct. One very successful social studies teacher, for example, taught principles of justice by having his students stage a mock trial at which a woman was being tried for the death of her arteriosclerotic husband. Was it suicide, as the woman claimed, or murder? The old man's mind had been going, and he was aware enough of what was happening to despair of life. But then the woman was beneficiary of a fat life insurance policy. . . . Everyone in the class had a role to play, from judge to juror, and participation required them to understand the roles of the others, too. Reading materials regarding the background of the case and the procedures and responsibilities of a jury trial were distributed, and these were used to prepare for the proceedings. The prosecuting attorney won the case, incidentally, by producing a charred journal that revealed the wife's true machinations.

English teachers can produce plays, edit literary journals, have students create and exchange their own anthologies, set up paperback libraries to which students contribute books, and hold literary discussions with refreshments. Science teachers have laboratories and equipment to work with and a world from which to collect specimens or in which to make observations. One day spent on the grounds collecting leaves can provide material for a project in classification, and reading can be related to this project in much the same way that an explanation of sanding techniques is related to a wood finishing job. Mathematics resides in all the shapes, dimensions, and relationships that surround us wherever we are, and a student who has trouble grasping solid geometry can learn a lot by applying what the text says about a cube to the room he is sitting in. And always there is the possibility of talking about what has been read, using interesting formats that provide specific roles in groups small enough to allow everyone to participate.

But it isn't always possible to introduce a three-dimensional task for students whose minds begin to doze whenever material becomes purely verbal. In these instances, worksheets can provide the specific guidance that some students need. Often a learner will benefit from having his attention focused on some particular aspect of a reading assignment so he feels as secure in handling it as he does a piece of wood. These worksheets should be given intermittently so the reader does not become wholly dependent on this kind of aid, and they should vary enough so he does not develop too narrow a learning set. He can, however, learn the set of starting out with a specific purpose, which will provide an initiation into the art of bookthinking.

Henry definitely has possibilities, and it is worth the teacher's time and effort to try to make the most of them. But what about Henry's friend, Hopeless George, who throws blocks of wood in shop, leaves his government book under his chair the first day of class, and for whom no secret literacy has yet been revealed? This is the student whose problems are great enough to require the help of specialists, and the content teacher cannot be expected to meet his needs through improved teaching practices alone. To help students who apparently don't read at all, the content teacher should be aware of the special services available in his school or district.

SUMMARY

The operational definition of comprehension presented here states that comprehension involves putting together the message of the text with what the reader already knows, retaining this product in a form accessible to recall, and being able to use it in constructive thinking. This concept of comprehension implies that a communication process is being shared by reader and text.

When we think of comprehension as communication in this way, it is useful to distinguish between three levels or types of operations: literal, inferential, and elaborative. Literal operations are closely tied to the explicitly stated information in the text and are often described as recall or recognition responses. Inferential operations go beyond the surface structure of the text and pick up on such text characteristics as implied information, structural properties, writers' purposes, and other aspects of writing which are indirectly communicated. Elaborative operations involve going beyond the text into new associations or ideas in response to the text.

It is probably more useful to think of these types of operations as interacting with each other rather than in terms of a hierarchy: The literal level indicates close adherence to the text itself; inference indicates reading "between the lines" and realizing the author's purposes and intents; and elaboration indicates going beyond the text into ideas of one's own. There is obviously much interdependence among these three "ways" of comprehending. Teacher questioning should reflect an awareness of these three reading operations and give students experience with all three. Models for teacher questioning are discussed, including Guszak's classification of teachers' questions and Bloom's and Barrett's taxonomies. Finally, ways of promoting comprehension by reluctant readers are briefly discussed.

DISCUSSION QUESTIONS

1. Why are understanding, retention, and ability to use information all important in formulating a concept of reading comprehension?
2. Why do some students have trouble when asked to operate at inferential and elaborative levels of thinking? Why is it important that they be given experience in all three kinds of thinking operations?
3. What is the relationship between teacher questioning and student learning?
4. How do texts differ in the kinds of responses they elicit from the reader?

Suggested Readings

Bruner, Jerome. "Going Beyond the Information Given." In *Beyond the Information Given*, edited by Jeremy Anglin. New York: Norton, 1973.

In this essay Bruner discusses his concept of "generic learning," which entails the development of a coding system that permits the learner to select essential features from various items and form abstract concepts. For teachers, this means providing students with the opportunity to "go beyond the information given." Only in this way can they develop the kind of code needed to build abstract structures.

Ennis, Robert. "A Concept of Critical Thinking: A Proposed Basis for Research in the Teaching and Evaluation of Critical Thinking Ability." *Harvard Educational Review* 32:81–111.

In this article Ennis discusses twelve aspects of critical thinking: (1) grasping the meaning of a statement, (2) judging whether there is ambiguity in a line of reasoning, (3) judging whether certain statements contradict each other, (4) judging whether a statement is specific enough, (5) judging whether a statement is actually the application of a certain principle, (6) judging whether an observation statement is reliable, (7) judging whether an inductive conclusion is warranted, (8) judging whether a problem has been identified, (9) judging whether something is an assumption, (10) judging whether a definition is adequate, (11) judging whether a statement made by an alleged authority is acceptable. Ennis believes that each of these aspects has three dimensions (logical, criterial, and pragmatic). The lists of aspects and criteria are to be used for developing tests and designing questions for instruction purposes.

Goodman, Kenneth S. "Reading: A Psycholinguistic Guessing Game." In *Theoretical Models and Processes of Reading*, edited by Harry Singer and Robert B. Ruddell. Newark, Del.: International Reading Association, 1970.

In this essay Goodman rejects the idea that reading is a precise process of decoding from a written to a sound representation of language. Instead, he views reading as a *selective* process which involves prediction from a minimum of processed cues. Reading is a continuous process of prediction and self-correction; hence, he calls it a "guessing game."

Ruddell, Robert B. "Psycholinguistic Implications for a System-of-Communications Model." In *Psycholinguistics and the Teaching of Reading*, edited by Kenneth S. Goodman and James T. Fleming. Newark, Del.: International Reading Association, 1968.

Ruddell proposes a model to account for the four language processes—speech, listening, reading, and writing. He views comprehension and production as reversed processes of the same basic model. He assumes that reading involves a continuous process of hypothesis testing, evaluation, and revision of strategies. He relates surface structure to manipulations in short-term memory and deep structure to long-term and structural memory.

Sherbourne, Julia Florence. *Toward Reading Comprehension*, 2d ed. Lexington, Mass.: D. C. Heath and Company, 1977.

This is a textbook intended both for students in developmental reading classes and for teachers preparing to provide instruction in study-reading techniques.

Chapters are presented as "how to" discussions and cover study skills, rate flexibility, vocabulary development, organizing techniques, critical (evaluative) reading, and adapting to different materials. Although intended for college-level students, ideas are also applicable to the secondary level.

Smith, E. Brooks; Kenneth S. Goodman; and Robert Meredith. *Language and Thinking in School*, 2d ed. New York: Holt, Rinehart and Winston, 1976.

The purpose of this book is to help teachers establish a theoretical foundation for relating language and cognition. The authors' thesis is that language is the primary means by which the individual organizes and makes sense of his environment. By means of language one builds an "ordered world" and has a "map" for reference. Teachers should be concerned with the use of language to develop thought. The writers of this book present a well-developed explication of the psycholinguistic position.

Smith, Frank. *Comprehension and Learning*. New York: Holt, Rinehart and Winston, 1975.

One of the leading proponents of a cognitive approach to reading, Smith has as his purpose here to present an informal model of the learner that teachers can use as a basis for developing instructional strategies. He brings together psycholinguistics and information-processing theory to present a concept of comprehension as "the condition of having cognitive questions answered" and of learning as "the revision of a theory that does not work." Meaning does not reside in language but in the thought processes of the language user. Teaching is described as "an effort to make comprehensible."

9

Study Skills:
The Key to
Independent Learning

What are some specific ways in which content teachers can help students learn to study in their classes?

How can students become independent learners?

The key to effective study is independence. Details of content learning may be forgotten over time, but methods for finding and reviewing information for specific purposes will remain with the student as he continues to learn. Using textbooks as sources of information, establishing effective study habits, and developing library skills are extremely important parts of a student's education. A primary goal of content instruction should be to help students become independent in learning.

STUDYING CLASS-ASSIGNED
MATERIALS

Many students who enjoy reading for personal reasons don't particularly like studying, at least in some subject areas. In fact, this is almost a universal

251

phenomenon. For virtually every student, there are some classes for which the required reading is at best a chore, at worst an exercise in futility.

Study-reading is a special brand of that multifaceted activity we describe as "getting meaning from print." Among its special characteristics are these: It is assigned by someone else; its materials are selected by someone else; and someone else is going to be testing one's knowledge of the material—that "someone else" being, of course, the teacher. Yet the real objective of study-reading has nothing to do with someone else at all. The reader's real purpose is to establish a structure of knowledge in his own mind which will become a more or less permanent part of his thinking.

Studying for classes and individual teachers should be viewed as means to the end of building one's own organization of knowledge about a subject. As they mature, students should gradually come to realize that individual assignments provide the means for them to develop their own thinking. This realization is more likely to occur if students learn useful strategies for dealing with this special kind of reading that we call studying. Strategies that students understand and can use will give them control over reading material.

A BASIC PROCEDURE
FOR STUDY-READING:
THE PARS TECHNIQUE

Any task seems simpler when one has a procedure to follow for carrying it out. One popular procedure for studying is the SQ3 (or 4)R technique, which means "survey, question, read, recite, review." The fourth R is "reread" after an interval of time has passed, or sometimes "write" spelled in 3-R fashion. This technique is a sound one and has proved to be successful with advanced high school and college students. It is highly recommended in medical schools where students must absorb large amounts of essential information, and it is regularly presented in college-level study-skills courses.

For younger students, however, who are just beginning to develop strategies for study-reading, the five or six steps of the SQ3(4)R technique may be too complicated to follow through on a regular basis. For junior-high and most secondary students, a simpler procedure that accomplishes essentially the same purpose will work much better as a strategy the student can use on his own. For this reason, we are presenting an alternate approach, called the PARS technique, which consists of four logical steps for study-reading. These steps are to set a *P*urpose, to *A*sk questions related to that purpose, to *R*ead in order to find answers to the questions, and to *S*ummarize what has been learned in one's own words. These four steps will be discussed more thoroughly below.[1]

---

[1] The author thanks Bobbie Brinson for her many ideas on the use of the PARS technique.

Purpose

The first step is for the student to decide why he needs to read. Most students will have a ready response to this question: "Because I have to." This may be true enough, but it is not very helpful. The student must go beyond this to other truths, beginning with the question: "What can I, personally, gain from reading this assignment?"

At the beginning, students will probably need help verbalizing their own personal reasons for reading something. One way for the teacher to help is to share with the class *his* reasons for reading in this subject field. Why does he find this subject personally rewarding? What would he expect to gain from reading the same assignment? The teacher himself can provide a good model for finding a purpose for reading and show how he uses the title and subheads to clarify his purpose.

When they are first learning this technique, students should be encouraged to discuss purposes they can set for reading, perhaps in conjunction with some prereading activities such as those discussed in chapter 7. What are some purposes that students can set for reading in different content areas? While ideally these purposes should come from the students themselves, it should not be forgotten that they are newcomers to the subject area and will need some guidance at first. The following possibilities are given to help the teacher provide such guidance when it is needed.

Purposes of Reading in English

Literature

To understand how others act and feel.
To understand a way of life other than one's own.
To understand oneself better through the experiences of others.
To extend one's experience to times and places that are remote from the reader's present situation.
To understand different modes of expression, such as poems, short stories, and plays.
To discover how others have solved problems that might be comparable to one's own.

Writing

To understand basic units of written expression such as sentences and paragraphs.
To find ways of presenting one's own thoughts and ideas.
To understand how others have organized their ideas and presented them.
To learn standards of "correctness" for putting language into written form.

Purposes of Reading in Social Studies

History

To understand how important events happened in the past.

To understand how people have lived according to the circumstances of their times and locations.

To learn about particular people who have had a major influence on the lives of others.

To understand how past events have affected our present lives.

To understand how history is being made today.

Contemporary Cultures

To understand other societies and how people live in them.

To compare ones' own way of life with that of others.

To realize the particular problems with which various societies must deal.

To understand the connections among different cultures of the world.

American Society

To understand different institutions that affect every citizen's life.

To learn how the individual can participate in public decisions.

To understand various subcultures that exist within our society.

To understand specific values of our society.

To understand important problems that the nation as a whole must deal with.

Purposes of Reading in Science

Life Sciences

To understand how particular forms of life continue as part of the overall system.

To understand the variety of kinds of life.

To understand relationships among different forms of life.

To understand how changes affect the balance of nature.

To understand man's role in the ecology of the earth.

Physical Sciences

To understand fundamental forces that act upon the world of living things.

To learn basic laws that have applications in our experience.

To understand particular aspects of technology that affect our lives.

To go beyond outward appearances to levels of understanding that could be discovered only through science.

Purposes of Reading in Mathematics

To learn certain mathematical operations.

To learn how to solve certain problems.

To learn how mathematical principles can be applied.

To learn the special "language" of mathematics, such as tables and graphs, the slide rule, and the calculator.

Purposes of Reading in Vocational Education

To understand the nature of particular tools, equipment, and materials.

To learn how to perform certain procedures.

To learn how to find the causes of certain problems.

To find out precautions that must be taken to ensure personal safety or avoid damage to equipment.

To understand underlying principles of operation.

To understand models, diagrams, specifications, and other technical information concerning products.

Ask

The next step is to ask questions. These will be related to the purpose the student has set and will also involve him directly in the reading material before he actually reads it. Questions can be thought of as road signs. Putting up these signs tells a reader where he's going and whether or not he's reached his destination. In other words, questions set up an initial structure for reading, which tells students what to do with information as they read along.

Two kinds of questions will be discussed here. The first are questions that can be applied to almost any expository prose (writing that is primarily explanatory)—that is, to most textbooks. The second kind are questions related to specific content.

For almost any piece of writing, the reader may ask about the author's purpose in writing, the accuracy or authenticity of his information, his main ideas, his conclusions, and his evidence. Some questions might be these:

1. What was the author's purpose in writing this?
2. What are his main ideas?
3. How are these ideas supported?
4. What assertions does he make?
5. What conclusions does he reach?
6. What evidence does he give for his conclusions or assertions?
7. What important facts are given?

Questions related to specific content can be derived from the organizational cues given by the writer of the text. One way to formulate questions is to convert chapter subheadings into question form. For example, the subheading outline for a textbook chapter on nuclear fission could be converted into the following questions:

I. What is the nature of nuclear fission?
  A. How and with what consequences can the nucleus of an atom be split?
  B. What is meant by the separation of U-235?
  C. What is the significance of critical mass?
  D. What is the nature of nuclear reactors?
  E. Why is heavy water the best moderator?

F. What is the significance of plutonium?

G. What uses can be made of nuclear reactors?

II. What applications can be made of nuclear radiations?

A. What are some consequences of dangerous radiations from nuclear reactors?

B. How is radioactivity measured?

C. What are radioisotopes?

D. What is the technique for radioactive dating?

III. What is the nature of nuclear fusion?

A. How does nuclear fusion produce energy?

B. What is the nature of the hydrogen bomb, a product of nuclear fusion?

For practice, try converting these subheadings into questions:

Religion influences medieval thought about the universe _____

European history reflects certain trends _____

Internal combustion engines _____

All machines waste energy _____

The components of style _____

Building a unified paragraph _____

The ontogenetic development of geometric illusions _____

Tests of cognitive and S-R interpretations _____

Reading as a cognitive and affective experience _____

Developing special comprehension skills _____

Read

With his purpose set and his questions in mind or on paper, the student is prepared to read. He has a plan for processing the information and ideas. If he uses his plan, his reading will be much more active than if he had simply started cold with the first word and plodded on through to the end, usually with no clear idea of what he was doing or why. The structure he is able to apply will help him to remember the content better for classroom purposes.

More important, the organization he imposes upon the material will help him to make sense of it in his own terms, and this is essential for long-term learning.

Reading now is part of an overall effort to get organized to learn. When a person reads a novel, a letter, a newspaper, or a recipe, he easily provides his own context of personal interests and needs. Study-reading however, will probably require a conscious plan to set up a context, because it is not immediately relevant to the student's own life. When students learn how to set up their own contexts for reading, they can gain the confidence to believe that they can cope with textbook reading, and will prepare themselves with paper, pencils, reference books, and so forth to achieve their end. As they learn to establish purposes on their own and to devise their own questions, they can even begin to relate personally to the task of acquiring textbook information.

Summarize

Learning will be "fixed" in the student's mind when he can put principal ideas into his own words. This is the importance of summarizing. In a summary of the material, the student should be able to say how he has accomplished his purpose for reading and to answer the questions he asked. He should also be able to state the main ideas in the text material, the general significance these ideas have for him, and perhaps other ideas or information they suggest.

The summary represents the form the content has taken in the reader's mind. Over time, he is much more likely to remember his own summary rather than the details of the text itself. The summary represents the reader's individual processing of the material, which is the way in which he makes it his own.

PARS

P Set a *purpose* for reading.
Make it relevant.

A *Ask* questions about the text that will guide your thinking as you read.

R *Read* with purpose and questions in mind, with a sense of how you will use the information.

S *Summarize* in your own words what you have read.

This, then, is the PARS technique, a procedure for study-reading that is simple enough for young readers to use, yet applicable to reading at any level. Students will need guided practice in learning to use this technique, but once they have acquired the habit of approaching reading assignments systematically, they will be well equipped for independent study. There is perhaps nothing more valuable that they can gain from a class.

Application

Select a chapter from any textbook you are currently using and apply the PARS technique. If possible, select material which has little intrinsic interest for you or which you consider difficult. How does a systematic approach to such material differ from less-organized reading? Does it make you feel that your reading was more profitable? Do you feel that your study time was more effectively used?

EFFICIENCY READING TECHNIQUES

The PARS technique is a method to be used for covering required material that is assigned to be read in detail. It makes possible the systematic processing of material so that students will be able to grasp the content of the entire assignment.

Other kinds of techniques are useful for other purposes. For example, there will be times when a student needs to scan a lot of material to find a few items of information relevant to his particular purpose. This would be the case if he was doing library research for a report on trying to find particular topics in a daily newspaper. For these kinds of tasks, which will become more common as the student progresses through school, efficiency-reading techniques are very useful.

Generally speaking, efficiency reading emphasizes speed. It is based on the assumption that a person can read at many times his usual rate and still comprehend well enough to derive the basic meaning from a text. Some claims made for speed-reading, for example the claim that a person can learn to read as fast as he can turn the pages, seem questionable, or at least not applicable to most readers. But students in high school and college frequently demonstrate speeds from 1,000 to 5,000 words per minute under conditions of controlled practice.

While a speeded-up rate is not appropriate to all purposes in reading, the ability to go over material at a fast rate is certainly a useful skill to have. For regular reading assignments, speed-reading can enable one to read something twice instead of once in approximately the same amount of time. Thus the first reading can serve as a preview of the second. This can be especially useful in reading material such as fiction that does not especially lend itself to the PARS technique. It can also be used as a technique for reviewing material just before a test or other recitation.

Skimming is distinguished from speed-reading in that it is usually more selective. The student may skim for major ideas, for specific content, or for new or important words. What he is looking for depends on what he has decided he wants to find. Or the student may skim in an evaluative way to see whether a piece of writing suits his purposes and is worth the time for closer study. Skimming will also be useful to the student in adult life when he might need to determine work priorities, seek information for specific purposes, or handle a great amount of correspondence. The adult will also use skimming when he browses in a bookstore or library.

The principles underlying speed-reading and skimming are simple and essentially the same. The reader forces himself to go at an uncomfortably fast rate, grasping what he can of the content without allowing his eyes to regress. As he continues to practice at this uncomfortable rate, he adjusts to it cognitively, so that he is able to make more and more effective use of the material he sees as his eyes hurry along. He learns to take in more information with each eye fixation and actively to construct meaning as he goes along. Eventually, if all goes well, his comprehension catches up with his speed. Then it is time for him to begin practicing at an even faster rate. To convert speed-reading into skimming, one need simply have a particular objective in mind so that one is trying to spot certain items in the text rather than process all of it. A student's skimming should always be faster than his speed-reading.

The content teacher may want to give students practice in these efficiency techniques and can do so in only a few minutes a week. Timed readings can be administered to an entire class with a stop watch and a set of cards showing a count by tens from 0 to 400 (or more, depending on the reading ability of the students and the length of the passages used for timed readings). The teacher gives the students a prepared reading for which the words have been counted. Initial readings should have no more than 900 to 1,200 words. But, as students improve their reading rates, longer passages can be used. When the class begins reading, the teacher clicks on the stop watch. The click of the watch can be the signal to begin. As the class reads, the teacher holds up a card in sequence every ten seconds; the number on the card shows the number of seconds that have passed. As each student finishes, he notes the number of the card being shown, which tells him how many seconds it took him to read the text. This can be converted to words-per-minute by the following formula:

$$\frac{\text{words read}}{\text{seconds}} \times 60 = \text{words read per minute}$$

Before students compute their WPM scores, they should be given a brief comprehension check to let them know how well they are understanding at the speed they have reached. This kind of speed practice can be given in a few minutes once a week, and, over the school year, students can record their progress. Many students get very much involved in this kind of activity and will push themselves to see their speed increase over a period of time.

Sample Rate Record

DATE	SELECTION NUMBER	WPM	COMP. SCORE

A simple chart for recording speed-reading progress encourages students to work on rate improvement.

The teacher can provide practice in skimming techniques by having students try to find particular items in a text through rapid reading. For example, in the following passage, students could be directed to any one of a number of specific tasks:

Find a scientific explanation of mirages in 30 seconds.
In one minute, find as many examples of mirages as you can.
In 30 seconds, find an explanation of a double mirage.
In one mintue, find two examples of mirages seen on the sea.

Nature played an old trick on Charles Lindbergh, the first man to fly alone across the Atlantic Ocean. Toward the end of the long flight, the tired flier was happy to see green hills and beautiful trees. At last, he thought, he had safely reached Ireland.

"But a few minutes later," Lindbergh said, "this false land disappeared. I found before me the long stretch of the silent sea." When the vision had appeared, Lindbergh was 200 miles from the coast of Ireland!

Fliers have often reported mysterious, shadowy airplanes flying near them. "When my plane comes out of the clouds, with the sun behind me," one pilot said, "I have noticed a second plane 30 or 40 yards ahead of me. Though I know it is my plane's shadow, it always surprises me. The shadow looks exactly like my plane.

"Often it is surrounded by a circle or rainbow colors."

On mountain tops, travelers may see their own shadows as "ghosts," when sun and mist appear at the same time. On the thick mist, the sun casts a huge shadow of the traveler. Colored circles, or halos, may be around the head of this ghost.

Even an experienced traveler may be fooled by such strange images, called mirages. In 1906 Robert E. Peary, the famous explorer, thought a mirage was a new land in the Arctic. He even gave it a name—Crocker Land! Nine years later, other explorers found that "the faint white summits of a distant land" described by Peary was a mirage.

A mirage is not imaginary, though your imagination may play a part in what you think you see. It is a real expreience, caused by unusual conditions in the air.

Light rays are bent when they pass through layers of different thickness or density. When you thrust a straight stick halfway into water, the part below the surface appears to be bent sharply upward. The light rays from the lower part have passed from water to air before reaching your eye. Because water and air are of different densities, these rays have been bent from their usual straight paths. The part of the stick below water appears to be removed from its real position.

Cool air, denser than warm air, acts like the water in the case of the stick. Rays of light are bent in passing from one layer of air to another. So, whenever air layers are of widely different temperatures, mirages may be seen.

On the desert, for example, the hot sand causes a layer of very hot air. Above, the air is usually cooler. The traveler may see what looks like a reflection of trees in a lake. The image is out of place because the hot air bends the light that brings the image to his eyes. The "lake" is sky.

An explorer in northern Canada suddenly saw a camp pitched on top of a mountain, above the clouds. The camp was upside down! Examining it with his telescope, he noticed several dogs around it. After half an hour's travel on flat ground, he found an Eskimo camp. It was the very one he had seen upside down in the air.

In the arctic seas, three ships may sometimes be seen where there is really only one. The first is the real ship. Above it, upside down, is the first reflection. Above that is another reflection, right side up. When warm air passes over frozen seas, it becomes sandwiched between two layers of cold air. So, a double mirage may be seen.

When a layer of warm air rises to great height, the most striking of all mirages—a "loom"—may appear. In one of these looms, off the New Jersey coast, sand dunes thirteen miles away were clearly seen in the sky. In Arizona, a loom showed the Grand Canyon in the air. In Wisconsin, Milwaukee appeared above Lake Michigan.

In a mirage sometimes seen off the coast of Italy, castles appear in the sky, with towers reaching dizzy heights. This beautiful mirage is simply a reflection of buildings on another shore![2]

Help students periodically review their efficiency reading techniques by using a checklist like the one that follows.

---

[2] From H. C. North, "Mirages—Tricks of Nature," in Franklyn M. Branley, ed., *Reader's Digest Science Reader* (Pleasantville, N.Y.: Reader's Digest Services, Inc., 1962), pp. 119–122.

Efficiency-Reading Checklist

	NOT SURE	NEVER	SOMETIMES	USUALLY	ALWAYS
1. I read easy books rapidly and with understanding	—	—	—	—	—
2. When reading rapidly, I look for main ideas	—	—	—	—	—
3. Before reading, I preview material to see what rate I should use	—	—	—	—	—
4. I change reading rate from one selection to another as needed	—	—	—	—	—
5. I skim when looking for a single fact or other item	—	—	—	—	—
6. When skimming, I try to infer meanings from context	—	—	—	—	—
7. I read silently without subvocalizing	—	—	—	—	—
8. I read groups of words rather than one word at a time	—	—	—	—	—
9. I do not look back at material already read	—	—	—	—	—
10. I try to keep increasing my rapid-reading speed	—	—	—	—	—

NOTE TAKING

The basic principle of effective study is to take the meaning from a text or lecture and make it part of one's own thinking. Meaning becomes part of the reader/listener's thinking when he can put it into his own words. Therefore, good note-taking strategies are an important part of good study techniques, and the learner will benefit from guided practice in how to take notes.

Note taking consists of extracting essential meaning cues in a form that can later be used in reconstructing a more comprehensive version of what was read or heard. For this task of reconstruction, organization is very important. The better organized a set of notes is, the more sense the notes will make when consulted later. Students also need practice in using their notes. Because a full set of notes represents a condensation of material covered over a period of time, the task of interpreting them is actually a special kind of reading that students must learn to do.

Perhaps the most effective way to organize notes for later use is to put them in a modified outline form—modified in the sense that the outline combines topical, sentence, and even paragraph form. Major topics and subtopics can provide the basic organization for the notes, while supporting ideas, facts, and definitions are put into more complete form. At the same time, students should be encouraged to make their notes as concise as possible and to put ideas into their own words rather than copy or quote extensively verbatim. The basic guiding principle should always be kept in mind: Make something your own by putting it into your own words.

Following are some examples of how notes might look. You should notice that outlining is used to give structure to the notes but does not become an end in itself.

Notes from a chapter on prehistory (first 4 pages of a 15-page chapter).

"The Dawn of Man"
  I. Origins of the universe
      A. What is the Big Bang theory?
          1. Countless galaxies created when a single original mass of matter exploded (10 billion years ago).
          2. Galaxies now rushing outwards at high speed.
          3. Elements formed at time of "bang."
      B. How did the solar system develop?
          1. Condensation of cloud and dust particles (4.5 billion years ago).
          2. Formation of central and satellite masses.
          3. Contraction and rising of temperature of central mass.
          4. Surrounding masses became dependent planets.
      C. What is the impact of scientific theories?
          Great—most people accept them. Most religions find scientific theory compatible with their beliefs.

  II. Beginnings of life and man
      A. How did Darwin believe life evolved? (Key ideas)
          1. *Struggle for existence:* Animals must compete for limited food supply.

2. *Survival of fittest:* The strongest are able to stay alive and bear young.
3. *Natural selection:* Animals with particular characteristics that help them in their environments will be the ones to survive and reproduce.
4. *New species:* Over millions of years, animals of a species become so different because of different environments they are no longer the same species. That's how new species come into being.

B. What did scientists find out about early man?
Raymond Dart and Robert Leakey, anthropologists:
1. *Australopithecus*—S & E Africa, 2 million years ago.
2. *Homo erectus*—500,000 years ago, more advanced, used fire, hunted big animals.

For notes on reading, students can begin with the outline they construct from the subheadings in a reading assignment. In the example above, these subheadings have been converted into questions. At first, the teacher might want to duplicate a worksheet on which the outline appears with sufficient space for notes to be filled in. A similar format can be used for practice in taking notes from a lecture. The teacher can plan a lecture that is well organized and then provide students with a basic topical outline that provides space for taking notes as the lecture proceeds. Later, of course, students should provide their own outlines.

Since outlining is such a valuable skill, you may wish to spend extra time helping students perfect their technique. The following procedure will help students gain an understanding of the function and construction of an outline that is formally structured and relatively complete.[3] Although carefully constructed and detailed, outlines are not always called for in note taking. Focusing on the formal aspects will enable students to grasp the concept of outline organization more clearly. Having mastered the concept, they will then be able to use it more effectively for their own purposes.

Procedure for Teaching Outlining Skills

Directions: Provide students with an outline that is complete through the first three levels. Their task at this stage is to compare the outline with the text, noting form and the relation among elements of the chapter.

[3] The outlines presented here are taken from Kenneth D. Wann, Henry J. Warman, and James K. Canfield, *Man and His Changing Culture* (Boston: Allyn & Bacon, 1967), pp. 108–128.

Chapter 4   "Ancient Cultures in the River Valleys"

I. The Tigris-Euphrates River Valley
   A. Conditions in the valley promoted settlement
      1. Rich soil (silt) was provided by the flooding rivers
      2. Rivers provided moisture for dry land
   B. The Sumerians were first to live in the valley
      1. Developed good water-control system
      2. Irrigated dry land
      3. Built cities of sun-dried bricks
      4. Food surpluses led to specialization
      5. A way of writing was developed
      6. The Semites conquered the Sumerians

II. The Nile Flood Plain of Egypt
   A. Physical features of the region
      1. Little rainfall in Egypt
      2. Flooding covered land with silt
      3. The Nile River begins in mountains of central Africa.

The second step in this procedure is to provide students with an outline that contains labels for major sections and a list of the number of points to be found under each label. Students must provide the information that is missing from the outline.

Chapter 5   "Cultural Gifts of the Ancient Greeks"

I. Greek Lands
   A. Physical features
      1.
      2.
      3.
      4.
   B. Sources of food
      1.
      2.
      3.

II. A scattered nation
   A. Greek city-states
      1.
      2.
   B. Sparta
      1.
      2.

The third step is to provide students with an outline that contains only a list for major sections and subsections. The student must complete the information that has been omitted.

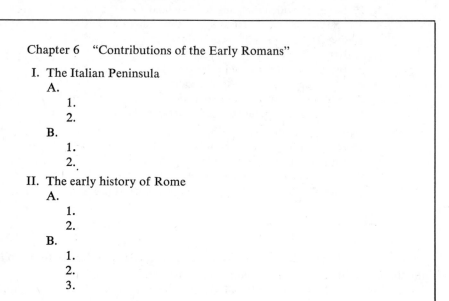

Next the students can supply all of the labels for an outline. Only the form of the outline is given, with the number of points in each section indicated.

After the teacher leads students step by step through the elements of outlining, they should be ready to attempt an entire selection on their own.

When students are first learning note-taking techniques, it is especially important for them to have their notes checked occasionally by the teacher. Oral feedback is often sufficient. While the students are engaged in note taking from reading, for example, the teacher can move among them and comment briefly on the notes they are producing. Listening notes can be collected for a brief check. The main things to look for are the extent to which students are avoiding mere copying from the text and whether they are getting the main ideas. Students should be reminded frequently that the purpose of their notes is to enable them to recall later the substance of what they are reading or listening to now.

To acquire good organizational habits, students should have a specific place where they keep their notes (always dated, in sequence), either in a notebook or a filing folder. For younger students it may be a good idea to begin with a folder that is kept in the room and later switch to a notebook which it is the student's responsibility to keep. As in other kinds of bookthinking activities, a main objective in note-taking instruction is guidance toward increasing independence.

Application

Construct a note-taking worksheet for students based on a chapter of a textbook in your subject field. Then outline a lecture you might give and design a note-taking worksheet based on that.

Practice in making use of notes is just as important as practice in taking them. One way of providing such practice is to have students use their notes to write their own prose versions of what they learned earlier. Notes can also be used for class or small-group discussion. Just before a test, the teacher can conduct a review in which notes only are used. The more students are required to rely on their notes as a record of what they have learned, the more likely they are to develop note-taking strategies which really work for them. They will become more adept at grasping the structure of a text or lecture (or providing their own structure when this is necessary), recognizing key ideas, putting concepts into their own words, and using notes effectively for review. Note taking is another way of gaining control over material, and practice in note taking will prove invaluable to the student as he continues to learn in school.

ESTABLISHING AN
ENVIRONMENT FOR STUDY

One of the reasons study can be difficult for adolescents is that they are physically active people with a great interest in interacting with others. In other words, like most of us, they would rather be "goofing off" than toiling over a task, especially one which requires them to be quiet and alone. Sitting down in the company of a book and sheet of paper may have considerably less appeal than other available activities. Most teen-agers still have much to learn about the benefits of solitary communication with the written word, especially when it is required textbook reading.

Young learners are much more likely to persist when they have a setting and a system for study. The setting will reduce the influence of competing attractions in the environment, and the system will get them through the task efficiently so there is time for those attractions as well. If students can devise their own rituals for study, they are much more likely to make it a regular and even an important part of their lives. Following are some suggestions that should help students in this respect:

Setting

1. If possible, have a place set aside for studying. Preferably, this will be a desk in a quiet corner. This study area should be equipped with good lighting, pencils, pencil sharpener, supply of paper, dictionary, and anything else you find useful in studying.
2. Music played low on a radio or record player may be a helpful accompaniment to study, but television and talk should be avoided. A person cannot effectively process language from different sources at the same time, and he will get through the study task more quickly if there is no competition with the language in the book. Similarly, turning up the volume on the stereo will only make music competitive with study.
3. Let other members of the family know that you do not wish to be disturbed while studying except in emergencies.
4. Maintain order at your place of study. Since organization is what studying is all about, you can positively influence yourself by avoiding clutter and the accumulation of extraneous objects where you work.

System

1. Prepare to study by arranging your materials, sharpening your pencils, and composing yourself mentally for the task.
2. Allocate time for various subjects and assignments in accordance with the requirements of your classes. Maintain a calendar of assignments that enables you to plan each day's study in advance. Above all, don't let assignments pile up.
3. Use a study strategy appropriate for each assignment. This might be the

PARS technique for study/reading, efficiency reading for periodic review, interpretation of study notes in preparation for a test, or on-paper planning for a writing assignment or other project. The main thing is to have an approach to each study task.

4. Plan short breaks at regular intervals. If you know a break is coming, you are more likely to concentrate while you are at work. Study is most effective when done intermittently—that is, with occasional breaks that allow the mind to relax.

5. If possible reward yourself for a good study session. You deserve it! Save your dessert, talk to a friend, watch a good television show, or schedule some other enjoyable activity as a reward for achieving your study goals. Remember that positive reinforcement is a very effective practice in learning.

Help students develop their awareness of personal study habits by having them fill out a checklist at the beginning of each new grading period. Then they can reach their own conclusion about where improvement is needed in the weeks to come.

Study Habits Checklist

Name _____
Date _____

SETTING: Where I study	Yes	No	Sometimes
1. I have a place set aside for studying.	—	—	—
2. I keep materials needed for studying at my place.	—	—	—
3. I have good lighting and a quiet atmosphere.	—	—	—
4. I can avoid distractions at my study place.	—	—	—
5. Others understand that I am not to be unnecessarily disturbed while studying.	—	—	—

SYSTEM: How I study	Yes	No	Sometimes
1. I make sure I have what I need at hand before I begin to study and organize myself for each task.	—	—	—
2. I plan ahead and schedule my study time.	—	—	—
3. I keep a calendar of assignments and tests for all classes.	—	—	—
4. I set specific purposes for each assignment.	—	—	—

5. I use a study strategy appropriate
to each assignment. — — —
6. I concentrate while I am working and
plan short breaks for relaxation. — — —
7. I reward myself *after* I have
accomplished my study purposes. — — —

Teachers can help students organize themselves for study by giving them assignments and test dates well in advance, perhaps even making up a monthly "calendar of events" for the classroom. Planned study sessions at which specific study techniques are applied will help students devise their own study routines. The experience of sitting down and applying a particular strategy can be transferred to home study. Teachers can also show students how to work in pairs or small groups, using questions and answers to rehearse material. The main principles to apply to this kind of study are: Have students formulate their questions, and make sure that they participate as both question askers and answer givers.

USING THE LIBRARY

The next time you are in a school, visit the library. It may well be one of the most inviting areas in the building: walls of books, wide tables for study, interesting displays, a quiet atmosphere, and, above all, order. All the materials and resources in this richly equipped room are cataloged and arranged so that one person can find anything—provided, of course, that he or she knows how to use the system on which the order is based.

Also while you are in the library, ask yourself this question: Is it being used? Often a visitor will notice that the school library seems rather empty, as if it were there to be admired rather than disturbed. But like a home, a library should be not only attractive but lived in. It should be a place where students feel comfortable because they can use it for their own purposes. The library should be a center for independent learning.

But a library will mean little more than shelves of books and required silence to a student who does not have the skills needed to find materials. No matter how well stocked, a library is as useful as the knowledge he has of how to use it, and no more. For this reason, every student should have a variety of library experiences throughout his school years, in different classes, so that he can learn to use the library in different ways. Through experience, his grasp of basic library skills will be reinforced while he learns to use the resources available for specific purposes.

A student can learn a lot about using a library from his content teachers because they can provide guidance for using materials in their subject areas. The content teacher can assign projects that will get students involved in library use and can also show students how a library can help them meet personal information needs.

For example, Becky, a serious eighth grader, tells her science teacher that she wants to be a veterinarian. With his guidance, she can find information on this career possibility in her school library and also be directed to the kinds of reading she will do as she pursues this interest—books and articles about animals, biology, and other scientific areas that a veterinarian must understand. She can learn about educational requirements and the high school classes that will help her get ready for college study. In this way, she can base her planning on something more specific than a fondness for dogs and cats. Even if Becky has not really made her final career choice at the age of thirteen, she can learn much about how to follow up on an idea and base further decisions on real information. And, if she remains serious about her choice, she will have a head start on a demanding course of study.

The first step in teaching library skills is for you to become thoroughly familiar with the library facilities in your school. Spend some time in the library to get a feel for using it, as if you were going to write a term paper and had only these resources to use. What reference books are available? Which ones do you want your students to learn how to use? What books and periodicals in your field does the library have? Is the card catalog complete with subject, author, and title cross-references? Does the library have several encyclopedias? Does it have a newspaper collection? Does it have career information? Are there books related to your field in the fiction section, and, if so, how can students find them?

While you are in the library, get to know the librarian, for this person will be invaluable to you when you begin to plan instruction centered on library use. The librarian is a resource person who can give your class an introduction to this particular library and a review of basic information-finding strategies. It may be possible, working with the librarian, to plan projects designed to give students practice in specific skills. In addition, you can find out from the librarian how you can request materials to be added to the library collection.

Generally, library skills fall into two main categories: how to find materials in the library, and how to make use of them once they are located.

LOCATING INFORMATION

The three primary ways that students will use to find materials are (1) consulting the card catalog, (2) using other indexes such as the *Reader's Guide to Periodical Literature,* and (3) browsing among books on shelves.

In many school libraries, the card catalogs may be the only general reference system available, although juniors and seniors should have the opportunity to use other kinds of indexes. Browsing is effective when students can find their way around in the shelving system of the library.

A complete card catalog will list each book in the library by title, author and subject—three cards for each book. Students should have practice finding books all three ways. Simple exercises with activities such as the following can help students gain basic familiarity with the card catalog:

Title: Find the name of a book by John Gunther that is about life in America.

List the titles and call numbers of all the books by _____ (any particular author).

Author: Who wrote the book entitled *The Invisible Pyramid?*

Who wrote a book about the French Revolution?

Subject: Find the names, authors, and call numbers of five books about Africa.

Find the author, title, and call number of the book you think would be useful if you wanted to find out about America in the 1930s.

These problems will appear to be straightforward if students have some familiarity with catalog cards. To provide this familiarity, duplicate for each student a sheet on which an author, a title, and a subject card for the same book are shown. As students gain experience using the catalog, they can attend to other kinds of information given on the cards, such as the following:

1. Specific abbreviations, such as *c1973*, meaning "copyright 1973," or *192p illus*, meaning that the book has 192 pages and illustrations.
2. Information directing students to other potentially useful sources.
3. Information concerning the author.
4. Call numbers, which make it possible to find the book on the shelves.

Most libraries use the Dewey Decimal system for classifying books, and the call numbers of the book refer to this system. In the past, some students have been kept temporarily out of mischief by being made to memorize the Dewey Decimal system, but probably the only long-term learning that took place was an aversion to the task. Students need only learn the general arrangement of books in the library so that they can track down a particular call number or browse productively. They can understand the basic function and organization of the system from a chart indicating the major classifications:

000–009	General Works
100–199	Philosophy
200–299	Religion
300–399	Social Sciences
400–499	Language
500–599	Pure Science

600–699	Applied Science or Technology
700–799	The Arts
800–899	Literature
900–999	History

Because this type of chart is usually on display in the library or can easily be duplicated for students, there is no need for them to memorize even this much of the system. They do need to be able to use it as a map for finding their way around. The content teacher will also want to familiarize students with subcategories related to his subject matter. Using a more detailed listing of a major classification, students can learn to survey a section of related books. This strategy is especially useful when a student is narrowing down a general topic to a specific idea and wants to skim through the materials available.

The student should also learn what materials besides books are available in his library, for example, filmstrips, pictures, maps, records, magazine collections, and special learning kits or other resource packages. He should be familiar with the reference section where he will find encyclopedias, atlases, large dictionaries, directories, and other special volumes.

To gain an idea of the scope and diversity of a large library, older students who have comfortable command over the resources of their school facilities should be taught to use public and university libraries in the area as well. Again, members of the library staff can be recruited in this effort. Few of us fully appreciate how useful public libraries usually are, and even you as the teacher will probably learn something new about how the library can serve professional and personal needs.

Using Books

When they use the library to find information from different sources, students are engaging in research. They will need to be able to find relevant information, record it for future use, and eventually synthesize what they have found into a single, coherent report. All of these steps can be taught as a part of content learning.

The table of contents of a book provides a structured outline of its subject matter. Sometimes a table of contents will simply list the titles of chapters. But often other kinds of information such as subtitles or major units or brief summaries will also be included. By reading the table of contents, the reader can asse. the appropriateness of a book to his particular needs.

Sometimes a book will list illustrations, figures, and maps separately. If so, the student can make a judgment concerning the usefulness of this kind of information to his needs. Using both the table of contents and lists of graphics, the student can turn to introductory sections in the book or find captions that summarize information. The teacher can help students use these organizational aids by paging through several chapters of a book with them and pointing out such organizers and how they inform. Used in conjunction with skimming, organizers provide an excellent means for locating information in a book.

One of the most important reference aids in a book is the index, which gives a more exact location of the information the reader seeks in a book. An index is nearly indispensable for using a book that contains information, especially when the reader needs to be selective. Students can practice using the indexes in their textbooks. Instruction can begin with the simple task of locating specific terms in the alphabetical index and noting a specific page number. Later, students can practice using cross-references, identifying entries that might provide information on a topic, and employing multiple indexes in the same book.

A set of volumes, such as an encyclopedia, might have a separate index and outline for the whole series. Sometimes this indexing system can be quite elaborate. For example, *Encyclopaedia Britannica III* has a *Propaedia*, a single volume outlining human knowledge with references to specific volumes; a *Micropedia,* ten volumes which give short articles on subjects with extensive references to other volumes in the set; and a *Macropedia*, nineteen volumes which provide lengthy discussion of important topics. Students can learn a lot about research simply by becoming familiar with the system of this set of encyclopedias.

Recording Information

The note-card technique for gathering information is a good way to keep research notes organized in a form for future use. Following is a procedure for developing a set of notes that can be used conveniently:

1. Keep bibliographic references on 3 by 5 cards, using one card for each reference. These can then be kept in alphabetical order by author's name as new references are added. The following information should be recorded for each entry:

   Author, last name first. Title of book, underlined. Publisher, copyright date.
   Page numbers consulted.
   Call numbers of the book.

2. Use 4 by 6 or 5 by 8 cards for reading notes. Each card should be headed as follows:

   Topic   Author or reference work   Page reference

With this information at the top, cards can be sorted according to topics. The author's name provides a reference to the appropriate bibliography card, so it is not necessary to repeat bibliographic information here. The page reference is important for giving proper acknowledgment of the source of a quotation or idea.

3. Record information concisely on one side of the card only. A second card should be used if more room is needed. Cards are much easier to use if they can be laid out flat with all information immediately available to the eye. Information should be paraphrased economically with quotations used sparingly and for specific purposes, for example, when it seems necessary or most effective to use the author's own words. The following cards illustrate notations from two articles from the *Encyclopaedia Britannica*:

Lunar Craters   *Britannica*, Vol. 12, 420–22

Types of Craters:

Bowl-shaped craters: usually less than 20 kilometers (12 miles) diameter. Up to 3 kilometers deep, raised rims.

Saucer craters: very shallow.

Crater pits: no raised rims.

Ray craters: center of systems of rays "now known to consist of numerous small bright craters and blocks of light-toned rock." (p. 421) Rays up to 1,900 kilometers.

Dark-halo craters: have dark rings around them possibly volcanic deposits.

Dome-top craters: located on top of a swelling.

Parasitic or ringworm craters: in the walls or ridges of other craters.

Chain craters: a line of craters of the same type.

Rille craters: craters or chains that "form part of lunar rilles, which are trenchlike features" (p. 421).

Deepest & largest craters mainly in the meridional belt of the moon's southern hemisphere. Various theories to explain craters. They seem to be systematically arranged.

Michelangelo   *Britannica*, Vol. 12, 97–98

Early life & Works

Born 1475 in Caprese. Four brothers, father mayor of town.

1488: became apprentice to painter Domenico Ghirlandajo.

Studied sculpture under Bertoldo di Giovanni.

Became known to Medicis, spent time in household of Lorenzo Medici in Florence. Gained reputation as a "Medici man."

Early Works

Madonna of the Stairs (relief) about 1490
Battle of the Centaurs (relief) about 1490
Sleeping Cupid (disguised & sold as antique) 1494
Crucifixion (wooden statue) 1494

(continued on next card)

Note cards can be sorted and used as the basis for writing an outline for a report. Many students will need guidance in using their note cards the first few times, and class time will be well used for that purpose. The teacher might also demonstrate how to write notes in card form on the blackboard or overhead projector. Similar demonstrations of how to arrange cards and derive an outline will also be very helpful.

KEEPING TRACK
OF INDIVIDUAL STUDENT
PROGRESS

The ability to use a book as a source of information is so important that it is well worth the time to monitor each student's progress in the skills involved. By using books and other materials for specific purposes, the student will develop his critical reading skills and acquire the habit of setting purposes. By regarding regular written work and classroom observation as a source of diagnostic data, the teacher can build his awareness of individual student progress. A checklist like the one that follows, adapted to particular content needs, can be used to keep track of observations.

Student's name

Rating key
1. Has great difficulty with this.
2. Making progress but still in need of help.
3. Has a grasp of all essential elements and needs occasional checking.
4. Completely independent of all assistance.

   I. Organization
      Can the student do the following?

    a. Take notes

    b. Determine relationships between paragraphs

    c. Follow time sequences

    d. Outline single paragraphs

    e. Outline sections of a chapter

    f. Summarize single paragraphs

    g. Summarize larger units of material

    h. Make generalizations

    i. Draw conclusions

    j. Derive "drift" of unit from table of contents, topical headings, topic sentences, and so on

II. Knowledge and use of reference materials

    Can the student do the following?

    a. Use the dictionary

    b. Use indexes of books easily and efficiently

    c. Use encyclopedias

    d. Use library card catalog

    e. Use other library reference systems

    f. Understand the purpose of footnotes and bibliographies

    g. Use the following sources to locate materials:

        1. Atlas

        2. World Almanac

        3. Glossary

        4. Appendixes

        5. _____

        6. _____

        7. _____

        8. _____

III. Following directions

    Can the student do the following?

    a. Follow steps in sequence

    b. See relation between purposes and directions

IV. Specialized skills

    Can the student do the following?

    a. Follow a table by reading across and down from given points

    b. Understand the purpose of lines and bars in graph measurement

    c. Relate graphics to written text

    d. Interpret diagrams

    e. Read maps and map keys

    f. Interpret topographical features

    g. Measure distance, areas, and elevation

    h. Interpret special maps such as these:

        1. Outline map

        2. Population map

        3. Agricultural map

        4. Mineral production map

        5. Climate map

V. Other specialized skills

Can the student do the following?

a. Understand the significance of pictorial aids
b. Observe and infer from picture representations
c. Read and interpret charts
d. Read and interpret cartoons
e. Read and interpret diagrams
f. Read and interpret scales

g. _____
h. _____
i. _____
j. _____

UNDERLYING PRINCIPLES OF LEARNING

One of the best ways to help students acquire effective study behaviors is to understand some basic principles of learning that underlie the study strategies discussed in this chapter. Such principles are central to human learning at all levels and can be incorporated into instruction in many ways. Students can also learn to understand these principles themselves and therefore develop their own theoretical base for devising effective strategies. A few of the most important learning principles are discussed below.

Learning Principles[4]

1. *Learning to make old responses to new stimuli is a basic condition for positive transfer:* As students apply specific study strategies to various materials, they will be establishing their knowledge of methods as well as learning content. Every time they use a strategy effectively, they will increase their chances of applying it successfully to new material.

2. *Humans may show strong persistence of old habits in new situations where they are no longer appropriate:* This is the other side of the coin from the principle stated above. Too restricted a range of reading and study behaviors may be difficult to expand. Habits are hard to break, and students will not easily give them up or resist relapses into old, less effective ways of doing things. By the time the student gets into junior or senior high school, he has many years of habit learning behind him. Helping him become more flexible in his responses to various learning situations may require persistence on the teacher's part.

3. *The key to effective memory is direct practice in the retrieval process, that is, in producing the information:* Input is not all that is important in learning. A student can read a text ten times and not do better on a test than if

---

[4] From Henry C. Ellis, *Fundamentals of Human Learning and Cognition* (Dubuque, Ia.: William C. Brown Company, 1972).

he had read it only once. He needs to practice output as well. He needs to practice saying and/or writing what he has learned. The problem that most people have with memory is not so much *storage* of information as *retrieval*.

4. *Human memory can process only about seven "bits" of information at a time, but if you "chunk" or group information into categories, you can process a greater amount of information:* The better a student can organize information into ideas and concepts, the more efficiently he will be able to learn. For example, seven words can be a single "bit" of information if they form a sentence, but they remain seven "bits" if they have no apparent relationship to each other. If the student can relate items into larger structures, his learning capacity will be increased. Therefore, it is important to emphasize relationships in teaching content material.

5. *Concept learning requires that the learner come to respond to the relevant dimensions of the concept and to ignore irrelevant dimensions:* To learn a concept, students must understand its essential, defining features. Positive examples, which show how the concept is applied, help them to identify the common relevant features. Negative examples, which show how the concept does *not* apply, help the student realize which features are irrelevant to defining that concept. Both positive instances and negative instances are important.

6. *Distributed practice facilitates the acquisition of skills:* While this principle applies specifically to motor skills, it can also be applied to other kinds of skill learning. It states that short practice periods distributed over an interval of time will be more effective than a single long practice session, although the same amount of actual time may be spent in both cases. The best way to teach a skill is to arrange for brief practice activities at regular intervals rather than try to teach the skill thoroughly at one time.

7. *As the degree of motivation increases, problem-solving efficiency increases up to an optimal point, beyond which increases in motivation produce a reduction in problem-solving efficiency:* Too high a level of motivation is like anxiety in its effects and can have similar paralyzing consequences. Students should be calm and collected when they study, an outlook they will be more likely to achieve if they have confidence in their study strategies. It will also help if teachers de-emphasize grades and competition in favor of less emotionally charged forms of feedback.

8. *Thinking refers to a class of covert activities that involve the manipulation of symbols. For man, the most important symbols are language and concepts:* This principle is fundamental to everything said in this book. Teachers of all subjects at all levels are engaged in the common enterprise of helping students develop conceptual knowledge and language facility.

SUMMARY

A primary goal for every class should be to help students become independent learners. Most students will need some help to develop effective strategies for doing academic work, and this kind of help can be an integral part of content learning. A recommended general study procedure, especially for younger students, is the PARS technique (*Pur*pose, *A*sk, *R*ead, *S*ummarize). To help teachers guide students in this procedure, the PARS technique is related here to specific subject areas. Examples of purpose setting and question asking are given.

Uses of and techniques for efficiency (speed) reading are discussed. Other aspects of study covered are note taking, organization for study, using the library, using reference books, and collecting information for papers and other projects. The major point emphasized is that students can learn and apply specific techniques that make learning in school easier and more directed.

A number of generalizations from learning theory are summarized. These are as follows:

1. Students will be able to transfer study techniques from one situation to another.
2. Students need a lot of practice to break old habits and establish new, more effective ones.
3. Recall can be improved by practice in retrieving information.
4. Learning will become more efficient as students learn to organize information into ideas and concepts.
5. Both positive and negative examples are important in concept learning.
6. Short practice periods distributed over time will be more effective than a single long practice session.
7. Too much motivation to succeed has effects similar to those of anxiety and can reduce learning efficiency.
8. Developing conceptual knowledge and language facility is the basis of school learning.

DISCUSSION QUESTIONS

1. Why do students often need specific strategies for dealing with required reading?

2. In this chapter, reference is made to "gaining control over material." What is implied in this phrase?

3. How can "overmotivation" be counterproductive in learning? In your judgment, what is the optimum motivation for school achievement?

4. What are some study strategies that seem especially important in your content area?

Suggested Readings

Gilbert, Doris Wilcox. *Study in Depth.* Englewood Cliffs, N.J.: Prentice-Hall, 1966.

The purpose of this book is to provide an orientation to serious study with advice for effective planning and scheduling as well as specific study strategies. Other practical skills covered include taking notes, using the library, learning from textbooks, and key points on reading in various content fields. Of special interest is a listing of selected references for setting up a reading-study laboratory.

Pauk, Walter. *How To Study in College.* 2d ed. Boston: Houghton Mifflin, 1974.

This is an excellent tool book for the older student who is interested in taking an organized approach to academic learning. Chapters include an analysis of the academic setting, general memory and concentration skills, and specific advice for study in various subject areas. Other strategies discussed are notetaking, paper writing, and studying for exams. Throughout are practical illustrations and formats for applying the skills discussed.

Scholastic's Go Series: An Instruction Skills Text Series for Grades 4 Through 8. Englewood Cliffs, N.J.: Scholastic Book Services, 1976.

Each book in this series includes selections from four content areas—literature, math, social studies, and science—to show students that skills are applied differently in different subjects. Self-checking exercises, high-interest readings, and practice opportunities help students acquire the skills they need to understand basic concepts in the four areas and to apply reading and reasoning skills. For the content-area teacher, skills are outlined and procedures worked out step by step so that they can be presented by teachers with little or no training in this aspect of reading instruction.

Smith, Nila Banton. *Read Faster and Get More from Your Reading.* Englewood Cliffs, N.J.: Prentice-Hall, 1957. Paperback edition: *Speed Reading Made Easy.* New York: Popular Library, 1957.

This is a self-help book intended to help its user improve in a variety of study techniques including skimming, scanning, selecting main ideas, and reading for details as well as increasing speed. Each chapter provides a number of exercises that enable the reader to practice the techniques explained. The clear explanations and accompanying practice pages make this an excellent book for secondary students, especially those preparing for college.

Spache, George, and Paul Berg. *The Art of Efficient Reading.* 2d ed. New York: Macmillan, 1966.

The aim of this book is to help students increase their reading flexibility. Techniques are presented that, while they do increase speed and understanding, also emphasize the need to adapt to different purposes in reading. The book constitutes a training course for college-bound students and contains many suggestions that could also be adapted to junior high and secondary classes.

10

Characteristics of Subject-Matter Bookthinking

How can a student analyze a text to learn better from it?

What different characteristics can be found in the writing of one subject matter versus another?

When a student begins to take classes in content areas, he must learn to use reading as a primary means of learning. This means that he is expected to be able to read independently. It also means that he must be able to adapt his reading to different kinds of materials.

A writer of a mathematics textbook, for example, may want his reader to stop after every statement and solve a problem, while the writer of a short story may want his reader to "hear" the rhythm of his sentences and so read nonstop over long passages. Other textbook writers ask questions as they go along or put parenthetical information in footnotes, altering the reader's pace and response. Sometimes a science writer will develop the logic of an explanation so tightly that the reader must go over it several times to grasp all the connections. If the content of a text happens to be about human affairs, as in social studies material, the reader can make personal associations. But if it happens to be about microbes or galaxies, he must deal with it using the tools of abstraction.

Any content area can be looked at in two ways: (1) as a particular body of material, composed of concepts and information, and (2) as a set of strategies for thinking. The view of this chapter is that a subject area book is a body of material that provides the vehicle for acquiring thinking strategies. In other words, materials should be used as a means for teaching students ways of thinking.

A VIEW OF LEARNING

"Learning" in a content area, according to this view, does not mean mastering a certain body of information. It means developing the ability to absorb new information and ideas, to relate them to what is already known, and to make applications. It means weaving a fabric of understanding, not simply collecting threads. As a teacher, you have the important task of guiding students in the development of reading/thinking strategies that will enable them to read independently in the kinds of materials characteristic of your field.

Typically, at the beginning of the second year, a student is issued a textbook in each of his classes. He then has a tall stack of heavy books with which to deal as he makes his way from one grading period to the next. Looked at from the student's point of view, the prospect can appear rather formidable. Each textbook provides its own challenge—or, as the case may be, obstacle in the student's experience.

Teachers are often as baffled as students when it becomes apparent that many young readers cannot handle the amount and diversity of reading that has befallen them. Even students who have acquired sound basic reading skills may have difficulty making the adjustment to the varied reading assignments they receive in different classes. They need preparation, guidance, and specific strategies for reading and learning in each content area. In this way, their development in bookthinking can proceed.

The first step in this development is teacher awareness. The teacher should understand the nature of materials in his area and the demands these make upon the student. He should then plan ways to prepare students for his reading assignments. Getting students to read particular material is an important part of instruction. It can mean the difference between losing a large percentage of the class on homework assignments and keeping them involved as active learners.

This chapter examines the general characteristics of reading in different content areas and uses samples from a variety of middle school and secondary texts. A strategy for analyzing a text in any area to find ways to help students deal with that material is also presented. The final part of the chapter will discuss preparation and follow-up activities that will help the teacher integrate reading with classroom instruction.

Bookthinking in English Classes

Diversity of reading selections is the rule in English classes. Students read stories, novels, poetry, essays, and plays—in addition to texts on grammar and writing. Literature as taught in English classes is the most direct extension of the kind of reading experienced in earlier grades, with an emphasis on narrative content and concepts relating to personal and social experience. Through this kind of reading, the student is invited to extend his personal experience by entering into the experiences of others. He looks into the mirror of literature and sees a reflection of his own life, as well as many other aspects of human experience that he might not previously have understood.

Besides literature, most English classes have instruction in communications skills per se, including the rules or conventions of writing. Material in this area tends to be explanatory and sometimes prescriptive. This is in contrast to material calling for a very personal, reflective response. Writing exercises often require the use of models or the application of specific instructions to original work. This emphasis on technique and the development of rather abstract skills makes reading them a quite different task from that of more literary selections in English.

A third area often found in the English curriculum is instruction in the nature of language. This can be grammar in the traditional sense, or a more philosophical approach that attempts to go beyond the prescriptive level of standard grammar texts. In the latter case, these materials represent beginnings of studies in linguistics and communications. The reader often is made aware of the human being as a verbally communicating animal— that is, of the importance of language to us as thinkers.

From the student's perspective, mixing those three rather different kinds of materials into a single "subject" may be rather confusing. But undoubtedly there is a relationship. Learning to write goes along with the reflective thinking encouraged in literature study, and because both writing and literature make the student conscious of language and communications, it is appropriate to focus on language as an object of study too.

In most ways, however, English emphasizes the personal response. The student learns to extend his own experience through reading and writing. Consider the following excerpt from a short story by Wilbur Daniel Steele, "Footfalls," anthologized in a secondary literature text:

Footfalls

Nothing in his life had been so hard to meet as this insidious drain of distrust of his own powers; this sense of a traitor within the walls. His iron-gray hair had turned white. It was always this now, from the beginning of the day to the end of the night: How was he to know? How was he to be inevitably, unshakably sure?

Curiously, after all this purgatory of doubts, he did know them. For a moment at least, when he had heard them, he was sure. It was on an evening of the winter holidays, the Portuguese festival of *Menin Jesus*. Christ was born again in a hundred mangers on a hundred tiny altars; there was cake and wine; songs went shouting by to the accompaniment of mandolins and tramping feet. The wind blew cold under a clear sky. In all the houses there were lights; even in Boaz Negro's shop a lamp was lit just now, for a man had been in for a pair of boots which Boaz had patched. The man had gone out again. Boaz was thinking of blowing out the light. It meant nothing to him.

He leaned forward, judging the position of the lamp chimney by the heat on his face, and puffed out his cheeks to blow. Then his cheeks collapsed suddenly and he sat back again.

It was not odd that he had failed to hear the footfalls until they were actually within the door. A crowd of merrymakers was passing just then; their songs and tramping almost shook the shop.

Boaz sat back. Beneath his passive exterior his nerves thrummed; his muscles had grown as hard as wood. Yes! Yes! But no! He had heard nothing; no more than a single step, a single foot pressure on the planks within the door. Dear God! He could not tell!![1]

The reader of this story is being asked to do a number of things: to share the perceptions of the main character, who happens to be blind; to imagine a scene that is set in a foreign culture; and to sense the growing doubt and anxiety that keep Boaz from acting. The writing attempts to involve the reader emotionally, but makes definite cognitive demands too. The sentences are complex, and the vocabulary sometimes difficult. The reader must make good use of his imagination to place himself in the experience of the main character. At the same time, he must understand the premises underlying that character's thoughts and actions.

Now consider an excerpt from a secondary writing text, in which the author is trying to convey a particular technique for paragraph development.

Developing with Examples

The author of the following paragraph collects words in the same way that someone else might collect stamps and old coins. In this paragraph he tells about a prized part of his collection, words that are unfamiliar but refer to things which everyone recognizes. He cites several examples to illustrate what he means.

WARREN WEAVER
in "THE CASE OF THE WAYWARD WORDS"

Still another part of my (word) collection, and one of which I am particularly proud, since I invented the category myself, contains nouns which, as a mathematician might put it, "maximize the product of the familiarity of the unfamiliarity of the object's name." In other words, these are very unfamiliar names of very familiar objects. All of us are familiar with the underside of a

---

[1] From Wilbur Daniel Steele, "Footfalls," in *Exploring Life through Literature* (Chicago: Scott, Foresman, 1964), pp. 17–31.

staircase; but apart from a few doublecrostic fans, how many people know that it is called a *soffit*? In at least an impersonal sense we are all familiar with the bottom of the sea, but do you know the name *benthos*? Everyone with trees and shrubs to care for is familiar with the long wooden pole with a pruning shear on the end of which is a blade operated by pulling a rope, but have you ever asked your wife where the gardner put the *averruncator*? Most persons are familiar with the strangely curved handle of a scythe, but few call it by its proper name, which is a *snath*.

The Writer's Craft

1. What is there about the topic in this paragraph that makes it especially suited for development with examples?

2. Suppose the writer had used one example and had stopped with his mention of *soffit*. What would the paragraph have lost by not including *benthos*, *averruncator*, and *snath*?[2]

This passage asks the reader to look at the application of a concept and derive his own generalizations from it. He is also being given a model to use in writing paragraphs of his own. But first he must understand the model—that is, be able to read the specimen paragraph with understanding. If he can understand it, he then must be able to analyze it and then apply his analysis. These are really quite sophisticated operations. The textbook author has tried to state his own concept very simply and then ask questions that would help the student to make his analysis. Even with this help from the writer, however, the process may be very abstract for many students.

The next passage calls students' attention to emotional attitudes toward words:

Please Pass the . . . Ah! Hmmm . . . Drumstick

In the nineteenth century, polite society became so horrified at vulgarity and ashamed of sex that people shuddered at the mention of anything physical. Instead of being *pregnant*, women were in a *delicate condition*, *in a family way*, or *expectant*. Their children were not *born*; the *little strangers* were *brought by the stork, came into the world*, or *saw the light of day*.

Prudishness reached its golden age in the straitlaced Victorian era. In rural American, *bull* was considered an indecent word, and the proper substitute was *he cow*, *male cow*, or *gentleman cow*. Rather than use such an improper word as *leg*, the Victorians referred to *limbs* even when talking about the legs of a piano or chicken. If someone wanted the leg of a chicken, he asked for the *drumstick* or *dark meat*. If he wanted breast of the chicken, he asked for *white meat*.

Since someone sitting on a chair rests a "shameful" part of his body on the chair, *chair* became a taboo word and was replaced by *seat*. But then seat also became associated with the *backside* (another euphemism) and was judged an improper word. Even *couch* got a bad reputation. It was replaced by *davenport*. It makes you wonder if the Victorians ever did sit down.

---

[2] From Harold Fleming and Allan A. Glatthorn, *Composition: Models and Exercises, Book 10* (New York: Harcourt, Brace & World, 1965), p. 21.

Such extreme squeamishness sees indecency where indecency does not exist. It suggests the editor of *The Century* magazine who insisted on cutting from *Huckleberry Finn* such "dirty" lines as *"I was in a sweat"* or *"Dern your skin!"* Nearly anything can be made embarrassing or improper by those who wish to make it so.[3]

This entire passage actually explains one vocabulary item that is buried in parentheses two thirds of the way through the article. That word is *euphemism.* The reader is also asked to understand, mainly through inference, the powerful emotional effect that words can have on people for cultural reasons. Readers in another culture (or time) can hardly understand what the fuss was about. But also by drawing inferences, readers can understand that the same principle applies to their own time and culture. There are always some words that are "taboo," and understanding why gives psychological insight into a culture. A passage such as this, then, requires considerable critical response, and the ability to go beyond the information given into various related ideas.

Bookthinking in Social Studies

Social studies as a content area focuses on the human dimension of the environment. An important purpose of social studies instruction is to impart to students the social consciousness and understanding they will need to think as members of groups, communities, the nation, and the human race as a whole. Reading in this area, then, is a way for students to expand their sense of personal relationship to the world, going beyond the immediate environment in both space and time. Reading also helps them to understand the larger structures and institutions of society that are difficult to comprehend unless placed in perspective. People who do not have this kind of knowledge tend to be intimidated by institutions and helpless to change unfavorable conditions that affect them personally. An important task of the social studies teacher, then, is to enable students to interpret and act upon the complex society of which they are a part.

There was once a time when history was associated with memorizing dates and social studies with making up lists of the principal products of remote nations (tin comes from Bolivia), while the study of government was mainly a salute to a narrowly defined patriotism. Since then there has been a revolution in the writing of social studies materials with a new emphasis on concept formation and problem solving. In addition, it is now recognized that almost any kind of material can be used including newspapers, magazines, novels, plays, government documents and publications, nonfiction paperbacks, and even comic books. Moreover, social studies is bolstered by the medium of television, which has been teaching children

---

[3] From Joseph Fletcher Littell, ed., *Gaining Sensitivity to Words* (Evanston, Ill.: Littell & Company, 1973), p. 53.

to extend themselves beyond their immediate environment from an early age.

Nevertheless, social studies materials present a special challenge in reading because this subject requires constant growth of critical thought. Students are often asked to think abstractly on subjects about which they are used to thinking concretely. For example, everyone is familiar with a bank as a place where one keeps or borrows money, and perhaps has a safe deposit box. This concrete notion of a bank can be so firmly impressed by the time the student encounters a course in economics that the real impact of banks on our society is difficult to comprehend. Or a student might have acquired very definite personal attitudes toward certain groups that get in the way of understanding the interactions of different kinds of people in the whole society.

One might say that the content of social studies material asks the student to relate personally to events remote in time and space, and to think abstractly about immediate experiences. This is the paradox that makes social studies teaching a challenge.

Reading material in social studies also emphasizes inferential thinking. There is considerable use of diagrams, tables, graphs, flowcharts, and models to present complex concepts and information. Secondary and primary sources are often combined, as in a chapter on revolutionary change in an American history book that quotes the American Declaration of Independence, the Constitution and Bill of Rights, Thomas Carlyle's description of the storming of the Bastille, and Thoreau's essay on civil disobedience. This means that the student is exposed in one assignment to a variety of styles. He might also be called upon frequently to draw generalizations from particular instances or to reason analogically, as when two political events are compared to each other. If there is a word for social studies materials, it is *potpourri,* but it is the variety that provides such excellent opportunity for teaching critical thinking and for developing strategies for reading different types of material.

Here is a passage from a secondary economics text which presents information on the American system of banks. Note that the emphasis here is on information, of which there is quite a lot in this short passage:

Commercial Banks

The 14,244 commercial banks in the United States are private corporations operating like other corporations formed for the purpose of making profits for their stockholders. In order to establish a bank corporation, the prospective bank stockholders must obtain either a national bank charter from the federal government or a state bank charter from the state government. A commercial bank cannot be operated unless a charter is obtained first. The decision to incorporate under state or federal law depends on the preference of the organizers and stockholders of the bank.

The state banking laws vary a great deal from state to state but are largely patterned on the federal legislation governing national banks. In most cases, however, the state regulations are not as stringent as those of the federal government. Most of the larger commercial banks have national charters; and although less than one-third of all commercial banks have national charters, they hold about 60 percent of all deposits. If you receive a national bank charter, you must also become a member of the Federal Reserve System. State banks may join the Federal Reserve System if they meet the standards set up by the system.[4]

This passage and the material that follows it present specific facts from which the reader is to build a concept of the national banking system. To do so, a student must have some prior concepts of large institutions in our society and the rules by which they operate. He must understand the concept of a corporation. He must also have some understanding of state and federal government. This is an example of reading that is firmly embedded in prior learning. Over the long run, the specific facts that seem to be the main content of this passage are not as important as the general concept of banking the reader is able to derive from them. Many students will need guidance to get beyond the specific facts of a passage like this.

The next passage is more narrative in style but also largely composed of specific facts:

The Dutch Lost Their Colony

Colonists from Sweden settled on the Delaware River, near what is now Philadelphia. Soon, Dutch soldiers marched from Manhattan Island, captured a fort from the Swedes and took over their land.

New Amsterdam, in turn, was captured by the English in 1664. In that year, an English fleet arrived at the settlement. Peter Stuyvesant (sti v sent), the Dutch governor, ordered his soldiers to fire on the English ships, but they refused. England took over New Amsterdam and the colony of New Netherlands. The name of the colony was changed to New York, in honor of the Duke of York, the brother of the English king.

The Dutch influence on life in New York was strong, even though they had lost their colony to the English. Brick houses with tile roofs, looking much like those in Holland, were used long after the English took over. For more than a hundred years, the Dutch language was spoken in New York. Dutch people continued to go to Dutch churches, and their children attended Dutch schools.

The land that became the colony of New Jersey was first claimed by the Dutch. Later people from Sweden started a settlement there. New Jersey was finally taken over by the English.[5]

Here the reader is to build a concept of the development of a life-style during a period of political changes. The time is in the past, remote to the

---

[4] From Richard W. Lincoln and Paul Driscoll, *Our American Economy*, 4th ed. (New York: Harcourt, Brace Jovanovich, 1970), p. 316.

[5] From Clarence L. Ver Steeg, *The Story of Our Country* (New York: Harper & Row, 1965), pp. 113–118.

reader. Yet he is asked to visualize a particular setting and relate this to swift changes in national rule. This in turn would require some understanding of the international struggles going on during this period. What were the actions of settled countries when new lands were being found and claimed? What does it mean to say that one nation took over from another? Even though the text is clearly and simply written, it may be difficult for students to relate to a sequence of events that affected so many people in the remote past.

The next passage is interesting because it does try to get the student involved in understanding the concept behind a fact. But as you look at this, ask yourself whether you can answer the question posed at the end of the short text (Figure 10–1). What kinds of thinking does this question seem to require?

Here the reader is being asked to respond critically to two diagrams that illustrate mechanical processes. This requires the analysis of nonverbal, visual information. It may be difficult for a reader at any level to appreciate the differences between the two mechanisms as they are pictured here. To begin with, one cannot assume that a reader knows the function of rods and pistons. If he does not, he obviously can't go on to make a judgment concerning the efficiency of their operation. While this kind of illustration may be very useful in helping students understand the "why" of an event, the students may need help in understanding the diagram itself.

Bookthinking in Science

From the time of Aristotle, western civilization has been shaped by its "scientific mode of thought," characterized by controlled observation, analysis, and careful reasoning. Yet, while science is the basis of western thought, many citizens are scientifically illiterate, and students often have difficulty dealing with science materials.

One of the reasons for this is that comprehending science materials usually requires a background of formally acquired knowledge. Almost any reader has had some personal and social experiences that can help him to fill in associations that will make English or social studies material meaningful, but most areas of science have primarily academic connections in the student's mind.

Consider the following passage from a physics text. (Try to assume the point of view of a naive reader if your background is in science.)

> *The concept of matter.* In the study of science, the composition of the universe is divided into two entities, matter and energy. In keeping with the scientific method, we must truthfully admit that there may be something in the universe besides matter and energy, but so far science has not found such a third component. Matter includes the materials in the universe: the rocks,

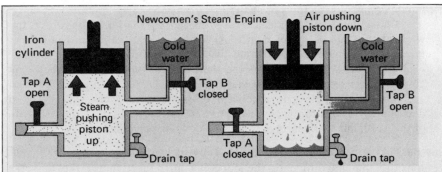

To start, Tap A was opened to let in enough steam to push the piston up. Then Tap A was closed and Tap B opened to let cold water in to condense the steam. Air then pushed the piston down. The water was drained and the process started again.

One of the new machines was an engine run by steam. In 1705 Thomas Newcomen invented a steam engine that could make rods go up and down. Sixty years later, James Watt was repairing a steam engine like the one Newcomen invented. Watt realized he could improve Newcomen's engine. He made a faster, more powerful steam engine that used less fuel. Compare the drawing of Watt's engine with the drawing of Newcomen's engine. Can you figure out why Watt's engine worked better?

When steam pushed the piston to the top of the cylinder, Tap A closed. Tap C then opened to let steam into a side cylinder. Air pushed the piston down. Tap B was opened to let cold water into the side cylinder to condense the steam. The water was drained and the process repeated.

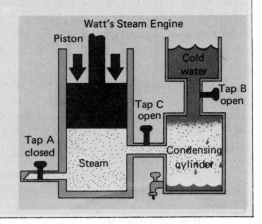

Figure 10-1. From *Inquiring About Technology: Studies in Economics and Technology*, Holt Databank System, edited by William Fiedler (New York: Holt, Rinehart and Winston, 1972), p. 47.

the water, the air, and the multitude of living things. Anything that is solid, liquid, or gaseous is a form of matter.

Classifying something as a form of matter does not mean, however, that we know the real nature of matter. As we have seen, the chemist takes matter apart to determine its building blocks and the physicist wants to know what holds these building blocks together; but the fundamental particles and laws of matter seem to be ever a challenge.

The best way to gain a concept of matter is to work with it and to describe its various forms. A description is not a definition in the real sense of the word, but it brings an abstract idea down to concrete terms.[6]

This passage is not difficult to read at a literal level of comprehension, and yet consider the magnitude of the concepts introduced here: the universe, matter, energy, fundamental particles, and fundamental laws. What do these terms really mean to the young reader? If he attempts to assign his own personal meanings, these are likely to be inadequate. In science, the personal perspective is not enough and may have to be set aside because it is misleading. From the personal perspective—today no less than 500 years ago—the earth is flat and arched by the path of the sun. We know otherwise, most of us, not because we are sophisticated but because we have been indoctrinated from an early age. In our culture, it is easier to reject the notion of a deity than the model of a solar system. Yet both are articles of faith for most persons.

Science is, essentially, an enterprise in which logic is used to make the most of a small amount of evidence, with careful testing to find the accuracy and power of the logic. Reading material in science, then, often represents a great amount of compressed thought. Years of hypothesis building and testing can be compressed into a single statement. The young reader often feels the weight of this compression without being able to respond to it. In other subjects, personal elaborative responses to material are encouraged, but in some science areas the student must often suspend his own responses and try very hard to match his thinking processes to those of the author.

In science classes that emphasize an experiential approach to learning, reading can be quite different. Here the reader may be asked to draw concepts from his experience and perform experiments that lead him to further understanding of these concepts. In this case, as the following passage shows, reading is very closely integrated with personal response:

How about Classifying Living Things?

1. Would location be a good system? Can we put all African animals in one group and all South American animals into another group? Explain.

How about pattern? Perhaps we can put all striped animals into one group and polka-dotted animals into another group.

---

[6] From John E. Williams, H. Clark Metcalfe, Frederick E. Trinklein, and Ralph W. Lefler, *Modern Physics* (New York: Holt, Rinehart and Winston, 1972), p. 9.

2. Do you think pattern is a good system? Explain.

The process of putting related objects, such as organisms, into similar groups is called *classification*. One system used today to classify organisms can be traced back to a set of books published in 1758 by the Swedish scientist, Linnaeus.

3. What do you predict is the preferred system used by scientists to classify living things?

B. *WHO'S RELATED TO WHOM?*

Obtain the same collection of cards used in the last investigation. Each card will have the picture of an animal on it, the name of the animal, and some information about the animal.

Sort through the deck of cards and find the 15 cards that are different.

You will be given 15 data punch cards like the sample shown on top of the next page.

Transfer the information from each of the animal cards to the data punch cards. The procedure is as follows:

a. Write the name of the organism on the punch card.

b. There are names of structures on the edge of the punch card. If the organism has any of the structures listed, cut a "V" in the hole above the structure. *Do not make a cut if the structure is absent.*

c. Repeat this procedure for the remaining 14 animals.

d. Leave the line after "Group" blank for now.

You now have 15 data punch cards, all punched in different ways. Is there any order to the differences? Let's see.[7]

The reader is led through a series of questions designed to elicit his own present understanding of the topic, classification. Then he is given a set of procedures to follow so he can apply what he knows to the classification of animals. Reading that calls for response in such a direct way will mean little unless the student actually does express his response. It is usually not enough that he try to answer questions in his own mind as he reads along. It is also important to give him the opportunity to talk about the concepts he infers from a task such as this.

Bookthinking in Mathematics

In his mathematics text for students who don't like math, Harold Jacobs tells the story of a mother who was concerned about her son's lack of progress in this subject. It was not so much that he did not understand mathematics, she said, but rather that he just didn't seem to believe it.

What she meant, perhaps, was that mathematics seemed so abstract and remote from the world of concrete experience that it fell into a

---

[7] From Harry K. Wong and Melvin S. Dolmatz, *Biology, Ideas and Investigations in Science* (Englewood Cliffs, N.J.: Prentice-Hall, 1971), pp. 66–69.

credibility gap. Indeed, it is not uncommon to hear someone confess that he has forgotten everything that he learned in a math course although he "did all right" when he was taking it. In mathematics, thinking is condensed to logic, and the emphasis is on performing logical operations rather than storing information and ideas. In this sense, learning mathematics is somewhat akin to language acquisition. One can do long division without being able to explain the logic of the progress, just as one can produce grammatical sentences without being able to explain the syntactical relationships involved. Mathematics has its own symbol system, vocabulary of word concepts, and syntax, which one must learn to be able to read in this subject.

What does learning to use the language of mathematics entail? Some of the basic features of the task are these:

Learning the vocabulary of special symbols and notations.
Understanding the syntax of equations and formulas.
Recognizing the equivalency of alternate forms of the same mathematical statement (just as one recognizes that two sentences worded differently can have the same meaning.)
Separating variables in a problem that can be solved using mathematics.
Understanding mathematical concepts, including theorems and axioms.

Mathematics enables the student to practice basic logical operations that can be comprehended better, it seems, through practice than through explanation. Therefore, the prose in mathematics textbooks tends to be terse and disconnected into separate statements or short explanations, so that students spend more time in the application of concepts than in the reading of them. Texts feature specific concepts to be applied to problem-solving, step-by-step procedures that represent logical chains and verbal problems that have specific solution strategies. Often, too, there is graphic supplementation to written explanations.

Following is a passage from the book mentioned earlier, Jacobs' text for students who don't like math.[8] You will note that the conceptual load is low in comparison to that of other types of texts discussed here. But the concepts that are presented are quite abstract and require considerable manipulation by the student to comprehend.

Logarithms

Although we now know the logarithms of the numbers from 1 through 10, we still don't know the logarithms of any numbers larger than 10, except for those numbers that are multiples of 10: 100, 1000, and so on. Many other logarithms can be found by simply adding the ones we already have. For example, the logarithm of 12 is equal to the sum of the logarithms of 3 and 4, since $12 = 3 \times 4$.

1. Find the logarithm of 12 by adding the logarithms of 3 and 4.

---

[8] From Harold R. Jacobs, *Mathematics: A Human Endeavor* (San Francisco: Freeman, 1970), p. 161.

2. Since it is also true that $12 = 2 \times 6$, the logarithm of 12 can be found by adding the logariths of 2 and 6. Check your answer to problem 1 by doing this.
3. Find the logarithm of 36 by adding the logarithms of 4 and 9.
4. Check your answer to problem 3 by using the logarithms of 3 and 12.

Copy each of the following equations, and fill in the missing number. Then find the logarithm of the number on the left of the equal sign. To save space, we will abbreviate the "logarithm of n" as "log n."

5. $\log 20 = \log 4 + \log$ _____
6. $\log 20 = \log 10 + \log$ _____

Reading here is definitely subordinated to actually working with the problems given. At the same time, however, it is essential that the student process everything written in order to develop his understanding. He is also reading when he deals with equations. All this reading assumes that he has grasped the concept of the logarithm itself. Because the student is operating in a symbolic and conceptual system different from that of his natural language, he may have difficulty grasping the concepts involved as he attempts to solve specific problems.

Bookthinking in Vocational Education

Learning to use technical materials is an important part of job training. When he is on the job, the student will need to be able to read manuals, catalogs, instructions printed on equipment, employee notices, and a host of other written communications.

Teaching the students to deal with textbooks in vocational-education classes, therefore, is an important part of preparing them for a job. These texts, however, can be difficult to read for several reasons. The first is that every occupational field has its own technical vocabulary, which the student must learn as part of his training in that field. This relatively large proportion of new terms can interfere with fluent reading. Another reason is that technical books frequently combine verbal and pictorial information, and the reader may need to learn techniques for dealing with this kind of presentation. Diagrams, models, photographs, and step-by-step illustrations of procedures are common. In addition to relating verbal and pictorial information, moreover, the student often must relate both to real objects that may have only a general correspondence.

Another common characteristic of vocational education reading is that it is presented as factual material which is to be accepted at face value rather than considered more critically, as materials in English or social studies classes usually are. The writer is usually an expert in his field with command over a great amount of technical information, and his objective is to convey as much of this information to the student as he can. As a result, texts in vocational-education courses often have heavy conceptual content, and this is combined with the large number of vocabulary items the reader must learn. Anyone who looks through a vocational textbook in an unfamiliar field realizes the density of the material. Yet students must acquire this technical information if they are to become competent in the field, and they must learn to use their books as references in preparation for using on-the-job materials.

Following are some examples of typical kinds of materials found in vocational-education textbooks (Figures 10–2 and 10–3). A relatively high vocabulary load is illustrated in Figure 10–2, an explanation of free electrons from a text on electricity and electronics.

Looking at the technical vocabulary alone, we found the following terms that must be understood for this short passage to make sense:

electrons	positive terminal
conductor	voltage source
atom	negative terminal
polarity	positive charge
voltage	impulse
insulator	

In addition, the student must infer a complex process from a highly schematic illustration that accompanies the text.

Figure 10–3 illustrates the combination of verbal and pictorial information. This is a rather complex example, for the student must not only identify the parts of the machine shown but also visualize the relationships among the parts and their operation.

The fact that the information in vocational textbooks is applicable to hands-on tasks, or can be related directly to later job success, is an advantage to teachers of technical subjects. Students with a high level of motivation and working experience may not have appreciable difficulties with vocational-education materials. But inexperienced students who are poor readers probably will. Any student will benefit from specific guidance in the acquisition of technical vocabulary and the use of nonverbal information. He should also become used to reading instructions, descriptions, and rules. The vocational-education teacher should be especially alert to those aspects of the text that are most like the reading the student will encounter on the job and then help him to prepare for this aspect of employment.

A STRATEGY FOR ANALYZING STUDENT TEXTS

Any unit of instruction should begin with a careful analysis of the materials that students will be given to read. On the basis of this analysis, assignments

Free Electrons

Voltage causes electrons to be removed from some atoms. When electrons leave their atoms they are called free electrons. A conductor is a substance which contains many electrons which can be fairly easily removed from their atoms. When this happens within a large number of atoms, the free electrons move through in a direction determined by the polarity of the voltage that is applied to the conductor.

An insulator is a substance with very few free electrons, or none at all.

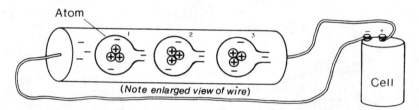

Fig. 23-4. In a conductor material, voltage causes some electrons to be removed from their atoms. These electrons then flow through and along the conductor.

How Electrons Flow

Figure 23-4 shows the action of the atoms within a metal conductor through which electrons are flowing. The positive terminal of the voltage source attracts some of· the electrons from atom 3. At the same time, some of the extra electrons upon the negative terminal are repelled. These extra electrons move into the conductor.

Atom 3 now has a positive charge that attracts other electrons from atom 2. The positive charge of this atom, in turn, attracts electrons from atom 1. During this time, the electrons repelled from the negative terminal move into the atoms which have lost electrons. This action takes place within all of the atoms of the conductor, producing a steady drift of free electrons through it.

Electrons drift through a conductor under the influence of voltage at a rather slow rate, usually less than 1 inch per second. However, an electrical impulse travels through a conductor at the speed of light, or 186,000 miles per second. In other words, when voltage is applied to the ends of the conductor, electrons begin to flow through all points along the conductor at the speed of light. This means that a 186,000-mile-long conductor has electrons flowing through all parts of it steadily one second after the proper value of voltage has been applied to its ends.

Figure 10-2. From Peter Buban and Marshall L. Schmitt, *Understanding Electricity and Electronics*, 2d ed. (New York: McGraw-Hill, 1969), pp. 128–129.

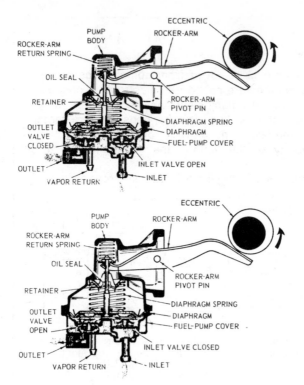

Fig. 17.5 When the eccentric rotates so that it pushes the rocker arm down, the arm pulls the diaphragm up. This pulls fuel into the space under the diaphragm. The inlet valve opens to admit the fuel.

Fig. 17.6 When the eccentric rotates to allow the rocker arm to move up under it, the diaphragm is released. Now the spring pushes down on the diaphragm, creating pressure on the fuel under it. This pressure closes the inlet valve and opens the outlet valve. Now fuel can flow to the carburetor.

In Figs. 17.5 and 17.6 you can see where the vapor-return line is connected to the fuel pump.

In Fig. 17.5 the rocker arm has pulled the diaphragm up, producing a partial vacuum in the gasoline chamber under the diaphragm. The inlet valve is pulled open by the partial vacuum, and gasoline enters from the fuel tank.

Now look at Fig. 17.6. Here the big part of the eccentric has moved out from under the rocker arm. The diaphragm spring pushes the diaphragm down, producing pressure in the gasoline chamber. The pressure closes the inlet valve and opens the outlet valve. Gasoline is pushed out of the fuel pump and into the carburetor.

17.5 Fuel Pump Operation. Now let's go over fuel-pump operation more closely. Look at Figs. 17.5 and 17.6, which show the two extreme positions of the pump. First, study Fig. 17.5, which shows what happens when the big part of the eccentric pushes the rocker arm down.

17.6 Vapor Return Line. Many cars have a vapor-return line. This line allows vapor that has formed in the fuel pump to return to the fuel tank. Fig. 17.7 is a view from the top of a car frame, showing the location of the fuel tank, the fuel line, and the vapor-return line.

Figure 10-3. From William H. Crouse, *The Auto Book* (New York: McGraw-Hill, 1974), pp. 190–191.

can be composed that will purposefully direct reading, study guides provided, and questioning strategies determined. Below is a general procedure for performing a text analysis.

1. First *survey the ideas* and information contained in a reading assignment to determine what it is the writer hopes to convey to the student. Identify key concepts, supporting material for these concepts, and new vocabulary items. It is also important to determine what prior knowledge the text seems to assume. What terms, concepts, or specific information is the student expected to know already?

2. Next, *look at the way the text is written* and put together. Check to see what aids to learning the writer has provided. Organizational aids might include chapter organization; use of subheadings and marginal notes; typographical devices to signal key ideas such as italics, boldface, different type sizes, or specially set-off portions of the text. Other aids might include introductory or summary material, study questions, and follow-up suggestions. The teacher should also look at the graphics used and how these relate to the written text.

3. Then *make a decision regarding the kind of student response* the text seems to call for. Is he being asked to acquire factual information? Is he being asked to formulate concepts? Does the text call for critical thinking? Does it require the student to relate his personal experience to the material? Does it ask him to carry out specific procedures as a result of his reading?

4. Perhaps most important of all, *decide what the students should be able to do* as a result of this reading. This would include activities done as a class, small-group activities, and individual projects. If class discussion is a desired outcome, the teacher should decide how this discussion will be carried out. Or the teacher may want the student to apply to specific problems the information gained from reading. Reading might be used as input for carrying out projects or writing assignments. Whatever the purpose of the reading, the student should understand what the activity will be and how his reading relates to it.

Application

Select a chapter from a student text in your subject area and analyze it according to the procedure given above. The object of this activity is for you to find out how much you can learn about the material that students will be asked to read. An outline for a text analysis is given as an appendix to this chapter. This analysis may be more elaborate than your purposes require, but it illustrates the various dimensions of textbook prose that *can* be used as a basis for planning.

GUIDING CONTENT READING

There are ways in which the teacher can help students prepare for reading their texts and respond to them as they read. These methods are based on the principles of structure and prior knowledge, both of which are essential to learning. To acquire new material, the student must be able to organize it in his own mind and relate it to what he already knows. The following discussion points out ways in which the teacher can make use of his text analysis to help students organize and relate their reading.

Reviewing Previous Learning

In virtually every reading assignment there are assumptions of previous learning. Students will often need to be reminded of what they know. Reading new material will be more meaningful to them if concepts they have learned earlier are fresh in their minds.

A good technique for reviewing earlier learning is to ask questions that require students to respond in their own words. In this way they discover for themselves what they already know. Such student-centered questioning should be based on a clear idea in the teacher's mind of what previously learned material is important for understanding new reading. The questioning should then be carried out as a probe to get students to really think about topics being reviewed.

Using Organizational Cues in the Text

Students can learn much about the contents of a text without actually reading it. Simply by observing the organizational cues given by the writer, they can gain an overview of the material before reading it in detail. Such cues include introductory material, subheadings, marginal notes and other set-off information, illustrations, and summary material.

An introductory paragraph often gives an overview of the main concepts in a chapter, which students can use as an advance organizer to reading. An advance organizer is any material that provides a general framework to which to relate specific ideas. The following introductory paragraph to a chapter discussing the impact of the early Middle Ages in Europe is an advance organizer that gives an overview of the main events of that 1,000-year period. Note too the topical review preceding this paragraph, which is also an advance organizer:

Awakening of Western Europe

Chapter Focus

The Crusades: Christianity and Islam in Conflict
The Growth of Towns and the Rise of a Middle Class

The Rise of Universities
Advances in Science and Technology
Medieval Folk Songs and Literature
The Legacy of the Middle Ages

In the Early Middle Ages (500–1050 A.D.) in Western Europe was a pioneer society struggling to overcome invasion, disorder, and weak government. Trade, town life, and learning declined. Nevertheless, during these
centuries of confusion, the foundations of a new civilization were taking
shape. It took centuries for medieval civilization to mature, and in the twelfth
century it entered its golden age. In the last three sections of this chapter we
shall examine the achievements of this civilization—its philosophy, literature,
science, technology, and architecture.[9]

Reading over subheadings through the chapter can be very helpful for gaining knowledge of what is in a text. Subheadings often constitute an outline
of the text, and sometimes it is useful to have students copy this outline on
a separate sheet of paper to use as a study guide. Also the class can discuss
the topics indicated in the subheadings to find out what students already
know or to have them formulate their own questions. The following extraction
of a subheading outline from a chapter on nuclear energy, which did not
have an introductory advance organizer, demonstrates how subheadings can
be used for this purpose:

Nuclear Energy

I. Nuclear Fission
   A. Splitting the atomic nucleus
   B. The separation of U-235
   C. Critical mass
   D. Nuclear reactors
   E. Heavy water is the best moderator
   F. Plutonium, a fissionable element
   G. Uses for nuclear reactors
   H. Types of reactors
      1. The boiling-water reactor
      2. The pressurized water reactor
      3. The high temperature gas reactor
      4. The liquid-sodium reactor
II. Nuclear Radiations—Their Applications
   A. Nuclear reactors produce dangerous radiations
   B. Units for measuring radioactivity
   C. Radioisotopes
   D. Radioactive dating

---

[9] From Marvin Perry et al., *Man's Unfinished Journey: A World History* (New York:
Houghton Mifflin, 1971), p. 151.

III. Nuclear Fusion
    A. Energy from nuclear fusion
    B. The hydrogen bomb is a product of nuclear fusion[10]

Skimming Illustrations

It is also worthwhile to look at specially set-off material and illustrations in advance. This will help students gain some advance knowledge of the text, and it will also prepare them to make use of such supplementary information while they are reading. If the text refers to an illustration or table, the student is much more likely to relate this to his reading if he is already familiar with it. Previewing the material in advance simplifies the task of reading when it calls for attention to different parts of the page. The teacher should also be aware of references to illustrations and tables in other parts of the book and have students review these in advance too. These techniques help the student learn to integrate textual and pictorial information. In his independent reading, the student is much more likely to use various kinds of information if he has been given specific guidance in how to do so.

Advance Organizer

Often it is a good practice to turn to the end of a chapter first and see how the author has summarized the content. A well-written summary can serve the same function as an overview introduction, and often it is more complete. After observing the main conclusions reached in a chapter, the student can read the text with the purpose in mind of finding out how these conclusions were reached. He can use the summary section as a basis for formulating questions and identifying key concepts. Students will find using a summary section as a preview to be a study technique that they can apply to many kinds of reading throughout their years in school. The following summary section from a chapter on force in a science text illustrates the kind of summary that can also be used as an advance organizer:

> There are many kinds of forces around us at all times. Friction and gravity are two such forces. Even a body at rest has at least two forces constantly acting upon it. A body at rest or in uniform motion is in equilibrium, with no net force and no net torque acting upon it.
>
> A vector represents a quantity such as a force that has magnitude and direction or velocity. Vectors are added in a special manner to find their resultant, which is a single vector that can replace others.
>
> A machine is any device used to change the amount, speed, or direction of a force. Simple machines include the lever, pulley, wheel-and-axle, in-

---

[10] From G. Tracy, H. Tropp, and A. Friedl, *Modern Physical Science* (New York: Holt, Rinehart and Winston, 1970), pp. 130–141.

clined plane, wedge, and screw. In the operation of any machine, whatever is gained in force must be lost in distance or speed. Friction reduces the efficiency of machines. The amount of energy or work that is put into the machine is always greater than the amount of work that the machine does. This is in keeping with the law of conservation of energy.[11]

Preteaching Vocabulary and Important Concepts

Another way of getting at the structure of a chapter is to look at the vocabulary items it presents, for these are usually associated with the main concepts of the chapter. Going over these items in advance with students will enable them to deal with the words more effectively in the flow of connected discourse. At the same time, such instruction will provide an overview of the key ideas in the chapter. Often a chapter will provide a list of terms important to the understanding of the material. At other times, the teacher must provide the list himself. In both cases, his supplementary explanations of the terms will be very helpful in getting the student ready to deal with these terms in context.

The following lists of vocabulary items—one from a chapter in an economics text discussing money and banking and the other from a short story in a literature anthology—illustrate how the sheer number of new terms make them an important factor in reading a text. The list also gives an idea of the conceptual load of each text and a means for previewing main concepts:

ECONOMICS TEXT	ENGLISH TEXT
medium of exchange	gratuitous
measure of value	paradoxical
store of value	herculean effort
currency	disconcerting
legal tender	perambulation
bullion	incessant
standard money	irony
token money	tympanums
silver certificate	oracular
gold certificate	promontory
Federal Reserve Note	formidable
promissory note	travail
demand deposit	impervious
time deposit	didactic

[11] Tracy, Tropp, and Friedl, pp. 367–368.

Presenting Concepts in Discussion
Before Reading

Following are illustrations of how a particular concept might be explained and then demonstrated with examples. Examples are important because a concept is a kind of category, and a variety of examples will help the student to learn what goes into that category. Also, examples can be thought of as applications of the concept. This explanation is keyed to the passage from the physics textbook analyzed in the section on text analysis in science.

Science

Concept to be taught: Scientific knowledge is always a matter of probability; there is no certainty in science.

Explanation of the concept: Scientists do not look for absolute certainty regarding a phenomenon being studied, but rather for the highest degree of probability that they are right, which gives a maximum amount of predictability. Thus, scientific discovery is more a matter of eliminating wrong answers than finding right ones. The more that one eliminates error from an explanation, the more certain he can be that what remains of it has some accuracy and will be useful in predicting events.

Examples of the concept:

1. Because modern physics attempts to interpret all observed phenomena in terms of the behavior of atoms, molecules, electrons, protons, etc., the purpose of experiments is to supply details about a conceptual scheme of particles that cannot be directly observed. Since physicists do not have direct access to the material they are studying, they must deal in probabilities. They infer the properties of these elements from the results of controlled experiments, but they must always continue to refine their conceptualization of particles.

2. Even when a prediction works today, scientists cannot be sure that it was always true. Thus, the age of rocks is estimated by their helium content, on the assumption that this has been accumulating from radioactive disintegrations at the same rate over the past billion years. However, it cannot be proved that the rate has been steady, and so this assumption is only a convenient working hypothesis that scientists have no basis to refute. But if evidence were to be discovered that changed this view, scientists would have to give up or change their method for dating rocks.

3. Currently there are phenomena in the universe which scientists are trying to explain, but they must rely on inference from observa-

tions using special apparatus. Recently strange objects have been discovered called quasars and pulsars. The quasars seem to be objects with so much compressed energy that ordinary laws of physics cannot account for them. Pulsars, flashing objects, seem to be fragments of previously exploded stars that have collapsed to great density. From these phenomena, and the conclusions reached regarding them, one can make further predictions regarding the dynamics of the universe. However, there is no way that the scientist can be absolutely certain regarding the nature and history of quasars and pulsars.

English

Concept to be taught (from "Footfalls"): Confidence in one's own perceptions is an important part of intelligence.

Explanation of concept: Our senses are our windows to the world, the means by which our brains make contact with reality. Even though we know that perceptions may fail, still they provide us with necessary evidence for interpreting experience. Therefore, an important part of intelligence is to learn to see, hear, feel, etc., as accurately as possible, and then to trust one's own perceptual abilities. If one does not have confidence in the accuracy of his perceptions, he will be too uncertain to make sense of his surroundings and act upon them.

Example 1: When a person first looks through a microscope, he is not used to seeing objects in this perspective, and it looks like an undifferentiated mass. But as he gains practice in identifying different elements, he gains confidence in his ability to perceive in this way. The longer he continues to practice seeing in this way, the better able he is to interpret the world of microorganisms, and he becomes an intelligent observer of this kind of life.

Example 2: In a game like tennis, it is important for a player to know where the ball is at all times. For the beginner, however, this is difficult because he is concerned with so many different things—his own physical movements, the position of his opponent, and all the various objects that are within his field of vision. Eventually, though, he gains the ability to concentrate on the ball, and his perception in this regard is strengthened. As his confidence to keep the ball in focus grows, he becomes a better player.

Example 3: In stories about life in the wilderness like Cooper's *The Last of the Mohicans*, Indians tended to have a remarkable ability to interpret sounds. This ability to find meaning in sounds that seemed arbitrary to others made them more intelligent in the forest than people whose auditory perceptions were not trained. The Indians learned to have confidence in their ability to understand what they could not see in the wilderness, and so it did not baffle or frighten them as it did others.

Social Studies

Concept to be taught: Money is a fundamental measure of value in our society that affects almost every citizen in some way.

Explanation of concept: People tend to be defined according to the amount of money they earn, have stored, or have invested in other material possessions. Monetary value provides a convenient standard for comparing the worth of different items, and often it supersedes other less objective ways of defining value. An item is marked by the price that is put on it, and when the price changes, the intrinsic value of the item seems to change too, although the item itself remains exactly the same. Similarly, people are often regarded as more or less "important" according to the net value of their assets or the amount they earn regardless of personal characteristics.

Example 1: A talented art forger made a handsome living by copying the styles of modern masters like Picasso, Cézanne, and other Impressionists. People bought his paintings believing that they had been done by the famous painters whose names he forged on them, and even experts were fooled. When the man was discovered, the monetary value of these paintings (for which he had collected large sums) dropped, and his customers felt themselves cheated. Yet they had enjoyed the paintings before they knew about the forgery. In time, perhaps, this forger will be considered famous in his own right because he could copy styles so exactly, and then his copies will regain some of their former monetary value. At this point, perhaps, their owners might begin to enjoy them again.

Example 2: Every so often, a report comes out stating the salaries of the faculty and administration of a large university. This report establishes a scale of value that ranges from $12,000 per year to about $50,000. When it comes out, every professor and administrator reads it with great interest to see how his salary compares with that of others in his rank, and how his department compares with other departments. This report therefore provides an index of each man's worth to the institution and becomes a measure of his professional success.

Example 3: In the movie *Treasure of the Sierra Madre*, Humphrey

Bogart plays a prospector who becomes so greedy after his first strike that he steals all the gold dust from his partners and takes off alone, calculating the dollar value of his treasure as he starves and stumbles his way along. Eventually he is ambushed by Mexican bandits, who scatter the dust in order to steal the burros and skins he was using to transport it. Throughout the movie, the value of the treasure is nothing more than the dollar value assigned to it in the minds of the men who found it, and when it no longer had this value assigned to it, it turned to mere dust.

COMPOSING ASSIGNMENTS
THAT PURPOSEFULLY
DIRECT READING

The sample worksheet given below shows how you might help students establish a purpose for reading by tying their thinking to explicitly stated objectives. This worksheet asks the student to evaluate for himself how well he seems to have achieved the objectives. It also provides space for the student to ask questions in response to the reading, questions that can be returned to the teacher via the completed sheet. This assignment/worksheet is keyed to the text analysis for the excerpt from the short story, "Footfalls," given in the section on text analysis in English. Examples from other content areas follow:

English

Reading Assignment: Read "Footfalls" by Wilbur Daniel Steele, pp. 17–31.

Following are three objectives for you to achieve in reading the assignment. Read these before you read the story, and then afterwards comment on how well you think you have achieved each objective. If you don't think you have achieved an objective as well as you would like, try to think of some questions that would lead to a better understanding.

Obj. 1. The student will understand some of the literary devices used by the author such as point of view, clues for interpreting character, and use of implicit information.

Obj. 2. The student will understand the kind of intelligence that the main character, Boaz, has.

Obj. 3. The student will be able to relate what this story tells him about human nature to experiences of his own.

Your questions:

Social Studies

Assignment: Chapter 13, "Money and the Banking System" in *Our American Economy*, pp. 296–322.

To find how well you have grasped the overall purpose of this reading, answer the following questions. Each of these questions is related to a major objective in your reading. After you have answered the questions, try to determine what these objectives are:

1. What is the difference, if any, between your everyday concept of a bank and the concept presented here?

Objective: _____

_____

_____

_____

2. In what sense do banks "create" money—that is, determine the amount of money in circulation?

Objective: _____

_____

_____

_____

3. What is the role of money and banks in our total economy? Consider here why the kind of economy that we have requires an institution like the banking system.

Objective: _____

_____

_____

_____

Your questions: _____

_____

_____

_____

_____

Science

Assignment: Chapter 1, "Matter and Energy," in *Modern Physics*, pp. 1–18.

Your primary objective in reading this chapter should be to gain a general understanding of what the field of physics is about. Of course, this is only an introduction. Your concept of physics will continue to develop as long as you study or think about the subject. To see how well you have gained the primary objective, write down how you would respond to each of the following situations after you have read the chapter:

1. An adult who has never studied physics asks you what the course is about.

_____

_____

2. Look up the word energy in the dictionary and look at its various meanings. Then describe how you would explain the difference between the concept of energy in physics and the concept of energy as it is used in each of the following phrases.
     a. a person with a lot of energy.
     b. the energy crisis.

_____

_____

_____

_____

_____

3. It is easy to say that energy and matter are relative, but hard to really conceptualize what this means. Think of an example that would help explain this concept.

_____

_____

_____

_____

_____

Your questions: _____

_____

_____

_____

_____

Mathematics

Assignment: Chapter 4, "Large Numbers and Logarithms" in *Mathematics: A Human Endeavor*, pp. 140–183.

This chapter has two primary objectives:
1. To help you understand the nature of a logarithmic scale.
2. To show you how this kind of scale is useful in measurements where huge numbers are involved.

After you have studied the chapter, test the first objective by explaining the *concept* of logarithmic scales in your own words:

_____

_____

_____

_____

_____

_____

Then test the second objective by listing as many practical applications of logarithmic scales as you can think of or find, including those given in the book.

_____

_____

_____

_____

_____

_____

_____

Your questions: _____

_____

Providing a Context for Reading

Following are some items that could be included on a one-page worksheet designed to aid students in reading a section of material assigned from their texts. This worksheet focuses the student's attention on selected concepts and vocabulary items, and could be expanded to include more according to the purpose of the lesson. Or several worksheets could be used for one reading assignment to cover all concepts and terms presented in the reading unit. This worksheet is keyed to the chapter on money and banking analyzed in the section on text analysis and social studies.

Social Studies

Assignment: Read Chapter 13, "Money and the Banking System," in *Our American Economy*, pp. 296–322.

The primary purpose of this chapter is to make the reader aware of the nature of money and the role that banks play in our overall economy. Briefly state, in your own words, what you think the nature of money and the role of banks in the economy are:

_____

_____

_____

_____

_____

_____

_____

What forms of money do we use in our society? _____

_____

_____

How do banks control the amount of money in circulation? _____

_____

_____

What is the purpose of government regulation of banks? _____

_____

_____

What are the duties of the Federal Reserve System? _____

_____

_____

How does the writer define (or seem to define) each of the following terms:

1. legal tender: _____

_____

2. demand and time deposits: _____

_____

3. clearinghouse: _____

_____

4. discounting: _____

_____

English

Assignment: Section One: "The Paragraph," in *Composition: Models and Exercises*, pp. 3–42.

This chapter attempts to make you aware of some specific techniques you can use in paragraph writing. It also makes the point that a paragraph should have a unifying idea or theme. With this in mind, write your own explanation of what a paragraph is:

_____

_____

_____

_____

_____

How is unity achieved in each of the following kinds of paragraph development?

Descriptive: _____

_____

Expository: _____

_____

Narrative: _____

_____

What is the usual function of a topic sentence? _____

_____

Your questions: _____

Science

Assignment: Idea 2: "Evolution," in *Biology*, pp. 41–98.

The main purpose of this chapter is to help you understand the concept of evolution. Evolution can be defined as change over time in response to the environment. In your own words, describe how some living thing (for example a horse, a house pet, or a human being) has changed over time to its present form:

What kinds of evidence do we have about life in the past?

What is the relationship between an organism and its environment? That is, how does the environment shape the form that life in it will take?

_____
_____
_____
_____
_____

Your questions: _____

_____

STRUCTURE AND ORGANIZATION

Students will be better able to learn complex material if they can grasp its internal structure and organize (rather than try to memorize) its content. To do this, they need two things: some understanding of the elements of the text (analysis) and direction as to how to put it together in their minds (synthesis). George Miller, a well-known scholar of language and communication, describes a problem-solving experiment conducted by an earlier researcher named Maier. The subjects in this experiment were divided into four groups and given the task of building a structure that would support two pendulums, each swinging over a designated spot. To do this, they were given some pieces of equipment including poles, braces, and string. The first group was given no help at all, just the equipment. The second was given instructions in how to use the different pieces of equipment, such as combining poles with a brace and making a plumb line by attaching a small brace to the end of a line. The third group was given a hint: They were told that the task would be easy if they could simply hang the pendulums from nails in the ceiling, although unfortunately they had no nails. A fourth group was given both the instructions and the hint.

Of the four groups, only the last had any appreciable success with the task. They used the clamps and pole to construct a T-shaped frame braced against the ceiling, from which they suspended the pendulums over the required spots. Why were they able to succeed? Because they had both a procedure and an idea. With these together, they were able to approach the task creatively and successfully.

SUMMARY

"Learning" in a content area consists, in large part, of developing the ability to read and use materials in that area. Many students need to learn specific strategies for dealing with the various kinds of subject matter assigned in different classes. To aid the teacher in helping students develop sound strategies, this chapter has examined the general characteristics of reading in various content areas with examples from texts at different levels. Suggestions and formats for readiness and follow-up activities were given. The idea emphasized here is that reading should be embedded in a context of preparation, discussion, and application of ideas. Finally, a detailed guide for analyzing any text is given in Appendix A. This can be used in whole or in part depending on the teachers' purposes.

(*Note:* Application and discussion questions are provided in the text rather than at the end. The reader is referred to these and also to the study guide models for discussion.)

Suggested Readings

Dillner, Martha, and Joanne P. Olson. *Personalized Reading Instruction in Middle, Junior and Senior High Schools.* New York: Macmillan, 1977.
This is a self-instructional, problem-oriented approach designed to help secondary classroom teachers develop skills for teaching reading. This book contains many specific suggestions for teaching and materials development under five major sections: Understanding the Meaning of Reading, Matching Reading Needs to Classroom Materials, Planning Diagnostic-Prescriptive Instruction, Developing an Effective Reading Program, and Practicing Teaching Reading.

Eash, Maurice J. *Reading and Thinking: Using Supplementary Books in the Classroom.* New York: Doubleday, 1967.
This book is useful in two ways: It discusses the use of trade books in specific content areas, and, as the title implies, it emphasizes the relationship between reading and cognition. Each identifies five basic cognitive abilities as understanding, utilizing, discriminating, chaining, and judging and in this way provides the teacher with a framework for observation. Each of these abilities is explained fully but in nonspecialized terms, and author Eash focuses on one central theme: how these abilities can be developed through the reading of supplementary books. This theme is carried out through Eash's own chapters, which provide the main theoretical discussion of the book, and the four chapters dealing with specific content areas, each written by a person knowledgeable in that field. Eash also provides a good discussion of the difference between textbooks and tradebooks as sources of information, and the book contains many practical suggestions for teaching.

Herber, Harold L. *Teaching Reading in Content Areas.* Englewood Cliffs, N.J.: Prentice-Hall, 1970.
Herber argues against what he calls "preassumptive" teaching, by which he means instruction in which the teacher simply assumes a minimum background of knowledge and reading development among students. Instead, he

advocates the use of "study and reasoning guides" which direct the student in his effort to learn from printed materials. Besides providing examples of these in the major content areas and giving suggestions for their use, Herber discusses the rationale upon which his approach to teaching reading in content areas is based.

Piercey, Dorothy. *Reading Activities in Content Areas: An Ideabook for Middle and Secondary Schools.* Abr. ed. Boston: Allyn & Bacon, 1976.

This book is, as the title suggests, a collection of techniques and activities for teaching the language of content areas. Its main focus is on vocabulary development. The first section discusses general concepts and strategies for a language-oriented approach to teaching content. The second describes activities related to nine specific content areas: business; English, speech, and journalism; foreign languages; health; home economics; industrial and vocational arts; mathematics; science; and social studies. The concrete ideas given may suggest other ways of using novel materials and approaches in teaching content language.

Robinson, H. Allan. *Teaching Reading and Study Strategies: The Content Areas.* Boston: Allyn & Bacon, 1975.

This author places emphasis on the characteristics of text materials in specific content areas. After a section dealing with general strategies for pre-teaching in the content classroom, he provides a discussion of writing patterns and strategies in four major content areas, with a fifth chapter devoted to a few minor ones. Useful for analyzing text material, the text gives some specific suggestions for teaching in each of the content areas discussed.

Smith, Richard J., and Thomas C. Barrett. *Teaching Reading in the Middle Grades.* Reading, Mass.: Addison-Wesley, 1974.

This book is addressed to classroom teachers responsible for teaching reading in content classrooms in grades four through eight. Each chapter includes both theoretical discussion and suggestions for teaching application. Topics include comprehension, skill development, motivation, the poor reader, and evaluation. The book has a practical orientation to make it useful to the classroom teacher.

Thomas, Ellen Lawar, and H. Alan Robinson. *Improving Reading in Every Class.* 2d ed. Boston: Allyn & Bacon, 1977.

This book is a practical classroom aid, designed for easy reference and usability according to the teacher's specific needs. It contains a wide range of instructional suggestions keyed to specfic content areas and/or reader problems. The goal of the book is to show teachers how they can integrate reading into content instruction as a way of increasing students' critical thinking powers.

Appendix A

Outline for Text Analysis: For Lesson or Content Units

This analysis is rather elaborate, but its purpose is to be both comprehensive and adaptable to specific purposes. The individual teacher should use it first to become aware of the various dimensions of textbook writing and then selectively according to his instructional needs.

I. *Content analysis:* First survey the ideas and information contained in a reading assignment to determine what it is that the writer is hoping to get across to the student.
   A. *Key concepts:* The first time you go through the text, select a limited number of major concepts that are the principal content of the instruction. These form the main contours of what is to be learned. Four to eight is a reasonable number to work with.
   B. *Primary supporting material:* Now go back over the text and look at information and ideas that are important in the support and development of the key concepts. In listing these, key them to the concepts to which they relate.
   C. *Vocabulary items to be taught as part of content instruction:* These should be listed and briefly defined.
   D. *Assumptions of prior knowledge:* What does the text take for granted about the reader? What terms, concepts, or specific information is he already expected to know? These assumptions and any references in the text to prior learning should be checked for review.
II. *Structure and style analysis:* Now look at the way the book is written and put together. Check to see what specific aids to learning the writer has provided.
   A. *Organizational aids:*
      1. Chapter organization (how has the author chosen to organize his material overall?)
      2. Table of contents (how completely does it outline the content or explain the material in the chapters?)
      3. Use of subheadings (do these provide organizing cues?)
      4. Use of typographical aids to signal key ideas (various typefaces, italics, capital letters, indentations, etc.)
      5. Index (name, topical, etc.)
      6. Glossary
      7. Other _____.
   B. *Written aids to study:* In addition to the text itself, what has the author provided to help guide the student's understanding of the material?
      1. Introductory and summary material.
      2. Questions, problems, and follow-up activities.
      3. Marginal notes and footnotes.
      4. Other _____.
   C. *Graphics:* What is the relationship between written and visual material in the book? What kinds of graphics are used—photographs, pictures, cartoons, graphs, tables, charts, diagrams? Do these supplement the text, repeat information, or add interest?

      1. Types of graphics used.

      2. Relationship of graphics to text.

III. *Cognitive operations:* Using the cognitive operations outline presented in chapter 2 and discussed in chapter 6, determine the kinds of intellectual response to the material you wish to emphasize:

    A. *Principal level of comprehension.* (See discussion and examples in chapter 6.)

    B. *Cognitive operations to be emphasized at each level:*

      1. Concrete

      2. Critical

      3. Elaborative

IV. *Planned applications of reading:* Now that you are thoroughly familiar with the concepts, supporting material, organization and cognitive operations to be emphasized in the reading of this material, decide what you expect your students to be able to do as a result of reading it. This would include activities done as a class, small-group projects, and individual assignments.

    A. *Discussion:* In what format and at what level of comprehension do you want students to be able to discuss the material?

    B. *Problem solving:* The book or the teacher may give specific problems to which the student would apply information gained from reading.

    C. *Projects:* Reading might be used as input for planning and carrying out more elaborative activities.

    D. *Writing assignments:* Essays and papers that might be the result of certain readings should be planned in advance of the reading assignment so that students know that they are reading in order to write.

    E. *Other:* _____.

11

Writing and Bookthinking

What is the relationship between writing and thinking?

What is the role of writing in content instruction?

How can teachers provide experiences for students without becoming submerged in paper grading?

I don't remember exactly how it started—but I wanted to write. Not just to be writing but to put down an idea—a story—something of my own . . . I became extremely interested in this idea & commenced on my first crack at a novelette—or short book . . .

I had already written a memoir of myself in Kentucky when I was 12—but writing as a regular thing was a new experience for me in which I wanted to explore.

I began writing on Country Boy at sometime in 1962 & took notes on my ideas and wrote and rewrote and corrected to the best of my ability—what at the time was not much to speak of. I got Brenda to help since she could type—& borrowed Theresa's typewriter—which I kept for a good while, & we proceeded with the first copy of *Country Boy*—a 23 page manuscript . . . which was never actually finished.

It was actually written by Brenda and myself. As I dictated to her the story as I read my notes and all—she added a few remarks of her own as we went along.

I gave up on that particular deal & while down in Kentucky—I went out into the yard for a wonderful cool day—with a pad & pencil—& wrote down another good portion to add to the Country Boy story.

I wrote it all down and completed it within about two weeks. . . .

The character in CB was much like that of J. R. Salamanca's character of his book Lost Country or Wild in the Country . . .

I wrote an odd science fiction after CB—then completed the book I called 3 in 1 by writing the biography of Elvis Presley.

I went on an exciting vacation to Detroit & described it in detail in the comical memoir, "Vacation in Livonia."

Earlier that summer I conceived the idea for writing a book about a hillbilly who finds that life is quite confusing . . . in

EBBY & WOLF

I later made this into a 218 page book handprinted entitled—"The Country Gentleman." Close to one year after I conceived the idea . . .

In October of 1963 I began writing on what was planned on being my first *big* book . . . but gave up the idea of rewriting Country Boy . . .

I began writing songs to a 6-a-month extent around in July of 1964 . . . when I grew to love writing and plan it as a career, moreso when I was on my vacation and had much interest in a girl by the name of Sandy Conlin.

NOTE: Much of this will be explained in my 500-page memoir of 1964.

I wrote the book Sandy, which wasn't completed for certain complications.

I wrote an interview on my little cousin.

I wrote to a publishing company and they sent back a brochure telling me to send my manuscripts in when finished.

I took an extreme interest in getting down my memoirs and made plans for an over 2500 page series adding up to one complete book.

I read much & my reading influenced my type of writing & my vocabulary & my writing ability.[1]

This excerpt from a teen-ager's personal journal conveys the excitement he felt when he discovered that he could write. As the last statement suggests, for him there was a natural relationship between writing and reading; one led to the other. Mark's journal also describes how he learned to love reading. When he was fourteen, he happened to find a paperback novel on which an Elvis Presley movie had been based. Up to that point, he had confined his reading to comic books, but now he thought that he "would take a crack at reading those books without pictures—and when I did, it opened up a whole new world that fascinated me."

This world quickly expanded to include science fiction, mysteries, adventures, everything written by Harold Robbins to date, and other books

---

[1] From the unpublished "Memoirs" of a sixteen-year-old, quoted here by permission of the writer, Mark Mann.

inspired by his admiration for Elvis Presley. Then he began to write, which led to more reading, itemized in his journal with pride: *Hawaii, From the Terrace, Gone With the Wind, The Violet Season, Pioneer, Go Home, The Lost Country, Lilith, Anthony Adverse, Peyton Place, Kid Galahad, Memoirs of Casanova, Tom Jones,* and *The Prize.* And from the reading came more writing.

Reading and writing *are* naturally related and should be brought together in the classroom just as Mark brought them toegther for himself. They should inspire each other. Just as no one would happily go through life simply listening to what others had to say without saying anything himself, no student should go through school merely absorbing written language without using it as a medium of expression. If we think of writing as a system in itself, it is clear that reading and writing go together in the same way as listening and speaking.

Educator James Moffett believes that all academic subjects teach essentially the same thing—the central process of using symbols. That is to say, they are all concerned with the teaching of discourse:

> Because one discourses in his native language about *all* matters and at many abstraction levels, there is really only one subject (aside from art, music, and physical education), and that subject is discourse itself, of which science and social studies are subclasses. The latter are correctly viewed either as bodies of content (symbolized) or as ways of processing information (symbolizing). As content, they are what one discourses about; as process, they are acts of discovery. Either way, they are not subjects separate from and coordinate with the native language, but specialized examples of the functioning of language.

He adds that "the most important things that children of today will need to know when they are adults are how experience is abstracted, communicated, and utilized, whether the data are recurring phenomena of nature and society or the private truths of the heart."[2]

WRITING IN CONTENT AREAS

Many content teachers rightly feel that teaching the technical skills of writing is not their job. Teaching grammar, sentence and paragraph construction, matters of style, and all the other technicalities of the craft is the job of the English teacher. But writing is not merely a set of technical skills, although these are important in order to communicate. Writing is a basic mode of

---

[2] From James Moffett, *Teaching The Universe of Discourse* (Boston: Houghton Mifflin, 1968), p. 212.

expression which becomes increasingly important as the individual matures. It is a way of deliberately bringing language to the service of thought. The ability to use language in this way will develop only through practice.

The use of written discourse as a means of learning is fundamental to all subjects. The learner must structure the knowledge he gains into a framework of understanding that is his own, and language is his primary tool for doing this. Through writing, he develops his ability to grasp concepts, think abstractly, organize his thoughts, and explain them completely. With practice, writing becomes a way of thinking and learning. It involves the deliberate use of language to reveal ideas as the writer strives to put his own thinking into a form that can be comprehended by others. That process of reconstructing his knowledge forces a writer into an act of learning (Piaget, 1951).

But the question may still be asked, how can it be done? How can a teacher who sees 150 different students a day give them the experience in writing that they need? It cannot be done, obviously, by making frequent, lengthy assignments that are corrected and critiqued in detail. Rather, the content teacher's objective should be to provide practice in using writing so that it becomes a natural medium of expression. From this point of view, even the writing of a sentence or paragraph is a valuable experience if its purpose is to convey a thought clearly. Copying a lengthy report out of one or two reference works will provide little more than practice in penmanship or typing. But a carefully considered paragraph of the student's own will put him in touch with his own thought and language.

The following pages give practical suggestions on ways that content teachers can incorporate writing into their regular class instruction. These suggestions come from three sources: the teaching experience of the writers of this book, the experience of other teachers who have been generous in sharing their ideas, and the experience of high school graduates who found certain writing assignments especially valuable as part of their secondary education. As these students testify, nobody seems to like writing assignments when they are given, but almost everyone appreciates the experience in retrospect, when he realizes the effect that practice has had on his ability to express himself.

Suggestions are grouped into four categories: (1) short writing activities that can be integrated into daily lessons, (2) writing for tests, (3) independent writing, and (4) longer writing. For the last category, suggestions are given for some specific content areas. Following this section is a review of ways that teachers can minimize the amount of time and effort spent grading papers.

SHORT WRITING ACTIVITIES
THAT CAN BE INTEGRATED
INTO DAILY LESSONS

Short writing activities can be made a part of daily class instruction. These should be regarded as part of continuous developmental experience for each student. To make use of short writings in this way, the teacher or student should keep a folder in which writings are filed in chronological order. If the short writings accumulate quickly, the teacher can check the folders periodically for a general assessment rather than try to respond immediately to each paper. If students understand this procedure, they can adjust to it and learn to monitor their own writing.

1. At the end of a class period, have students write a paragraph describing a concept or fact they have learned that day. Books and other materials may be consulted, but copying is not acceptable. This exercise will be more effective if students are told at the beginning of the class that they will be asked to write a brief statement at the end. To provide an ongoing experience, this activity should be done systematically once or twice each week.

2. Following a lesson in which instructions for a procedure have been taught, give students a list of the directions in scrambled order and have them rewrite them in proper sequence. Let them check and revise their own work by giving them a handout that lists the directions in the correct order. This idea could be adapted to any material that explains a process in steps.

3. Have students listen to a paragraph read out loud—or some longer piece of prose—and then write the meaning in their own words. This can be good practice for note taking. If a teacher often puts an outline on the board, eliminate the outline occassionally and have the students try to produce one for the day's lecture that matches the teacher's.

4. Show students a picture related to the content they are studying and ask them to write an idea suggested by the picture. For example, show a magazine advertisement for a Cadillac or other large car following a discussion of energy use, or a picture depicting rural poverty in relation to a lesson on social problems. Randomly selected students can read their statements to the group.

5. Give students a key term from the content lesson and have them write definitions in their own words. Use clearly definable terms such as *cell, sonnet, properties of matter, supply and demand,* or *sphere* (in the geometrical sense).

6. Have students communicate with each other in writing using a question/answer strategy. First have each student formulate in writing a question based on the content material being learned. Then collect papers, redistribute them randomly, and have each student answer in writing the

question he receives. Return the answers to the originator for reactions and discussion.

7. Have students write a fifty-word comment on any matter of current interest in the class with emphasis on getting across a point in a few words. This exercise can give practice in directness and conciseness of expression. Select a few for class reaction to clarity and conciseness.

8. Ask students to give their own opinion about something learned in class, whatever it may be. They should also give at least one reason for this opinion.

9. Give students a worksheet with three or four questions requiring analysis and have them select one to answer in a paragraph. For example, these questions might follow a discussion of energy problems in America: How did the record-cold winter of 1977 affect people's thinking about energy? What is the connection between energy and employment? What is the role of the individual in energy conservation?

10. Review a concept learned in class and have students write down at least one example of how that concept operates or can be applied. After learning the concept of symbiosis, for example, students could describe one instance of two species living interdependently or contributing in some way to each other's welfare.

11. Reversing the process, give students examples of applications for which they provide an explanatory concept. For example, after learning about one writer's version of an ideal society, students could listen to brief accounts of other such visionary writings and then write their understanding of the concept of *utopia*.

12. Have students write down questions that they would like the teacher to discuss at a future class meeting. But each question should be accompanied by a paragraph explaining what background information the student brings to the question.

Essay Tests and Short-Answer Questions

Of course, it is easier and faster to check a multiple-choice or true/false test, and sometimes considerations of time and efficiency must come first. It should not be forgotten, however, that it is the teacher, not the student, who provides the answers to these kinds of questions. A teacher who does a good job of composing an objective test will develop his own writing skills in the process, but he should also provide students with the opportunity to develop theirs.

Objective questions can focus on specific recall of factual items when this is considered important. For example, a teacher may want a student to say whether or not (true or false) a liter is larger than a quart, or to pick out from a list (multiple choice) the current value of an English pound in

U.S. dollars. But if he wants to know something about the student's conception of the metric system, the true-or-false technique won't do. And designating the equivalence of two national money scrips does little to reveal the student's understanding of the economic relationship involved. Students need to be required to express conceptual understandings in their own words. Otherwise, they are encouraged to focus their attention on specific facts without formulating the underlying concepts that give these facts meaning. The kinds of responses they can be expected to make will strongly influence the kind of reading and listening they do (Harris and Smith, 1976).

Essay and short-answer responses on tests can be viewed as another kind of short-writing experience for students. Even one question that requires a student to construct his own answer from scratch will be valuable to him. Such a question can relate to the material reviewed in objective questions, enabling the student to pull together the various facts he has identified into a synthesis of his own. This will give the whole examination a significance that goes beyond the recognition of correct or incorrect responses to specific questions.

For example, following a series of objective questions on natural sources of energy, the student can be asked to explain how man has made use of these sources, or to comment on the problems that particular kinds of energy entail. A particular period or event in history can be reviewed by objective questions, followed by a request for the student to describe the event in his own words. The objective part of the test can provide an analysis of the material, while an essay question calls for synthesis. This format can make test taking a more significant experience for the student without unduly complicating the teacher's grading task.

Independent Writing

Another part of content instruction can be independent writing for which separate class credit is given. One way of doing this is to have students keep a class journal in which they write regularly, describing events that have happened within a given interval. Part of a period each week can be set aside for writing in the journal. The teacher should keep one too. In this way, the teacher provides a model. Just as a reading period in which the teacher also reads books helps to convey the value of reading, a writing period in which the teacher writes will demonstrate his commitment to this mode of expression. The teacher should also share his writing with the class by making his journal available for them to read, reading aloud from it periodically, or duplicating parts of it for the class. Occasionally the teacher might use an overhead projector to show students what he does when he writes and what some of them have done in their journals.

Like folders, individual journals can be checked periodically at the convenience of the teacher. Some parts of them may be shared with other students if this seems appropriate, always, of course, with the permission of the writer. It might be interesting, for example, to compare how different students have perceived the same topic or event. Sometimes a student comes up with an observation that would be helpful or interesting to other students. The teacher might even have an "observations of the week" section on a bulletin board where relevant journal excerpts are posted.

Another way to provide for independent writing is to make students responsible for writing a certain number of short essays—say, half a page or one well-developed paragraph—within a grading period or other time limit. Students can select from a list of topics that can be treated in a short discussion, preferably topics that call for thinking on the part of the student and can't be found easily in a reference book. Topics of this sort might be as follows:

Why Houseplants Often Sit on Window Sills
The Dangers of Flip-Top Lids on Beverage Cans
Thank You for Not Smoking
If I Had Been Born 100 Years Sooner (or Later)
What's in a Cup of Instant Hot Chocolate? (or other convenience food?)
What is a Dollar Bill?

These papers can be filed by the students in their folders to be checked periodically by the teacher, with appropriate reminders when work isn't coming in. It is important for students to have a wide variety of topics to choose from as well as the opportunity to suggest topics of their own. As a beginning, the teacher might require no more than five independent writings during a grading period, and then increase the quota by two or three each subsequent period. Eventually, students themselves might select the ones they want used for grading purposes at the time of evaluation. These folders of writings can also be used for student conferences, especially after enough writing has been done for some development to be apparent.

LONGER WRITING

In addition to regular practice in written expression of ideas, students also need some experience in composing longer pieces of writing such as essays, term papers, and project reports. Many students, especially those who continue their education beyond high school, look back on these writing assignments as among their most valuable school experiences. They especially appreciate being taught specific procedures for finding and using information. Many also value assignments that allow for personal creativity.

Report-writing projects should be planned to avoid the traditional encyclopedia and/or textbook excerpts that students frequently confuse with report writing. Students should have the experience of using the information they gain from reading, but they should not be encouraged simply to copy chunks of material from various sources. Rather, they should learn techniques for gathering and using information.

One way to approach true report writing is to have students compose a discussion of a subject in which they compare information from two or more sources. In this way, they learn to distinguish their own writing from that of their information sources and give proper form and credit to the latter. They can learn to set off quoted material and provide their own context of explanation. A simple format in which the student provides a general introduction, properly introduces and quotes his various sources, and writes his own conclusion can be a beginning to this kind of information reporting. Students at more advanced levels can increase the number of their sources and learn to compress the length of the report by paraphrasing rather than using long, direct quotes. Specific practice in paraphrasing, another kind of short-writing exercise, will be very helpful. (See chapter 2 on study skills for other suggestions for teaching research and report-writing strategies.)

Students can also respond to assignments that call for creative thinking on their part and encourage them to use information in novel ways. Such formats might include news articles, letters, fictionalized accounts of an event, journals by imaginary writers, plays, dialogues, and descriptive narratives. Imagine a news article published in some advanced part of the universe on the day that life first appeared on earth. Imagine a letter written home by a soldier in some historic battle. Suppose you are a dinosaur contemplating the problem of survival, a pioneer crossing the Great Divide, Isaac Newton discovering the principle of gravity, or Charles Darwin explaining evolution to a fundamentalist. How about a dialogue between a tree and a squirrel concerning the relative merits of each one's way of getting nourishment? Or a monologue in which a shark defends his character? Have an ant and a republican compare their concepts of social order. Describe the American family from the point of view of a house cat, an automobile, and a telephone.

Have students pretend they are either an advice-column writer or a person with a problem. Half the class can write letters seeking advice (real, imagined, or humorous) to be answered by the other half of the class. On another day, the roles can be switched. This activity can be tied in with specific content material, for example, the social problems studied in a civics class. Students can also assume the role of a well-known news commentator or a talk-show host and write an interview with a character from a novel, short story, or history lesson.

Some students will need starters for assignments like these, but most will have fun with them and try to use sound information in developing their accounts. Starters can be in the form of opening paragraphs, head-lines, or descriptions of settings in which actions or dialogues are to take place. For plays or conversations, let students work together in small groups, each providing the point of view of a particular character. Other kinds of imaginative writings can be done in small groups too. Students can get together to pool ideas, with the help of a circulating teacher, and then write on their own. All of these ideas are applicable in all subject areas.

Below are some suggestions for essay and other types of full-length writing assignments that apply to specific content areas. These can be used as "base" ideas that the teacher adapts to specific material or purposes. Also, many of these suggestions can be adapted to more than one content area.

Social Studies

Group News Reports on Current Events. Working in groups, students select a current news topic and compile a collection of newspaper articles, magazine stories and TV-radio reports. This collection of materials is then used as reference sources for writing interpretive reports on the topic. Both the refer-ence articles and the interpretive reports can then be arranged in notebook form to share with other members of the class.

Composing a Class Editorial Section. After reading several newspaper edi-torial pages, have the class put together its own editorial section on current problems. Items can include syndicated columns, comments by local editors, guest editorials, humorous columns, editorial cartoons, and letters to the editor and replies. Let each student select the type of piece he wants to write and encourage representation of a wide range of viewpoints.

Personal Value Papers. In political science, philosophy, civics and other classes in which students examine the role of the individual in society, have them formulate their views of their own responsibilities and expectations as citizens. They should be especially concerned with why they hold certain beliefs and how to provide good support for their ideas. One student who had done this kind of writing stated that it was very helpful in helping him shape his own humanistic concepts.

Comparing Two Basically Different Cultures. Students can gain information about a totally different way of life and insight into their own culture by comparing it to one which is appreciably different. One student, for example, compared a day in the life of a midwesterner with a day in the life of an Australian aborigine. This kind of assignment also provides a very definite basis for organization, which is helpful to students in the development of expository skills. Some categories of comparison are food, earning a living, family life, social order, law, and police protection.

Comparing a Current Situation with a Historical One. For example, a student might compare racial segregation in America today (or in recent times) with segregation in the past, or segregation in the old South with recent apartheid policies in South Africa. Or students can compare a twentieth-century civil war with the American Civil War, or the assassination of a contemporary leader with an assassination of the past, such as that of Abraham Lincoln. This kind of writing/thinking experience will help the student to realize that there is a relationship between the present and the past and that people do not learn the lessons of history as well as they might. He learns, too, that his subject authors are trying to communicate similar messages.

Other Comparisons Across Time. Students can explore the relationship between some facet of life in early America or any time and place in world history and the same phenomenon today. An example might be violence as a part of frontier development and violence as a social problem today. Students can try to find how the current situation developed out of the historical one.

Looking at Two Sides of a Situation. Have students assume both sides of a "debate" and write a pair of complementary essays in which they explore first one side of a situation and then the other. For example, students can look at both the beauty and the ugliness of modern cities. The positive and negative sides of life in any setting would provide interesting topics.

Modifying the Constitution. Have students draw up a set of amendments to the Constitution that they think should be added to fit modern times. They can also be asked to prepare an argument in defense of each of their proposed amendments and present these at a "constitutional change convention," in which the delegates are other members of the class. An alternative to this topic is to draw up a bill of rights that is appropriate to contemporary society.

Instituting Social Reform. Students assume the position of some reformist of the past or present, for example, an abolitionist during the Civil War era, and write a program for solving the social problem under consideration. This can be related to a discussion of the value of hindsight.

Using Primary Sources of Information—People. Have students conduct a survey among members of an older generation regarding their experience during historical events or eras in the recent past, for example, the Depression, World War II, or the McCarthy hearings in the fifties. This will help students to realize how close they are to events that have now become history.

Science

Writing Descriptions of Laboratory Experiences and Independent Projects.
This kind of writing can focus on accuracy, clarity, and completeness. It
will help students direct their attention to the procedures they learn in science
and develop an appreciation for detail.

Research Reports. Students can learn something about using reference
materials in a given area of science by elaborating on topics given general
coverage in class. Students in advanced courses such as physics or chemistry
will find this introduction to scientific writing especially useful.

**Descriptions of Observable Phenomena in the Laboratory or Natural Environ-
ment.** Have students exercise their powers of observation by concentrating
on a particular object or scene and finding out how much they can say about
it. For example, in one biology class, students were asked to make a slide of
a drop of pond water and then write a description of everything they saw
when they viewed it under a microscope. Students can make the same kind
of observation by selecting one aspect of their normal environment, such as
a particular tree observed at various times, the daily habits of a house pet,
or changes in the sky on a particular day.

Reports on Human Problems. One student described as a valuable experience
the compiling of a report on human diseases, which was also presented to
the class. Not only did the student find a lot of information considered
personally relevant, the assignment opened a "new world of vocabulary to
me."

The Personal Side of Science. Many biographies and autobiographies of
scientists reveal the inner experience of people struggling to gain a clearer
understanding of some phenomenon or achieving the insight necessary to
solve a problem. Students, too, can keep a journal account of their efforts
to gain scientific understanding through observation and experimentation.
These notes can be used as a basis for their own scientific autobiographies.

English

Writing a Prose Version of a Narrative Poem. If the poem is set in the past,
the writer may "modernize" it, retaining the basic plot but changing setting
and language to refer to a contemporary situation. In this way, the student
may gain deeper understanding of the durability of human experience over

time. Other forms of literature can also be used for this kind of personal adaptation.

Writing Children's Stories. Students are actually creating literature when they write for a real audience. These stories can be edited and put into booklet form for gifts. Artists in the class can provide illustrations and cover designs.

Describing Contemporary Life for a Visitor from an Alien Planet. Students assume that the visitor is completely ignorant of modern American culture and will be especially interested in the details of daily living most people take for granted. Students will become aware of the challenge of describing things they know a lot about but have never put into an expository context.

Making Up Short Stories in Response to Music. These should be shared with others in the class. Students will discover that several produce similar themes for the same musical scores. They will also be interested in comparing unique or especially imaginative responses. Letting students suggest music or provide records will increase their interest in this activity.

Expositions of Personal Values. Students select some belief or value they consider important to their philosophy of life and develop it with supporting evidence. These, too, can be shared as a way of communicating personal values to others and learning to understand their values. These writings and related discussion can foster the development of mutual understanding and respect among students.

Variations of Book Report Writing. Have students assume the role of publishers or book promoters, making up "advertisements" to persuade other members of the class to "buy" the book. They can design posters or magazine layouts that combine pictures and written copy. Those who are not artistically inclined can write an imaginary interview with the book's author. Or, because many new books are now being used as the source material for television programs, some students may enjoy describing a possible show or series to be derived from the plot and characters of a novel. Similarly, a news documentary could be based on a nonfiction book.

WAYS TO REDUCE TIME
SPENT GRADING PAPERS

While feedback on written work is important, teachers should find a reasonable balance between the amount of writing students do and the time spent responding to student papers. There is no law stating that a teacher must give a thorough critique to every piece of written work before another is undertaken. On the contrary, students will not benefit from a barrage of corrections and critical comments.

Students will learn more if they can focus on particular aspects of writing and gradually develop their understanding of such elements as style, clarity, completeness, and other components of good writing. Applying this principle may also simplify the teacher's reading task, so both students and teachers will benefit from a selective approach to grading. Below is a review of some ways in which a teacher can cut down the amount of time spent grading papers while giving students the amount of writing they need and the kind of feedback they can benefit from.

Selecting a Specific Criterion. Have students focus on a particular purpose such as accurate paraphrasing of an idea, clear sentence or paragraph structure, development of an idea, or providing good support for a point. Make sure that students understand this criterion in advance and then check papers only for success on this point.

Random or Student-selected Grading. Collect all written work in a folder and select a certain percentage for grading purposes. Or have students designate certain papers that they would like to have evaluated for grading purposes. A variation of this idea is to have students rank their papers in order of their preference with the understanding that only those on the top will be used for grading.

Student/Teacher Conferences. At regular intervals, schedule time for individual conferences to discuss the contents of each student's writing folder. Together, the teacher and student can agree on a few aspects that need attention during the interval until the next conference.

Student Responses to Student Papers. Again, specific criteria should be given in advance of the writing and the same criteria used for student evaluation. This is simply a way of getting students to communicate with each other as well as with the teacher and thus can give the writer's task more reality. It will also give students more than one kind of practice in understanding and applying specific standards.

In-class Oral Reading of Written Work. This can be beneficial when students are trying to express basic concepts in their own words. Oral reading, either by the students themselves or by the teacher, will enable students to compare different ways of expressing an idea. As a variation, let students work together in small groups using their individual writings to come up with an "ideal" explanation of a concept.

USING A DIAGNOSTIC FRAMEWORK FOR ASSESSING STUDENT WRITING

The main thing a teacher should look for in writing is evidence of growth. Writing reflects thinking, and over time students should show progress in their ability to incorporate detail and complexity in their writing. Explanations should become more fully developed. Supporting detail should be brought increasingly into use. Relationships between sentences and paragraphs should become clearer.

There should also be progress in the student's ability to express abstract as well as concrete observation. For example, describing a personal experience represents thinking at a concrete level, while the ability to interpret that experience and derive some general observations from it requires abstract thinking. One student wrote a wryly humorous account of a teacher who seemed to be almost sadistically demanding of his tender-minded students. The description was good in itself as a piece of personal, concrete expression, but the writer made even more of it by explaining, at the end, that this is the kind of teacher from whom students learn in spite of themselves and therefore a good example of how teachers should be. He had moved from the particular to the general, demonstrating his ability to abstract meaning from personal experience.

Students should also demonstrate increasing proficiency in organization. They should show that they can perceive any composition as having parts that can be consciously manipulated. At the same time, they should be becoming conscious of style and originality.

A simple checklist will enable the teacher to look at student writing diagnostically to determine whether he is growing in his ability to achieve completeness, detail, abstraction, organization, and style in his expression. The following six-point scale can be used to keep a record on each student, using the data sheet given. (See Figure 11–1.) The scale and data sheet can be used as given or adapted to the teacher's own analysis of what demonstrates growth through writing in his subject area.

Scale

1 = Minimal communication: The writer gives only a few simple utterances which he does not attempt to develop in any way. Writing is extremely brief.

2 = Some development of communication: The writer expands the number of statements and achieves some complexity but lacks evident organization or an overall idea of what he wants to get across. Writing is still quite brief.

3 = Some development and organization of communication: The writer is achieving order and completeness at the sentence level but still lacks a clear grasp of overall structure. Writing is rather brief.

4 = Evidence of abstraction along with orderly presentation: The writer includes interpretive comments of his own along with a coherent presentation of information. Writing now seems complete.

5 = Communication that combines orderly presentation of information, development of ideas, interpretation beyond a concrete level, and strong overall organization: The writer can provide cohesive sentences organized into paragraphs (for longer writing assignments). Overall organization shows a clear beginning and end with a well-developed body. Writer has produced a complete and organized statement.

6 = Communication that includes the criteria of number 5 along with originality of expression or idea, or a polished writing style that adds clarity and personality to writing.

Where appropriate, the teacher could underline those aspects of a composition that are particularly weak and circle those that show growth. A combination of the scale with underlining and circling gives specific feedback to the student but does not require a written commentary from the teacher.

This checklist will help the teacher "think diagnostically" about students' writing development. Students who are writing at stage one have at least made a beginning in using written language as a medium of expression. They have not yet begun to explore the possibilities of using written language as a vehicle of thought, but at least they are bringing pens into contact with paper, which is the point at which everyone must start. These students probably find writing a very difficult mode of communication and should receive much encouragement to keep trying.

Students at the second stage are beginning to develop their written language. Although their efforts may fall short of even the most generous literary standards, the fact that they are willing to go beyond a minimal effort is important. Some instruction in the use of a simple outline (one primary idea and two or three supporting ideas) should enable them to concentrate on further expansion of ideas. This is the most important kind of experience for them at this point. Primarily, they should be encouraged to write freely and fluently just to find out how much they can say on a topic.

Students at the third stage are just beginning to bring it all together, combining the development of ideas with a beginning notion of overall structure. The teacher should be sure to acknowledge both aspects, encouraging the student to continue to think in terms of both organization and details. This writer still lacks full command over writing as a medium of thought and expression, but he is learning to communicate clearly. This in itself is a tool that will prove valuable to him in many ways, and he should be made aware of the importance of this achievement.

Students at the fourth stage of development are beginning to discover the value of writing as a way of thinking. They are going beyond report writing and integrating information with their own thinking. At the same time, each piece of writing is being treated as a unit in itself, and grasp of overall organization is firm. Students who achieve this level of written communication in high school are doing well. They should be encouraged to explore their own ideas and reach toward increasingly original productions. Practice, feedback, and encouragement are extremely important at this stage.

At the fifth stage, students are developing real strength as writers and showing excellent control over this mode of thought and communication. They need to be challenged with assignments that call for greater length and complexity of ideas. These students will also benefit from critical response in the form of suggestions of new approaches they might try. If they have developed this far, they are probably interested in improving their abilities even more and may even have a special interest in writing. They are also fairly independent and can respond on their own to challenging assignments, so the teacher need only use his imagination to provide interesting experiences for these students.

The rare student who reaches the sixth stage may well be a better writer than the teacher and deserves the teacher's appreciation and respect. Adolescence is a creative stage in life, and students with literary talents may turn out some extremely competent work. The student at this stage is quite independent and requires assignments that will make him put forth his best efforts. He is likely to be highly conscious of writing as a mode of thought development and personal expression and may even prefer writing to oral communication. He will benefit from being introduced to readings that provide diverse models of written expression, vocabulary development at a high level, and responses directed toward style and quality of ideas. This student should also be encouraged to keep trying new forms and approaches and in this way discover how much he can do.

Students should know what stages of development the teacher uses for evaluating their compositions. The explanations may be stated in simpler terms than the checklist given in Figure 11–1, but the criteria for progress should be part of the student's view of his task as well as in the view of the teacher. Thus a similar checklist for the student might by very appropriate. It could be used for personal review or for offering constructive suggestions to a classmate.

Perhaps the individual student is the best possible source for reducing the teacher's chore in correcting compositions and for increasing the learning done by the student. If each student had his own set of criteria for proofreading or for reviewing his own writing, he could be asked to reread his paper and mark on it the number of the scale that seems to represent what he did. The teacher could then glance at it quickly to see whether it achieved the level that the student had given it. If the teacher agreed, the evaluation could stand and both would know what must be done next time to achieve a higher number on the scale. If the teacher disagreed, they could confer or the

STUDENT WRITING DATA SHEET   Student's name _____

Assignment (briefly described)   *Date*   *Rating*

	1	2	3	4	5	6
1. _____						
2. _____						
3. _____						
4. _____						
5. _____						
6. _____						
7. _____						
8. _____						
9. _____						
10. _____						
11. _____						
12. _____						

Comments:

Figure 11-1

student would have to review and rewrite (or scale down) to achieve the level he had posted.

Students should practice writing throughout their years in school and receive guidance toward ever-increasing clarity and completeness in this mode of communication. There is more at stake, moreover, than the ability to fill out a job application at some future date or write coherent correspondence once employment is secured, although these skills are certainly important too. Writing is more than a handy skill. It is a way of thinking and, therefore, an important means of intellectual development. Through writing, one learns to construct his ideas using the materials of language, relying on these alone. To do this, the writer must understand both language and his own thoughts, becoming consciously involved with both. He learns to structure his ideas, to deal with relationships as well as specific concepts, to elaborate, and to follow through on ideas to see where they might lead. Writing enables one to develop a train of thought without interruption or distraction and to find out for oneself the value of an idea. Writing is, ultimately, an important form of communication with oneself. It is also the most enduring way of communicating with others.

Content teachers do not have to double as English teachers to provide suitable writing experiences. This idea arises from the misconception that language development can be confined to one subject, that it involves only technicalities, and that each subject is a self-contained area of knowledge. Knowledge as it grows in the mind of the learner is not subdivided along the lines of a daily class schedule. Students who go from one class to another as if they were switching channels are likely to become confused. Students need to remain in touch with their own thinking as they are exposed to different learning experiences. One very important way to enable them to do this is to give them many opportunities for self-expression through writing. As one student put it:

> I strongly feel that students, regardless of what grade . . . are the ones that need to express themselves in the classroom. Instruction is one thing, but expression is yet another. Give the student the chance to write how he understands the subject.

SUMMARY

Reading and writing go together as naturally as do listening and speaking. The content teacher can and should incorporate writing as an integral part of classroom learning without trying to teach writing "skills" or unduly burdening himself with papers to read and correct. The important thing is to give students writing experience in all content areas.

This chapter presents practical suggestions for providing writing opportunities, grouped into four categories: (1) short writing activities that can be integrated into day-to-day work, (2) writing for tests, (3) independent writing, and (4) longer writing. Suggestions are also given for efficient ways of keeping track of student writing and progress. The emphasis is on student effort and experience. Every piece of writing need not be critiqued in detail, and, in fact, this kind of heavy marking will probably be counterproductive. The best approach is to give the student one or two writing objectives to concentrate on at a time and lots of practice.

A six-point scale of writing development is described. This should help the teacher understand each student's writing performance and give him the kind of encouragement and direction he needs.

DISCUSSION QUESTIONS

1. How are reading and writing related to each other?
2. How does writing differ from speaking as a form of communication? What are its special advantages and limitations?
3. Why is writing important across the curriculum rather than just in English classes? What is the relationship of writing practice in content areas to the formal instruction given in English classes?
4. It has been said that school is the only place where a person will receive the instruction and practice he needs to develop his writing abilities. Does this mean that writing is not really important in life? Will the person who does not get sufficient writing experiences in school be missing something important? Does it matter whether or not Johnny can write?

Suggested Readings

Burgess, Carol et al. *Understanding Children Writing*. New York: Penguin Books, 1973.

The ten authors of this book have brought together many examples of student writing representing different ages, writing abilities, and curriculum areas. The authors are interested in how students write, that is, the process of writing as well as the product. Part III, "Handling Information," is especially applicable to subject-matter instruction. Although the analytic discussion in this book gets rather deep, it is an excellent short reference for teachers who want to know more about the nature and possibilities of student writing.

Harris, Larry A., and Carl B. Smith. *Reading Instruction: Diagnostic Teaching in the Classroom*. New York: Holt, Rinehart and Winston, 1976.

Moffett, James. *Teaching the Universe of Discourse*. New York: Houghton Mifflin, 1968.

The purpose of this book is to propose a sound theoretical foundation for teaching communication. Moffett emphasizes the concept of structure and the process of abstraction, which he believes underlie all stages of information processing. Through abstraction, the mind's "materials" are arranged in hierarchies of classes and subclasses. This depends on selection, a deliberate singling out of some features of the environment and ignoring of others. Students need to practice in this process of abstracting with the freedom to learn through trial and error. Moffett also presents his analysis of different kinds of discourse, ranging from the most concrete to the most abstract. He believes that progressing toward greater abstraction is a natural tendency that will be developed through organized practice.

Richards, Bertrand F. Writing From the Mind Out. Paper read at a conference of the National Council of Teachers of English, 1974, at New Orleans. Available from the ERIC Document Reproduction Service, P.O. Box 190, Arlington, VA 22210.

This paper describes a method for developing writing fluency and ease of communication by having students write for quantity four days of the week and then select one item for polishing on Friday. In this way, they are able to separate the development of ideas from the mechanics and yet concentrate on both. Although this program is intended for English classes, the idea can be adapted to other content areas.

E. Brooks Smith, Kenneth S. Goodman, and Robert Meredith, *Language and Thinking in the Elementary School.* Second Edition. New York: Holt, Rinehart and Winston, 1976.

The purpose of this book is to help teachers establish a theoretical foundation for relating language and cognition. The authors' thesis is that language is the primary means by which the individual organizes and makes sense of his environment. By means of language, one builds an "ordered world" and has a "map" for reference. Teachers should be concerned with the use of language to develop thought. The writers of this book present a well-developed explication of the psycholinguistic position.

part 4

Organizing and Evaluating

12

Selecting Books and Coping with Them

What criteria are useful for selecting books for students?

How can a teacher match books to the interests and academic needs of students?

How does a teacher instruct students to cope with the books they use?

BOOKS AND FREEDOM

In the book *Roots* by Alexander Haley, the masters of Kunte Kinte (Toby) several times talked about the need to keep slaves ignorant and illiterate, "Otherwise, they will get ideas. And no telling what they might try then." One of the frustrations in reading the book is the knowledge that Kunte Kinte's attempts to escape are doomed to fail because he doesn't know where to go or what to do besides run.

What is the difference between him and Aleksandr Solzhenitsyn? In a very real sense, Solzhenitsyn was enslaved in a Siberian labor camp and forced to work, without pay, without rights, without reprieve. But he was literate. He could write. He could read. Through books and through his own manuscripts he maintained contact with the outside world—a contact that eventually became his road to freedom. Through men like Solzhenitsyn we know that books are the dread of Russian leaders, for books may contain seeds of dissent. Members of the Politburo know, as did Hitler, that to control the flow of information is to control the mind. Those who keep a sense of free-

343

dom alive in a totalitarian state are the ones who can read something beyond the party line. They stay alive mentally through books.

What then are we to say to people who predict that the world of the future is a printless world? McLuhan broadcast that message and seemed to approve the idea. Others, including some teachers, are telling us to "tone down the reading bit because the kids of the next generation won't need reading anyway." The importance of reading diminishes as radio and television increase their capacities to deliver the ideas that people need. Even if I believed that the future could eliminate books, I would cry out, Anathema! and Abomination!

Who will determine what comes to my children over radio and television —the only source of information and entertainment my children will receive in a bookless society? Who determines what goes into the government audio-cassettes that teach my children in their schools? Even today—in those classrooms where teachers say that content books are too difficult for their students to read and therefore they will give them all they need in lectures and in films—what are those teachers doing to their students? They are starving them! They are depriving them of a student's primary avenue to independence —the use of books. Unwittingly those teachers are trying to enslave their students' minds just as the masters and the dictators have enslaved peoples' bodies.

For those who predict that the future will be a readerless world, let us persuade them to do all in their power to fight the trend they predict. For those, especially teachers, who actively promote learning without books, let us attack them—with reason—vigorously, for they are dangerous. They are spreading a poison that will slowly strangle us all. In human development it is a movement backward.

In our turn, let us search out and promote attractive, invigorating, fun-loving, mind-boggling books that will convince our students that the meats and sweets of intellectual freedom are found in the libraries and bookstores all around them.[1]

SELECTING BOOKS AND MATERIALS

Assuming you agree that books are the protein of a school's diet, you need to decide how to incorporate books into your classroom scene. It is now time to bring together the ideas, activities, and philosophies discussed so far and develop an image of how they work in the classroom. This chapter and the next one try to coordinate the books, people, space, and time that each teacher must organize for effective learning. Though these two chapters give examples and suggestions, it is with the realization that each teacher must decide what will work best for himself and his students—given their backgrounds, personalities, and the setting in which they work. It is with

---

[1] From an address by Carl B. Smith to the Wisconsin State Reading Association, 1977.

that intent that we ask you to examine the function of books, how to cope with them, and how to promote a beneficial interaction among them, students, and the daily time schedule.

Picture for yourself two classrooms. In the first, the chairs are neatly arranged in rows; the teacher's desk sits at the front near the chalkboard; a permanent projection screen is mounted over the chalkboard; several notices, including the fire-drill regulations, are pinned to the bulletin board; a dictionary and a 1957 encyclopedia occupy the bookshelf along one wall; on another wall there is a topographical map of the United States. The teacher's desk has on it a notebook, a textbook, and several overhead projection transparencies.

In the second classroom, there are two well-defined areas: about 60 percent of the space has student chairs circling the teacher's desk; the other 40 percent of the room looks like it might be a study-family room in a private home. There is a narrow display table covered with magazines; bookshelves hold reference works of various types, including a dozen dictionaries; newspapers hang from swivel arms attached to the wall; a table is covered with books (topical labels on the table help keep the books in suitable categories); a couple of beanbags are bunched into corners; a small rug and a plant are near each beanbag; student papers and maps are hanging all around the room; a two-drawer file cabinet is labeled "book file" on one drawer and "student records" on the other.

Question: If you were a teacher in that school, in which room would you want to work? If you were a student, in which room would you want to work?

The visual impact of the two classrooms not only suggests how students and teachers discuss social studies topics but also indicates the attitude of the teacher about books and materials and the role those resources play in secondary-school learning. In the first room, the only visible resource is the textbook and, of course, the teacher as a lecturer and discussion leader. Because other books and materials are not readily available, is it likely that students and teachers are going to explore other avenues on a regular basis? In the second room, however, the very fact that a major portion of space is occupied by such materials as books, magazines, newspapers, student work, and maps, states graphically that a considerable amount of time should be spent in learning from those resources. The presence of those materials shows that even incidental learning from them could be substantial if the teacher regularly provides independent work time.

SUCCESS IN BOOKTHINKING

In the second classroom, books are not placed simply to envelop the student in a pleasant academic environment. They are selected and arranged to achieve more specific purposes—to meet the needs of the youngsters who come to class to learn about health, or the modern short story, or the history of the United States. Becoming aware of information resources in an area is a significant part of learning. Knowing there are books and materials to suit a student's particular style and level is an equally important factor in helping him develop into an independent thinker. Books are there for information, for verifying statements, for personal unhurried perusal. But to achieve that atmosphere, to communicate the value of becoming an independent learner in, say, history, the teacher needs to make a concerted effort to make available appropriate books and other print materials.

The teacher's responsibility in the book-learning process includes selecting books and magazines that do indeed match students' background and competency besides conveying desirable information about a topic for discussion. More than that, a class has no single face: There are students who devour books and those who won't even taste them, students whose book-thinking skills are highly efficient and those who can't make use of the table of contents to find a chapter title. Within that diversity the teacher still wants to make books and periodicals come alive because they have messages and authors vital to the enterprise of learning his subject. It is only when a student realizes that books are the faces of live people and that magazines contain ideas that feed mind and emotion that books will in fact sport some flesh and muscle.

Creating that kind of awareness is one of the simplest tasks related to this discussion: Two minutes given at the beginning of each class (or right after an initial vocabulary activity) will start ideas rolling. The teacher tells the class what he found interesting or important in an article or a book he has been reading. When finished with his one-paragraph statement, the teacher places the book or magazine on a rack or a table reserved for special-interest items and proceeds with the class. Any student can peruse the book later if he wishes. Those brief moments on "interesting things I've been reading" are not just for the teacher. In fact, students ought to have first opportunity. If they don't have an item to comment on, the teacher can present his reading. Depending on the class and the attitude of the teacher, some of those shared ideas wouldn't even have to be related to the particular subject, or perhaps they relate to some aspect of teenage life. An occasional sign that the teacher knows they are growing up might convince them that French II isn't as remote from life as they thought at first.

Helping books come alive for a wide range of people and interests is no simple task. Too often we interpret the task as one of motivating students through displays of thunder and lightning: dramatic demonstrations, provocative pictures and magazines covers, book reports where intensely interested readers try to sell their latest book to the class, and other attention-getting devices. These are helpful and teachers should certainly make use of them to open students to the world of books. Students do enjoy and respond to such techniques but they really expect more from reading than an occasional dazzling fireworks display.

A student's perception of success in reading and his view of the value of books and other print material can be characterized as follows:

1. He wants to be teased into reading some books.
2. He wants to observe his progress as a bookthinker.
3. He wants independence in choosing his reading (Smith, 1976).

In other words, the student recognizes that often he needs external stimulation to attract his attention to a book or to a series of articles. He sees that even seduction is part of the game that is played in school, as society pressures him to become a useful citizen. Once hooked on a subject or on a book, the student will often pursue it on his own. But he is also mature enough to want the stages of competence identified for him and his progress marked off as he works through those stages. When the learner has a sense of how to grow and of what steps he can take or which practice activities promote his progress, then it is that he wants independence because he knows how to use it. Each of these three characteristics of success deserves some elaboration.

Reluctant Readers Come Alive

A book doesn't necessarily come alive for a student simply because the teacher puts it on a reading list.

In an experiment to test the notion that students respond to being teased into reading, one graduate class at Indiana University took the theme "Come Alive Through Books" and asked local teachers to identify their reluctant readers—not the students who couldn't read, but the ones who would not read. Once the experimenter had identified the student and the manner in which he avoided reading, the experimenter devised an approach or a gimmick for getting the student to try a book. In one ninth-grade classroom, for example, an English teacher pointed to a boy at the back of the room who normally made an ugly display when asked to read a story with the rest of the class. When the teacher said, "OK class, take out your books, turn to page thirty-two, read that story, and then we'll discuss it," good old Harry in the back of the room snapped his book shut, crossed his arms, put his head on his chest, and slid down in his seat for a little nap. The lights were out; he was out of business.

One experimenter took a skinny book back to Harry, threw it on his desk and said aloud: "Harry, I want you to hold this book for me. Don't read it. Just hold it while I work with someone in the front of the room. I'll come back and talk to you later. But don't read the book."

A moment after the experimenter had returned to the front of the room, some of the students around Harry shouted: "Hey, he's opened the book. He's started to read it." The trick to getting Harry into that book was not simply the loosely veiled challenge: "Don't read it; just hold it." On the front of that skinny book was stamped (as with a rubber stamp) TOP SECRET. "Do not open this book, for it contains secrets that cannot be disclosed." (See Figure 12–1.)

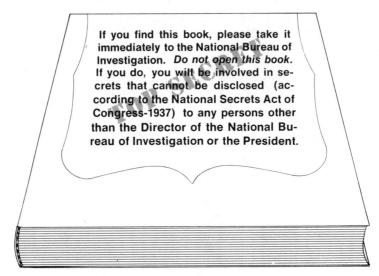

If you find this book, please take it immediately to the National Bureau of Investigation. *Do not open this book.* If you do, you will be involved in se-crets that cannot be disclosed (ac-cording to the National Secrets Act of Congress-1937) to any persons other than the Director of the National Bu-reau of Investigation or the President.

Figure 12-1. "Top secret" book as a reading teaser

The TOP SECRET book itself was a tease. In combination with the chal-lenge, "Don't eat the apple," the book cover lured reluctant Harry into the book to see what it was about. And he began an adventure that led him through FBI files and across the Atlantic in a chase after a spy. A book was used instead of a game or a machine or a film or some other means for seducing the student into reading.

We are not suggesting that one incident in the life of a reluctant reader will convince him that books are alive and that he ought to become an avid reader. But the incident gave the experimenter and the teacher an opportunity to ask Harry why he read that book but would not read when the teacher said, "Take out your books, turn to page thirty-two, and read the story." We might hypothesize from many incidents like the one with Harry the book-snapper that some students want to be convinced that the books proposed by the teacher are worth it. If they are, some of these stu-dents reason, then the teacher should spend some of his vitality on selling them to the class. Strange language for the academic world? In context, perhaps not. Today's students have grown up in the world of television where they are sold something every eight to ten minutes. To the student, most ideas and most books have no apparent intrinsic merit. They may be required to suffer through a course in order to fulfill graduation require-ments, but that fact doesn't make the ideas and the books come alive for the students. They have to be convinced that learning is exciting. That's part of today's learner makeup, and it is linked to everyone's personal need to be recognized as someone important. When a teacher says to a student, "I read this book and thought of you," he is saying more than, "This snappy book has excellent illustrations of paramecia." He announces that he thinks enough of that student as an individual to select something special for him. The book comes alive because the teacher acknowledges that the student is alive and valuable, maybe even interesting. Obviously, the teacher must read widely to be able to offer personal book suggestions to his students. But teachers can find numerous book ideas in teacher magazines and in book-review sections of professional teaching journals.

Reluctant readers and other students can be teased into reading by means of media other than books and magazines. Films, filmstrips, tape recordings, lab work, and demonstrations serve as the attention-focusing activities. Once the students are interested, the teacher can point to books or chapters where they can learn more or finish the experiment. With appropriate self-restraint (it's difficult for one to avoid telling all), the teacher can present a beginning of the concept and send the students to find the conclusion on their own in the assigned reading or in books available in the classroom or the library.

In any discussion about motives for learning, teachers must realize that the "preoccupying motives for most American adolescents revolve around resolving uncertainty over sexual adequacy, interpersonal power, autonomy of belief and action, and acceptability to peers. The urgency of these questions dominates the weaker desire to acquire competence at mathematics, history, or English composition" (Kagan, 1971). But there are some students, perhaps 20 percent in a typical classroom, whose belief in academic values makes them unwitting partners with the teacher in encouraging reading. The clever teacher will spread that influence by identifying the believers through interest and attitude inventories (see chapter 4) and placing them in small-group activities with some of the nonbelievers, by encouraging those students to share ideas from their reading (see chapters 4, 13).

Seeing Progress

The second main characteristic of success is seeing evident progress. Students, like the rest of us, need demonstrable signs that they are advancing. A third-grader once told us that reading success to her was "a skinny book." She could get through a skinny book in a hurry and, to her, finishing a book was demonstrable progress. Textbooks tend to be large, heavy volumes that no one gets through. It's like digging a tunnel through a mountain. You never get there on schedule and the effort seems exorbitant. Why is it, for example, that U.S. history teachers never get to World War II? How many physics teachers work until May on the first ten chapters of a nineteen-chapter physics text and then skim over the last nine in three weeks? Those texts may provide an excellent guide for the curriculum in U.S. history and in physics, but from a reader's viewpoint, she never sees much progress. This is especially true for the slower reader who probably views the whole task of text reading as a frustrating experience. That frustration and snail-like pace can be alleviated by having students read short, easy books on the same topic as the text or related topics. Finishing the short book becomes a demonstrable sign of progress and helps the student keep her energies in gear for other tasks.

For students to see that they are making progress through reading, they have to move quickly through materials: magazine articles, short topical books, topical books written at vocabulary levels where the students can absorb the concepts without huge amounts of effort. When the effort to read a text exceeds any clear payoff, the student is compelled psychologically to reject the book and probably to reject the subject along with it. Even if he is making progress, to him it is so imperceptible and so slow he cannot see anything happening. But by getting the student into short books with clear objectives, the teacher gives him a way of checking off something he has accomplished.

This explains the popularity of reading exercises and reading-practice books that focus on a specific skill such as finding the main idea or drawing conclusions. Those practice books are often limited to from thirty-two to forty-eight pages of selections and questions aimed at improving one skill. A pre- and post-test of the skill is provided so that the student and the teacher know how well the student can perform the skill after he has gone through the exercises. Once finished, he can put the book aside and check off that item on his list of reading skills. He has shown himself that he is making progress.

The same would hold true for reading skills related to specific content. A set of exercises in reading graphs, for example, will give the student a sense of reading progress and will give him renewed energy to tackle a new set of reading activities in the same subject area. Appendix A, Materials for Specific Skills and Subjects, lists numerous materials in a variety of content areas. Books and other materials are categorized so they can be used to teach and used for practice in aspects of bookthinking. Grade-level designations can help a teacher with decisions about practice at the students' reading level.

The Student Progress Checklist (Figure 12–2) shows how one teacher not only guided students in various reading skills related to a social studies class, but also helped the students see that they were making progress toward reading competence in that area. The teacher selected five areas to work in: charts and graphs, maps, drawing conclusions, technical vocabulary, and reading speed. Initially he gave the students some sample exercises in each area. The students did an analysis of their performance in the exercises. The teacher then identified materials—kits and books—in the classroom that

ASPECTS OF BOOK-THINKING[a]	PRACTICE ACTIVITIES[b]				EVALUATION[c]
	1	2	3	4	
Reading charts and graphs	social studies lab II section 3	section 5	section 9	section 15	
Reading specialized maps	Reading maps and globes Book II, pp 13–16	pp 29–32	pp 40–45	pp 61–69	
Drawing conclusions	B-L Practice Books Drawing Conclusions Bk E 1–5	Bk E 6–10	Bk F 1–5	Bk G 1–5	
Using technical vocabulary	E-B Vocabulary Set— Social Studies Group B	Vocabulary Group C	Vocabulary Group D	Vocabulary Group E	
Reading speed	"Speed and flexibility," timed exercise 1	Timed exercise 2	Timed exercise 3	Timed exercise 4	

[a] From the pre-test, a discussion with your teacher, or your knowledge of your strengths and weaknesses, work on the skills during your independent study and reading times. Select those activities that add to your abilities.

[b] The activities listed are available in the classroom. Check off each box in the chart above as you complete what is listed there. Then go on to the next exercise that you and/or your teacher have decided you need.

[c] After completing as many activities as you need, rate your ability with that skill; 1–4, low to high. Depending on your sense of progress, either ask the teacher for additional work or for a test to demonstrate that you can perform that skill.

Figure 12-2. Student Progress Checklist

had activities for each of the areas in which the students had tested themselves. He said that each student should work on at least three of these
bookthinking areas over the semester during the time for independent study
and reading that he had built into the class schedule. The remainder of the
directions were written on the bottom of the form (Figure 12–2) that he
gave to each student as a personal record. The checklist guided the student
in making choices, in giving him specific directions for work activities, and
in asking him to evaluate himself before he turned to the teacher for additional help or evaluation. Another teacher might choose different skill areas
and other books or teacher-designed practice activities, but the format illustrates how relatively easy it is to organize for and to demonstrate a student's
progress while he works on reading and thinking—a very complex aspect of
the school's responsibility.

It would probably be a helpful exercise for readers of this text to work
out a student progress checklist for their own subject specialty, perhaps
using Figure 12–2 as a model and finding targeted materials in Appendix
A, Materials for Specific Skills and Subjects.

Need for Independence

The third characteristic of reading success is the student's need for independence. Although most students want to be with their peers for most
learning experiences, they want regular opportunities to make choices of
their own. Whether it is working on a project different from the others, or
selecting a book that is different, or working on a skill that is identified as a
personal need, the middle- and secondary-school student views that sense
of independence as part of his picture of success in reading.

A sense of independence may be achieved by working with a variety of
books and materials, showing the student by implication that he can find
something that matches his interests. The teacher can offer the student
choices by providing regular, free reading time. So long as the student reads
within the subject area, both his interest in the subject and his sense of
success should be enhanced. By sharing important ideas that are being
learned from multiple sources, students stimulate one another and display
a wider assortment of books than a single teacher could. That type of free
reading shouldn't be reserved for the English class. It encourages a kind of
independence and exploration that every teacher should claim as part of his
teaching goal. Other ways to encourage self-selection include assigning
differentiated reading tasks among members of the same project or the same
study group, building study teams who help one another by each doing
different kinds of reading and explaining, making individuals responsible for
collecting books and periodicals on a topic and bringing them to class for
others to read during free reading time, and so on. See Figure 12–3, Planning
Independent Reading Time, for one way of building independent study into
the weekly schedule.

Along with other learning opportunities, independent (free) reading should become part of each week's plan. Alternative plans can be worked out. Two are shown here based on a 50-minute period.

Weekly Plan A

50-minute class period	M	T	W	Th	F
5 minutes	1	6	7	6	7
15 minutes	2	4	2	3	4
15 minutes	3	8	4	8	4
15 minutes	5 Free reading	8	5 Free reading	8	5 Free reading

Legend

1. Vocabulary development
2. Background concepts or new explanations
3. Assigned study-reading for a given purpose
4. Problem solving and discussing
5. Independent (free) reading
6. Sharing book ideas
7. Working on bookthinking skills, e.g., PARS technique
8. Project work

Plan A spreads free reading and sharing book ideas across the week. Plan B sets aside one full period each week for reading and sharing. Students are chosen at random to state briefly what was important or interesting to them about the book or selection.

Plan B

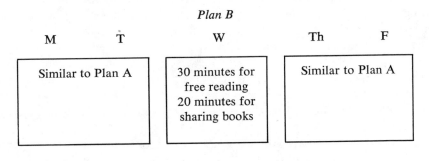

M	T	W	Th	F

Similar to Plan A

30 minutes for free reading
20 minutes for sharing books

Similar to Plan A

Figure 12-3. Planning independent reading time

POOR READERS AND NONREADERS

As the chapter on helping poor readers indicates, one of the conditions for success with them is to help them maintain their self-respect. Because reading stands as a public signal that a person can make his way in society, no poor reader or nonreader wants to have the world (his classmates) know that he can barely get through a third- or fourth-grade book, much less the ninth- and tenth-grade books that are thrust upon him. It is incumbent on the teacher, therefore, to devise means for having those assignments executed without forcing students to constantly rub their noses in their own embarrassment. Poor readers will appear in every class, so the teacher should learn to spot them quickly with a minimum of trumpet blowing. (Techniques for identification are found in chapter 5 on assessment and in chapter 6 on helping the poor reader.)

It might appear initially that simply displaying assignment options for a class would provide a way for handling the poor reader who wants to participate as actively as he can in the class. But the options available must, by deliberate action, include some that can be done by very slow or very poor readers; otherwise the specific problem will not be solved. The kinds of reading materials available determine whether a reading assignment on the topic can be managed by a poor reader. See Appendix B to this chapter, High-Interest Low-Readability Materials, for a list of books that can be used for supplementary practice with the poor reader. It would be beneficial to develop a list like that given in Appendix B for each subject area, using the appendix, a local library, and the publications of the subject matter teachers' association, perhaps the National Council of Teachers of English. For example, a chapter taken exclusively from the writings of Aaron Burr, the American Revolutionary figure, is not likely to lend itself to any direct participation by the poor reader. The poor reader may be able to read something written about Aaron Burr, but the language of an eighteenth-century intellectual, as pertinent as he may be as an original source, would pose innumerable problems for a twentieth-century poor reader. Where original source material is used, perhaps the poor reader can be helped comfortably by another student who works as part of a team or a group, each contributing what he can to the class and to each other. (See chapter 13 on student teams.)

But when everybody is reading, then the poor reader must have something to read, too. And his book or periodical must have a respectable appearance. The book may be filled with illustrations and have reduced exposition, but those illustrations must look like ones that a fifteen-year-old or a seventeen-year-old would have in his book bag; otherwise the effort will fail. It is easy to say that a teacher ought to provide high-interest, low-vocabulary materials for the poor reader, but quite another matter to purchase them and use them effectively. There are several lists of books in many categories that would be helpful. (See Appendix B to this chapter.) In fact, many of the professional associations for teachers publish lists of books and materials that can be used for different levels of student performance. It would be useful to write the national office of the association of teachers of English, or of social studies, or of science, and ask for their lists of books and periodicals for the slower reader. The National Council of Teachers of English has published lists in book form. Understandably there are hundreds of books in the field of English that are designed for the poor reader but have content and intent for the teen-ager.

For the poor reader it cannot be stressed enough that the success characteristics mentioned above be prominent guidelines for the teacher in trying to encourage reading among those individuals. Brevity, simplicity, evident progress—these are easily understood prerequisites for success. But we should not forget the need to tease, to sell the reader on what we think it is important for him to read. More than other students, he has less chance of seeing the relationships that show why a subject should be read and studied. It is usually this reader who truly tests a teacher's ability to teach a subject with imagination and originality.

Other print forms, including TV, posters, movies, tape recordings, and newspapers and magazines could be used to provide the poor reader with the information he needs to succeed in a class. The teacher or students in a class, for example, could tape record important passages from the text, thus enabling the poor reader to hear the concepts and to read along. In this way he not only gets the concepts through listening but also practices reading (a necessary ingredient for improvement) at the same time. Tape recordings for helping slow readers should be placed in the school library/media center for continued use. In the library their availability and the privacy afforded is a real boon to the student who may be more sensitive than others about his reading difficulties.

EVALUATING PRINT MATERIALS

The textbook. It should go without saying that a textbook should be chosen for the students. But experience and studies that have been conducted on content texts suggest that the student is not always clearly in mind when some textbooks are chosen. In chapter 1, Matching Students and Books, studies were listed that indicated that many texts are rated considerably higher in difficulty than the grade level of the students for which they were chosen. That speaks only of the level of difficulty. Additional guidelines are given below.

A text for students should be appropriate in developing concepts tied to the background of the students.[2] The text should be clear in organization and in style and should be readable enough to compete with similar stimuli that the student encounters in related fields. In other words, a textbook has to be evaluated first in terms of the students, their characteristics, their backgrounds, and the kinds of textbooks they are accustomed to reading. *The text is a tool for learning and not a resource book for the teacher.* Though a teacher most often uses a textbook for an orderly presentation of the curriculum, it should be selected because it does communicate to the student.

Guidelines for Evaluating Books and Periodicals

A few brief guidelines for the selection of materials will serve as reminders of the need to use several criteria for evaluation instead of simply seeing whether a book or periodical "covers" the content or organizes it to suit the teacher. The major principle in evaluating materials is that they match or satisfy the objectives selected for the students in a school or in a class. In other words, the selection presupposes that considerable thought has been given to the needs of the students and that the teacher has in mind a clear image of what has to be accomplished. There is strong evidence that clearly identified objectives and procedures are highly correlated to successful teaching (Rosenshine, 1971). See Figure 12–4, Student Needs Checklist, for a reminder of student characteristics to consider in choosing textbooks.

With that guiding principle as a backdrop, a teacher considers instructional values, content values, and format and utility factors. To say that a teacher considers these matters oversimplifies choosing a text, especially one to be chosen as a basic text. In many states today and in some federal projects, parents and other members of the community must be enlisted as part of the selection committee for adopting textbooks. A given parent's concern will most often rest with the content of the books, because the incidental learning that occurs through reading textbooks may often appear as a more powerful influence on the student than the actual technical content of the subject. For that reason, the current preoccupations of society such as sex bias, fair distribution of cultures and races, traditional ethnic values, and similar matters must be built into the checklist of criteria to be used in judging materials. Healthy is the setting where the teacher provides expert technical advice and then joins his voice with that of the community to work out the related content criteria which will guide the group in selecting the best books for the students of that school.

---

[2] The term "text" is used here to mean any formally prescribed book or print material purchased for classroom instruction. Whether a 400-page book or a 40-page pamphlet, the same principles apply to evaluating them.

Determine how many or what percentage of your students fit into the subcategories on this checklist. Those estimates indicate what to look for in the books and other print materials you will use. Consider these areas of students needs!

1. *Reading level*

   beginning   grades 2–4   intermediate 5–7
   advanced 8–11   mature 12+

2. *Background concepts and vocabulary*

   lacks experience   cultural deprivation prevented
                             development
   flat but adequate   strong

3. *Interest in subject or topic*

   only if it flashes lightning
   another thing on the schedule
   his favorite

4. *Sense of Purpose*

   none   vague   on target

5. *Use of book parts*

   no system   occasional   systematic

6. *Author-reader relationship*

   stillborn   limping   healthy

7. *Attention span*

   only watches commercials
   needs a drink when it's time for the commercials
   watches educational television

Figure 12-4. Student Needs Checklist

Given below are sample questions for evaluating academic materials. These or similar statements might be converted into a checklist for the review and selection of materials which students are expected to read and study.

Criteria for Selecting Print Materials

Instructional Values

1. Do the materials fit the population?

Is the reading level appropriate? For which students?

Do the concepts match the students' background? Or account for limited cultural experiences?

Are there ways for the students to work out the technical vocabulary problems? Terms in context, glossaries?

2. Are the instructional tasks arranged in an order that the student can follow?

Are the objectives clear—at the student level? Do they help him establish purposes?

With teacher guidance can the student then work through many tasks independently? With his attention span? Are there frequent checkpoints?

3. Does the material lend itself to differentiated assignments and various levels of learning?

Are there subheads and other textual notations?

Are the pages illustrated for instructional purposes? Will they provide needed background?

Is there an appropriate balance between presentation of ideas and practice? Is it paced right for these students?

Content Values

4. Does the content include all or most of the objectives for the course?

5. Does the content present social concerns in a reasonable manner?

See the discussion above. Even math books can show pervasive bias through illustrations if, for example, all the tough problems are solved by boys.

6. Does the content include motivational and interest factors suitable to the age and culture of the population?

(Horse stories may be high in popularity in the seventh grade, but they will give way to acne and other issues by the ninth grade.)

7. Does the content lead to a continuing interest in and appreciation for the subject?

[Both the style of writing and the examples or the experiments should lead a student to say, "Gee, I didn't know this could be so much fun" (so intriguing).]

Format and Utility

8. Are the materials sufficiently attractive for their purpose?

Reading appeal is also related to eye appeal. The typeface should be clear and open. Illustrations should be inviting and helpful, not distracting or dismal. Are there enough illustrations to give the materials a sense of openness and movement? Will they appeal to students?

9. Are different typographical techniques used to help the reader?

A variety of heading sizes, the use of italics and boldface type should help the reader distinguish among ideas and points of emphasis. Will such devices guide those who are weak in using book parts?

10. Are the materials easy to handle?

> Will they lie flat for easy reading? For easy use? Are they appropriate in size for the purposes of the class?

Supplementary Materials

The core text and related materials deserve considerable attention from a committee responsible for choosing books. A core text carries a major load by providing the basic content and probably the primary organization for the curriculum in the subject. For that reason the ten guidelines given above should be applied in an orderly fashion when one is evaluating core books. But in today's world, that's only the beginning. Books, magazines, and newspapers that can be used for classroom instruction surround us in libraries, homes, bookshops, drugstores, supermarkets—almost everywhere. It takes only a minimal imagination to find ways of using those plentiful resources to help students in every subject area. Any teacher today who says, one book (one idea?) for all students is all he has available either is a bullheaded elitist or is dodging his responsibility to provide information resources that his students can use.

The problem is certainly not lack of material. The problem for the teacher is selecting and gathering materials from the wide range that is available. A visit to the publishers' exhibits at a teachers' conference quickly reveals the overwhelming variety that school publishers now offer teachers of every subject. The larger the conference, the larger the number of exhibitors. At the annual meeting of the International Reading Association, for example, three or four hundred publishers display books, magazines, games, and equipment that can be used to stimulate, direct, or correct reading competencies. A sample of supplementary products that publishers have had on the market for several years is given in Appendix A. The Appendix was constructed simply to give examples of the types of things available for various students in different subject areas. It does not begin to identify the books that the listed publishers have developed to help with reading needs in the secondary classroom. The appendix could be used as a beginning checklist for the decisions a teacher must make about supplementary materials and as a guide for the teacher to search through a school library and resource center, thereby becoming acquainted with various options.

Funds for Materials

Teachers may not receive individual budgets for supplementary materials, but that should not prevent a teacher from getting money.

Funds can often be found or generated through the school's discretionary monies. Ask the principal: he has some. Money might come through PTA, the librarian, or special board of education funds. Ask the curriculum

director or the consultant. Money is available through federal and state
grants that come to every school system. Librarians and curriculum directors
are regularly looking for someone who has a special list so they don't have
to rummage through publishers' catalogs and try to guess what the teachers
and the students will need. In one school system with about nine thousand
students, the curriculum director went to a local foundation and asked for
$40,000 to establish a materials depository to aid content reading, and she
got the money. Her teachers now have $40,000 worth of books, magazines,
tape recordings, and so forth to supplement their texts. More to the point,
she asked the teachers for lists of materials they thought would serve them
and purchased what the teachers submitted.

Students themselves can often help build a classroom library or provide
sets of useful practice material. Some teachers ask students to donate books,
and their names are written on special nameplates pasted in the books.
Libraries have duplicates, bookstores have overstocks, secondhand stores
have boxes of donated books, attics have treasure boxes—all are sources of
materials free or available for pennies on the original dollar. Make a list
of what you want and send your students out to find them, offering no more
than 10 percent of the original purchase price. Supplementary books
have a clear mission of helping students learn independently. Supplementary
materials should carry forward one or more of the success characteristics
discussed earlier in this chapter: lure students into reading, help them
see progress as bookthinkers, provide choices to increase their sense of
independence.

The Teacher as Manufacturer

In every discussion on supplementary materials, someone invariably says
that the classroom teacher should be creating "a lot of his own stuff." That
remark seems intended to develop guilt feelings in those who use a lab
text or a skills workbook. The statement, often made by a supervisor, is
probably intended to ward off "busy work," the assignment of workbook
tasks just to keep the kids occupied. Implied in the comment is the assumption that in his basement at night the teacher will develop some creative and
exciting game or activity that will involve the student in a very useful learning experience. And such an original creation may indeed arise from an
hour in the basement on Tuesday night. But more likely, given the time,
energy, and resources that most teachers have remaining after a day in the
classroom, they will use a stencil duplicator master and type up a fill-in-the-
blank exercise modeled after the "despised" workbook, run it off and give
the students a faded purple-printed sheet that strains the eyes, contains
typographical errors, and bores them with its pedantic phrases. That is not
meant to discourage teachers who want to develop their own materials. It
is directed toward an unfair attitude about what constitutes effective, that is,
creative teaching. The teacher who seeks out books and magazines and news-

papers that speak to the issues and to their students will need to exercise considerable imagination and creative energy. For the teacher, creativity must be measured in his ability to interest and push the student forward, not in the number of spirit-duplicating masters he can type up on Tuesday night.

A teacher's resourcefulness—and that is certainly creativity—should be encouraged by the school through giving him funds for magazines, newspapers, and paperback books which he can distribute to his pupils. In a sense, the teacher should regard everything he reads in his subject as potential learning materials to be passed along to his students. His motto should be: *Books are to be given away!* Articles from the newspaper, features in journals and magazines, and paperbacks are prime examples. Simply by dropping a copy of the *Scientific American* on a student's desk and suggesting that he might be interested in an article in that issue gives the student a sense of importance and a personal obligation to find out what the article is about. One industrial arts teacher constantly used his copy of *Popular Mechanics* as bait and through that technique made *Popular Mechanics* the most popular magazine in the school library. A newspaper article on a recent election campaign can be given to one small group of students and a detailed analysis of the campaign from *U.S. News and World Report* to another group. Each group is asked to come prepared to discuss the information and the point of view presented to them. The teacher gave the newspaper article to those who had difficulty in reading; the magazine analysis went to those who were more proficient. The ensuing discussion between the two groups of students illustrated the contrasts between the respective writers, taught the students about election politics, and had each group reading reasonably close to its performance level. That's a resourceful teacher—a creative teacher who uses his manufacturing time for ideas that help students.

SCREENING MATERIALS

Like any professional person, the teacher stays current by reading, both in the subject he teaches and in the books that will communicate to his students. Ads in teachers' journals and publishers' catalogs and exhibits at conventions alert the teacher to the possibilities. Books that appear to be appropriate can be acquired for examination. But the search should not mean an omnivorous grabbing of everything in sight. Selectivity is needed, else the poor teacher will be inundated with information and materials that he cannot even warehouse. One of the main threads throughout this chapter has been how important it is for the teacher to determine the needs of his students so that he can make intelligent judgments on what books to select.

The lists of books in the two appendixes for this chapter indicate some of the criteria for making appropriate selections. Level of readability and topical interests are self-evident criteria. So, in the perusal of a catalog or a visit to a convention exhibit, those two factors should be the first notations to be made on a book-selection checklist. After that the teacher should list the more specialized requirements such as practice in vocabulary, outlining, summarizing, locating or recalling specific information, map reading, graph reading, organizing to assimilate information, and so on. As to the usefulness of the list, a good test is to ask yourself how you would go about explaining any of the items just listed. Then find a teacher's guide or a student book that proposes to teach the same thing. Was there a reasonable match? Or are there skills that you need to bring more to the front of your consciousness and that you need to learn how to explain to students?

COPING WITH CONTENT BOOKS

Assuming that a teacher has purchased, borrowed, or inveigled basic content texts as well as supplementary materials, he still has the responsibility of helping his students to cope with those books. Coping means to contend with or to do what one can under the circumstances. As noted periodically in this text, the difficulty of books, the abilities and skills of students, and the dynamics of classroom activity make *coping* a useful word for teachers and students alike. Simply having a large selection of books does not get the right student and the right book together. Nor does it show the right student what to do with the right book once he has it. Chapter 13 will discuss aspects of organization that brings students, books, teachers, and learning activities together in a beneficial format. Here we deal with the problem of helping the student do something worthwhile once he has the book in his hand.

As with any group-learning experience, no one example or model will satisfy the needs of all students or all teachers. What is presented here must be adapted to the personal style of each teacher and to those students making up the teacher's class. In an effort to make is possible to adapt to a wide range of learning environments, we are presenting here a picture of a classroom where the teacher combines two elements—a typically structured-content curriculum interspersed with projects the students choose to work on. Your own teaching style may lean more to the structured-content curriculum. That's where your adaptation of these ideas takes place.

THE I–YOU RELATIONSHIP

No matter what the student is reading, he must be conscious of the relationship that exists between author and reader. In some very personal styles of writing that "I–you" relationship is quite evident. A personal letter, for example, and the personal essay which uses the second-person pronoun in addressing the reader makes the reader quite conscious of the personality of the writer. The reader begins to attach feelings to what is being said and interprets, develops, imagines, and constructs his own ideas based on those of the writer. Can you imagine, for instance, anyone reading a love letter in a passive, sponge-like attitude? No, the reader-lover hovers around every phrase and every word, interpreting, reading into, adding meaning that may not even have been in the mind of the writer. The "I–you" relationship in this case is so strong that the two of them—writer and reader—build together something greater than either had before they came together.

As the prose becomes more abstract, more academic, and therefore less likely to evoke a personal image of the writer, there is a human tendency to ease back, become more passive, and try to soak up the message rather than attempt to wrestle with the writer's mind. In a college text like this one, for example, its academic character may make you think of it more as a pile of ideas than a message from a person. To counter that notion we have from time to time talked to you directly, as we're doing right now. But we must emphasize that a writer's style is often governed by the conventions of the audience for which he writes, as in the case of college textbooks. And so the burden of the "I–you" relationship rests on the reader's head. Figure 2–5, Bookthinking: Author-Reader Relationship, will remind you of the things that we have said in this text about the nature of that relationship, and therefore indicate the areas in which teachers and students must work to cope with various kinds of reading materials. (See chapter 2 for a discussion of Figure 2–5.)

One advantage of shorter, more pointed, better-targeted reading materials for the middle-school and secondary student is their potential for maintaining a personal attitude. A five- or six-hundred-page textbook is akin to a warehouse. And nobody gets too cozy with a warehouse. But he can feel quite snug and comfortable with a couple of short books or articles on marine life, like the personal knicknacks in his room.

Whatever is used, however, the student must learn to cope, and to try to foster the "I–you" relationship.

STRUCTURE AND CHOICE

In Figure 12–3, a weekly plan is shown that incorporates learning activities which are assigned by the curriculum and the teacher and activities which demand student choices. Although there are other learning activities that could appear there, the weekly plan includes:

Vocabulary development
Providing background concepts
Explaining new concepts
Assigned study-reading for a specific purpose

Problem solving and discussing
Independent reading
Sharing ideas from books read
Working on bookthinking skills
Project work

Applied to any given subject, Figure 12–3 provides a time-and-task plan which uses assigned and free-choice reading-study opportunities. It is not presented as an ideal plan—only a workable one. And it helps create a concrete image of why teachers need to help students cope with the books and periodicals used in the classroom. Whether assigned or free choice, the objective of reading is to help the student arrive at new ideas. (See Figure 2–5.) The new ideas represent success for the student, and he should certainly have success in both assigned and free-choice materials.

The helpful aspect of the plan is that it enables the teacher to guide students in their study through assigned reading and also provides time for hints on how to cope with the bookthinking problems which they encounter in their free-choice and project reading. Each type will be discussed separately.

Assigned Reading

Whether reading in the textbook—warehouse—or in other selected materials, the student reads to achieve objectives demanded by the curriculum or by the teacher. The curriculum, or the book, or the teacher provides a structure for learning. Thus, certain purposes and outcomes are determined by someone other than the reader, though obviously he can add his own. The point is, however, that the teacher can guide or direct the student through the material in order to achieve certain outcomes—a score on a test, answering certain questions, applying the information to the real world. The teacher can accomplish those ends by providing personal oral directions and engaging in group discussion or by developing written guidelines in the form of study guides or worksheets.

Outcomes

One of the easiest ways to visualize how to teach students to cope with assigned reading is to list the desired outcomes, and to record them at various levels of performance. If student needs vary, it is because their strengths and weaknesses vary. For any one topic or objective, then, expectations will differ. In a science unit on the topic, the inclined plane, for example, a teacher might expect these three outcomes from three groups of students in the class:

Group 1:   (Concrete thinkers. Little scientific experience.) Be able to find examples of an inclined plane in the textbook and to list some examples in real life.

Group 2:　(Have some scientific experience. Understand themes but are not critical thinkers.) Be able to explain the main idea and definition of an inclined plane and its value in specified areas of our lives.

Group 3:　(Have experience and ability to do abstract thinking.) Be able to analyze the usefulness of the inclined plane in the examples given in the text and to describe its value in several fields of work in the real world.

With those outcomes in mind, the teacher tries to plan activities that will enhance the "I–you" relationship discussed earlier. As he prepares for each group, the teacher asks:

Concept—Do they have the background to understand?

Vocabulary—Which words are difficult and important?

Language—Is there anything about the writing style or the presentation style that doesn't match their language?

Message—Can the students follow the organization of the message or do they need help? What purpose shall they read for?

Followup—Is there a way that I can help them assimilate or use this information?

A planning worksheet helps the teacher keep those items straight as he prepares to show his students how to cope with the reading that he wants them to do.

CONCEPT	GROUP 1 PREFACE ACTIVITY	GROUP 2—OK	GROUP 3—OK
Vocabulary	Teacher list on worksheet. Student list	Define list in study guide	Personal checkoff in study guide
Language	Complex. Read samples aloud to get used to pattern	Ask them to adjust rate base on complexity	OK
Message	Find examples in illustrations and in text	Use outline as advance organizer	Identify inductive logic. Study guide
Followup	List examples and applications in student's life	Discuss main idea and applications	Discuss and write applications. Study guide

In each block the teacher can pencil a note that guides his work with a group on that particular aspect of bookthinking. (The term "groups," as used here, does not mean that the class should be divided into three separate working groups—though that is a possibility. Groups is used here to refer to identified needs and ways of speaking to those needs through assigned reading activities.) Take background concepts as an instance. The teacher knows that the experiences, vocabulary, and mental structures from those experiences are key ingredients in the way a student approaches the assigned text. If the teacher doubts the student's capability to dive into the text because he lacks the experience or the framework to do so, then the teacher provides an experience or an explanation that makes up for the deficit. One teacher, for example, develops what she calls "preface activities" for some members of her class. Her preface activities are designed to use an experience in the students' lives as a way of getting them interested and of leading them up to an understanding of the main concept of the assigned reading. She usually constructs a brief description and then asks that students respond in a brief answer form to show whether they have grasped the concept she was working on. A sample taken from her "Inclined Plane Preface" and one worksheet appear as Figure 12–5.

This preface activity is another form of advance organizer, that is, a capsule idea that helps the student organize his language or his mind for the passage he is to read. Other forms of advance organizers are discussed in other places in this text. In the teacher's judgment, some of the students may not need introductory concept development, and so they may work on vocabulary or setting a purpose for reading.

For each of the factors that helps to establish the interaction between reader and writer, the teacher decides how to help the student progress. In vocabulary, for instance, the teacher may use a worksheet and ask the students to review the material and select other words they want to discuss or pronounce. The students simply skim over the pages and collectively identify the words they think will cause trouble or will need advance definition. For a second group, the teacher may use a study guide with vocabulary to be defined. And for a third group, a list of words may be used that the student checks off if he thinks he knows them. Those he doesn't know he is asked to research on his own before reading. And so on down through the list for each group.

Study Guides

There are other ways to differentiate reading assignments besides using study guides. Some of those ways are treated in other chapters in this text. A study guide enables the teacher to have all students work from the same text, when the teacher deems that to be desirable. Or students can work on the same topic with readings and activities from a variety of sources—each geared to the needs of the student (see chapter 1). Study guides for different levels or for different needs can be a group project for a subject matter department, then used for differentiated reading study by all the students taking a course under the same label. Efficiency! But probably the most important benefit of a study guide approach is that it forces the teacher to think carefully through how to lead a student with given capabilities through the reading to some desired outcome. It forces the teacher to explore the learning dynamics in the reader-author connections, especially the dynamics that exist as learners of differing competency try to read the same author.

The outline above in which three groups are analyzed across several aspects of bookthinking demonstrates one way that a teacher could organize a study guide. Through the use of a guide, the students are led systematically from concept to vocabulary to purpose to message and so on. Depending on the students' needs, the teacher adjusts the activity in each of those categories, all the while directing the students toward a preconceived outcome. Each aspect of the outline could become a sheet of directions or a worksheet in a study guide.

Another approach to a study guide can be seen in the work of the science and English departments of the Cleveland, Ohio public schools. Their reading-study guides for the middle group in science start and end with a test (pre-test and post-test). The results of the pre-test can be used by the teacher to determine which students need specific help in various aspects of the other parts of the study guide. Sample pages from one of their units on levers are included in Appendix C, Study Guide for Physical Science. The pre- and post-tests have not been included, nor have some supplementary activity sheets. Their guides follow this pattern:

First day: Pre-test over concepts and problems in the unit.

Second day: Guide questions for reading a three-page segment. Answers are required on the sheet.

Third day: Problem solving over material from second day. Answers can be checked in the text.

Fourth day: Inquiry problem—an extension and explanation.

Fifth day: Worksheet to identify aspects of the topic, "Identifying Types of Levers."

Sixth day: An explanation and a lab demonstration of the concept, "The law of the lever."

Seventh day: A group problem and discussion, "Archimedes' lever problem."

Eighth day: Post-test.

The Cleveland guides also include supplementary activities for those who need further practice or additional problems as indicated by the post-test or by teacher observation.

Study guides need not be as elaborate as the sample in the appendix. Using a single guide, a teacher could stimulate students to read within their personal strengths and restrictions. Using the headings and the explanations in the outline below, a teacher could distribute the same guide to all students. Differentiation occurs primarily in the reading assignments from different books and in the kinds of questions assigned to each book.

Anna Jeff

This Spring weather has been great
for bike riding. Do you ever bring your
bike over to the school yard and ride it
around here? I did that over the weekend
and while I was here I saw Jeff and
Anna riding their bikes down by the baseball diamond. As I was watching them,
they stopped to talk about something.
They pointed first to the school building
and then in the other direction toward
the new high school. All of a sudden they
both turned on their bikes and Jeff
started riding up the hill toward the door
of the school that leads to the sixth
grade classrooms. while Anna was riding
up the hill that leads to the high school.
Guess who won? Right! Anna got to the
top of her hill first. It was an easier
hill to ride eventhough it was longer.
Jeff had a hard time with his hill
because it was so steep.

Figure 12-5. Preface activity. This advance organizer uses examples from the
student's environment to introduce a concept. Used with the permission of the
. teacher, Linda Crafton.

The hills that Jeff and Anna were racing up can be given special names. Inclined planes. Anna's inclined plane let her get to the top of her hill with a lot less effort than did Jeff's. The less the angle of the inclined plane, the longer the distance and the less the effort needed.

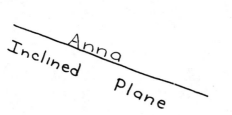

Which of the following are inclined planes?   (answer with a ✓)

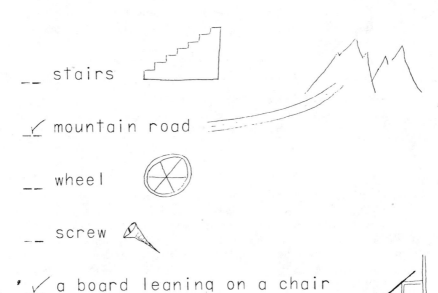

__ stairs

_✓ mountain road

__ wheel

__ screw

'_✓ a board leaning on a chair

Constructing a Single Guide with Different Assignments

1. Concept and vocabulary

In a group discussion or with a preface activity (see above), the teacher introduces the concept. From three sources, he lists pages where students can find material on the topic. They are to skim the pages and make a list of the vocabulary terms that seem difficult or part of the technical development. Those terms are then discussed, defined, and used in context as the students write them on an assignment sheet and note the definitions each thinks he will need.

2. Message organizer

One sheet of the study guide contains a simple outline of the topic and its major features. This serves as an organizer for reading and continued discussion.

3. Reading for a purpose

The reading assignment sheet is divided into three parts with different questions for each part. Each of the three parts is to be read from a different source, different text.

> *Part one.* Read Text A, pages 38–42. Answer these questions. The questions that follow call for specific examples and concrete details. Concrete level.
>
> *Part two.* Read Text B, pages 88–94. Answer these questions. The questions that follow ask for the theme, important details, some interpretation. Analysis level.
>
> *Part three.* Read Text C, pages 136–147. Answer these questions. The questions ask for analysis, evaluation and application. Application level.

The students are directed to read one of the three parts according to the teacher's plan or by a system of self-selection and teacher guidance. As they read, the students are reminded to use the PARS technique (see chapter 9).

4. Problem solving

Each of the three reading groups is given a problem to solve which is then brought back to the whole group for discussion and review. The teacher's role is to roam the room showing individuals and groups how to make the most of the guide and their readings to meet the desired outcomes. The teacher has time to explain and to demonstrate how the student can get the most out of his text, given his particular capabilities. The disadvantage of this assignment technique is that a student may get locked into the concrete level (part one) and never be asked to evaluate concepts, even though he is capable of doing so. A general class discussion should open up an opportunity for him to engage in those kinds of questions, even if his study guide doesn't call for them.

Independent Reading

In our discussion of assigned reading, it is assumed that the student often reads alone with the aid of a guide, a purpose, or a list of questions. Independent reading refers to the student's opportunity to choose what he is going to read and then to devise ways to cope with his choice. What he is choosing is indicated in the form, Planning Independent Reading Time, as project work or free reading. Project work, either individual or group projects, supports the subject or the topics being discussed. The student chooses an aspect to work on and then searches out the books and print materials that enable him to develop his or the group's theme. Free reading, usually related to the topic but with no specific direction or text implication, is an activity intended to expand the student's personal awareness and interest in the subject. His only responsibility is to share some of those ideas with the class when called upon to do so.

During independent reading time, the student must make decisions about what to read and how to get the most out of those books. In brief, that's what this book is all about: providing a definition of mature reading and ways the classroom teacher can help students become effective mature readers, ways they can cope with various bookthinking problems. As shown in the form, Planning Independent Reading Time, the teacher has two time slots for helping students. During the project and free-reading time slots, the teacher can confer with individuals on how to be more effective in the kind of reading they are doing. Those brief conferences enable the teacher to use the ideas that appear in this book. The other usable time is the five-minute period at the beginning of each class hour. Those periods can be used for group instruction in a particular aspect of bookthinking—anything from increasing reading speed and flexibility to ways of understanding a technical dictionary, which will help the student use the technical vocabulary he finds in his books.

Instructional Centers

To make the independent reading and study more personalized, the teacher may construct instructional centers to accomplish subject content objectives and/or bookthinking objectives.

The extrinsic appeal of books, magazines, and problem-solving materials can solve many problems in the classroom under one condition: the student thinks that he can make a choice. Having locations in the classroom where coordinated materials on a topic can be found provides a structure for instructional centers where students can make choices. In a foreign-language class, for example, where one center has readings on historical works, another on modern works, and still another on the use of current periodicals from a country in which that language is used—all give the student an opportunity to practice reading in the language and make a personal choice at the same time. One math teacher, for example, established three types of application centers—one with cards carrying descriptions of daily-life problems, another with cards describing problems from space explorations, and a third with problems taken from the standard textbook. The individual student chose the set of problems on which he wanted to work. Or in a science class, the life chain was studied with three optional routes—one emphasizing plant life, a second, animal life, and a third, microscopic life. Each center was organized to lead the student through a cycle and to a similar conclusion, but the student had a choice of reading about the type of life that appealed to him most.

Examples of techniques like these could be multiplied. They need not apply only to the student's need for independence. Instructional centers should appeal to the student's need for progress. As in programmed learning, a center could concentrate on offering a series of carefully sequenced, small learning steps that offer the student the opportunity for frequent positive reinforcement. Or, like the fisherman who selects different lures for different fish at different times of the day at different seasons of the year, the teacher uses sets of materials in learning centers to "lure" students into reading. That is an important objective. Above all, teachers must remember that practice in reading, practice in using books, contributes heavily to competence in reading.

Properly devised, instructional centers in the classroom give teachers freedom to work with individual students and also give their creative energies an outlet for exercise and display.

Steps in Developing Instructional Centers

1. Determine the purpose for the center.
2. Describe for yourself what outcomes you are expecting and what is the best way to achieve those outcomes.
3. Select the books and other materials that will provide the ideas to which the student is to react.
4. Write clear and simple directions for the student. Lead him carefully through each stage of the center.
5. Test the directions on a few students to make sure they are intelligible. Is it clear how to exit successfully?
6. Put all the materials and the directions in a box, a set of envelopes, or some other format that can be easily transported and displayed.
7. Place the learning center in the classroom and explain how it works and what the choices are.

There are innumerable ways in which teachers can repackage, reorganize, and thus enhance the instructional value of the flood of books and magazines available in today's schools. Or, teachers can compose their own written exercises if they are so inclined.

TEACHER ON THE MOVE

As the students work, the teacher confers with them and also spends time searching for additional books and materials that make the independent work more valuable for individual students. As that happens, more and more students will become interested, enthusiastic, and successful.

Thinking about getting students to become independent, most teachers will want to use a combination of assigned and independent work, gradually moving them toward more free choices. Thus a plan like that given earlier, the form called Planning Independent Reading Time, stands as a reasonable outline on which most teachers can build to bring books into the service of the student and that of the school's curriculum.

SUMMARY

Instructional books and periodicals can be classified as *core,* that is, containing the basic topics and curriculum, and *supplementary*, that is, helping to fill out the program or meet special needs of students in class. Both core and supplementary materials should be chosen to assist teachers in carrying out the major instructional decisions they have to make:

1. To meet the reading and maturational level of the student;
2. To communicate and practice a chosen set of skills and processes;
3. To motivate the student to continue his progress in the subject area.

Those decisions are related to the students' expressed desire to see that they are (a) making progress, (b) being teased into reading and learning by means of a book as they are through television, and (c) making personal reading choices as an expression of their growing sense of independence. For their part, teachers can systematize their search for appropriate materials by categorizing them as titles and other descriptions are seen in catalogs or at conventions. In those ways, the reluctant readers, the average readers, and the eager readers will have books, newspapers, and magazines to help them because their teachers engage in a creative effort to select and organize those materials for individual use and for use in learning centers. At times teachers will compose their own materials to fill a gap or to satisfy their own creative urges.

Once the books are available to the students, the teacher must help the student cope with them, that is, use them for purposes within his capabilities. Most teachers will want to combine assigned reading and independent-reading activities to provide better guidance in the content curriculum and in bookthinking operations. Several techniques for working on coping skills are discussed in this chapter.

DISCUSSION QUESTIONS

1. For your subject area, how would you catalog supplementary books that you would want students to use in your class?
2. What are two ways in which a teacher can help students cope with the variety of print materials used in his subject?
3. Take several representative secondary books from a subject area and discuss their value, using a set of evaluation criteria.
4. Make a list of several bookthinking operations useful for a subject and then use appendixes A and B to begin a list of materials that help accomplish those operations.
5. Describe a typical class and then explain how to incorporate a wide variety of books into assigned reading and independent-reading activities.

Suggested Readings

Carlsen, Robert. *Books and the Teen-Age Reader: A Guide for Teachers, Librarians and Parents.* New York: Bantam Books, 1967 (revised 1971).
This is a very readable examination of literature for adolescents based on an analysis of how reading relates to the process of becoming an adult. It is largely a discussion of the literature that teenagers find appealing at various stages of maturity—good book talk with extensive annotated bibliographies at the end of each chapter. Of particular interest is the writer's description of the "stages of life" of a young reader. Difficulty might arise if a reader gets "stuck" at a particular stage, and the writer has some suggestions for ways of moving him on. Although this book was written in 1967, it has gone through several printings and been periodically updated, so the extensive bibliographic material is a fair reflection of what is currently available.

Fader, Daniel N., and Elton B. McNeil. *Hooked on Books: Program and Proof.* New York: G. P. Putnam's Sons, 1966.
This is a very readable account of a high school English program designed for students with little achievement motivation in which reading and writing were incorporated into content instruction in a natural and successful way. More important, the discussion delves into the basic issue of how books and reading can be of personal value to students and relate to their lives. The author's major premise is that surrounding students with interesting materials from which they make their own choices will lead them to discover their own values in reading.

Weiss, M. Jerry, et al., eds. *New Perspectives on Paperbacks.* Monograph No. 1. The College Reading Association, 1972. (Available from Strine Printing Co., Inc., 391 Greendale Road, York, PA 17403) Topics covered include censorship and ways to cope with it; books dealing with the experience of the physically or mentally different individual; the black experience for young children; teachers' attitudes toward contemporary literature and how these attitudes might turn students off reading; the problem of television as a competitor to books and ways that both TV and movies can be used to encourage reading; the issue of the "obsolescence" of print and suggestions for countering this trend; the flexibility that paperbacks make possible in particular subject fields; and advice on choosing literature that will help adolescents mature into perceptive adults. This is a stimulating collection of ideas presented in short discussions with ample reference to current paperback literature. Each chapter is followed by a substantial bibliography of materials available, and the monograph features title and author indexes and a publisher's directory.

Appendix A

Materials for Specific Skills and Subjects

Any list of materials related to reading skills must be limited to examples because the flood of available materials would overwhelm this book. Thus, presented here are only a few samples of learning materials available in several skills categories. Organized by publisher,[a] the books and materials will be designated according to their intended grade-level usage: *grades 5–8, grades 9–12,* and *remedial.* The remedial category includes those designed for middle-school and high-school use but provide practice in elementary skills with very simple reading selections. Other categories and their descriptions are:

> *Attending:* listening, developing attention, and concentration.
> *Word pronunciation:* word analysis, phonics, pronunciation skills.
> *Vocabulary:* developing and expanding word meanings.
> *Recall:* finding the basic message and details.
> *Critical:* inferences, conclusions, judgments.
> *Rate:* developing speed and flexibility.
> *Content:* G = general, L = literature, Sc = science, SS = social studies, M = math.
> *5–8:* grade levels 5–8.
> *9–12:* grade levels 9–12.
> *Remedial:* readability levels below fourth grade but designed for secondary students.

---

[a] Addresses of publishers can be found in *Literary Market Place*, R. R. Bowker Company, 1180 Avenue of the Americas, New York, New York 10036.

TITLE	ATTENDING	PRONUNCIATION	VOCABULARY	RECALL	CRITICAL	RATE	CONTENT	5–8	9–12	REMEDIAL
Addison-Wesley										
Reading Development Kits A and B		X	X	X	X		G	X		
Associated Educational Services										
The Short Story as a Listening Form	X		X	X	X		L		X	X
Baldridge Reading Instruction Materials										
Reading and Study Techniques for Academic Subjects							L	X	X	
Barnell Loft and *Dexter, Westbrook*										
Specific Skills Series	X	X	X	X	X		G	X	X	
Supportive Reading Skills	X	X	X	X	X		G	X	X	
Benefic Press										
Thinking Box					X		LM Sc SS	X	X	
Better Reading Program										
Rapid Reading Kit				X		X	G	X	X	
College Skills Center										
100 Passages To Develop Comprehension				X	X		G		X	
How To Develop a College Level Vocabulary			X				G		X	
Communacad										
Word Craft 1, 2, 3			X				G	X	X	X
Coronet										
Listening With a Purpose	X						G	X	X	
Curriculum Research Associates										
Reading as Thinking— Paragraph Comprehension				X	X		G		X	
Developmental Reading										
Developing Reading Efficiency			X	X	X	X	G		X	
Educational Developmental Laboratories										
EDL Study Skills Library					X		Sc SS	X		
Listen and Read	X				X		G	X	X	
Reading 300	X	X	X	X	X	X	Sc SS	X	X	
Educational Progress										
Audio-Reading Progress Laboratory: Levels 7 and 8		X	X	X	X		LM Sc SS	X		
Educators Publishing Service										
A Vocabulary Builder Series			X	X			G	X	X	

TITLE	ATTENDING	PRONUNCIATION	VOCABULARY	RECALL	CRITICAL	RATE	CONTENT	5–8	9–12	REMEDIAL
Efficient Study Skills							LSc SS		X	
The Structure of Words		X	X				G	X	X	X
Educational Record Sales										
Sound Skills for the Upper Grades		X					G	X		
Eye Gate House										
Advanced Reading Skills	X		X	X			G	X		
Fundamentals of Vocabulary Building		X	X				G	X		
Field Educational Publications										
The Kaleidoscope Readers			X	X			G	X	X	X
Checkered Flag Series				X			G	X		X
Classroom Audio-Visual Kits	X						G	X		X
Follett Publishing Co.										
Success With Language		X	X	X			G	X	X	X
Garrard Publishing Co.										
Read and Say Verb Game	X	X	X	X			G	X	X	X
The Syllable Game	X	X					G	X	X	X
Ginn & Co.										
Word Enrichment Program Levels 3–7		X					G	X	X	
The Globe Book Co.										
Programmed Reading				X	X		G	X		
Grolier Educational Co.										
Reading Attainment Systems	X	X	X	X			G		X	X
C. S. Hammond and Co.										
Building Reading Confidence	X	X	X	X			G	X		
Harcourt Brace Jovanovich										
Design for Good Reading A, B, C, D			X	X	X	X	G		X	
The New World Series			X	X	X	X	L	X		
World Attack: A Way to Better Reading	X	X	X				G		X	X
Harper & Row										
Design for Reading Levels 17–20			X	X	X	X	MSc SS	X		
D. C. Heath and Co.										
Efficient Reading, Revised			X	X	X		G		X	
Guide to Effective Reading		X	X	X	X	X	G		X	
Toward Reading Comprehension		X	X	X	X	X	G		X	

TITLE	ATTENDING	PRONUNCIATION	VOCABULARY	RECALL	CRITICAL	RATE	CONTENT	5–8	9–12	REMEDIAL
Holt, Rinehart and Winston										
Increasing Reading Efficiency		X	X	X	X		G		X	
Realizing Reading Potential		X	X	X	X		G		X	X
Houghton Mifflin										
Trouble Shooter	X	X	X	X			G	X	X	X
Laidlaw Bros.										
Study Exercises for Developing Reading Skills		X	X	X	X		G		X	
Learn Inc.										
Rapid Comprehension Through Effective Reading		X	X	X	X		G		X	
Learning Materials										
Literature Sampler		X	X	X	X		L	X		
Lippincott										
Reading for Meaning			X	X			G	X	X	
McGraw-Hill										
Critical Reading Improvement					X		G		X	
Macmillan										
Advanced Skills in Reading 1, 2, and 3			X	X	X		G	X	X	
Audio-Lingual English	X	X	X	X			G		X	X
Charles E. Merrill Books										
Improve Your Reading Ability		X	X	X	X		G		X	
Oxford Book Co.										
Enriching Your Vocabulary		X	X	X			G		X	
Vocabulary Workshop		X	X	X			G		X	
Prentice-Hall										
Be a Better Reader:							ScL			
Series I through VI		X	X	X	X		SS M	X	X	
Increase Your Vocabulary		X	X				G		X	
Random House										
Random House Reading Program Green, Blue, Tan, Olive		X	X	X	X		G	X		
Reader's Digest Services										
Grow in Word Power			X	X		X	G	X		
Help Yourself To Improve Your Reading Levels 1–4			X	X		X	G	X	X	
The Reading Laboratory										
The News Read Series			X	X	X		G	X	X	X

TITLE	ATTENDING	PRONUNCIATION	VOCABULARY	RECALL	CRITICAL	RATE	CONTENT	5–8	9–12	REMEDIAL
Scholastic Magazines										
Go			X	X	X		LM Sc SS	X	X	X
Pattern for Reading		X	X	X	X		LM Sc SS	X	X	
The Action Kit		X	X	X			G	X	X	X
The Action Libraries		X	X	X			G	X	X	X
Science Research Associates										
Cracking the Code		X	X				G	X		X
Dimensions: Man Power and Natural Resources			X				SS	X	X	
Dimensions: We are Black		X	X				SS	X	X	X
How to Improve Your Reading			X	X	X	X	G		X	
How to Read Factual Literature			X				G	X	X	
Learnings in Science			X	X	X		Sc	X		
Streamline Your Reading				X	X	X	G		X	
Basic Reading Skills for Junior High		X	X	X			G	X		
Basic Reading Skills for Senior High		X	X	X	X		G		X	
Tactics in Reading I, II, and III		X	X	X	X		G		X	
Silver Burdett Co.										
Building Your Language Power		X	X	X			G		X	X
Steck-Vaughn Co.										
Reading Essentials: Progress in Reading		X	X	X	,		G	X		
Teachers College Press										
Gates-Peardon Reading Exercises Books A, B, C, D				X			G	X		
Fern Tripp										
Reading for Safety: Community Signs		X	X	X			G	X	X	X
Webster Division, McGraw-Hill										
New Practice Readers				X	X		G	X		
Programmed Reading for Adults		X	X	X			G		X	X
Winston Press										
Power Reading II		X	X	X	X		G	X	X	X
Power Reading III		X	X	X	X		G		X	

Appendix B

High-Interest/Low-Readability Materials

These materials are usually used as supplementary practice.

1. Series or collections of high-interest/low-readability materials:

Addison-Wesley	Reading Development Series
Allyn and Bacon	Breakthrough
American Guidance Service	Coping with Series
Bantam Books	Bantam Perspective Series
Barnell Loft (Dexter-Westbrook)	Incredible Series
Benefic Press	Mystery Adventure Series
	World of Adventure Series
Berkeley Books	Tempo Books
Bowmar	Reading Incentive Series
Childrens Press	". . . and Hereby Hangs the Tale" Series
Dell	Laurel Leaf Library
	Mayflower Books
	Yearling Books
Ed-U Press	Comics on Drugs, Sex, Venereal Disease and Birth Control
Fearon	Pacemaker Series
Field Educational Publications	Americans All
	Checkered Flag Series
	Deep Sea Adventure Series
	Happenings
	Kaleidoscope
	Morgan Bay Mysteries
	Reading Motivated Series
	Interesting Reading Series
Follett	*American Folklore*
Globe Book Co.	*Four Complete Teen-Age Novels*
	Insight and Outlook and other titles
Harper & Row	American Adventure Series
	Myths and Tales of Many Lands
	Paperback Classics
	Scope/Reading
Harr-Wagner	Reading Motivated Series
D. C. Heath	Teen Age Tales
Hertzberg New Method	General Collection of Interesting Topics
Holt, Rinehart and Winston	Impact Series
Houghton Mifflin	Directions
	Interact
	New Riverside Literature Series
	They Helped Make America
Learning Research Associates	Literature Sampler, Junior Edition

Leswing Communications

Macmillan

McGraw-Hill

Charles E. Merrill

National Association for the Deaf

New Dimensions in Education

Noble and Noble

Penguin Books

Pyramid Publications

Rand McNally

Random House/Singer

Your Own Thing Series
Series r Solo Books
What Job for Me? Series
Mainstream Books
Classics for Low Level Readers
Name of the Game
Crossroads Series, Springboards
Puffin Books
Hi-Lo Books
Voices
Alfred Hitchcock Mysteries
Aware
Challenger Books
Gateways
Green Interest Center
Blue Interest Center
Red Interest Center
Landmark Books
Landmark Giants
Pro Basketball Library
Punt, Pass and Kick

Scholastic Book Services

Action Libraries
Arrow Books
Biography
Black Literature Program
Contact
Dogs, Horses, Wildlife
Especially for Boys
Especially for Girls
Ethnic Reading
Fantasy
Favorites Old and New
Fun and Laughter
History, History Fiction
Making and Doing
Modern Stories
Mystery
Myths and Legends
People of Other Lands
Pleasure Reading Libraries I and II
Reluctant Reader Libraries
Science
Science and Fiction
Scope Play Series
Tab Books

Science Research Associates

An American Album
Countries and Cultures Kit
New Rochester Occupational Reading

	Pilot Libraries, IIb, IIc, IIIb
	We Are Back
	Manpower and Natural Resources
Scott, Foresman	Something Else
Silver Burdett	Call Them Heroes
Steck Vaughn	Books for Specific Subjects
Washington Square Press	Archway Paperbacks
Webster	Everyreader Series
	Reading for Concepts
	Reading Incentive Series
	Reading Shelf I and II
Xerox	The Way It Is

2. Booklists for high interest/low readability:

A Place to Start. Robert Leibert. Reading Center, University of Missouri, 52nd and Holmes, Kansas City, Mo. 64110. Lists thousands of titles appropriate to school subject areas, especially social studies. Annotation includes reading level, interest level, author, and publisher.

Children's Books for $1.50 or Less. Association for Childhood Education International, 3615 Wisconsin Ave. NW, Washington, D.C. 20016.

Fare for the Reluctant Reader, Anita E. Dunn and others. Capitol Area School Development Association, Western Ave., Albany, N.Y. 12203, 1964. Annotated list selected for junior and senior high readers. Books chosen to reflect teen-age interests.

Gateways to Readable Books. Ruth Strang and others, 4th ed. Wilson, 1966. The H. W. Wilson Co., 950 University Ave., Bronx, N.Y. 10452. Annotated graded list on many topics for adolescents who find reading difficult.

Good Reading for Disadvantaged Readers. George Spache, Garrard, 1972.

Good Reading for Poor Readers. George Spache. Garrard, 1972. Garrard Publishing Co., 1607 N. Market St., Champaign, Ill. 61820. Useful in elementary and junior high school.

High Interest-Easy Reading for Junior and Senior High School Reluctant Readers. Raymond E. Emery and Margaret B. Houshower. National Council of Teachers of English (NCTE), 1111 Kenyon Rd., Champaign, Ill., 61801, 1965.

High Interest-Low Vocabulary Booklist. Education Clinic, Boston University School of Education, 322 Bay State Road, Boston, Mass. 02215.

Hooked on Books. D. Fader and E. McNeil. G. P. Putnam's Sons, 200 Madison Ave., New York, N.Y. 10016, 1966.

Mod-Mod Read-In Book List. Hertzberg New Method, Inc., Vandalia Road, Jacksonville, Ill. 62650. Fifty titles with one-line annotations prepared especially for black potential dropouts.

"Offbeat Paperbacks for Your Classroom," George J. Becker, *Journal of Reading* (November, 1971), 127–129.

Vocations in Biography and Fiction: An Annotated List of Books for Young People. Kathryn A. Haebich. American Library Association (ALA), 50 East Huron St., Chicago, Ill. 60611, 1962. 1,070 titles, mostly biographies. Includes some titles of high interest, low reading level for grades 9–12.

3. Magazines of interest at middle school and high school:

American Girl. Girl Scouts of America, 830 Third Ave., New York, N.Y. 10017.
Boys' Life. Boy Scouts of America, North Brunswick, N.J. 08902.
Children's Digest. Parents' Magazine Enterprises, Inc., 52 Vanderbilt Ave., New York, N.Y. 10017.
Cricket. Open Court Publishing Co., 1058 Eighth St., LaSalle, Ill. 61301.
Kids. 747 Third Ave., New York, N.Y. 10017.
School Bulletin. School Service, National Geographic Society, Washington, D.C. 20036.
Nature and Science. The Natural History Press, Garden City, N.Y. 11530.
Newsweek. Newsweek, Inc., 444 Madison Av., New York, N.Y. 10022.
Read. American Education Publications, Education Center, Columbus, O. 43216.
Reader's Digest. Reader's Digest Services, Pleasantville, N.Y. 10570.
Scope. Scholastic Book Services, 904 Sylvan Av., Englewood Cliffs, N.J. 07632.
Seventeen. 320 Park Av., New York, N.Y. 10022.
Sport. Sport Magazine, P.O. Box 5705, Whitestone, N.Y. 11357.
Time. Time-Life, Inc., Time and Life Building, Rockefeller Center, New York, N.Y. 10020.
World Traveler. 1537 35th St., NW, Washington, D.C. 20007.
Young Miss (formerly *Calling All Girls*). Parents' Magazine Enterprises, 52 Vanderbilt Ave., New York, N.Y. 10017.

4. Newspapers:

Junior Review. Civic Education Services Inc., 1733 K St., NW, Washington, D.C. 20036.
Know Your World. American Education Publications, Education Center, Columbus, O. 43216. Reading level for grades 2–3. Interest level for grades 5–12.
New York, New York. Random House, Inc., 201 East 50th St., New York, N.Y. 10022. Reading level for grades K–8. Interest level for grades 5–12.
News for You. A and B Editions, Laubach Literary, Inc., 1011 Hartson St., Syracuse, N.Y. 13210. Edition A: reading level for grades 2–3. Interest level for grade 7–adult. Edition B: reading level for grades 3–4. Interest level for grade 7–adult.
You and Your World. American Education Publications, Education Center, Columbus, O. 43216. Reading level for grades 3–5. Interest level for grades 9–12.

Appendix C

Study Guide

PHYSICAL SCIENCE   DAY TWO
LEVERS   WORKSHEET

GUIDE QUESTIONS
Pages 172–174

A. Read "Levers and Work" on page 172. Answer the following questions:
   1. a) Name the fixed support of a lever.

   b) Explain how the fixed support is used.

2. There are two forces which act upon a lever: the resistance and the effort. Using photograph 1 on page 172,
   a) Identify the effort
   b) Identify the resistance

3. The Principle of Work states: work input is equal to work output if you disregard friction.

> Work Input = Work Output
> Effort × Effort Arm = Resistance × Resistance Arm
> $E \times A_e = R \times A_r$

Use the information in the box above to answer the following questions:

   a) Work input = _____ × _____
   b) Work output = _____ × _____
   c) Effort = 4 lb   Effort Arm = 3 ft
      What is the work input? _____
   d) Resistance = 6 lb   Resistance Arm = 2 ft
      What is the work output? _____
   e) Compare your answers to questions c and d.
      Work input is (equal to, less than, more than) work output. _____

4.

Effort	×	Effort Arm	=	Work Input		Resistance	×	Resistance Arm	=	Work Output
3 lb		?		3 ft-lb	=	3 lb		1 ft		?
1 lb		2 ft		?	=	4 lb		½ ft		?
8 lb		10 ft		?	=	?		2 ft		?
?		1 ft		?	=	15 lb		?		5 ft-lb

PHYSICAL SCIENCE   DAY TWO
LEVERS   WORKSHEET

GUIDE QUESTIONS
Pages 172–174

B. Read "Mechanical Advantage of Levers" on pages 172–174. Answer the foling questions:

   1. After reading "An Apprentice Investigation into Levers" on page 173, define the following terms:
      a) Effort
      b) Effort arm
      c) Resistance
      d) Resistance arm

2. Mechanical Advantage is a measure of how many times a machine multiplies a force. Levers give us a mechanical advantage.
   a) What is the formula for actual mechanical advantage?
   b) Effort (E) = 9 lb   Resistance (R) = 18 lb
      What is actual mechanical advantage (AMA)?
   c) What is the AMA of a machine that requires a 100-pound force to move a 200-pound barrel?
      1) Effort = _____ pounds
      2) Resistance = _____ pounds
      3) $AMA = \dfrac{R}{E}$

         $AMA = \dfrac{?}{?}$

         $AMA =$ _____
   d) A boy uses a lever on which he exerts a 50-pound force to move a 250-pound rock. What is the AMA of this lever?
      (follow the same procedure as in question c)
3. a) What is the formula for ideal mechanical advantage?
   b) Effort arm (A_e) = 10 ft   Resistance arm (A_r) = 2 ft
      What is the ideal mechanical advantage (IMA)?
   c) A man must push a crowbar down 24 inches to raise the lid of a crate 2 inches. What is the IMA of the crowbar?
      1) Effort arm = _____ inches
      2) Resistance arm = _____ inches
      3) $IMA = \dfrac{Ae}{Ar}$

         $IMA = \dfrac{?}{?}$

         $IMA =$ _____

PHYSICAL SCIENCE   DAY THREE
LEVERS   WORKSHEET

LEVERS AND MECHANICAL ADVANTAGE

1. Label each diagram   2. Find the mechanical
   R = resistance   advantage of
   F = fulcrum   drawings *F* and *I*.
   E = effort

PHYSICAL SCIENCE
LEVERS

DAY FOUR
WORKSHEET

INQUIRY PROBLEM

Purpose

To investigate how a first-class lever multiplies force.

Materials

Wooden block, wooden ruler, pencil

Procedure

1. Place a wooden block on the desk or a table. With one of your fingers lift the block by its edge. (Fig. 1)

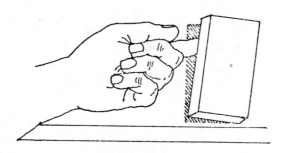

FIGURE 1

The resistance force is the force pressing down on your finger. The upward force applied by your finger is the effort force. The effort force must just barely overcome the resistance force in order to raise the edge of the block. Notice the amount of force needed to lift the block with your finger.

2. Place one end of a wooden ruler under the edge of the block. Slip a pencil under the ruler about 4 cm from the edge of the block. (Fig. 2) Press down with your finger on the other end of the ruler to raise the block.

PHYSICAL SCIENCE   DAY FOUR
LEVERS   WORKSHEET

INQUIRY PROBLEM

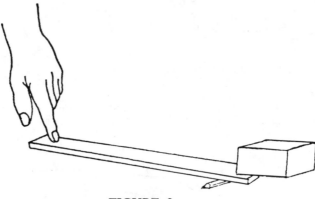

FIGURE 2

What do you notice about the force necessary to lift the block, using the ruler, compared to the force needed to lift it directly with your finger?

_____

3. Move the pencil about 5 cm from the edge of the block and press on the end of the ruler again. Is more, or less, force needed to lift the block than in procedure 2?

_____

4. Repeat, moving the pencil about 20 cm from the edge of the block. What did you notice this time about the force required to lift the block?

_____

5. Repeat procedures 2, 3, and 4, and observe how far the block moves in comparison to how far your finger moves.
   a) What effect does the position of the pencil have on how far the edge of the block moves in comparison to how far your finger moves?

_____

PHYSICAL SCIENCE
LEVERS

DAY FIVE
WORKSHEET #2

IDENTIFYING TYPES OF LEVERS

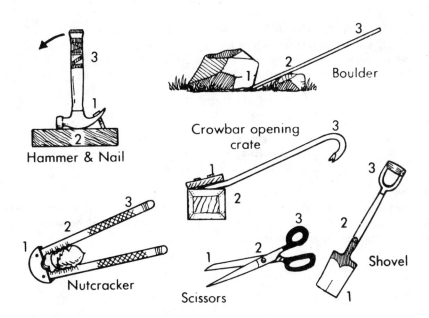

Identify the effort, the fulcrum, and the resistance of the following levers:

LEVER	1	2	3	IDENTIFY EACH LEVER as a 1st, 2nd, or 3rd-class lever.
Hammer and nail				
Boulder				
Shovel				
Crowbar opening crate				
Nutcracker				
Scissors				

PHYSICAL SCIENCE   DAY SIX
LEVERS   WORKSHEET

LAW OF THE LEVER

Introduction

The Principle of Work applies to levers. Work input is equal to work output. With the first-class lever, the relationship is between the weights and distances of the effort and the resistance. This relationship can be expressed mathematically. The effort times the effort arm equals the resistance times the resistance arm.

$$E \times Ae = R \times Ar$$

Materials

Ringstand	Masking tape
Ring	12-inch wooden ruler
Thread	4 paper clips of equal mass

Procedure

1. Attach the ring to the ringstand. Tie a piece of thread around the exact center of a 12-inch ruler. Attach it firmly to the ruler with a small piece of masking tape. Suspend the ruler by the thread from the ring.

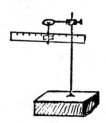

   The ruler should be balanced in a horizontal position. If it doesn't balance, place a small piece of masking tape on the side of the ruler which is raised. The ruler may be considered a first-class lever.
   a. Where is the fulcrum of the lever?

2. Form three paper clips in the shape of hooks so they can be suspended from the ruler.

PHYSICAL SCIENCE   DAY SEVEN
LEVERS   WORKSHEET

ARCHIMEDES' LEVER PROBLEM

Open a bottle with a bottle opener, pull a nail with a claw hammer, jack up a car
to change a tire and a simple machine is in use.

Archimedes was a Greek mathematician who lived more than 2,000 years ago.
One day he made the statement: "Give me a place to stand, and I will move the
earth."

Discussion

1. What would Archimedes have used?
2. Where might he have stood?
3. What else would Archimedes have needed to move the earth if an Apollo mission could have taken him there?
4. What would he have used as a fulcrum?
5. Which class of levers would Archimedes need to use?

13

Organizing
the Classroom

In what specific ways can better organization of time, activity, materials, and teacher cooperation enhance the reading instruction of students?

How do you get students to work with you instead of against you?

ORGANIZING FOR
DIFFERENTIATED LEARNING

Question: How can you expect me to be a competent, organized teacher when I personally have to supervise 150 students a day while lecturing for sixty minutes, five times a day? How can any one person handle the attendance taking, the materials gathering, the paper correcting, the lesson planning, the record keeping, and the individualizing I keep reading and hearing so much about?

Answer: Get a little help from your students and change your tactics.

Any teacher who can be replaced by a machine, probably ought to be.—Dwight Allen

Any teacher who can be replaced by a high school student probably ought to be.—Larry Mikulecky

Checklist for an Organized Secondary Classroom

1. Nobody seems to be obviously in charge and everybody seems to know where things are.
2. Directions are written out and posted in an easily accessible place.
3. Everybody seems to be involved with something, though not necessarily the same thing.
4. The teacher can leave the room or concentrate on an individual while group learning continues uninterrupted.

OVERVIEW

The message presented and developed in this chapter is two-fold. Initially, no one teacher can reasonably be expected to single-handedly teach individually nearly 150 students with varying levels of reading ability, interest, and motivation. Accepting this teacher limitation is a necessary first step. Second, this chapter outlines successful methods for a teacher of 150 students to use in organizing learning:

1. If he draws upon the resources of his students for help
2. If he plans his lessons with a maximum of student learning activity and a minimum of teacher-centered passivity
3. If he organizes the time and the space of the classroom to maximize the likelihood that most students will know what is supposed to be happening and where things are.

The trick here is to have reasonable expectations. It is not reasonable to expect a single teacher to meet the needs of all students encountered during an average school day. It is reasonable, however, to emulate the teacher in the oldfashioned one-room schoolhouse who knew she couldn't do it all. She also knew, however, that many students would love to be of use if they only had the chance. Students taught students. Small-group work was a necessity, not an innovation. Materials and tasks had to be clearly organized and clearly laid out, and individual students were responsible for a host of tasks as part of the daily class expectations. One of the spin-offs of such a well-organized school was a teacher who had large portions of time to devote to individual student attention.

Shared responsibility worked because it made sense and nearly everybody knew it. Having a single teacher as the regular center of attention and having the same assignment expectations for all student didn't work then, nor does it make sense now. Many teachers in today's schools are like little Dutch boys frantically rushing to plug all the holes in the dike at the same time. They are constantly busy, busy, busy. For those with a more philosophical bent, Schopenhauer once commented that a fanatic always redoubles his efforts when he loses sight of his goals. In plainer terms, the time has come to take a deep breath and give up the presumptuous fanaticism that makes us teachers think we can do it all. The time has come to take a careful look at what really needs doing and then ask for help from the young adults who are present and among the students in most secondary classrooms.

ORGANIZING ACTIVITY

At the beginning of this chapter is a quotation from Dwight Allen: "Any teacher who can be replaced by a machine probably ought to be." We would like to carry that idea a bit further: Any teacher who can be replaced by a high school student probably ought to be. The reasoning behind these statements is really quite simple. Most teachers have received at least four years of higher education and specialized training—many have received considerably more. Yet when observing many secondary-level classrooms, one finds well-trained teachers trapped by their own choice to become mired in tasks that could be completed successfully by any responsible twelve-year-old.

Such waste of trained-teacher time is nonsensical for several reasons. Besides stealing from teachers the time they need to give students individual attention, such teacher-centered activity has many other detrimental effects in the classroom. Students tend to become less involved with learning and hence grow passive or disruptive in the face of constant teacher overdirection. Opportunities for reinforcement are lost when students are deprived of the chance to teach other students. Questions that might have been asked in smaller student-centered groups go unasked (and unanswered) in larger teacher-directed classes. Finally, when the teacher is always the main focus of attention, the game of "How can I get by doing as little of what the boss wants as possible?" becomes the main game in class.

There are positive, constructive ways to teach and organize classroom activity that make considerably more sense for the teaching of subject matter and bookthinking. These approaches revolve around making an initial decision about what needs to be learned, deciding what needs to happen for that learning to occur, and then surveying the class as a whole for human and material resources.

A Reading-Writing Technique

This concept can be best understood through example. Two goals held by teachers in nearly every content area are: (1) Students should read and understand the material in the text, and (2) students should express the main ideas covered in the class through both oral and written expression.

These goals are often difficult for many class members to meet. The problems increase when texts are too difficult for the majority of students to comprehend independently. A student who is at frustration level in the main text will find it exceedingly difficult to understand, much less express, ideas he has read.

Typically, teachers have sought to deal with this reading problem by gathering easier supplementary materials, discussing or lecturing on major topics before assigning readings, setting purposes for reading, developing study guides and sometimes even rewriting chapters at lower readability levels. Good ideas all, but each is time consuming and depends on the teacher for the bulk of the preparation and work.

Consider an alternative that consumes less teacher energy. Students can be involved to a greater degree in their own learning by working in groups to rewrite and edit portions of textbook chapters. The teacher can organize the activity as follows:

1. Show the class how to use chapter headings and subheadings as aids in outlining a chapter. Students then rapidly preview and outline a chapter to be covered for the week (see chapter 10). During the last ten minutes of class, groups of two or three students exchange outlines, spot gaps, and make necessary corrections before handing outlines in. *During two-thirds of the period, the teacher has been free to move about the class giving individual attention.*

2. As a homework assignment or as a next-day classroom assignment, groups of three to five students are assigned portions of the chapter to rewrite and condense to two or three pages. The portions should be brief with more difficult sections appropriately assigned. The goal is to capture main ideas and use complete sentences. Students within each group correct each other's papers, make suggestions, and then select the two best papers. Some students may find it difficult to condense material and identify main ideas, but they will be getting immediate feedback from a number of other students and will be able to see what a good condensation looks like. Also, the main ideas of a chapter portion will be reinforced by three to five readings of other students' condensations. So, essentially, each student paraphrases a chapter portion and judges the quality of other students' paraphrases. Again, the teacher is free during the majority of this task to give individual attention and help.

3. The next step is begun on a third day. The paraphrased condensations of chapter parts are rotated among student groups. Each group reads the new set of papers, compares paraphrases to the original chapter, and selects the two best condensations from the set. Then the sets are rotated again. The rotation of paper sets continues until each group has rated the papers of all groups. The end result of this is a tremendous amount of reading on the part of all students. Main ideas of the chapter have been reinforced several times for each chapter portion, and comparisons with the original text have regularly occurred. Moreover, the teacher, by gathering together the most highly rated condensations, can compile several low-readability rewrite versions of the chapter to keep for use by poor readers. Typing classes might even use the manuscripts as part of a type-a-book project.

4. At this point, the teacher has had a chance to help virtually every student needing help and should have a clear idea of which portions of the chapter need most teaching attention. Study-guide questions can be posed at higher inference and application levels because nearly every student is now grounded in a literal understanding of main chapter ideas.

What should be especially noted about this particular assignment is that students did almost all of the reading, writing, comparing, correcting, and grading. The teacher was available as a second-line resource *after* each student had exhausted the resources of his own judgment and the judgments of other students. During the assignment, the teacher's task entailed carefully monitoring the directions of the groups, providing good examples, making suggestions, and keeping students on task. This assignment would be better tried *after* the teacher had used smaller assignments to train students to work successfully with each other in groups.

This reading-writing technique could be modified to accomplish several bookthinking competencies discussed earlier in this text, including the development of analytic and evaluative thinking skills. For example, instead of writing condensations, the students might be directed to list and define the key vocabulary in each section of the outline, or to write questions for each section so as to require judgments, inferences, applications, or some other type of thinking the teacher wants to help them with.

The point is that a reading-writing technique could be used occasionally as one of several options in any content area that employs textbooks. It could be modified for students as young as those in fifth or sixth grade or as mature as those of high school-early university age. The necessary ingredient is a teacher who views his or her role as an organizer and facilitator for learning.

Finding Learners

To develop a classroom atmosphere where cooperative learning can occur, that area must be seen as having several leaders. This is essential if the teacher is to be freed from answering every petty question and dealing with every minuscule problem. One way to develop a workable atmosphere is to create incentives for students to become leaders.

All over the world, people take on extra responsibility, work a little harder, and do some of the unglamorous nuts-and-bolts work of life, at least partially, for social rewards. These rewards can be dispensed in the form of money, social prestige, promotions, appreciation, or combinations of these. Classrooms can draw upon the strength of such motivations to foster more student leadership and less teacher babysitting.

For example, if at least part of a grade for a class is based on a point system, extra points might be earned by taking on a number of necessary tasks. Depending on the needs of a given school system, these could include one or more of the following:

1. Taking attendance
2. Recording daily work
3. Getting out materials and making sure materials are returned
4. Keeping track of what the week's assignments are for one's group or row (This is very helpful in getting absent students caught up.)
5. Serving as a tutor on particular assignments
6. Gathering supplementary materials for upcoming units.

The list should be limited only by the teacher's imagination. Most tasks done daily by a teacher can and probably should be done at least partially by responsible, trained adolescents. A student performing well on an important phase of classwork could earn an opportunity to try for an extra classroom job. The jobs should be seen as worth having. In addition, jobs should be rotated from time to time—especially if students are not performing well in particular roles. We have seen high school teachers who, by mid-semester, were able to leave the room for classroom emergencies without disrupting the learning process. Substitute teachers who enter such classrooms find themselves rapidly put to work by student leaders who see no reason why the substitute shouldn't do his or her share just like everyone else.

These tasks and jobs serve a number of constructive purposes. The teacher's freedom and ability to reach more students is increased. Students, especially poorer readers, have real opportunities to organize thinking, apply reading-writing skills, and receive positive reinforcement for using what they've just learned. The smallest job usually will serve constructively to help at least one or two students in a class. When all these purposes are served, the atmosphere in the classroom is healthier and more cooperative for both students and teachers.

Many teachers are uncomfortable with this approach and feel guilty about "using" students. The guilt, in some cases, is justified if a teacher doesn't use the new-found freedom to work with individuals. The real key to success or failure here is for a teacher to realize that his or her job is to create an environment where learning can occur. No teacher ought to judge his worth by how much of a classroom's necessary busywork he can single-handedly complete. The techniques discussed here necessitate an attitude that a significant aspect of teaching is organizing and facilitating learning; it is not simply being the center of learning.

Group Responsibility

In chapter 4, mention was made of a special sort of grouping suggested by Daniel N. Fader in *The New Hooked on Books*. Fader suggests that each student be part of a continuous, heterogeneous group of three students. The main task of the group is for the members to take care of each other. Papers are corrected and reviewed by the group before they are collected. Much of the classwork is group work and a lesser proportion individual work.

The spin-offs of this sort of arrangement are constructive and numerous. Initially, anonymity is dissipated, and a sense of responsibility for and from at least two other people is created. One of the truths about most learning is that it occurs in a relationship. Fader's groups create continuing relationships that are considerably more enduring than the nebulous relationships that are possible between one teacher and 150 students. Second, most work on grouping suggests that investment, participation, reinforcement, and the actual amount learned increase in small-group settings. Third, as students begin to ask group members about minute details, the teacher is freed to individualize his teaching. Finally, grouping encourages poor readers and students who are typically silent to ask questions of other group members. After all, group members who share grades have vested interests in seeing that the poor reader learns. Too often, poor students hesitate to ask questions of grade-giving teachers lest those questions make them appear stupid.

Posting Directions

We as teachers often let small unconsidered details completely destroy well-conceived and well-thought-out plans. A typical example of this is the teacher who wishes to encourage and teach student independence, but somehow always manages to create situations in which students must depend upon the teacher for the simplest information. Questions like "What are we supposed to do?" "What do we do next?" "What was yesterday's assignment?" "What page is that on?" can completely swallow up the time of a teacher who wants to individualize and have many activities occurring at once.

Creating groups and class leaders can go a long way toward providing alternatives to constantly badgering the teacher about every tiny detail. In many cases, however, if the teacher has all those trivial details in his head and nowhere else, he has unwittingly returned himself to the center of all activity. If someone forgets or was absent, the teacher is again the first source of information.

Much of the confusion and wasted time can be alleviated by posting assignments. The teacher might have written directions for each day's assignments placed in a particular file drawer or on a given wall. An even better idea is to have a designated student assume responsibility for recording assignments, showing them to the teacher, and then posting them. Reading now becomes a useful, utilitarian skill and the teacher is again free. The questions are still asked, but now the teacher can often choose to point to the appropriate place in the room while he continues to give individual help.

After two or three weeks of this routine, most students have got the idea and are that much more independent for it.

Whenever group work is to be the order of the day, step-by-step directions and expectations should be listed on the board. It is a rare individual who can listen and retain a complicated set of directions. Many teachers, however, are dismayed and even angry when sleepy or inattentive students have missed significant portions of five-part directions. Some teachers are so discouraged they give up group work altogether. By taking the time to clearly outline the steps of the day's group work on the board, a great deal of confusion and disappointment can be avoided. In addition, the posted directions help the teacher maintain some control over what is happening. He can simply ask, "Which groups have completed part three?" and get the information he needs to decide upon which groups to observe next. Noticing that other groups have been working is often enough to pull wayward groups back into the task.

Classroom Rituals

When a classroom moves from being teacher centered to being more actively student centered, there is a tendency for superficial disorganization to set in. A real sense of student and teacher discomfort can arise with so many things occurring at once. This discomfort may militate against the goals for which the individualizing was intended. The idea, after all, was for students to be encouraged to take on and feel comfortable with more independence. The discomfort of too much happening at once can set up a destructive tension in the classroom.

Much of that discomfort can be reduced by establishing a few regular rituals that everyone can count on. After all, don't we as adults simplify many of the complexities of our own lives through habit? We stop at red lights, signal for turns, appear for meals at fairly regular times. Beginning to provide some regular procedures in the classroom can simplify the demands of constant overchoice, of having to constantly consider: What happens next?

For example, if the class begins each day with a short five-minute vocabulary activity, with papers collected *immediately*, after five minutes have elapsed students begin to develop the habit of entering and getting settled down to work. Tardiness declines and there is less random commotion. Or, if projects are always due on Wednesday, material is less likely to be left in lockers or at home. Any teacher who doubts the importance of such ritualistic procedures needs only to change the free-reading day from Tuesday to Thursday. Many students will grow angry or feel cheated, and the likelihood of having as many students bring books on Thursday as did on Tuesday will be small. This is not to say that every minute of a class period should be inflexible. Spontaneous activities, surprises to maintain interest and enthusiasm, and other techniques should be incorporated to demonstrate the real-life values of bookthinking. Some regular rituals, however, should be maintained to regularize activity and reduce discomfort.

ORGANIZING TIME

The previous section described a number of ways to organize activities and students to create more time for teachers to individualize their teaching. Careful attention also needs to be given to how time is most effectively utilized. For example, in the previous section, several grouping activities or project activities were suggested. It would be very easy for a teacher to think of those activities in the traditional framework of one activity, one concept per class period. Given the fact that the attention spans of some secondary students are taxed after fifteen or twenty minutes, such an organization of time could prove disastrous. Bored, inattentive students learn little. Extending beyond the attention spans of students can be futile. Instead of being able to move from group to group giving individual help, the teacher may be forced into the counterproductive role of a police officer keeping students on task. Beginning attempts at fostering student responsibility and cooperation can be set back or even destroyed by ignoring attention span. In short, the duration of activity must match student attention span.

Stranding versus Traditional Time Blocks

In their own schooling and college training, most teachers experience traditional time blocks. Lectures usually develop a new topic or a new aspect of a large topic. Course syllabuses often use an organization much like that for building block towers. Concepts are arranged chronologically, or logically, or whatever and are presented one at a time, each block building on the previous block. Lectures are given twice a week and professors assume that students will take the time to assimilate concepts and reinforce lecture ideas with assigned or extra reading. By and large, the university system works for motivated, capable learners such as one finds in a university where students are normally paying for the opportunity to learn.

Similar conditions do not exist in most secondary schools, and similar methods for organizing time are correspondingly less likely to be successful. A logical conclusion: "Use methods that are more appropriate to the secondary-school situation." Changing methods is not easy for most secondary teachers, however, because they have internalized the one-topic-per-day pattern. It is difficult for many teachers to envision and attempt a new way of teaching that departs from the patterning experienced during so many years of their own schooling.

An alternative plan is *stranding,* a relatively simple technique for organizing time and goals. Rather than planning one academic goal and activity for Monday, another for Tuesday, a third for Wednesday, and so forth, a teacher lists his goals for the week and then *strands* them to spread them across the days of the week.

A few examples should make this concept more clear. A teacher of biology, for example, might have some of the following bookthinking goals:

1. Increased vocabulary (biological terms)
2. Mastery of major textbook concepts about one-celled life
3. Ability to read and follow lab-manual directions
4. Ability to observe, apply, and express text concepts in new situations
5. Increased interest in and reading of biology-related materials.

In a traditional time organization, a class period or perhaps two might be expended on the teaching of each goal. A day's period might be spent on vocabulary, a day or two lecturing or discussing the text, a day of lab work, and a day for a large end-of-unit test, with perhaps mention being made of extra-credit reading which is available in the library.

Each day in a traditional organization builds completely upon the preceding day. Material missed because of absence or inattention is difficult to recapture. Most information must be learned in one exposure, despite the established principle in learning theory that distributed learning is much more effective. And finally, the biology class is one of perhaps seven classes during a student's day. Each class makes the implicit demand: "Get it today because tomorrow we'll be covering another concept."

"Stranding," in contrast, considers academic goals in terms of several short activities which can be spread across the week. During any given day, the activity changes several times as each of several goals is touched upon. The change of activity keeps attention high, and the repeated reinforcement increases the likelihood of concept mastery while making a single day's absence less crucial.

In order to "strand," a teacher must resist a temptation to plan one day at a time and begin to consider priorities and goals for a unit or week.

The goals and activities for our biology class for example, might look something like these:

1. Increased biology vocabulary
   a. Five-minute exercise using special root words
   b. Textbook scavenger hunts to find key unit words in context
   c. Students spotting unknown words during brief chapter previews
2. Mastery of text concepts on one-celled life
   a. Ten to fifteen minutes of chapter preview for main ideas (perhaps brief outlining)
   b. Condensing portion of chapter to one or two pages

    c. Reading summary passages of other students
    d. Using text to answer student-supplied questions
  3. Ability to read and follow lab-manual directions
    a. Outlining major points of lab directions
    b. Explaining the directions to another student
    c. Being corrected by another student for missed portions
    d. Actually performing an observational experiment
  4. Ability to observe, apply, and express text concepts in other situations
    a. Identifying cell structures during lab procedure
    b. Creating and writing down comprehension questions based on the chapter
    c. Trading and answering other students' questions in discussion groups
  5. Increased interest in and reading of biology-related material
    a. Scavenger hunt for related articles in magazines and newspapers (homework)
    b. Extra-credit project of top students listing books, pamphlets, and articles available in library
    c. Letter-writing project—students requesting materials from appropriate medical, pharmaceutical, and biological supply companies
    d. Reading of appropriate science fiction novels
    e. Locating, reading, and summarizing on a 3×5 card interesting portions of other texts found in classroom or library
    f. Creation of a project of one's own.

Once the teacher has selected a few main goals and a variety of alternative activities for achieving those goals, time considerations can be sensibly entertained. The organization of activities to demonstrate this is based on a traditional fifty- to sixty-minute period and a five-day meeting schedule. Once a teacher has determined goals and activities, however, the activities can be *stranded* through any time framework. In examining the organizational plan given in Table 13–1, notice that each major goal is touched upon by a variety of activities.

The same kind of structure can be used for any content class. Because a major characteristic of stranding is having several activities directed to a few basic goals, the structure is flexible. If an activity doesn't seem productive, it can be dropped or exchanged for a different activity the next day. If an activity goes particularly well, it can be extended and another activity dropped or delayed. Because each major objective is approached from many different directions, there is no longer a necessity for each individual activity to be the final experience par excellence.

ORGANIZING TEACHERS

Until now, our discussion has dealt mainly with what the individual teacher and his students can do to organize a classroom for increased independence

TABLE 13-1 STRANDING MODEL—Biology Class

	MONDAY	TUESDAY	WEDNESDAY	THURSDAY	FRIDAY
0 min.—					Quiz on week's root words.
5 min.—	Five-minute vocabulary activity to begin class using special biology root words. ①				
10 min.—	Preview text chapter. 1. Make outline of main ideas. ②ᵃ 2. Locate unknown words in chapter. Turn in with page identified. ① and ②	Groups must rapidly locate and define teacher's selection from yesterday's unknown words (contest). ① and ②	Begin interest projects (Some students leave the room. Others stay to catch up on assignments.) ⑤	Brief lab 3 1. Follow directions. ③ 2. Identify structures. ④ 3. Try to answer student-generated questions. ② ④ 4. Use new vocabulary in write-up. ①	Group contest: Students must use books to answer questions prepared by other groups. ② ④
15 min.—					
20 min.—		Trade outlines for lab manual directions —check for what is missing. Terms graded as a unit. ③			
25 min.—	Groups of 2–3 students develop 5–10 questions about text based on outline. Place on 3 × 5 cards. ② and ④				
30 min.—					
35 min.—		Homework: Condense portion of chapter assigned you. 1–2 pages. ②	In groups of 5, students read each other's condensations to get an overview of the entire chapter. ②		
40 min.—					Teacher leads student through chapter pointing out key areas to study for next week's test. ②
45 min.—	Homework: Outline lab-manual directions —main points. ③	Teacher has selected best questions from 3 × 5 cards. Appropriate students write them on board. They are likely to be on unit test. ②		Homework: Read chapter with unanswered questions in mind. ②	
50 min.—	Read and select from alternatives for biology interest project. ⑤			Informal comments about progress of interest projects. ⑤	
55 min.—					

ᵃ Circled numbers indicate which general goals are being acted on.

403

and learning. Opportunities for learning on the parts of both students and teachers can increase still more if teachers can but organize themselves even minimally within a school. Such organization shouldn't necessarily be construed as involving policy changes or meetings. A simple recognition of shared predicaments and grass-roots cooperation in solving common problems is the key.

Shared Materials and Unit Planning with Other Teachers

A tremendous amount of duplicated effort occurs in a typical secondary school. Sometimes, within a single department, teachers on opposite sides of a wall are planning similar lessons for similar courses to be taught to similar students. Each teacher is overworked and each is disappointed at being forced to do a less-than-pleasing job because of excessive demands on his or her time and energy.

The solution seems obvious, but is uncommon. Those teachers could, at the very least, share materials they have developed and thus save each other countless hours. They might even derive a lot of enjoyment through brainstorming to plan thematic units for their classes. In most team planning situations, where the participants have a vested interest in working together, the whole is greater than the sum of the parts. The product of two or more working together is greater than what the teachers might have developed individually.

If cooperative work in materials creation and shared planning goes well, the teachers may decide to cooperate more. If scheduling permits, they may decide to trade classes for a few days so each teacher can teach a particular lesson that he or she has developed and perfected. If a lesson is extremely well done and captures student interest, one teacher may temporarily teach both classes while the other plans, gathers materials, works with a few "problem" individuals, or simply observes for the purpose of learning new teaching techniques. In a large secondary school, three or four teachers might work together in a similar fashion.

Conference-Hour Switches

Most secondary schools allow teachers one scheduled class period as a conference hour or as preparation time. An alternative and profitable use of the conference period is the conference-hour switch. The cooperation of three teachers, each interested in learning more about teaching from his or her colleagues, is required. During his conference period, teacher A substitutes in teacher B's class for the period. This frees teacher B either to observe in teacher C's class or perhaps even to teach a special lesson in that class. By covering each other's classes and returning the favor, a great amount of freedom and opportunity to trade techniques can be obtained.

A conference-hour switch can be especially useful if one or more teachers have had special training in content-area reading. The person with special training could demonstrate reading-improvement techniques in a wide variety of classes, thus enabling teachers to get first-hand experience in how to incorporate reading into their classroom activities.

The beauty of the conference-hour switch is that it can occur whenever two or three teachers decide they want to expend the effort to make it happen. Policies don't have to be changed, administrative permission usually isn't necessary, extra funds aren't required, and only those who wish to be are involved.

Interdisciplinary Cooperation and Teams

Informal and formal cooperation between members of different departments can serve to improve the reading instruction in a school. For example, if the English, social studies, and science classes can organize their units such that topics and skills learned in one class can be reused, reinforced, and reemphasized in other classes, learning increases. Novels can be read concurrently with study of appropriate historical periods and scientific discoveries. Reading skills and writing skills, main-idea sentences and supporting details, or perhaps the use of subheads can be emphasized in all classes. A few synchronized actions like these can go a long way toward dispelling the myth that each class is entirely separate, and that all knowledge will be forgotten after the test or after leaving the classroom.

Formalizing such cooperation by scheduling the same group of students to the same several teachers can increase the likelihood of success. If the teachers in the interdisciplinary team can also share lunch hours and planning periods, the chances of achieving a well-organized approach to student literacy are enhanced. Adding the reading teacher to some of the planning meetings and teaching demonstrations provides an opportunity for content teachers to observe at first-hand methods for incorporating reading into content-area classes. Even if the reading teacher cannot join the team, teachers who are sharing responsibilities and planning can learn from each other and offer each other the flexibility that comes with attempting to introduce both large-group and small-group activities.

The Bookthinking Committee

A capstone for reading improvement in the middle or secondary school is for teachers to organize into a bookthinking committee. Usually a building-level reading teacher will head such a committee, but anyone may assume leadership. Any school with a number of concerned content teachers can organize to survey the reading strengths and weaknesses of the school, assess the immediately available resources in personnel and materials, and establish some cooperative goals (see chapter 5). Having a concerned representative from each department is best, but a core group of five or six teachers with administrative support can do a lot.

A bookthinking committee operates to reflect the concerns and needs of those departments represented, while each member becomes more proficient in diagnosing and dealing with classroom reading difficulties. If a building-level reading specialist is available, special in-service training can be given to committee members who will then share their new training with other members of their departments. Such sharing can be done informally in classrooms or more formally during special departmental meetings.

If a trained reading specialist isn't available, teachers may take university reading instruction classes together. It is often possible to modify university class requirements to fit committee needs and the needs of the school. A university consultant could also be brought into the district to do in-service work with the bookthinking committee or the entire faculty.

One of the important goals of a bookthinking committee is fostering the active involvement of more faculty members with bookthinking improvement in classrooms. Periodically changing the makeup of the committee precludes charges that a professional clique has been formed. Moreover, changing committee membership broadens the base of support for content-area book-thinking within a school.

ORGANIZING MATERIALS AND RECORD KEEPING

Another important aspect of a classroom organization that aids the process of bookthinking is the way in which books and other reading materials are placed and used. It is well established that the use of and interest in books increase in proportion to their accessibility to the reader. Thus, the principle of availability and ease of access to books should guide classroom teachers in their efforts to help students expand their vistas and cope with varied reading tasks. As with assessment, the fundamental reason for organizing books and materials and for keeping records is to help make important instructional decisions. Some of those decisions revolve around specific outcomes that a teacher (or the school curriculum) want to achieve. They fit into a test-teach-test pattern. For example, competence in reading a topographical map in a social studies class may be one of those specific outcomes. A teacher discovers who cannot read a map, teaches them, and then tests their competence.

Other decisions concern the use of time in the class hour and how more effective use of time promotes an aspect of personal development important to the curriculum. The value of that type of decision is measured primarily by checking to see that time and materials were provided for the students. Free reading time to expand the students' interest in a subject is an example. A teacher may suggest categories for growth and encourage students to search out and examine each of the categories through library research, or by checking a book list or the books and magazines available on the classroom bookshelf. One English teacher, for example, gave her students regular free reading time. Then she suggested that, during the year, each student read at least one book in each of several categories listed on a sheet she distributed. The categories were depicted as spread around in a circle to represent a "well-rounded" reading program for that year (see Figure 13–1).

Figure 13–1. "Well-rounded reading program." When completed, write the book title and author in a matching wedge above.

In each space in the diagram, students were asked to write the title and author of books they read. The teacher then provided a bookshelf labeled with the categories shown in Figure 13–1. During free reading time, it was easy and natural for students to select books from that shelf. The purpose was not to limit choices to those in the classroom bookshelf but to provide readily accessible samples of materials available in libraries and bookstores. Time to read was provided as a desirable curriculum opportunity, and materials were available to make that opportunity a guided growth activity.

By changing the categories in a similar diagram, any teacher could use this device to promote personal growth in his or her subject area.

DECISIONS AND MATERIALS

Level

As stated in chapter 5 on observing students, many students will have considerable difficulty with a textbook designed for a specific grade. The teacher must provide appropriate materials and instruction for those students. If a second text is an option, that book should be easy enough to give most of those below grade level a chance to be successful. Where a second-text option isn't open, a bookshelf to match the topics being covered in the class would help greatly. Library books above, at, and below the level of the classroom text can be labeled to indicate their respective levels of difficulty.

Some teachers may find that playful labels work best for them: *quick and dirty, straight stuff, heavy duty.* Or, there is nothing inappropriate in labeling books as *easy reading, average* (at grade level), or *difficult.* In a similar way, library books can be identified in a classroom card-file system. Creating a card system or looseleaf notebook listing appropriate books would make a very serviceable workshop or in-service project for content teachers. This is another idea that could be pursued by the bookthinking committee. Most of the professional teacher associations issue annotated lists that could serve as guides or recommendations for a classroom topical book file. As a teacher herself reads new books each year, additional cards could be written and added to the card-file box. In using the file, students will learn that they themselves should be categorizing books for future reference, just as their teacher did, to help make the classroom more attractive and responsive to students. As they read books on a topic, the students can contribute to a subject card-file list and thus aid their classmates in future quests for appropriate books.

Vocabulary

Associated with growth in reading level is growth in reading vocabulary. Every classroom should have word-finder books on the reference shelf. A thesaurus, synonym dictionary, and other word-finding books are needed where students are asked to be creative—and how else does learning occur if not through an active construction of ideas?

Various vocabulary games, puzzles, and word lists should also be on a shelf for free-time use or for play or as a reminder of everyone's need to constantly expand his usable vocabulary. Scrabble®, crossword puzzles, double crostics, and so on, can be used in every subject matter (see chapter 7). As indicated earlier, students themselves can help to develop and manage these activities.

Skills Centers

Through commercial books and kits or through units developed by a teacher, a bookthinking skills center makes a helpful addition to a content classroom. When it is seen as part of lab activities, the teacher and students can work in the classroom skills center on a regular basis. Each student (or group of students) works on those skills he needs to learn or to review. Development and practice in commercial materials can be found for such things as reference skills (dictionaries, glossaries, encyclopedias), notetaking and outlining, reading maps, globes, and charts, increasing speed, generalized study skills, and so on. Vocabulary and word-skill books, filmstrips, and audiovisual tapes are also prime candidates for skills-center activities. Once organized with students having developed routines for using a skills center, it can operate with minimum teacher supervision. By employing answer keys, students can self-correct and keep records of their own progress. (The appendixes to chapter 12 list many materials suitable for skills centers in bookthinking.)

With more and more subjects, including lab activity, specified in the course plan, the establishment of a bookthinking skills center as a station in the lab makes good sense as a classroom management technique.

Room for Work

If we agree with Piaget (1952) that learning always involves construction, we should design our classroom in such a way as to emphasize its function as a workroom. By using movable bookcases, screens, and other dividers, a room can be segmented to provide various work areas and activities. The diagrams below indicate ways in which some teachers have rearranged their rooms to promote more individual work (see Figures 13–2, 13–3, and 13–4). By its basic concept, instruction that pays attention to the student instead of the teacher will provide for a variety of work and reading tasks. The actual physical arrangement of a classroom can suggest that students need to accept responsibility for their own learning, that they must use books and materials to assimilate the ideas of the course. Clearly not everyone can, nor should be expected to, use the same books. Thus, the effective classroom has a variety of content books and a variety of skill-development materials to help all students grow successfully rather than frustrating half of them by giving everyone the same book without ways to properly adjust to it.

Besides a typical large-group meeting area, every classroom should have at least a library-reference corner, a small-group meeting area, and an area for private study or writing. Those areas should be in the classroom proper

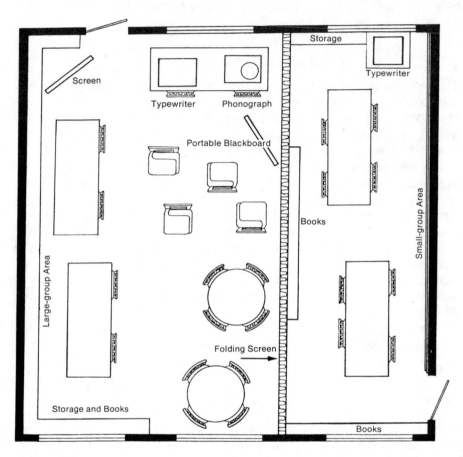

Figure 13-2. Classroom with folding wall.

or contiguous to it in a workroom shared by two or more teachers. A classroom can be divided into two rooms by means of a folding wall. (Money for the divider might come from the P.T.A. or from the principal's contingency fund.) One side of the room is for personal development and the other for group growth and learning. To achieve a more personalized reading and study plan, a teacher need not purchase a folding wall. A table and six chairs in one corner and a bookshelf divider in another are enough to get started. Some teachers enlist the advice and help of students to make the room more adaptable to learning. Perhaps a shop class would design the dividers, carrels, book holders, and so on. Thus, a teacher's room becomes not only a functional learning center but also a source of interest and pride for the students.

In some schools, teachers share rooms and have the opportunity to cooperate in mutual planning. No teacher should hesitate to suggest a change. The person with an idea to improve learning has a substantial advantage over someone who persists in walking the same cowpath day after day.

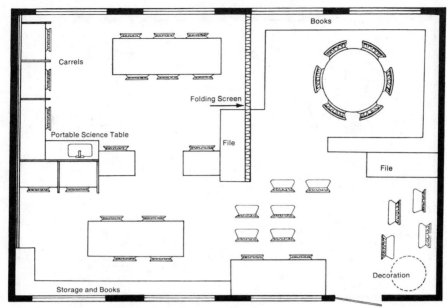

Figure 13-3. Classroom arranged for small groups.

Who knows? Your suggestion for change may win you some friendly help.

Creating learning centers also give teachers a chance to begin cooperative efforts with neighboring teachers. Among three contiguous classrooms, for instance, one might become filled with learning stations while the other two are used for large-group instruction. A coordination of three schedules and room use would be necessary, but that might be easier than at first appears.

Tutor-Conference Nook

The research on the efficiency of tutoring (Ellson *et al.,* 1965), makes tutoring, peer-tutoring, and teacher conferences on bookthinking activities that every teacher should explore. When a student restates a passage to someone, or has the opportunity to ask on-the-spot questions, he becomes more involved and makes plainer progress than when he must work out everything on his own. Schools usually have numerous nooks where tutors—and the books they need to work with—can work with students and help them with various bookthinking tasks. Offices, hallways, library conference rooms are appropriate. Directions or lesson plans to guide tutors in those bookthinking operations might be organized in a looseleaf notebook or found in existing guides for tutors of reading (Dapper and Carter, 1972; Smith and Fay, 1973). A teacher may want to organize a tutoring program that extends beyond his own classroom but, at any rate, ought to search out small conference areas where a tutor might be able to work or where the teacher can confer with an individual or a small group.

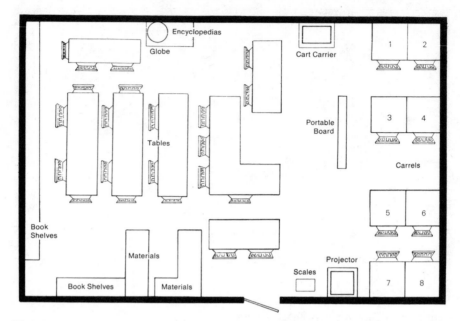

Figure 13-4. Department learning center. In schools organized around departmental areas, one classroom or the department commons could be organized for small groups and individual work.

KEEPING RECORDS

Adjusting instruction for a student or for a group of students is based on the premise that the teacher knows enough about the student's competence to determine what to do next. That means taking notes and keeping records —a job no teacher pursues with enthusiasm. It is a job of drudgery, a clerical task. And it seems that correcting papers and keeping records must be done after the teacher is exhausted from working in the classroom. But maybe that's the rub—the time and the attitude.

Record keeping requires attention to detail but need not be seen as a clerical task. Quite the contrary. Recorded observations about a student's competence represent a professional judgment. They are used to make additional professional judgments and also become a permanent record of what the student accomplished during his school years. The accompanying outline for making Informal Observations indicates the kinds of judgments, and therefore the kinds of observations, the teacher makes about a student's ability to read and understand the books used in a given class. The areas of observation in Figure 13–5 can be adjusted to suit the objectives of the class, but they do represent the level of decision making in which a teacher is involved. When it comes to mechanical scoring of tests and homework, stu-

I. *Vocabulary*
Recognizes common words (basic words) _____

Recognizes most words in grade-level material _____

II. *Special content considerations*
Defines new words _____
Breaks words into recognizable parts:

Compounds _____

Roots and affixes _____

Uses charts and graphs to solve problems _____

Uses special reference material—glossary, technical dictionary _____.

III. *Comprehension*
Gets the main idea _____

Remembers major details _____
Recognizes organizational structure, that is, chronological order, topical order, spatial order, logical order _____

Uses content to understand new words _____

Can reread to find specific answers _____

IV. *Capacity*
When he listens to a passage and is asked to answer comprehension questions, is his listening comprehension significantly better than his reading comprehension? _____
Listening comprehension is an indication of the student's language capacity. Would you rate his listening comprehension at or near grade level?

Figure 13-5. Informal observations.

dents themselves can collect that kind of data, as was described earlier in this chapter. But it is only the teacher who puts that information together with daily classroom observations to make the kinds of judgments represented in the outline of Informal Observations. From those judgments, classroom activity is planned, and conferences, tutoring, or small-group work can be set up for those who need growth in specific areas.

Time is not as large a problem as it appears, so long as a teacher pays attention to the student throughout the class period and arranges his note-keeping system so he can make quick incidental notes with little effort. They are not made, then, at the end of the day when all vital juices have drained from a teacher's body, but during the regular day when he is actively engaging

---

+ indicates seeing student perform adequately
− indicates seeing student perform inadequately

1. Is he familiar with many sources of information?
2. Can he choose the best sources for his purpose?
3. Is he able to use an index efficiently?
4. Can he use an elementary encyclopedia for locating information?
5. Can he interpret and evaluate the information he finds?
6. Does he recognize an author's purpose?
7. Does he read critically and judge the accuracy of his material?
8. Does he take intelligent notes?
9. Can he construct a two-step outline?
10. Is he able to organize and summarize information?
11. Can he interpret maps and diagrams?
12. Is he able to follow directions?
13. Is he able to use the glossary or dictionary efficiently in finding word meanings and pronunciations?
14. Can he use an atlas, a comprehensive almanac, and other references?

Figure 13-6. Inventory of study skills.

the minds of the students. Then a checklist on a clipboard for each class or for each group enables him to use a simple notation system, a plus and minus, for example, to record what he sees students do during the period. The illustrated Inventory of Study Skills provides a checklist type of record-keeping which a teacher could keep in front of him while working with students during the class hour.

SUMMARY

To fulfill the goals for subject-matter learning and for independence in reading, the classroom teacher needs to organize time, people, and space for those purposes. Something beyond the lecture-discussion format is needed to accommodate the variety of learners in a typical class. Several examples of student-centered organizational techniques presented in this chapter guide the teacher in using small groups, finding leaders (helpers) within the class, stranding and pacing activities across the week, involving other teachers in the organization of time and activities, rearranging the room, and keeping records that make continuing adjustments feasible. Two premises stand behind the organizational techniques of the chapter: First, content knowledge and varying student abilities must govern the organization of books, people, time, and activities in the classroom. Second, a teacher alone cannot manage a responsive classroom and so needs the assistance of students, other teachers, and flexible facilities to accomplish student-centered learning.

DISCUSSION QUESTIONS

1. Alone or in a group, list at least twenty necessary classroom tasks that a teacher could reasonably delegate to students.
2. How should a teacher deal with a student who reacts to group editing, rewriting, and correcting of papers by claiming such things are the teacher's job and not the student's job?
3. Agree or disagree with the following statement: "For the vast majority of teachers, the stress of actual teaching drives the teacher back to the model of his or her own high school teachers and causes the teacher to ignore methods learned during teacher training. We are locked into imitating past behavior."
4. If you wanted to make use of some form of tutoring (peer-tutoring, adult volunteers, and so on), what kinds of tasks would you have the tutors work on for your subject? To make tutoring beneficial, what sort of tutor assignment sheet would you hand each tutor as he reported to work with a student? Design a form that reminds the tutor to help the student with bookthinking skills as well as content objectives.

Suggested Readings

Dunn, Rita S., and Kenneth G. Dunn. *Practical Approaches to Individualizing Instruction.* Englewood Cliffs, N.J.: Prentice-Hall, 1971; Dell, Helen Davis. *Individualizing Instruction,* Chicago: Science Research Associates, 1972.
The books by Dunn and Dunn and Dell give many practical suggestions on managing classroom and students in a student-centered environment. These are nuts-and-bolts books that serve many teachers as course-planning handbooks.

Harris, Larry A., and Carl B. Smith. *Individualizing Reading Instruction: A Reader.* New York: Holt, Rinehart and Winston, 1972.
The readings in this book include general articles and studies relating to prominent issues in reading as well as those more specifically related to problems of individualization. Part V, "Higher Competencies in Reading," contains articles on critical reading, content-related reading, and reading flexibility. The first section of the book deals with organization for individualized instruction.

Hunkins, Francis P. *Involving Students in Questioning*. Boston: Allyn & Bacon, 1976.

This book provides hints for all kinds of activities that draw out students through questioning. Three chapters deal specifically with ways that the teacher can involve students in planning, using, and evaluating questions they construct themselves. These activities are designed to promote critical thinking about text reading and to place more responsibility for small-group learning on the shoulders of the students.

Smith, Carl B., and Leo C. Fay. *Getting People to Read—Volunteer Programs That Work*. New York: Delacorte Press, 1973.

Dozens of different tutorial patterns are reviewed in this book. A distillation of their successful organizational patterns might guide a teacher or a school in setting up its own tutorial program. Of specific value are the chapters on programs for teenagers and how to work with an individual. Endorsed by the International Reading Association and the American Library Association.

14

Progress
and Evaluation

Does the teacher have assistance outside the classroom in solving bookthinking (learning) problems?

How does a teacher evaluate the teaching of bookthinking?

Suppose you had the following students in your class:

Louise: Good student, average ability, college-bound, reads all her assignments in the same way, likes books but has little sense of how to adjust to their differences.

Tony: Does reasonably well in his work, very interested in self-improvement, both personally and academically; complains that he reads too slowly and foresees trouble ahead during his college and work years.

Beth: Reserved, does not participate in class, refuses to read aloud in class, very poor grades, seems overwhelmed by every reading assignment; her intelligence score is within the normal range.

What would you do to solve the reading problems of each of these students?

These students are likely to appear in every typical class. Helping each one make progress is the concern and the responsibility of the classroom teacher. The question is, just how can the classroom teacher respond to each of those three with the resources he has available?

417

Louise is the kind of student every teacher appreciates but pays little attention to. She does her work and passes tests reasonably well because she has the basic skills taught in the elementary grades. What she doesn't have are the thinking skills that would help her to set purposes and change her study and learning behavior from one class to the next. How to do that is something she should be taught in each class, because each "subject" justifies its place on the schedule by telling us that it is a distinct discipline with its own specialized way of looking at the world.

Tony, another type that teachers want in their classes, doesn't shine on tests, but he keeps the work flowing and he also talks a lot to his teachers. He keeps telling them that he is interested in learning more—if only. . . . If only he could read faster, he would take off on his own. The teachers may tell him to keep trying, which is similar to telling a kid who wants to be a 100-yard dash sprinter to keep jogging. "Just keep jogging, kid. Maybe something magical will happen." What is the school doing for Tony? There's a track coach for the 100-yard dash. Is there a coach for the kid who wants to double his reading speed?

Beth doesn't rate any rave reviews from her teachers, but they aren't upset with her either. She doesn't cause any trouble. So long as the teacher doesn't call on her to participate, she remains there quietly and accepts her poor grades. And she remains a confused and frustrated—but quiet— member of the class. Who in the school is going to help her adjust to group participation and to the confusion she experiences in her reading assignments?

All these students appear in the same class. Is the teacher expected to solve all the problems in the class—alone?

Throughout this text we have emphasized ways the teacher can promote progress in his subject content, no matter what the reading level of the student or what his competencies are. This final chapter makes a few comments on two little-discussed aspects of student progress: the school's special-service personnel and the feedback a teacher gets from evaluating his or her own teaching. As the teacher thinks about the total framework in which he will lead his students toward independent learning, he begins to realize that other people in the school system are there to help him. He also knows from experience that he will work hardest on those things on which he takes the time to evaluate himself.

Furthermore, the teacher realizes that the setting in which students work creates a backdrop against which special services and self-evaluation operate. Each school, like any large institution, has an image that is very difficult to alter or erase, even in small part. As an institution, the secondary school resists change, even though society and its students are changing. The crises of the past decade or two indicate the need for changing objectives and procedures in middle and secondary schools. This turmoil has led to some project-oriented schools, alternative schools, and various measures of accountability. In other words, despite elephantine resistance to new ideas, pressures from the community and from the students themselves are pushing teachers, administrators, and special-service personnel to work together for more independent student learning. Bookthinking operations rest right in the middle of that scene. Whatever the picture is in a given school, progress is based on that setting and not on some generalized "average secondary school."

IMPORTANCE OF THE CURRICULUM

Schools operate on the premise that they are designed to help all students grow. The curriculum for the upper grades, therefore, should reflect the diversity of the teen-age population in its levels, its background, and its evolving maturity. For the notion of bookthinking alone that premise would mean at least a three-armed outreach to the student community. In looking at the Curriculum Outline for Bookthinking in Figure 14–1, consider that (1) basic curricular experiences must be supplemented by (2) free-choice electives and by (3) individual help for those who ask for it or are judged in need. In his role as guide and advisor, the teacher directs students from basic course offerings to electives to special services as he sees those functions benefiting the students.

A comprehensive curriculum has been designed to provide the student with substance, with choice, and therefore with specialized help if he needs

The curriculum should provide basic growth and personal improvement electives for all students and special services for students who have critical problems in reading and learning.

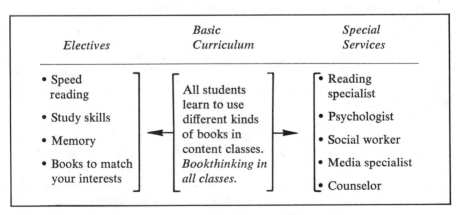

Figure 14-1. Curriculum outline for bookthinking

it. Throughout their school career, the students should benefit from continuing efforts to help them understand how books work, how authors think and how they can be more effective in learning from, and in using books and other printed material. That part of the load should be carried by every member of the teaching staff. It amounts to teachers working to answer the question, What can I do to foster student progress in learning how to think while they read the books in my subject area?

Elective courses fill a second need. Most secondary schools now offer electives from which a student can choose topics that appeal to him. Besides those that are clearly directed to the students' or the faculty's interests (such as "comic books as literature," "simulated space travel"), there should also be self-improvement options, such as "speed reading and study skills," "bookthinking and successful learning," "reading and memory improvement," "books to match your interests," and so on. Teachers and counselors could encourage students into these courses by helping them identify their need to sharpen skills that will serve them for the rest of their lives. Where those electives are not available, a teacher or "the reading committee" should work to get them into the curriculum.

The third aspect of a comprehensive effort entails the use of special services for the student who has serious problems with reading. Despite the negative influence that years of failure are bound to have on a student, the secondary school should spend some of its resources to rescue those students lest they flounder hopelessly. Specialized testing and clinical services should be administered to these youngsters to bring them as close as possible to the mainstream of school work. Counselors, psychologists, reading specialists, and learning specialists are the varied types of personnel who are most likely to design appropriate options for those youngsters. (See chapter 6 on helping the poor reader for further insights into ways of helping students who would benefit from this aspect of the school's program.)

GETTING SPECIALIZED HELP

Electives and ways to incorporate bookthinking into the basic courses have been discussed throughout this text. But the specialized services of a school have been given only a fleeting notation.

Too often the subject-matter teacher believes that all student problems must be solved in his classroom. That is far from accurate. Almost every school system hires special-service personnel whose job is to help students and teachers deal with the special problems and interests that naturally arise among a diverse group of youngsters. Of course, a school system does not intend to satisfy every whim that flits across the minds of teacher and pupil, but it does try to provide reasonable help in satisfying the curiosity of students

—that's where librarians shine—and in aiding those who have an intellectual, emotional, or physical handicap. What the school recognizes is that a basic set of curriculum objectives implemented by competent teachers is only part of the job. When teachers have exhausted their personal resources or when students cry out for additional help, there must be resources outside the classroom for both teacher and pupil.

Those special resources have two major functions: (1) to assign specialized personnel the responsibility of helping students with special problems and interests, and (2) to act as resources or guides to teachers as they work together for the benefit of all the students.

The special problems that students exhibit in the area of bookthinking are not unlike those they show in other areas of academic life such as having a major deficit in the skills their peers have developed, being easily distracted and unable to concentrate, wanting to pursue personal desires that are dramatically different from those recommended in the class, having emotional or physical handicaps, being hampered by strongly negative attitudes derived from their home or neighborhoods. And there are more. Those who evaluate, guide, tutor, and provide resources for these kinds of students are the counselors, reading specialists, psychologists, librarians and media specialists, and special education teachers. These specialists have the responsibility of actively developing contacts and programs to help these students.

Such specialists' second function as a teacher resource makes them active partners with the classroom teacher in developing in-class strategies and activities that will enable the classroom teacher to teach students more effectively. The reading specialist, for example, can demonstrate how to teach cause-effect reading and then give the teacher sources (or books) of activities useful in the continued practice of cause-effect reading in social studies, in science, or in whatever the teacher asked for.

Counselors might provide bibliographies of books in a career-education unit or show a psychology class how schools collect and use aptitude inventories and achievement tests in helping students understand themselves and their aspirations. Librarians/media specialists could demonstrate the use of the school's media center for a specific topic or could show the English teacher how the media center helps students narrow their search for books through providing interest inventories and selected questions about the difficulty of the books they have been accustomed to reading. Similar examples would apply to other specialists. All these are examples of bookthinking activities.

In the midst of all these specialists is the teacher seeking help and advice. He will not get valuable help, however, unless he first collects enough information to let the specialist know what the problem is. Any memo or telephone call to a resource person should start, therefore, with a description of the situation and conclude with a request for service. For example:

MEMORANDUM

To: Karen K., Reading Specialist
Re: Vocabulary with Greek and Latin roots

Ms. K., I want to help my tenth-grade science class learn how to use
Greek and Latin roots in learning to pronounce and in learning the
meanings of many science words. The kids don't know how to use
them and I don't know how to teach them effectively. Would you
teach a demonstration lesson to my fifth-period class? I'll then use your
approach and suggestions in other classes.

Thanks,
I. M. Bare

With a specific request, a careful description of the student, or other
helpful directives, a specialist gets a feeling for the problem and knows that
the teacher has invested enough thought and time to make the case worth
pursuing. Any of the following personnel would be inclined to act from such
a memo.

School Counselor

Tony, one of the students we introduced at the beginning of this chapter,
wants to improve his reading speed and study habits. The counselor at the
school, by request from a teacher or from Tony himself, should be able to
identify electives in the school's curriculum and resources in the community
that will help Tony learn to study and organize himself for more efficient
bookthinking. The counselor has that role and responsibility, but someone
must get Tony and the counselor together before that information can be
shared. The classroom teacher is the person most likely to initiate the contact.
A suggestion to Tony or a note to the counselor may turn the key on that one.

Like everyone else, counselors sometimes have to be reminded of their
opportunities and their responsibilities. When a teacher or a department
believes that there are quite a few "Tonys" in the school, they should ask
the counseling staff to conduct a survey or to examine the student records to
see if students need options or electives that are not currently offered. If a
teacher's intuition suggests that a course in study skills would be appropriate,
he should ask the counselors whether their interviews and their records
support the intuition. The tables could just as easily be turned around. The
counselors could identify the need and suggest that a faculty member or one
of the school's specialists offer a study skills course. Whether the counselor

or the teacher steps forward first is incidental. What is important to remember is that the counselor has information that should constantly serve the faculty and the student body in the development of targeted courses or programs.

Reading Specialist

In most middle and secondary schools, the reading specialist has two major functions: One is to diagnose and teach those students who have severe reading problems. The second is to act as a resource person or an idea person for teachers who want to know how to work out a specific problem in the classroom. The first function is served by selecting and teaching those students who cannot meet the existing criteria for reading adequately in the classroom. Those criteria may include receiving a significant deficit on a reading achievement test. Three or more years below grade level is often used by secondary reading specialists. Other criteria, usually more valuable, include the recommendations of the teachers and an examination of achievement information, especially as it seems to be attached to using textbooks. When it is determined that a student's performance indicates a problem beyond the scope of the classroom teacher, the reading specialist diagnoses and works with the student. Individual diagnostic testing and small-group teaching by the specialist should be followed with related learning in the regular classroom. To make this possible, the specialist needs to inform teachers of activities they can use in the classroom to reinforce work done in the clinic or lab. Instead of a possible discrepancy, the student then sees a salutary transfer of reading skills from clinic to classroom and is likely to conclude that his learning does have some real-life applications.

When the reading specialist and the classroom teacher together believe that the student can keep pace, the student returns to the regular school schedule without going for daily or weekly specialized instruction. At that point, the classroom teacher should insist that the specialist give detailed instructions on how the benefits of the specialized help can be continued. Transfer of those learning experiences can be assured by transferring the responsibility to the student's classroom teachers and by showing them how to use the techniques taught in the lab. Tough as that may sound, it is the only way a remedial program makes any sense. Keeping the youngster in a special reading class beyond the point where he can function in the classroom is inefficient and unreal. The classroom teacher should take the responsibility of adjusting instruction to various learners—always, of course, within the limits imposed by large classes coming through his doorway each hour.

The reading specialist's second responsibility, that of helping classroom teachers become more effective in bookthinking, means that the specialist must help teachers learn to adjust their classroom instruction by discussing with them techniques, skills, interests, and other factors related to the teaching of reading and bookthinking. It is quite appropriate, for example, for one department to request a demonstration of how to teach students to use the reading cues that are indigenous to the books of that department. Appendix A at the end of this chapter lists the cues a reader can use in reading mathematics, science, geography, and social studies. Explaining how those cues can be taught to students multiplies the expertise of the specialist (or others like him) by the number of teachers who see the techniques and use them in their daily lessons. The student, seeing similar practices employed in several classes, begins to think they may have some long-term value.

Librarian and Media Specialist

In some school systems the title *librarian* has been replaced by *media specialist*. In other schools they are two distinct titles and persons. Each is concerned with books and other media such as magazines, film strips, and recordings. Some schools have organized learning centers in the library or media center, and students are encouraged—nay, expected—to engage in independent study there. When it comes to using books, therefore, the librarian touches every student in the school. It is in the library that every student can find something pertinent to read. Whether he is searching for a unique project for his social studies class or simply looking for a book that matches his interests and his reading level, the librarian can help him. No longer a cataloguer of books, the school librarian acts as privy counsel to the personal, social, and academic interests of the students. With sufficient experience, a librarian can use an Interest Inventory like the one in Figure 14–2 and suggest books for any student who completes the inventory for her.

The librarian and the teacher can work together to gather special collections on a topic and include materials that can be read by all class members. Or the librarian can teach students the reference and location skills that serve the subjects they are reading. A school librarian is an integral part of the teaching staff and should be used accordingly.

Psychologist/Psychometrist

Ordinarily the psychologist is summoned when a teacher and the school's counseling staff question a student's mental or emotional ability to perform the tasks that are assigned in the ordinary classroom. If numerous attempts to get the student to participate in abstract tasks fail to produce positive results, the teacher may ask for an examination that will help determine the kinds of activities a student can handle. If, for example, a student appears to be unable to arrive at generalizations or to find the main idea of the simplest passages in the text, or to categorize concepts, or to do any thinking beyond a rote memory operation, then the teacher has sufficient evidence to request further testing.

1. What sports do you like to play? (circle your answers) What sports do you like to watch? (underline your answers)
   a. Roller skating
   b. Skiing
   c. Football
   d. Baseball
   e. Basketball
   f. Swimming
   g. Bowling
   h. Horseback riding
   i. Boating
   j. _____

2. Do you have pets? What kinds? _____

3. Do you collect things? (circle your answers)
   a. Foreign money
   b. Stamps
   c. Rocks
   d. Butterflies
   e. Dolls
   f. _____

4. Do you have hobbies and pastimes? (circle your answers)
   a. Writing letters
   b. Sewing or knitting
   c. Dancing
   d. Singing or playing a musical instrument
   e. Playing cards
   f. Working on cars
   g. Repairing things
   h. Drawing and painting
   i. Driving a car
   j. Cooking
   k. Making things with tools
   l. Experimenting in science
   m. Going for walks
   n. Fishing
   o. Hunting
   p. _____
   q. _____

5. Suppose you could have one wish that might come true. What would it be?

6. Underline the kinds of reading you enjoy most: history, travel, plays, essays, adventure, stories, science, poetry, novels, detective stories, fairy tales, mystery stories, biography, music.

Figure 14-2. Interest inventory

Testing of the student by a psychologist should not be aimed at merely producing some go, no-go decision for admittance into the special-education program of the school. What is desirable is the psychologist's analysis of the kinds of thinking operations the student can perform. With this kind of information, the classroom teacher can select printed matter and make assignments that will benefit the student. If a psychometrist instead of a psychologist is used, counselors and others who look at the test information should ask themselves what the student can do to make progress in bookthinking. The objective is to plan ways to help him use books. It is not simply to label him and then store him on some academic shelf—"Oh, he's a trainable. I can forget him."

In cases of emotional disturbance, the teacher has the same obligation as with requests for an academic examination. A request to the school psychologist or the counselor for personality testing or psychiatric referral (see the accompanying sample memorandum) ought to be accompanied by a listing of the kinds of behavior that arouse the teacher's concern and make him believe that the student is not functioning within the normal limits of classroom behavior.

MEMORANDUM

To: Counselor Wells
Date:
Re: Bobby M.

I am asking help for Bobby who is in my third-period English class. On numerous occasions, I have called on him to answer questions or to read a passage or to join in a class discussion, and he has always responded like a turtle. He slowly pulls back into a shell, eyes cast down, physically shrinking from whatever activity I ask him to participate in. When I press him to speak or to read, he mumbles in an inaudible manner and refuses to make plain whatever it is that he said —if anything. (I have seen him talk to one or two of his friends in the hallway, but never in class.) In checking with some of his other current teachers and previous teachers, I find that they get the same kind of behavior from him. When he passes me to leave the room, he turns sideways so he won't have to acknowledge my presence in any way. There is no way that I can evaluate his work under the circumstances. I need the advice of a psychologist or some other specialist in order to know how to deal with this lad in my classroom. Please advise me.

Sincerely,
Teacher Down

Social Worker and Others

Some students come to school and sleep—exhausted from lack of sleep at home. Others float into class on a regular high. Whether from drugs or alcohol, they are flying. Still others ignore or rebel against the teacher's entreaty to read a book. They are sullen or beaten and depressed. Perhaps something is going on at home: rows, drunkenness, myriad forms of abuse. A memo to the social worker is in order. "See what you can do to help this kid work around his home or his neighborhood problems. He sleeps in school and wants to blame his surroundings."

Where feasible and when the school provides other personnel, such as a learning-disabilities specialist and special-education specialist, the classroom teacher should think of them as people employed to *help solve* special problems. Note the emphasis on "help solve." In many instances these people will be offering expert advice to the classroom teacher, who must then carry out a plan of action. Advice and direction are given, but most of the action takes place in the classroom.

Most school special-services personnel are spread exceedingly thin, and they can deal directly only with the most severe cases. If there is only one reading specialist in a school of 1,500 students, that person can spend individual time with only two or three percent of the students if he is also working with teachers in the classroom. As for a psychologist, a school system may have only one psychologist for every 5,000 to 6,000 students. And so it goes for other specialists. It is clear that the teacher must continue to provide the direction and control for the majority of students who have learning problems. After all, that's where the challenge and the excitement of teaching lie—providing stimulus and instructional guidance for all of the students in the class.

PERSONAL EVALUATION BY THE TEACHER

It may be fairly easy to see that special services to the child and for the teacher help promote progress in learning, but it may not be all that clear how the self-evaluation habits of the teacher lead to student progress. Perhaps it is clearer when one asks himself what has caused him to make improvements in the past. Most of us are concerned about the image we present to others—and consequently the image we present to ourselves. Most people are outwardly conscious of others who evaluate them. That's the reason we ask ourselves, Is the boss impressed? Is my boy friend impressed? Is God impressed? What would my mother or father say? It is natural for us to try to measure up to the expectations that important people have of us.

As we mature, one of those important people who set standards for our behavior is our self. Gradually we develop a list of priorities for things that we want to achieve. They become measures of our success—to us if not to others. The more clearly we develop those standards about what we want to do as teachers, the more likely we are to measure success by those objectives. In addition to the standards that the boss (the principal, the supervisor, the school board) sets for our teaching, we want to establish personal images. In addition to things like keeping order, turning in reports on time, having students score well on tests, and keeping parental complaints to a minimum, we want to have some kids thrill to our subject as a special view of the world and to feel that through their own learning capabilities they can pursue it further. We hope that by now you have the goals of the individual learner and his progress as an independent learner as some of your teaching objectives, because we believe that if you have individual progress in bookthinking as part of your teaching image, you will keep measuring yourself against that image. You will engage in a self-evaluation of your teaching to see if you are, in fact, interested in individual learners.

As you look ahead, then, you must ask yourself how you will evaluate instruction, especially when some of your priorities don't fall within the confines of a paper-and-pencil test. There is no doubt that part of the answer about individual progress can come from tests. For example, if practically all the people in the class make significant advances, you must be doing something right. But part of the answer comes from other observations, such as the feelings, attitudes, and perceptions that both teacher and students have about the "way things are going."

The trick of evaluation is to turn the expression, "the way things are going," into data which are more definite than a general feeling. The means for measuring student performance and student attitude were discussed in chapter 5, Analyzing a Student's Bookthinking Behavior. Now it is time to review your objectives, decisions, and intentions to see how you will decide whether or not you are doing a good job, and to make that judgment on the basis of something more than a general feeling that "everything is OK." Now, there is nothing wrong with a general feeling of satisfaction as an indication of success. But a teacher who intends to grow in the science and art of teaching becomes more analytical in examining some of the specific objectives and procedures he or she uses in class. How do you know whether you are becoming a good teacher?

Start with a Definition

At various points in this book we have emphasized the value of working from a definition of bookthinking that will give direction to your observations about student performance and guide you in joining your subject matter with bookthinking. From our point of view, bookthinking is simply effective teaching. It does not entail the addition of some content to an already overcrowded curriculum. It directs teachers to make use of basic texts and supplementary materials more efficiently, more appropriately for each of the learners. Your definition, then, should be personal and operational—because you must make it work. Giving bookthinking a personal definition will help fix an image in your mind of how a teacher promotes learning. From that image, then, you can work out an evaluation plan for evaluating yourself as a teacher.

Think for a moment about those aspects of bookthinking you have examined in this text and those you have observed in the classrooms you have visited. Are you now able to outline bookthinking-reading in such a way as to guide you in observing students and in leading them to further understanding of how to use books and periodicals in your subject area? If they do not exhibit certain skills in bookthinking, are you now able to design teaching and practice activities that will overcome student weaknesses in the areas you have defined? As you formulate answers to those questions, think about the major factors that go into competent bookthinking and ways you might check on your work as a teacher. Refer back to chapter 2 and Figure 2–5, Author-Reader Relationship. In the teaching of bookthinking in the classroom, the author and reader interact in a communication called *reading*. And the content teacher can promote that interaction, retard it, or do nothing for it. It depends on the role the teacher is willing to play in this communication process. Your personal definition here will guide your application of the evaluation techniques described in the next few pages.

EVALUATION TECHNIQUES

So, what does your teacher image include? Will you encourage interaction? Do you see yourself giving explanations and demonstrations of how to *think while reading?* Are there some regular things you will do to prepare the students for their reading assignments, for example, work on vocabulary and purpose questions? Do you see your classroom as an organization that encourages more flexibility? Is there open time for reading in your schedule? Depending on what you see yourself doing—as important to bookthinking in your classroom—evaluation techniques follow.

This text cannot begin to present a full discussion of the evaluation of teaching. However, we can describe in simple terms some useful means for teacher self-evaluation, such as interaction analysis, to help you see if you practice the kind of interaction you want your students to carry on with an author. Or videotaping to let you see how effective you are in explaining and demonstrating some of the thinking operations you ask students to perform through the questions you ask them. Or introspective surveys to allow you to check off those things you said you were going to do. Can you recall doing them?

Classroom Interaction

During a discussion about a reading passage, students must be alert and thinking. The nature of comprehension operations requires interaction. The discussion period should be characterized by verbal exchanges, and that means at least as much pupil talk as teacher talk. During the reading period, a teacher might have a colleague observe and record who is speaking at every ten-second interval. A simple tally of teacher talk and student talk would quickly reveal whether students were active in the discussion. That's a start in measuring interaction.

Flanders (1965), Amidon (1967), and others have developed procedures for assessing the nature of classroom interaction. Expressed in somewhat oversimplified terms, the interaction-analysis technique requires that an observer classify the types of activities in a classroom according to who is speaking (for example: teacher, student, or no one), the nature of the talk (for example: lecture, giving directions, or taking directions), and the nature of the interaction (for example: acceptance of feelings, praise or encouragement, criticism, or acceptance and use of ideas of students).

Interaction analysis can be an effective tool for appraising a book-discussion activity. Interpretation of the results involves some subjectivity, but generally reveals the degree of teacher dominance in classroom activities and the kind of intellectual tasks students are asked to perform. For book-thinking it is crucial that students have numerous opportunities to talk, react, debate, and share. With respect to the type of thinking that is taking place, higher-level tasks, such as interpretation and synthesis, are preferable to memorization or simple recall. An analysis of the type of interaction found in the classroom can provide feedback on how well the teacher is following good instructional principles. A classroom teacher might tape record his lessons and conduct an interaction analysis of his own teaching in order to make this kind of assessment.

Video Taping

Videotape can be a helpful tool for one's self-evaluation of teaching. The opportunity to view a lesson as an observer has several advantages. First, the teacher can focus on different aspects of the teaching situation and see the same lesson a number of times. Second, with the press of teaching responsibilities removed, the teacher can observe his or her behavior with a degree of detachment not possible while a lesson is in progress. For example, the number of students participating in a discussion can be noted, or the adequacy of a vocabulary lesson can be checked. This technique enables the teacher personally to judge his or her performance and effectively plan a program of self-improvement. It would be especially helpful in analyzing the explanations or demonstrations the teacher gives on bookthinking operations.

Introspection and Surveys

Teachers are constantly in the process of evaluating their performance by introspective means. As a lesson proceeds, for example, the amount of attention exhibited by the class is noted and serves as feedback for self-evaluation. The sensitive teacher depends heavily on this useful approach to evaluation.

Systematic self-evaluation about bookthinking is more important for a subject-area teacher than for the general elementary classroom teacher. The reason is that, given the subject teacher's interest and training, he is unlikely to examine bookthinking skills unless he has set up a regular procedure for doing so. A checklist or an end-of-grade-period self-review brings those matters back into his thinking. Because it takes that kind of willful decision, you may want to examine the following checklist, Self-Evaluation of Bookthinking, to see which aspects you will try to review regularly. It will take a commitment, that is, a firm decision, to establish checklists and routines for self-analysis about bookthinking in your classroom.

Select the items you are willing to include in your regular examination of your taeaching effectiveness. Then make them into a checklist you will use to collect data about yourself and your teaching.

Decisions about the Classroom

1. Are there evidences of bookthinking around the room?
   Are there charts, sets of directions?
   Are there vocabulary charts?
   Are there charts to guide development of writing skills?
   Are there pupil- or teacher-made summaries?
   Are there displays of pupils' work?
2. Materials for independent reading
   Are there books of varying levels of difficulty and different topics?
   Are different types of books (for example, biographies, travel books, political analyses) attractively displayed and accessible?
   In planning, is there provision for encouraging independent study?
   Do we share ideas and enjoyment from what we've read independently?
3. Does the organization of my classroom lend itself to both individual and group work?
   Is there a library or reference corner?
   Is there space for book reviews and related student comments?
   Are there comfortable tables, chairs, and other furniture that invite students to read?
   Does the arrangement of furniture encourage large-group and small-group (individual) work?

Planning for Students

1. Do I provide for various reading levels?
   Have I assessed each student's instructional reading level?

Have I studied cumulative records for data, for example, objective test data?

Have I given a cloze test using my standard textbooks?

Have I used the above information in planning reading assignments?

Have I provided for project options and other differentiated reading-study assignments?

2. How have I provided for groups and for independent work?

Do I limit the number of lecture-discussion sessions in favor of project and independent activity?

Have I developed learning centers or study guides to provide for self-directed learning?

Do I include time for sharing ideas from various sources that I have identified for my students?

3. How do I make my lesson plans student-oriented?

Are my directions for reading sufficiently precise with specific, attainable purposes?

Do I get students ready to read through a theme, concepts, vocabulary?

Do my follow-up lessons elicit recall of purpose and opportunities to use vocabulary and concepts introduced in the original lesson?

Do I design pupil self-evaluation and teacher-pupil evaluation?

Figure 14-3. Teacher self-evaluation of bookthinking

No one is expected to thoroughly attend to all of the items in the checklist. Some are more appropriate to one subject than to another. Choose those in each category that make sense to you. Attach your list of criteria to your grade book, and review your performance when you review students' grades. Or attach the list to your planning book as a weekly reminder of what you have chosen to work on.

Library/Media Center

The ultimate test of a book-centered curriculum is the use of books. It may be the classroom teacher's responsibility to make the use of books an integral part of learning, but the number of books checked out of the library independently is a prime measure of the long-term effects of that effort. If a school were to make a concerted effort to improve bookthinking, the number of books used and checked out of the library or media center should be counted prior to the start of the effort and then counted again after it has been operating. Circulation figures should indicate a healthy increase in fiction and nonfiction areas. Book sales, assuming the school has a bookstore, should also indicate student attitude and interest in reading.

STUDENT PROGRAMS

Teacher self-evaluation cannot be judged solely on the reading achievement scores of students, but those scores can offer insight into what has happened. Year-end gains in raw score points on criterion lists can also indicate growth in skills taught. Informal measures as described in various chapters in this book would also reveal progress. Student products such as papers and lab reports could furnish evidence of growth over the semester or the year. A checklist completed at the beginning of the year could be compared to a checklist covering the same types of observations at the end of the term.

Thus, student progress serves as an indicator of teacher effectiveness. When coupled with other criteria discussed in this chapter, it adds important evidence to teacher effectiveness.

Teacher Insight

It should be clear from the discussions in this text that bookthinking has numerous variables and depends heavily on the teacher's clarity of purpose and insight into student behavior. To exercise that insight, he needs to define bookthinking for his subject and students. Then he must organize the room and lessons to attune his observations to student success. As the research shows—so says the logic of our argument—the individual classroom teacher remains the critical factor in determining how well students will read and use books effectively.

EVALUATION PATTERN

All of the techniques described above are fine for evaluating bits and pieces of your teaching. What you must do for regular improvement, though, is to map out a basic strategy for evaluation that will serve you over the years. Instead of reaching into the grab bag of evaluation techniques and pulling out one this time and a different one the next time, devise an evaluation system that helps you judge your progress and that of your students month after month. Consistency, after all, is the difference between making steady progress and the occasional indulgence of self-recrimination that most people do when they make a New Year's resolution—soon to be forgotten.

Instead of thinking of evaluation as a kind of year-end test, regard it as a series of concentric circles that always bring you back close to your starting point, yet making progress toward the center target. A continuous evaluation plan, unlike your final test, incorporates regular adjustments to your teaching program—adjustments that could change the objectives or the procedures that you started with. As soon as you see that something is not

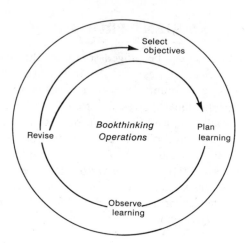

Figure 14-4. SPOR: continuous evaluation plan

going to work or is not working in the way you planned, make a change! Your concept of evaluation, then, could be represented by Figure 14–4. Your objectives are turned into learning moments or activities. Students act and you observe them in the learning activity. Based on what you see, you either change the activity to accomplish the objective or you change the objective. Changing the objective would stem from a successful accomplishment of the previous objective or from learning that the objective was ill-chosen for this student. A more appropriate target should be worked on. And so on and on.

The concept of a continuous evaluation plan and its stages of activity are fairly simple, but the execution of such a plan requires a disciplined mind. For bookthinking, an evaluation plan would start with a definition of what bookthinking means in your subject area. It would require you to develop mental images of how to create the author-reader relationship that is suggested in Figure 2–5, as reviewed earlier in this chapter, and shown in chapter 2. Practically speaking, it means that you must decide which aspects of bookthinking you are going to work on. Some decisions on priorities have to be made, and you have to decide what you believe is important. Suppose, for example, that for one group of students you chose vocabulary and establishing goals as teaching objectives for a grading period. With that in mind, your continuous evaluation plan can be turned into a kind of checklist which you use each week to see if you are making progress toward those objectives.

Evaluation Checklist

Select Objectives

Do I know clearly what I am looking for in vocabulary and in setting purposes?

Do I have evidence that there is a need for these students to work on these objectives?

Plan Learning

Did I locate or produce various activities for the students to work on the objectives?

Have I incorporated exploratory learning activities as well as directed learning activities?

Have I organized the environment as well as the books or activities?

Observe Learning

Did I observe the learner in the process of working on the vocabulary objectives? The purpose for reading?

Did the students know what they were to do and why?

Did the activities work?

What objectives have been completed?

Where were the confusions and frustrations?

Revise

Should we move ahead to the next objective? If so, which bookthinking objective is appropriate for these students?

Should I revise the learning activities? In what way? How can I clarify or make them less frustrating?

Though some of these questions are posed in the past tense, so as to represent a kind of weekly self-survey for the classroom teacher, we assume that the teacher will ask many of the questions daily as he selects, constructs, and observes. This Select—Plan—Observe—Revise (SPOR) outline is most valuable as an attitude developer. As a mental guide, it can shape the attitude of the teacher and remind him to analyze what he is doing in a consistent manner.

Was It Appropriate?

In this book, we have established that reading and, therefore, bookthinking are more than decoding and more than simple perception of words and phrases. As a person reads, he brings his own ideas and the author's ideas together. That process creates a resultant meaning that is both objective and personal. It is objective when the reader answers a question about something specific: for example, "How many people were killed in the battle?" And it is personal when the reader has to make inferences about the author's purpose or has to determine the impact of the ideas presented. Because there is a gradual change over the years in the level of difficulty in the writing presented to the student, and because he is personally changing and becoming more mature in his thinking, there are logical stages of development in bookthinking competence. In any discussion of evaluation, then, it seems proper to ask whether the objectives and activities were appropriate for the students. Not only age alone, but also the experience and past competence guide a teacher in selecting objectives and planning learning activities. Therefore, let us review briefly the gross stages of a student's development in bookthinking, to have us close as we began—focusing on the student.

Primary

During the primary years, students learn that speech can be represented by print, that a coherent idea or event can become a paragraph or passage, and that a story or a series of events can be represented in a book. The child's reaction to those phenomena is most likely to be personal—reactions of pleasure ("I like that."), surprise ("Wow! He got away."), and recognition ("We have flown kites at home.").

Intermediate

In the intermediate years, students learn that words have structure and can be manipulated in print to change meaning; that ideas are presented with some order in mind—for example, a main idea and supporting details, cause and effect, chronological order; that varied purposes are achieved with different kinds of presentations such as short stories, biographies, research articles. During the intermediate years, the students are more likely to include their peers and their families in their responses to the ideas they encounter in their reading.

Advanced

The junior and senior high school years, and beyond, usually mark a significant change in the way students interact with the ideas. Not only is their sense of community and society expanding to give them a broader reference base, but they are also more likely to see complex relationships among ideas and can therefore combine concepts and create applications at the abstract level. During these years, students learn that vocabulary can be technical as well as general in its application. They learn that authors' ideas may have implied meanings, as in figurative language and symbolic representations and that authors have styles and organizations to suit specific purposes. At this level, students can become conscious of the written message as a psychological entity with which they can analyze and interact just as they can with the physical and psychological beings who are their neighbors or friends.

SUMMARY

Table 14–1 shows stages in the development of a bookthinker. There is a tacit assumption that a teacher and student are working together

TABLE 14-1
Stages of Growth in Bookthinking

LEVEL OF STUDENT	ANALYSIS SKILLS	INTERACTION
Primary	Speech becomes print. Ideas lead to coherent passages. Story becomes book.	Personal
Intermediate	Words have structure. Ideas are presented with order. Purpose dictates type of book.	Peer and family included
Advanced	Vocabulary can be technical. Language includes implied meanings. Style and organization match purpose.	Society and relationships among ideas

to promote growth. Bookthinking does not emerge from the general experience of the youth like some academic artifact that springs up each new birthday. Ninth-grade youngsters, for example, will range all across the stages of analysis skills and will have to be brought forward toward the advanced skills by means of the curriculum and teachers who are conscious of their bookthinking abilities. A teacher realizes that his role is one of showing students how to become independent learners—a role that puts him right in the middle of the author-reader relationship.

Suggested Readings

Nielsen, Duane M., and Howard F. Hjelm, eds. *Reading and Career Education.* Perspectives in Reading No. 19. Newark, Del.: International Reading Association, 1975.
This handbook is a collection of papers on the role of communications in career education. The first major section provides a perspective on the concept of career education, followed by sections on reading requirements and exemplary programs. Many research and program studies are reported providing a broad overview of the role of literacy in preparation for adult roles in the world of work.
Tinker, Miles A. *Bases for Effective Reading.* Minneapolis: University of Minnesota Press, 1965.
This book tends to emphasize physical factors in reading, aspects that have been overshadowed by the more cognitive orientation of recent texts. However, Tinker's common-sense discussions of such issues as eye movements,

legibility and typography, lighting, and so-called visual hygiene still serve a practical purpose and suggest some contingencies that may be within the teacher's control. He also discusses reading flexibility and evaluation of reading performance at junior high and secondary levels.

Appendix A

Bookthinking Cues for Various Subjects[1]

Middle and high school curricula should include ways for students to grow in bookthinking competence. The middle school stands as an intermediary between the start-up skills taught in the primary grades and the skills for independent reading and learning that are emphasized in the secondary grades. In the middle school years, then, the curriculum objectives for all subjects should help the students become aware of (1) the wide variety of types of reading and (2) strategies available to engage the expanding array of books the student meets. Those objectives should likewise remind teachers to discuss reading assignments in a concrete way, but with a view to showing relationships among the ideas in the books and in the world around the student. It is quite appropriate, therefore, to discuss and demonstrate cause-and-effect relationships, using concrete examples that are in keeping with the experience of the class, or to show that a theme is supported by facts and/or arguments the writer marshals around the theme.

Secondary curriculum objectives should then take up the development of bookthinking. In all subjects students should be encouraged to analyze organizational differences, typographical differences, ways of analyzing terminology, and the kinds of thinking that seem to pervade the writing of books and articles in that subject field. Perhaps one of the clearest ways to translate bookthinking into workable statements is to look for cues that the reader can use to extract information and interact with the message. The cues for each subject matter vary. The teacher's responsibility, then, is to alert the students to those cues and to show them how to use such cues efficiently.

Listed below are examples of the kinds of cues that can be found in math, science, geography, and social studies. Not all of the cues for any one subject will be applicable in each article or chapter that the student reads. But teachers could use this list as a guide to asking questions, as a list of study aids they will review with their students, or as a checklist they will use to observe students and then help them with the cues with which they are unfamiliar. Note the major headings under which the cues are here presented: vocabulary, typography and

---

[1] From Larry A. Harris and Carl B. Smith, *Reading Instruction: Diagnostic Teaching in the Classroom* (New York: Holt, Rinehart and Winston, 1976), pp. 319–325.

location, kinds of reading, special considerations, and organization. Most of the headings are self-explanatory, with the possible exception of "kinds of reading." This heading suggests that the subject area may require different purposes for reading that need to be identified for an efficient extraction of information for a more intelligent response to the message given. These cues might become clear if you took a chapter from your subject text and tried to work through the cues given for your subject.

Math Cues

1. Vocabulary cues. Essential key words or phrases help to determine operations or sets to be utilized:
   Addition—total, sum, add, add to, in all, altogether, plus
   Subtraction—difference, left over, minus, subtract
   Multiplication—total, times, how many times, product
   Division—how many times more, divided by, how many would
2. Typographical cues (locational cues)
   a. Question mark (gives clue to location of question to be answered)
   b. Charts and graphs (give essential information for problem on page, often location in another area of the page)
   c. Illustrations (may act as road signs or directions for the problem)
   d. Signs (percent, decimal point, operational signs) indicate categories and mathematical operations
3. Kinds of readings—read for:
   a. Skimming for the purpose and for overall comprehension
   b. Question asked
   c. Key words or phrases
   d. Operation(s) to be utilized
   e. Key numbers (also eliminate extra numbers)
   f. Rereading problems to justify equations; redo if necessary
   g. Solving the problem
4. Special considerations
   a. The same term is not always used to indicate the same operation (for example, *and*, *added to*, and *plus* are interchangeable).
   b. The same term can indicate different operations (for example, *altogether* could indicate either addition or multiplication).
   c. Several technical terms have different meanings in general conversation (for example: square, mean, product).
   d. Mathematics entails understanding the many terms that remind the student of absolutely nothing and must be learned by memorization (for example: multiplier, divisor, radius, diameter, circumference).
5. Organizational guides. There is no special order, but certain structures appear in most mathematics problems:
   a. A situation is given.
   b. A numerical question is asked.
   c. An equation must be formulated from information given.

Science Cues

1. Vocabulary cues
   a. There are certain words and related concepts that all pupils
      should know in order to read almost any science material
      above the primary level:
      (1) Things *in common, characteristics, various, classified, simi-
          larities.* An understanding of these terms is quite help-
          ful in comprehending the data that follow the terms.
      (2) Common Latin, Greek, or other derivations:
          hydro-   *un-*
          electro-   *bi-*
          photo-
   b. Every new science lesson requires the teaching of terms perti-
      nent to that selection.
2. Typographical cues (locational skills)
   a. In most science textbooks there are good subtitles and chapter
      headings to use.
   b. Often there are good summaries at the endings of chapters.
   c. Typographical cues are especially important in the first survey
      reading.
3. Kinds of readings—read for:
   a. Surveying the material
      (1) Attention to pictures
      (2) How many main parts? Use the subheadings
      (3) Read the first paragraph and the summary, if given
      (4) Formulate questions for reading from the survey.
   b. Answering the questions
      (1) Appreciation of facts and objective data
      (2) Critical reading—what are the criteria?
   c. Reviewing the material read
      (1) The discussion and evaluation of the reading are probably
          the most important part of the lesson.
      (2) Pupils should be urged to report exactly what they have
          read; precision.
          "Most kinds of bats are useful to mankind because they eat
          harmful insects."
          "Some scientists believe there is life on Mars."
4. Special considerations
   a. Ability to read symbols. AuH_2O = goldwater
   b. Ability to follow diagrams. For example, a student must under-
      stand the idea of completeness as in an electrical circuit or
      a chemical equation.
5. Organizational guides. Various organizational approaches typical of
   science selections are:
   a. Generalizations are given first, then the examples and data; de-
      ductive.
      (1) All mammals have hair, they bear their young alive, and so
          on.

(2) The different kinds of mammals are listed.
   b. Examples and supporting data
      (1) Information on different mammals—their sizes, speeds, and
           so on.
      (2) In other selections—phenomena about light, heat, and so
           forth.
   c. Classification of data
      (1) Different classes of mammals, stars, and so on
      (2) Differences and similarities among the classes
   d. Often the data is given first, then the science writer builds up to
      classifying and generalizing; inductive.

Geography Cues

1. Vocabulary cues
   a. Extend the concept of a previously known word (for example,
      range, mountain range).
   b. Homonyms (for example, *plain, plane*)
   c. Refer to glossary.
   d. Develop vocabulary in context (for example, bananas are a
      tropical fruit.).
   e. Use illustrations to create perception of vocabulary.
2. Typographical cues
   a. Chapter headings, main headings, and subheadings are given.
   b. The format of the book includes illustrations, glossary, appen-
      dix, and index.
   c. The book is generally set up with two columns to make reading
      easier because of the shorter line of type and to facilitate
      scanning.
3. Kinds of reading
   a. Survey for overview
   b. Read to answer questions
   c. Skim to find specific answers and make generalizations (for ex-
      ample, What are the natural resources of Manitoba? How
      does this affect the industries of Manitoba?).
   d. Detailed reading of charts, graphs, maps, and so on.
4. Specialized considerations
   a. Statistical reading: This type of reading is developed through
      repeated use of statistics (for example, present statistical
      data and provide an exercise for using the data such as
      comparing the area in square miles of several given coun-
      tries).
   b. Symbolic language of maps (for example, a child's use of the
      map legend—see illustration).
   c. Recognize that a map is a ground plan drawn to scale.
   d. Interpret different kinds of maps (for example, population, po-
      litical, rainfall, topographical).

Political Map

❀ Capital

• Other City or Town

▲ MOUNTAIN

· *River*

A map legend

e. Reading graphs (for example, the reader learns to interpret data on various types of graphs—circle, line, bar, and pictorial).

f. Authenticating facts (for example, the reader must verify the data of statistical information, such as the population of a given area).

g. The reader cuts across the author's organization and makes his own groupings of factual material for a given purpose.

5. Organizational guides. The material in a geography book is generally organized in one of two ways:

   a. A specific area is given and all geographical aspects are examined (for example, the New England states would be thoroughly discussed as to topography, climate, population, industries, and so on).

   b. A geographical aspect is considered as it is found throughout the world.

Social Studies Cues

1. Vocabulary cues

   a. Pronunciation skills

      (1) Multisyllabic words (for example, as-tro-labe)

      (2) Foreign words (for example, *apartheid*)

   b. Meaning skills

      (1) Technical words (for example, *latitude*)

      (2) Abstract words (for example, *democratic*)

      (3) Concepts, abstractions (for example, *tolerance*)

      (4) General terms (for example, *elevator*—grain or passenger)

      (5) Mathematical terms (for example, *ratio*)

2. Typographical guides

   a. Headings and subheadings provide clues to the location of responses to questions.

b. Use the parts of the book as reference tools.

c. Relate text and graphic content such as maps, graphs, and cartoons to corresponding text material.

3. Kinds of readings. Read for:

a. Main idea and supporting details

b. Use of key words, concepts, and literal facts

c. Read critically:

(1) Appraisals

(2) Conclusions and inferences

(3) Propaganda

(4) Current events

d. Organize ideas to recognize relations and sequence of events; identify central issues.

e. Graphic skills (maps, graphs, charts, diagrams, and pictures)

f. Related reference skills (table of contents, index, cross-references, footnotes)

g. Related materials (periodicals and mass media such as radio, television, lectures, and field trips)

4. Organizational guides. General organization of the content:

a. Material in the social studies area is usually organized by the initial practice (for example, selection of the president by an electoral college), an event (for example, passage of the Eighteenth Amendment), or a method (for example, representative democracy).

b. Often a point of view is presented, usually subtly (for example, "private enterprise is best for the country"); in some cases it is presented straightforwardly (for example, "dictatorships are bad").

c. A relation often presented is one of conditions surrounding an effect: condition-effect relation.

d. Chronological order often meets the organizational needs of social studies material.

Bibliography

Abrahams, Roger D., and Rudolph C. Troike. *Language and Cultural Diversity in American Education*. Englewood Cliffs, N.J.: Prentice-Hall, 1972.

Alexander, J. Estill, and Ronald C. Fuller. *Attitudes and Reading*. Newark, Del.: International Reading Association, 1976.

Altick, Richard. *Preface to Critical Reading*. New York: Holt, Rinehart and Winston, 1969.

Amidon, Edmund, and John Hough. *Interaction Analysis: Theory, Research and Application*. Reading, Mass.: Addison-Wesley, 1967.

Ashton-Warner, Sylvia. *Teacher*. New York: Simon & Schuster, 1963.

Asimov, Isaac. *More Words of Science*. Boston: Houghton Mifflin, 1972.

Asimov, Isaac. *Words of Science and the History Behind Them*. Boston: Houghton Mifflin, 1959.

Atkin, J. Myron, *et al. Ginn Science Program, Advanced Level A*. Boston, Mass.: Ginn, 1975.

Bailey, Mildred H. "The Utility of Phonics Generalizations in Grades One Through Six," *The Reading Teacher*, 20:413–418 (February 1967).

Bamberger, Richard D. "Why People Read: The Reading Situation Worldwide," in Darryl J. Strickler (ed.), *The Affective Dimension of Reading: Resource Guide*. Bloomington, Ind.: Indiana University Reading Programs, 1977.

Baratz, John C., and Roger W. Shuy. *Teaching Black Children To Read*. Washington, D.C.: Center for Applied Linguistics, 1969.

Barrett, Thomas C. "Taxonomy of Reading Comprehension," *Reading 360 Monograph*. Boston, Mass.: Ginn, 1972.

445

Barrett, Thomas C. "A Taxonomy for Reading Comprehension," paper presented at the International Reading Association meeting, Anaheim, Calif., 1970.

Bernstein, Theodore. *The Reverse Dictionary*. New York: Quadrangle/New York Times Book Company, 1976.

Bettelheim, Bruno. *The Uses of Enchantment: The Meaning and Importance of Fairy Tales*. New York: Knopf, 1976.

Betts, E. A. *Foundations of Reading Instruction*. New York: American Book Company, 1957.

Blanton, William E., Roger Farr, and J. Jaap Tuinman (eds.). *Measuring Reading Performance*. Newark, Del.: International Reading Association, 1974.

Bleecker, Samuel E. "The Psychologist as Druggist," *Harper's*, 251(1507):117 (December 1975).

Bloom, Benjamin (ed.). *Taxonomy of Educational Objectives Handbook I: Cognitive Domain*. New York: McKay, 1963.

Bolinger, Dwight. *Aspects of Language*. New York: Harcourt Brace Jovanovich, 1968.

Bormuth, John. "Cloze Tests and Reading Comprehension," *Reading Research Quarterly*, 4(3):359–367 (Spring 1969).

Bormuth, John. "Cloze Tests as Measures of Readability and Comprehension Ability," unpublished doctoral dissertation, Indiana University, Bloomington, 1962.

Brown, James I. *Programmed Vocabulary*. Chicago: Lyons and Carnahan, 1965.

Bruner, Jerome. "Beyond the Information Given," in Jeremy Anglin (ed.), *Beyond the Information Given*. New York: Norton, 1973.

Bruner, Jerome. *The Process of Education*. Cambridge, Mass.: Harvard University Press, 1960.

Bureau of Curriculum Development, City of New York. *A Guide for Beginning Teachers of Reading, Grades 9–12*. New York: Board of Education, 1967–1968 Series.

Burgess, Carol, *et al. Understanding Children Writing*. Baltimore, Md.: Penguin, 1973.

Buros, Oscar. *Reading Tests and Reviews*. Highland Park, N.J.: Gryphon, 1969.

Byrne, Josefa H. *Mrs. Byrne's Dictionary of Unusual, Obscure and Preposterous Words*. New York: University Books, Inc., 1974.

Carlsen, G. Robert. *Books and the Teenage Reader*. New York: Bantam, 1972.

Carter, Barbara, and Gloria Dapper. *School Volunteers: What They Do; How They Do It*. New York: Citation Press, 1972.

Carver, Ronald P. "A Critical Review of Mathemagenic Behaviors and the Effect of Questions upon the Retention of Prose Materials," *Journal of Reading Behavior*, 4:93–119 (Spring 1972).

Chomsky, Noam. *Syntactic Structures*. The Hague: Mouton, 1957.

Cleveland Public Schools, Divisions of English and Science. *Science Reading Units II, Project Content-Cognition: Reading*. Cleveland, O.: Cleveland City School District, 1976.

Cline, R. "Reading Ability and Selection for Teacher Education Programs." *Journal of Reading*, 12:634–638, 678–680 (1969).

Clymer, Theodore. "What Is Reading?" in Helen M. Robinson (ed.), *Innovation and Change in Reading Instruction*, 67th Yearbook of the National Society for the Study of Education, Part II. Chicago: University of Chicago Press, 1969.

Cooper, J. D., L. A. Cooper, N. Roser, L. Harris, and C. Smith. *Decision Making for the Diagnostic Teacher*. New York: Holt, Rinehart and Winston, 1972, 1976.

Crosby, Muriel (ed.), *Reading Ladders for Human Relations*, 4th ed. Washington, D.C.: American Council on Education, 1963.

Crouse, William H. *The Auto Book*. New York: McGraw-Hill, 1974.

Dale, Edgar, Taher Razik, and Walter Petty. *Bibliography of Vocabulary Studies*, third rev. ed. Columbus, O.: The Ohio State University, 1973. A Payne Fund Communication Project.

Davis, Frederick B. "Psychometric Research on Comprehension in Reading," *Reading Research Quarterly*, 7(4):628–678 (Summer 1972).

Davis, Frederick B. "Research in Comprehension in Reading," *Reading Research Quarterly*, 3(4):499–545 (Summer 1968).

Dawkins, John. *Syntax and Readability*. Newark, Del.: International Reading Association, 1975.

DeBoer, John J. "Teaching Critical Reading," in M. King, B. Ellinger, and W. Wolf (eds.), *Critical Reading*. Philadelphia: Lippincott, 1967.

Dell, Helen Davis. *Individualizing Instruction*. Chicago: Science Research Associates, 1972.

Deutsch, Martin. "Early Social Environment: Its Influence on School Adaptation," in Daniel Schreiber (ed.), *The School Dropout*. Washington, D.C.: National Education Association, 1964.

Devlin, Joseph. *A Dictionary of Synonyms and Antonyms*. New York: Popular Library, 1961.

Dillner, Martha, and Joanne P. Olson. *Personalized Reading Instruction in Middle, Junior and Senior High Schools*. New York: Macmillan, 1977.

Dinnan, J. A., and L. E. Hafner. "Reading Interests and Abilities of College Students," *Reading Improvement*, 7:63–65 (Winter 1970).

Distad, H. W. "A Study of the Reading Performance of Pupils Under Different Conditions on Different Types of Materials," *Journal of Educational Research*, 18:247–248 (April 1927).

Don, Sue, *et al. Individualizing Reading Instruction with Learning Stations and Centers*. Evansville, Ind.: Riverside Learning Associates, Inc., 1973.

Donelson, Kenneth. "Adolescent Literature Revised After Four Years," *Arizona English Bulletin*, 18:3 (April 1976).

Draper, Arthur G., and Gerald H. Moeller, "We Think with Words," *Phi Delta Kappan*, 52:482–484 (April 1971).

Duffy, Gerald G. (ed.). *Reading in the Middle School*. Newark, Del.: International Reading Association, 1975.

Duker, Sam. "Basics in Critical Listening," *English Journal*, 61:565–567 (November 1962).

Dunn, Rita S., and Kenneth G. Dunn. *Practical Approaches to Individualizing Instruction*. Englewood Cliffs, N.J.: Prentice-Hall, 1971.

Dunwiddie, William E. *Problems of Democracy*. Boston, Mass.: Ginn, 1970.

Dutch, Robert A. (ed.). *The Original Roget's Thesaurus of Words and Phrases*. New York: Dell, 1962.

Eash, Maurice J. *Reading and Thinking: Using Supplementary Books in the Classroom.* New York: Doubleday, 1967.

El Hagrasy, S. "The Teacher's Role in Library Service," *Journal of Experimental Education,* 30: 346–354 (June 1962).

Ellis, Henry C. *Fundamentals of Human Learning and Cognition.* Dubuque, Iowa: William C. Brown Company, 1972.

Ellson, D. G., L. Barber, T. L. Engle, and L. Kampsworth. "Programmed Tutoring: A Teaching Aid and a Research Tool," *Reading Research Quarterly,* 1:77–127 (Fall 1965).

Emans, Robert. "The Usefulness of Phonics Generalizations Above the Primary Grades," *The Reading Teacher,* 20(5):419–425.

Ennis, Robert. "A Concept of Critical Thinking: A Proposed Thesis for Research in the Teaching and Evaluation of Critical Thinking Ability," *Harvard Educational Review,* 32:81–111 (Winter 1962).

Estes, Thomas H. "Scale To Measure Attitudes Toward Reading," *Journal of Reading,* 15:135–138 (1971).

Estes, Thomas H., and J. Vaughn. "Reading Interests and Comprehension: Implications," *The Reading Teacher,* 7:149–153 (1973).

Fader, Daniel N. *The New Hooked on Books.* New York: Berkley Medallion Books, 1976.

Fader, Daniel N., and Elton B. McNeil. *Hooked on Books: Program and Proof.* New York: Putnam, 1966.

Farr, Roger. *Reading: What Can Be Measured?* ERIC/CRIER Reading Review Series. Newark, Del.: International Reading Association, 1969.

Fiedler, William (ed.). *Inquiring About Technology: Studies in Economics and Technology.* New York: Holt, Rinehart and Winston, 1972.

Flanders, Ned A. *Teacher Influence, Pupil Attitudes and Achievement.* Washington, D.C.: Department of Health, Education and Welfare. (Superintendent of Documents, Catalog No. F.S. 5225:25040, 1965.)

Fleming, Harold, and Allan A. Glatthorn. *Composition: Models and Exercises, Book 10.* New York: Harcourt Brace Jovanovich, 1965.

Fry, Edward. "Graph for Estimating Readability—Extended," *Journal of Reading,* 21:1 (January 1977).

Fry, Edward. *Reading Instruction for Classroom and Clinic.* New York: McGraw-Hill, 1972.

Funk, Peter. *It Pays To Increase Your Word Power.* New York: Bantam, 1970.

Funk, Wilfred. *Six Weeks to Words of Power.* New York: Pocket Books, 1965.

Funk, Wilfred, and Norman Lewis. *Thirty Days to a More Powerful Vocabulary.* New York: Pocket Books, 1971.

Gallup, George. The *Gallup Poll.* New York: American Institute of Public Opinion, 1969.

Geeslin, R. H., and P. W. York. "Literacy Skills as a Barrier to Inservice Training," *Journal of Reading Behavior,* 3:9–11 (1970–1971).

Gibson, Eleanor J., and Harry Levin. *The Psychology of Reading.* Cambridge, Mass.: MIT Press, 1975.

Gilbert, Doris W. *Study in Depth.* Englewood Cliffs, N.J.: Prentice-Hall, 1966.

Gone, Chris H., and John L. Feiner. *General Shop.* New York: McGraw-Hill, 1969.

Goodman, Kenneth S. "Behind the Eye: What Happens in Reading," in H. Singer and R. Ruddell (eds.), *Theoretical Models and Processes of Reading*. Newark, Del.: International Reading Association, 1970.

Goodman, Kenneth S. *The Psycholinguistic Nature of the Reading Process*. Detroit: Wayne State University Press, 1967.

Goodman, Kenneth S. "A Communicative Theory of the Reading Curriculum," *Elementary English*, 40:240–242 (March 1963).

Goodman, Yvetta M., and Carolyn L. Burke. *Reading Miscue Inventory*. New York: Macmillan, 1972.

Graduate Record Examination: Preparation for Graduate Record Examination Aptitude Test. Chicago: Henry Regnery Company, 1973.

Grobstein, Clifford. *The Strategy of Life*. San Francisco: Freeman, 1964.

Guilford, J. P. *The Nature of Human Intelligence*. New York: McGraw-Hill, 1967.

Guilford, J. P. "The Three Faces of Intellect," *American Psychologist*, 14:469–479 (1959).

Gunning, Robert. "The Fog Index After Twenty Years," *Journal of Business Communication*, 6:3–13 (Winter 1968).

Guszak, Frank L. "Teacher Questions and Levels of Reading Comprehension," in Thomas C. Barrett (ed.), *Perspectives in Reading No. 8: The Evaluation of Children's Achievement*. Newark, Del.: International Reading Association, 1967.

Hamilton, Harlan B. "The Relationship Between Televiewing and the Reading Interests of Seventh-Grade Pupils," unpublished doctoral dissertation, Boston University, 1973 (Ed 095 524).

Harris, Albert J. *Casebook on Reading Disability*. New York: McKay, 1970a.

Harris, Albert J. *How To Increase Reading Ability*, 5th ed. New York: McKay, 1970b.

Harris, Larry A., and Carl B. Smith. *Reading Instruction*. New York: Holt, Rinehart and Winston, 1976.

Harris, Larry A., and Carl B. Smith. *Individualizing Reading Instruction: A Reader*. New York: Holt, Rinehart and Winston, 1972.

Hawkins, Martha, "Are Future Teachers Readers?" *The Reading Teacher*, 21(2): 138–140 (1967).

Herber, Harold L. "Reading in the Social Studies: Implications for Teaching and Research," in James Laffey (ed.), *Reading in the Content Areas*. Newark, Del.: International Reading Association, 1972.

Herber, Harold L. *Teaching Reading in Content Areas*. Englewood Cliffs, N.J.: Prentice-Hall, 1970.

Herndon, James. *The Way It Spozed To Be*. New York: Simon & Schuster, 1968.

Higgens, James E. *Beyond Words: Mystical Fancy in Children's Literature*. New York: Teachers College Press, 1970.

Hunkins, Francis P. *Involving Students in Questioning*. Boston: Allyn and Bacon, 1976.

Hunt, Kellogg. "Differences in Grammatical Structures Written at Three Grade Levels, the Structures To Be Analyzed by Transformational Methods," Cooperative Research Project No. 1998. Tallahassee: Florida State University, 1964.

Hunt, Lyman C., "The Effect of Self-Selection, Interests, and Motivation Upon

Independent, Instructional, and Frustrational Levels," *The Reading Teacher*, 24(2):148 (November 1970).

Hunt, Lyman C. "Evaluation Through Teacher-Pupil Conferences," in Thomas C. Barrett (ed.), *The Evaluation of Children's Reading Achievement*. Newark, Del.: International Reading Association, 1967.

Jacobs, Harold R. *Mathematics: A Human Endeavor*. San Francisco: Freeman, 1970.

Johns, Jerry L., Sharon Garton, Paula Schoenfelder, and Patricia Skriba (eds.). *Assessing Reading Behavior: Informal Reading Inventories*. Newark, Del.: International Reading Association, 1977.

Johnson, Donovan A., Viggo P. Hansen, and Wayne H. Peterson. *Applications in Mathematics, Course B*. Glenview, Ill.: Scott, Foresman, 1974.

Johnson, Marjorie, and Roy Kress. *Informal Reading Inventories*. Newark, Del.: International Reading Association, 1965.

Kagan, Jerome. "A Conception of Early Adolescence," *Daedalus*, 100(4):997–1012 (Fall 1971).

Karlin, Muriel S., and Regina Berger. *Successful Methods for Teaching the Slow Learner*. West Nyack, N.Y.: Parker Publishing Company, 1969.

Kennedy, Larry D., and R. S. Halinski. "Measuring Attitudes: An Extra Dimension," *Journal of Reading*, 18:518–522 (1975).

Kingston, Albert J., Wendell W. Weaver, and Leslie E. Figo. "Experiments in Children's Perceptions of Words and Word Boundaries," in Frank P. Greene (ed.), *Investigations Relating to Mature Reading*, 21st Yearbook of the National Reading Conference. Athens, Ga.: National Reading Conference, 1972.

Klare, George. "Assessing Readability," *Reading Research Quarterly*, 10(1):98–102 (1974–1975).

Kohl, Herbert R. *The Open Classroom*. New York: A New York Review Book (division of Random House), 1969.

Kohlberg, Lawrence. "Stage and Sequence: The Cognitive Developmental Approach to Socialization," in D. Goslin (ed.), *Handbook of Socialization Theory and Research*. Chicago: Rand McNally, 1969.

Krathwohl, D. R., B. Bloom, and B. Masia (eds.). *Taxonomy of Educational Objectives: The Affective Domain*. New York: McKay, 1964.

Labov, William. "Some Sources of Reading Problems for Negro Speakers of Nonstandard English," in A. Frazier (ed.), *New Directions in Elementary English*. Champaign, Ill.: National Council of Teachers of English, 1967.

Labuda, Michael (ed.). *Creative Reading for Gifted Learners: A Design for Excellence*. Newark, Del.: International Reading Association, 1974.

Laffey, James, and Carl B. Smith. *A Source Book of Evaluation Techniques for Reading*. Bloomington, Ind.: Reading Department, Indiana University, 1972.

Lee, D., and R. V. Allen. *Learning To Read Through Experience*. New York: Appleton, 1963.

Lefevre, Carl A. *Linguistics and the Teaching of Reading*. New York: McGraw-Hill, 1964.

Lindholm, Richard W., and Paul Driscoll. *Our American Economy*, 4th ed. New York: Harcourt Brace Jovanovich, 1970.

Littell, Joseph F. (ed.). *Gaining Sensitivity to Words*. Evanston, Ill.: McDougal, Littell & Company, 1973.

Lowe, A. J. "Recent Research Sources for Middle and Secondary School Reading Problem Areas," in L. Hafner (ed.), *Improved Reading in Middle and Secondary Schools.* New York: Macmillan, 1974.

MacGinitie, Walter H. (ed.). *Assessment Problems in Reading.* Newark, Del.: International Reading Association, 1973.

McCarthy, William. *Individualized Diagnostic Reading Inventory,* rev. ed. Cambridge, Mass.: Educators Publishing Service, Inc., 1976.

Malinson, George. "Research in Science Reading," in James Laffey (ed.), *Reading in Content Areas.* Newark, Del.: International Reading Association, 1972.

Mangrum, Charles T. (ed.). *How To Read a Book.* Newark, Del.: International Reading Association, 1970.

Manzo, Anthony. "The ReQuest Procedure," *Journal of Reading,* 13(2):123–126 (November 1969).

Mathews, Mitford M. *Teaching To Read: Historically Considered.* Chicago: The University of Chicago Press, 1966.

Meade, E. L. "Reading: The First R—A Point of View," *Reading World,* 12: 1969–1980 (1973).

Merriam-Webster Pocket Dictionary of Synonyms, The. New York: Pocket Books, 1972.

Mikulecky, Larry J. "The Developing, Field Testing, and Initial Norming of a Secondary/Adult Level Reading Attitude Measure That Is Behaviorally Oriented and Based on Krathwohl's Taxonomy of the Affective Domain," unpublished doctoral dissertation, University of Wisconsin, Madison, 1976.

Mikulecky, Larry J., and Jerilyn Ribovich. "Reading Competence and Attitudes of Teachers in Preparation," *Journal of Reading,* 20(7):573–580 (April 1977).

Miller, George. *The Psychology of Communication.* New York: Basic Books, 1967.

Moburg, Lawrence G. *Inservice Teacher Training in Reading.* Newark, Del.: International Reading Association, 1972.

Moffett, James. *Teaching the Universe of Discourse.* Boston: Houghton Mifflin, 1968.

Moorehead, Albert H. *Roget's College Thesaurus in Dictionary Form.* New York: New American Library (Signet), 1962.

Namekawa, Michio. "Children's Literature and Reading," in John E. Merritt (ed.), *New Horizons in Reading: Proceedings of the Fifth I.R.A. World Congress on Reading.* Newark, Del.: International Reading Association, 1976.

Nardelli, Robert R. "Some Aspects of Creative Reading," *Journal of Educational Research,* 50:495–508 (March 1957).

National Assessment of Education Progress: Reading and Literature General Information Yearbook. Washington, D.C. Government Printing Office, 1976.

Nielsen, Duane M., and Howard F. Hjelm (eds.). *Reading and Career Education.* Newark, Del.: International Reading Association, 1975.

Nurnberg, Maxwell, and Morris Rosenblum. *How To Build a Better Vocabulary.* New York: Popular Library, 1961.

Odland, N., and T. Ilstrup. "Will Reading Teachers Read?" *The Reading Teacher,* 17:83–87 (1963).

Onions, C. T. (ed.). *The Oxford Dictionary of English Etymology.* New York: Oxford University Press, 1966.

Partridge, Eric (ed.). *The Macmillan Dictionary of Historical Slang.* New York: Macmillan, 1974.

Partridge, Eric. *Origins: A Short Etymological Dictionary of Modern English.* New York: Macmillan, 1958.

Pauk, Walter. *How To Study in College,* 2d ed. Boston: Houghton Mifflin, 1974.

Pei, Mario. *The Families of Words.* New York: St. Martins Press, 1962.

Pei, Mario, and Salvatore Romondino. *Dictionary of Foreign Terms.* New York: Dell, 1974.

Perry, M., *et al. Man's Unfinished Journey: A World History.* Boston: Houghton Mifflin, 1971.

Piaget, Jean. *The Language and Thought of the Child,* 3d ed. New York: Humanities Press, Inc., 1959.

Piaget, Jean. *The Origins of Intelligence in Children,* Margaret Cook, trans. New York: International Universities Press, 1952.

Piaget, Jean. *The Psychology of Intelligence.* London: Routledge, 1950.

Piercey, Dorothy. *Reading Activities in Content Areas: An Ideabook for Middle and Secondary Schools.* Boston: Allyn and Bacon, 1976.

Postman, Neil. *Language and Reality.* New York: Holt, Rinehart and Winston, 1966.

Quandt, Ivan. *Self-concept and Reading.* Newark, Del.: International Reading Association, 1974.

Raim, Joan. "Rolling Out the Welcome Mat to Tutors," *The Reading Teacher,* 26(7):696–701 (April 1973).

Rankin, E. F., and J. W. Culhane. "Comparable Cloze and Multiple-Choice Comprehension Test Scores," *Journal of Reading,* 13:193–198 (1969).

Reading Disorders in the United States. Report of the Secretary's (Department of Health, Education and Welfare) National Advisory Committee on Dyslexia and Related Reading Disorders. Chicago: Developmental Learning Materials, 1969.

Reading Instruction in Secondary Schools. Newark, Del.: International Reading Association, 1964.

Reasoner, Charles F. *Releasing Children to Literature.* New York: Dell, 1976.

Reasoner, Charles F. *When Children Read.* New York: Dell, 1975.

Richards, Bertrand F. "Writing from the Mind Out," paper presented at a meeting of the National Council of Teachers of English, New Orleans, 1974. (Available from ERIC Document Reproduction Service, P.O. Box 190, Arlington, Va. 22210.)

Robinson, H. Alan, and Sidney J. Rauch. *Corrective Reading in the High School Classroom.* Newark, Del.: International Reading Association, 1966.

Robinson, Helen M. "Developing Critical Readers," in Russell G. Stauffer (ed.), *Dimensions of Critical Reading,* 11:1–11. Newark, Del.: University of Delaware, Proceedings of the Annual Education and Reading Conferences, 1964.

Robinson, Helen M. *Evaluation of Reading.* Chicago: The University of Chicago Press, 1958.

Robinson, Helen M. *Clinical Studies in Reading II.* Chicago: The University of Chicago Press, 1953.

Rosenshine, Barak, and Norma Furst. "Research in Teacher Performance Criteria," in B. O. Smith (ed.), *Research in Teacher Education.* Englewood Cliffs, N.J.: Prentice-Hall, 1971.

Rosenthal, Robert, and Lenore Jacobson. *Pygmalion in the Classroom.* New York: Holt, Rinehart and Winston, 1968.

Ruddell, Robert, in Kenneth S. Goodman and J. Fleming (eds.), *Psycholinguistics and the Teaching of Reading.* Newark, Del.: International Reading Association, 1968.

Scholastic's Go Series: An Instruction Skills Text Series for Grades 4 through 8. Englewood Cliffs, N.J.: Scholastic Book Services, 1976.

Schulwitz, Bonnie S. (ed.). *Teachers, Tangibles, Techniques: Comprehension of Content in Reading.* Newark, Del.: International Reading Association, 1975.

Severson, Eileen E. "The Teaching of Reading-Study Skills in Biology," *The American Biology Teacher,* 25:203–204 (March 1963).

Sherbourne, Julia F. *Toward Reading Comprehension,* 2d ed. Lexington, Mass.: Heath, 1977.

Shores, J. Harlan. "Reading of Science for Two Separate Purposes as Perceived by Sixth-Grade Students and Able Adult Readers," *Elementary English,* 37:461–468 (November 1960).

Shuy, Roger W. "Bonnie and Clyde Tactics in English Teaching: Linguistics, Cultural Differences and American Education," *The Florida FL Reporter* 7(1):81 (Spring–Summer 1969).

Silbiger, Francene, and Daniel Woolf. "Perceptual Difficulties Associated with Reading Disability," *College Reading Association Proceedings,* 6:98–102 (Fall 1965).

Silvaroli, Nicholas. *Classroom Reading Inventory.* Dubuque, Iowa: William C. Brown Company, 1976.

Simpson, R. H. "Reading Disabilities among Teachers and Administrators," *Clearinghouse,* 17:11–13 (1942).

Smith, Carl B. "Observing Reading Behavior—A Structural Observation," Occasional Paper (mimeographed). Bloomington, Ind.: Department of Reading Education, Indiana University, 1977.

Smith, Carl B. "How Do You Teach Comprehension?" *Reading in Virginia,* 4(2): 16–17 (September 1976).

Smith, Carl B., and Leo D. Fay. *Getting People To Read.* New York: Delacorte Press, 1973.

Smith, Carl B., and S. Smith. "Teacher Expectations and Student Responses to Reading Assignments," Secondary Reading Research and Opinion. Bloomington, Ind.: Department of Reading Education, Indiana University, 1977.

Smith, E. B., K. S. Goodman, and R. Meredith. *Language and Thinking in School,* 2d ed. New York: Holt, Rinehart and Winston, 1976.

Smith, Frank. *Comprehension and Learning.* New York: Holt, Rinehart and Winston, 1975.

Smith, Frank. *Understanding Reading.* New York: Holt, Rinehart and Winston, 1971.

Smith, Nila Banton. *American Reading Instruction.* Newark, Del.: International Reading Association, 1965.

Smith, Nila Banton. *Reading Instruction for Today's Children.* Englewood Cliffs, N.J.: Prentice-Hall, 1963.

Smith, Nila Banton. *Read Faster and Get More from Your Reading.* Englewood Cliffs, N.J.: Prentice-Hall, 1957. (Also available in paperback under the title *Speed Reading Made Easy.* New York: Popular Library, 1957.)

Smith, Richard J., and Thomas C. Barrett. *Teaching Reading in the Middle Grades.* Reading, Mass.: Addison-Wesley, 1974.

Spache, George. *Good Books for Poor Readers.* Champaign, Ill.: Garrard Publishing Company, 1974.

Spache, George. *Good Reading for Poor Readers.* Champaign, Ill.: Garrard Publishing Company, 1970.

Spache, George D. *Spache Diagnostic Reading Scales.* Monterey, Calif.: California Test Bureau, Del Monte Research Park, 1963.

Spache, George, and Paul Berg. *The Art of Efficient Reading,* 2d ed. New York: Macmillan, 1966.

Stauffer, Russell G. *The Language-Experience Approach to the Teaching of Reading.* New York: Harper & Row, 1970.

Stephens, Lillian S. *The Teacher's Guide to Open Education.* New York: Holt, Rinehart and Winston, 1974.

Strang, Ruth. *Diagnostic Teaching of Reading.* New York: McGraw-Hill, 1969.

Strang, Ruth. *Reading Diagnosis and Remediation.* Newark, Del.: International Reading Association Research Fund, 1968.

Strickler, Darryl J. (ed.). *The Affective Dimension of Reading: Resource Guide.* Bloomington, Ind.: Indiana University Reading Programs, 1977.

Tarter, Ralph E. "An Analysis of Cognitive Deficits in Chronic Alcoholics," *Journal of Nervous and Mental Disease,* 157(8):138–144.

Thomas, Ellen Lawar, and H. Alan Robinson. *Improving Reading in Every Class.* Boston: Allyn and Bacon, 1977.

Thomas, Lewis. *The Lives of a Cell.* New York: Viking, 1974.

Tinker, Miles A. *Bases for Effective Reading.* Minneapolis, Minn.: University of Minnesota Press, 1965.

Toffler, Alvin. *Future Shock.* New York: Random House, 1970.

Tracy, G., H. Tropp, and A. Friedl (eds.). *Modern Physical Science.* New York: Holt, Rinehart and Winston, 1970.

Tyler, Ralph W. *Basic Principles of Curriculum and Instruction.* Chicago: The University of Chicago Press, 1949.

Urdang, Laurence (ed.). *The New York Times' Everyday Reader's Dictionary of Misunderstood, Misused, and Mispronounced Words.* New York: Quadrangle/New York Times Book Company, 1972.

Veatch, Jeannette. *Individualizing Your Reading Program.* New York: Putnam, 1959.

Ver Steeg, Clarence L. *The Story of Our Country.* New York: Harper & Row, 1965.

Voight, Ralph Claude. *Invitation to Learning I: The Learning Center Handbook.* Washington, D.C.: Acropolis Books, Ltd., 1974.

Wallen, Carl J. "Independent Activities: A Necessity, Not a Frill," *The Reading Teacher,* 27(3):257–262 (December 1973).

Wann, Kenneth D., Henry J. Warman, and James K. Canfield. *Man and His Changing Culture.* Boston: Allyn and Bacon, 1967.

Wardhaugh, Ronald. "Linguistics and Reading," in Carl B. Smith and Ronald Wardhaugh (eds.), *Teacher's Resource Book—Series r*. New York: Macmillan, 1975.

Waters, Harry F. "What TV Does to Kids," *Newsweek*, February 21, 1977, pp. 63–70.

Weintraub, Samuel. "Children's Reading Interests," *The Reading Teacher*, 22:655–659 (April 1969).

Weaver, Warren. "The Case of the Wayward Word," adapted from a talk given before the Citizens' Advisory Committee of the New York Public Library. *Saturday Review*, March 8, 1960.

Weiss, M. Jerry, Joseph Brunner, and Warren Weiss (eds.). *New Perspectives on Paperbacks*. Jersey City, N.J.: The College Reading Association, 1972 and 1973. (Available from Strine Printing Co., Inc., 391 Greendale Rd., York, Pennsylvania 17403.)

Weitzman, David, and Richard E. Gross. *The Human Experience*. Boston: Houghton Mifflin, 1974.

Wentworth, Harold, and S. B. Flexner (eds.). *The Dictionary of American Slang*. New York: Crowell, 1975.

Williams, John E., H. Clark Metcalfe, F. E. Trinklein, and Ralph W. Lefler. *Modern Physics*. New York: Holt, Rinehart and Winston, 1972.

Williams, Raymond. *Keywords: A Vocabulary of Culture and Society*. New York: Oxford University Press, 1976.

Wolfe, Stanley, *et al. Concepts and Challenges in Science*. New York: CEBCO Standard Publishing Company, 1975.

Wong, Harry K., and Malvin S. Dolmatz. *Ideas and Investigations in Science: Biology*. Englewood Cliffs, N.J.: Prentice-Hall, 1971.

Index